Full-Power Thanks

...I'm saluting.

It's extremely difficult to make out, but...

KOYOHARU GOTOUGE

Hello! I'm Gotouge. Here's volume 13! It's happened due to everyone's support, so thank you. And as for the anime, the voice cast is rapidly coming together, and it's getting made! Recently, there have been many natural disasters, but amidst all that hardship, you picked up this manga and read it, so thank you very much. Painful things and things that must be endured come to everyone, but if you enjoy the series for even just a little while, and it gives you a positive outlook, I'd be happy.

DEMON SLAYER: KIMETSU NO YAIBA VOLUME 13

Shonen Jump Edition

Story and Art by
KOYOHARU GOTOUGE

TRANSLATION John Werry
ENGLISH ADAPTATION Stan!
TOUCH-UP ART & LETTERING John Hunt
DESIGN Jimmy Presler
EDITOR Mike Montesa

Printed in Italy

Published by VIZ Media, LLC
P.O. Box 77010
San Francisco, CA 94107

10 9 8 7
First printing, June 2020
Seventh printing, January 2022

ratings.viz.com RATED T TEEN

PARENTAL ADVISORY
DEMON SLAYER: KIMETSU NO YAIBA is rated T for Teen and recommended for ages 13 and up. This volume contains realistic and fantasy violence.

VIZ MEDIA
viz.com

SHONEN JUMP

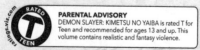

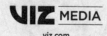

DEMON SLAYER!

KIMETSU NO YAIBA

13

TRANSITIONS

**KOYOHARU
GOTOUGE**

CHARACTERS

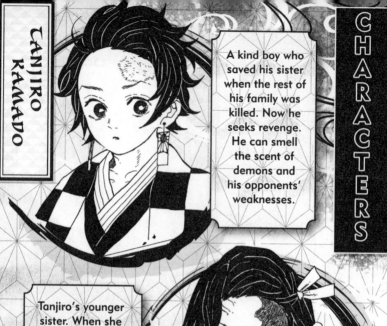

TANJIRO KAMADO

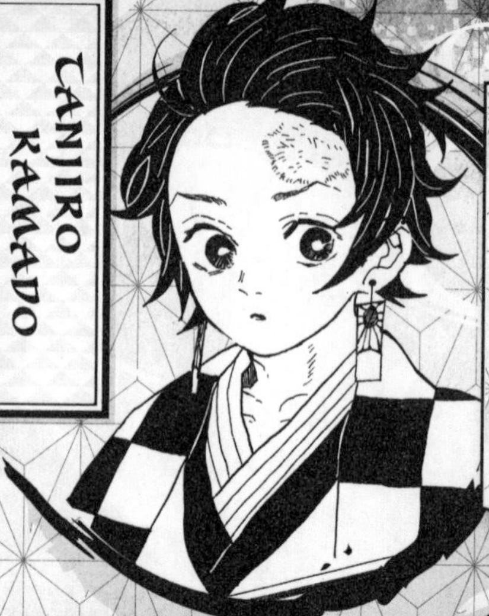

A kind boy who saved his sister when the rest of his family was killed. Now he seeks revenge. He can smell the scent of demons and his opponents' weaknesses.

NEZUKO KAMADO

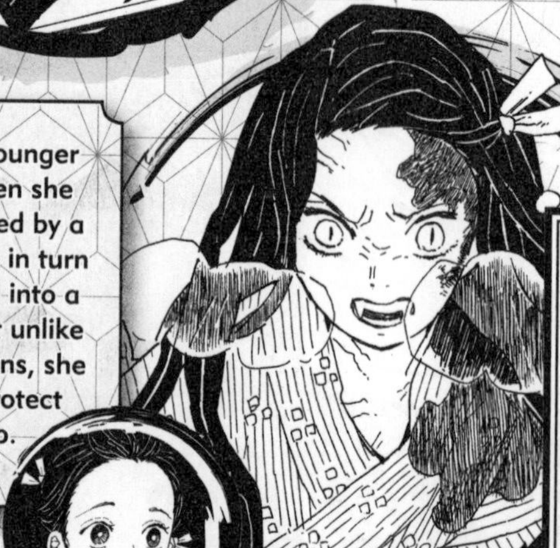

Tanjiro's younger sister. When she was attacked by a demon, she in turn was turned into a demon, but unlike other demons, she tries to protect Tanjiro.

STORY

In Taisho-Era Japan, young Tanjiro makes a living selling charcoal. One day, demons kill his family and turn his younger sister Nezuko into a demon. Tanjiro and Nezuko set out to find a way to return Nezuko to human form and defeat Kibutsuji, the demon who killed their family!

After joining the Demon Slayer Corps, Tanjiro meets Tamayo and Yushiro—demons who oppose Kibutsuji—who provide a clue to how Nezuko may regain her humanity. In search of a new katana, Tanjiro visits a hidden village of swordsmiths. But the Upper Rank 4 demon Hantengu and Upper Rank 5 demon Gyokko suddenly appear on orders from Kibutsuji! Tanjiro faces the demons with his peer Genya and the Mist Hashira, Tokito!

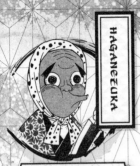

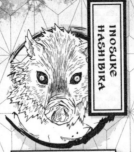

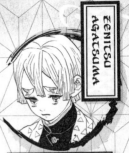

ZENITSU AGATSUMA

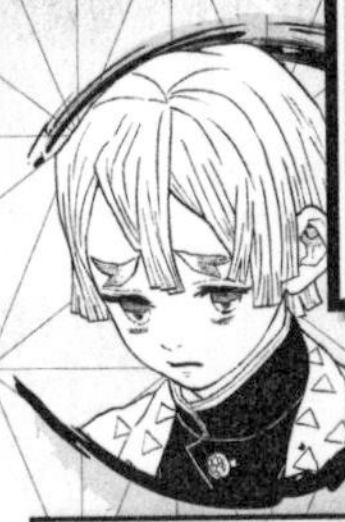

He went through Final Selection at the same time as Tanjiro. He's usually cowardly, but when he falls asleep, his true power comes out.

INOSUKE HASHIBIRA

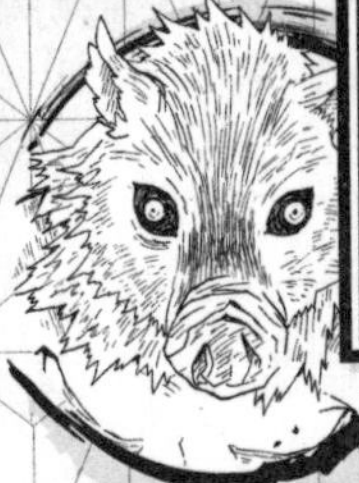

He also went through Final Selection at the same time as Tanjiro. He wears the pelt of a wild boar and is very belligerent.

HAGANEZUKA

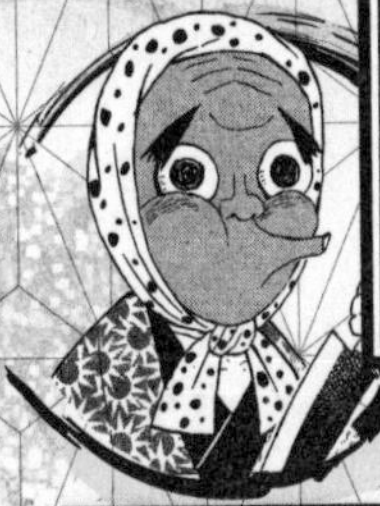

The swordsmith who makes Tanjiro's katanas. He has the soul of an artist, so he gets angry when a katana is treated poorly.

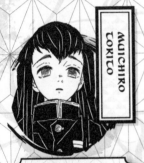

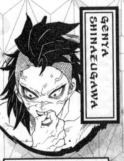

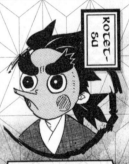

KOTETSU

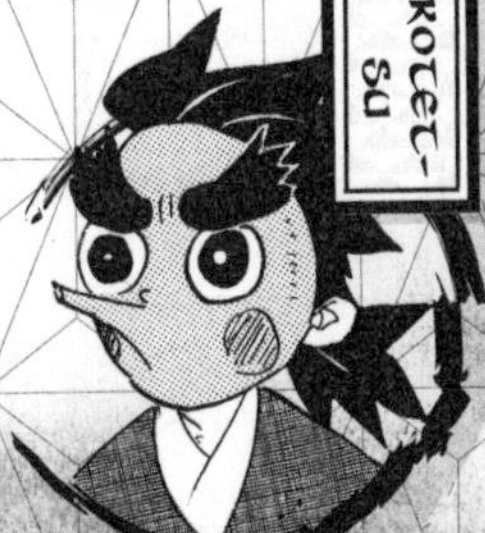

A boy from the village of swordsmiths. He aids Tanjiro's training using the clockwork automaton Yoriichi Type Zero.

GENYA SHINAZUGAWA

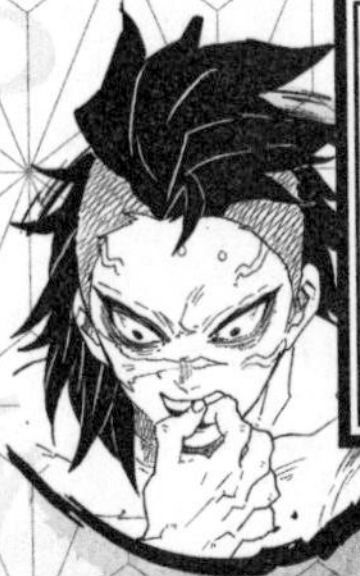

He went through Final Selection at the same time as Tanjiro. His elder brother is Sanemi, the Wind Hashira. He and Tanjiro meet again in the village of swordsmiths.

MUICHIRO TOKITO

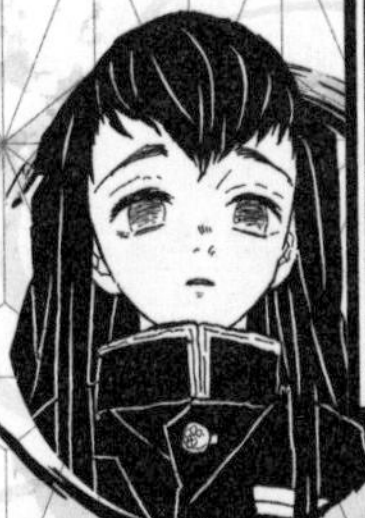

The Mist Hashira in the Demon Slayer Corps. He's the descendant of users of Sun Breathing, the first breathing technique.

MITSURI KANROJI

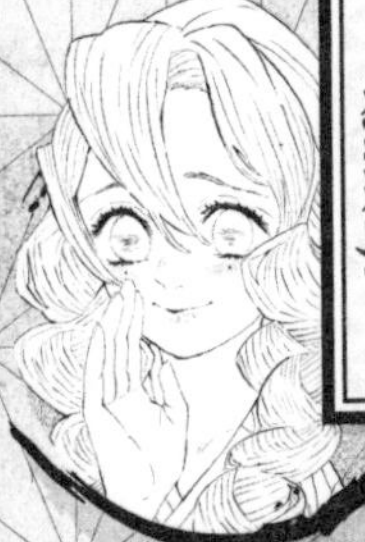

The Love Hashira in the Demon Slayer Corps. She joined the Corps hoping to find a man to marry.

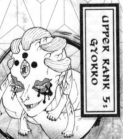

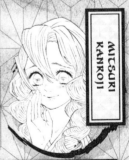

UPPER RANK 4: HANTENGU

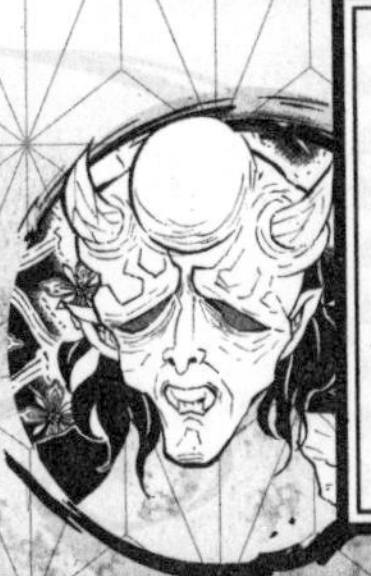

Together with Gyokko, he has infiltrated the village of swordsmiths on orders from Muzan Kibutsuji.

UPPER RANK 5: GYOKKO

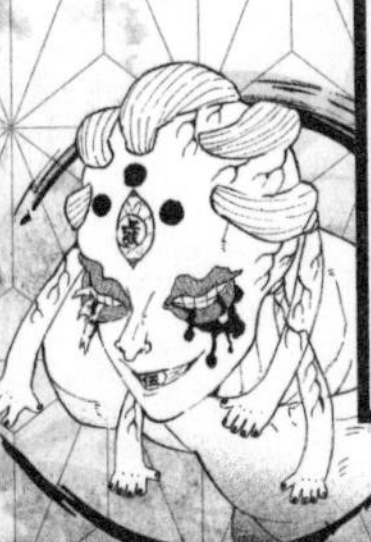

Together with Hantengu, he is attacking the village of swordsmiths in hopes of weakening the Demon Slayer Corps.

CONTENTS

DEMON SLAYER

KIMETSU NO YAIBA

13

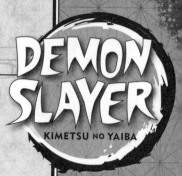

TRANSITIONS

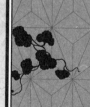

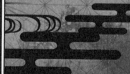

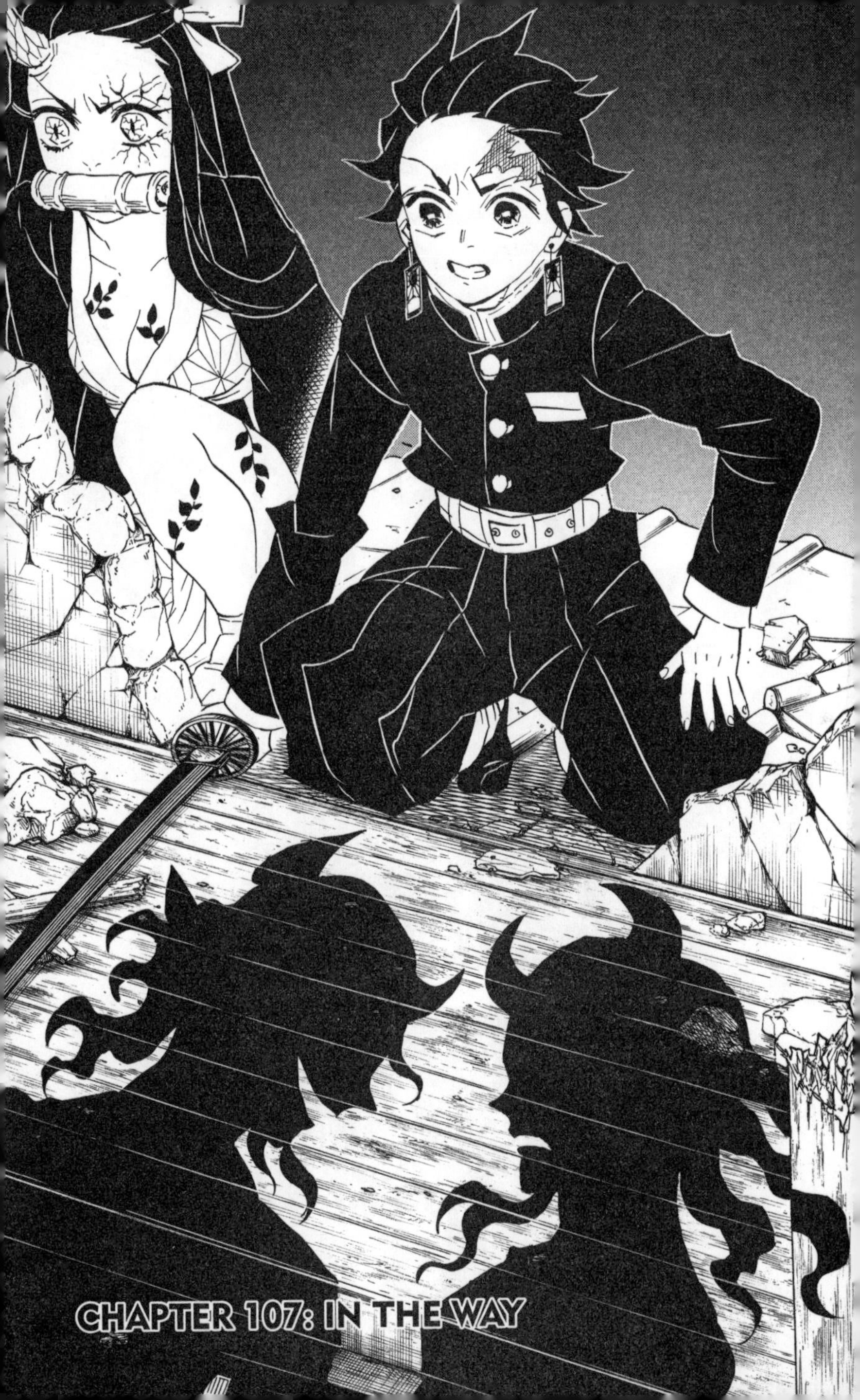
CHAPTER 107: IN THE WAY

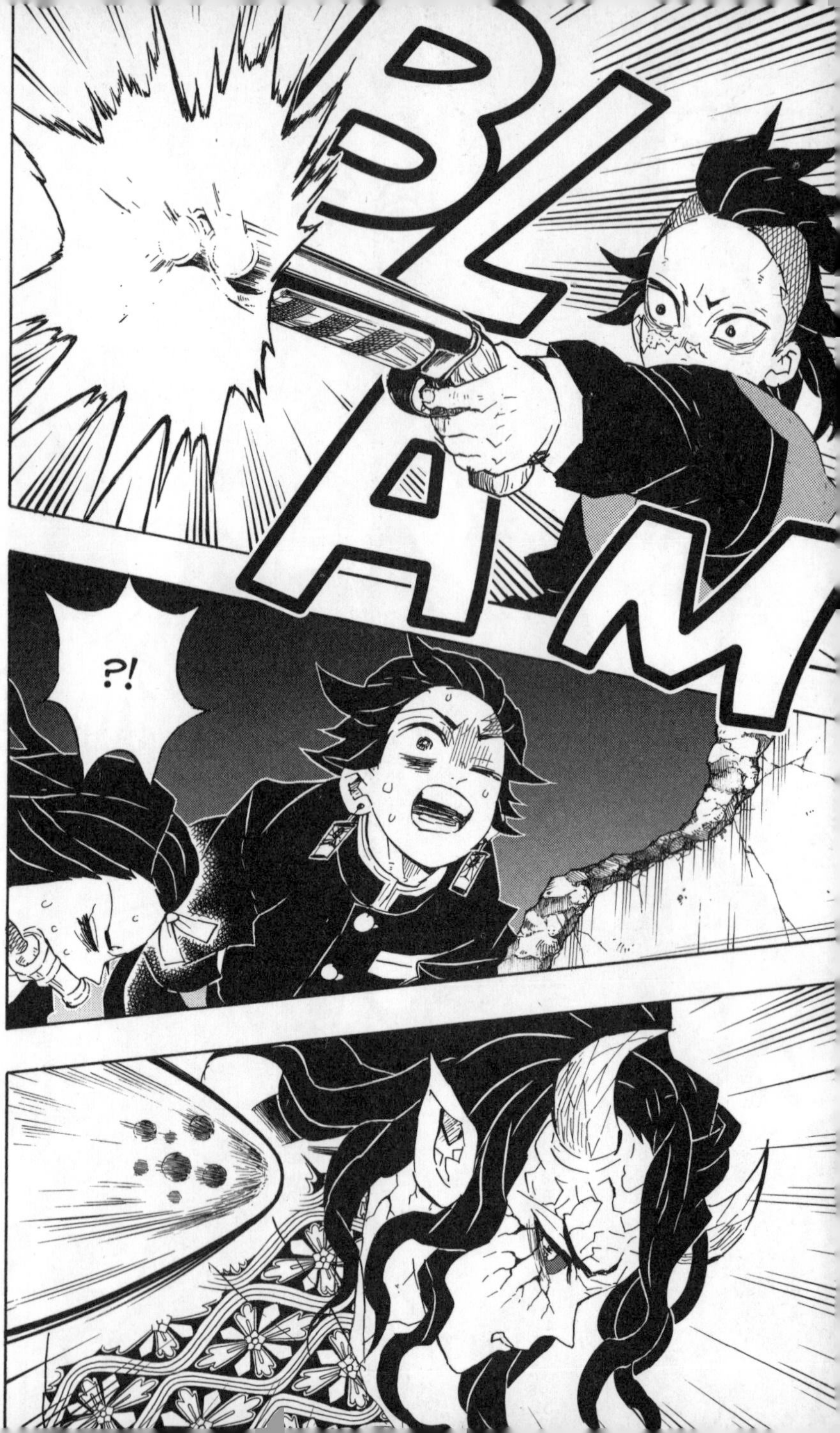
BLAM
?!

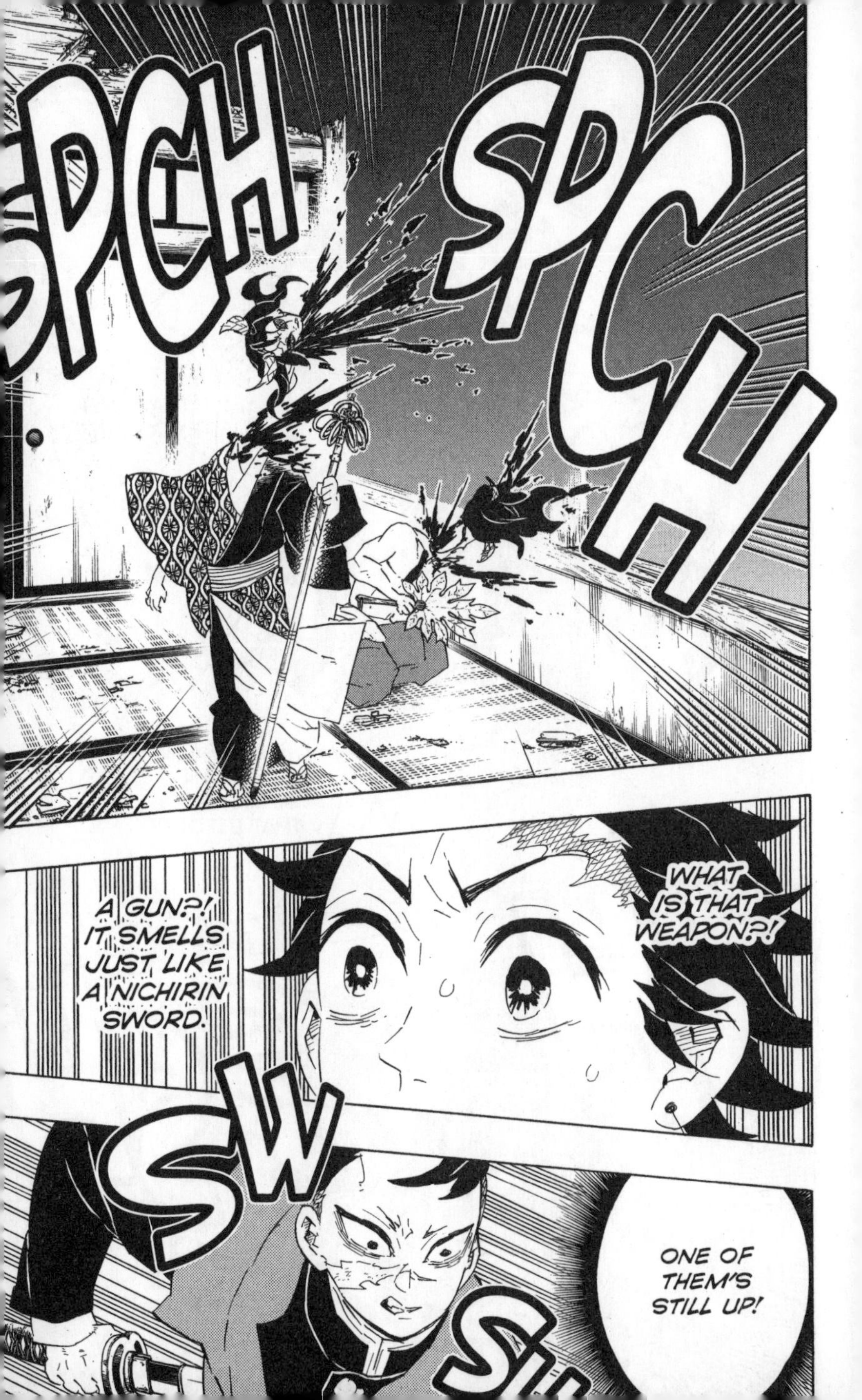
SPCH
SPCH
WHAT IS THAT WEAPON?!
A GUN?! IT SMELLS JUST LIKE A NICHIRIN SWORD.
ONE OF THEM'S STILL UP!
SW

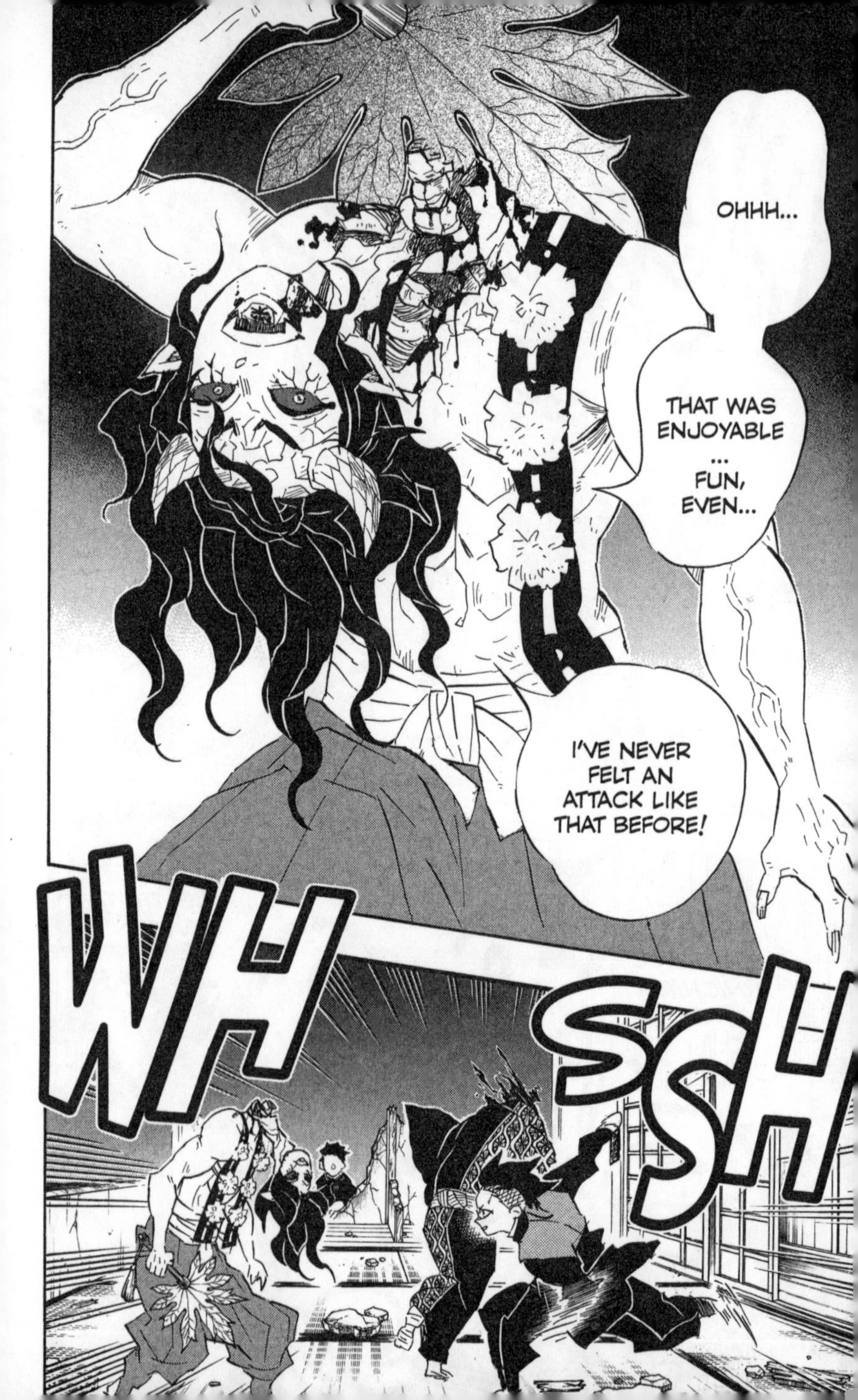
OHHH...
THAT WAS ENJOYABLE ... FUN, EVEN...
I'VE NEVER FELT AN ATTACK LIKE THAT BEFORE!
WHSH
SH

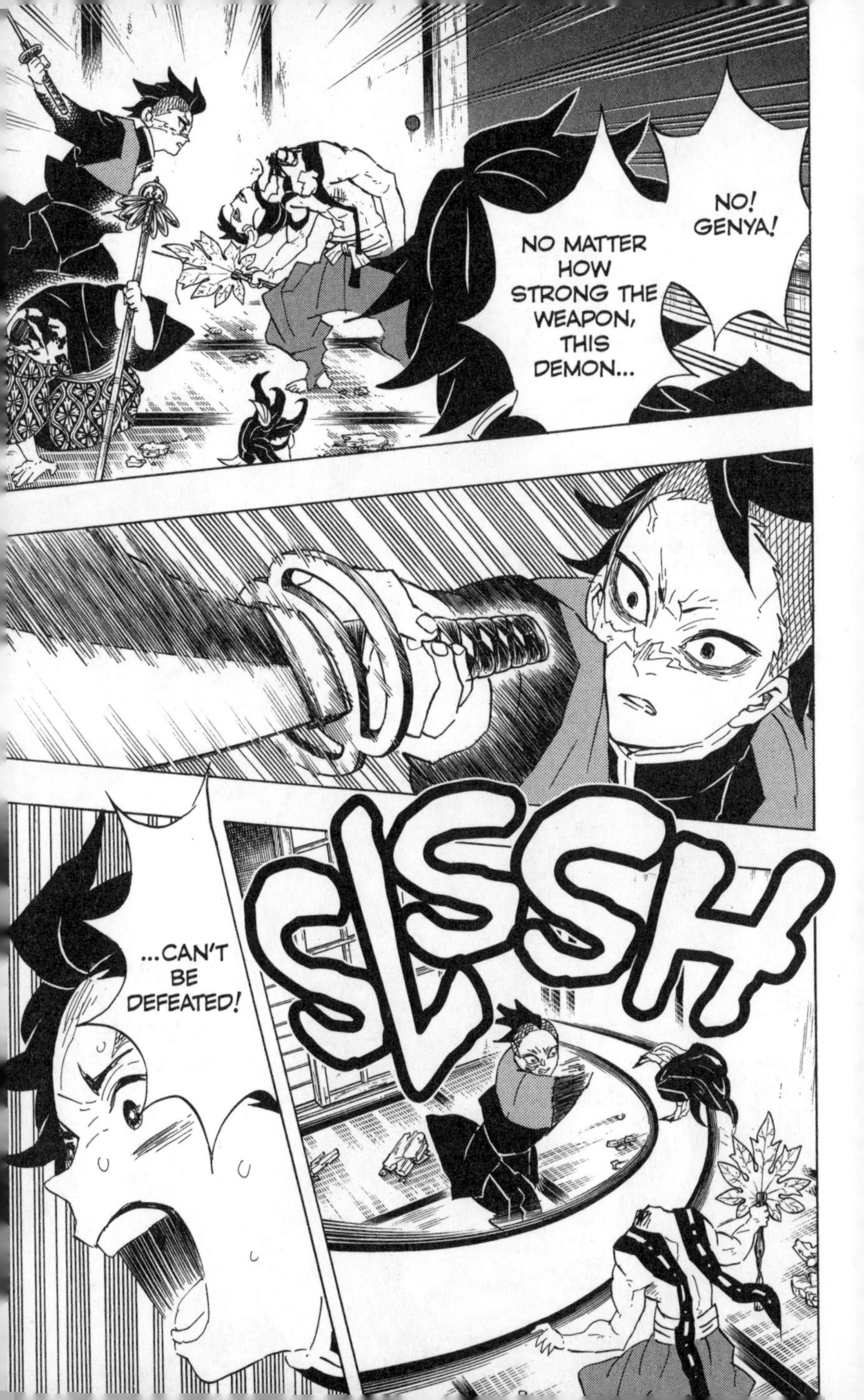
NO! GENYA!
NO MATTER HOW STRONG THE WEAPON, THIS DEMON...
SLSSH
...CAN'T BE DEFEATED!

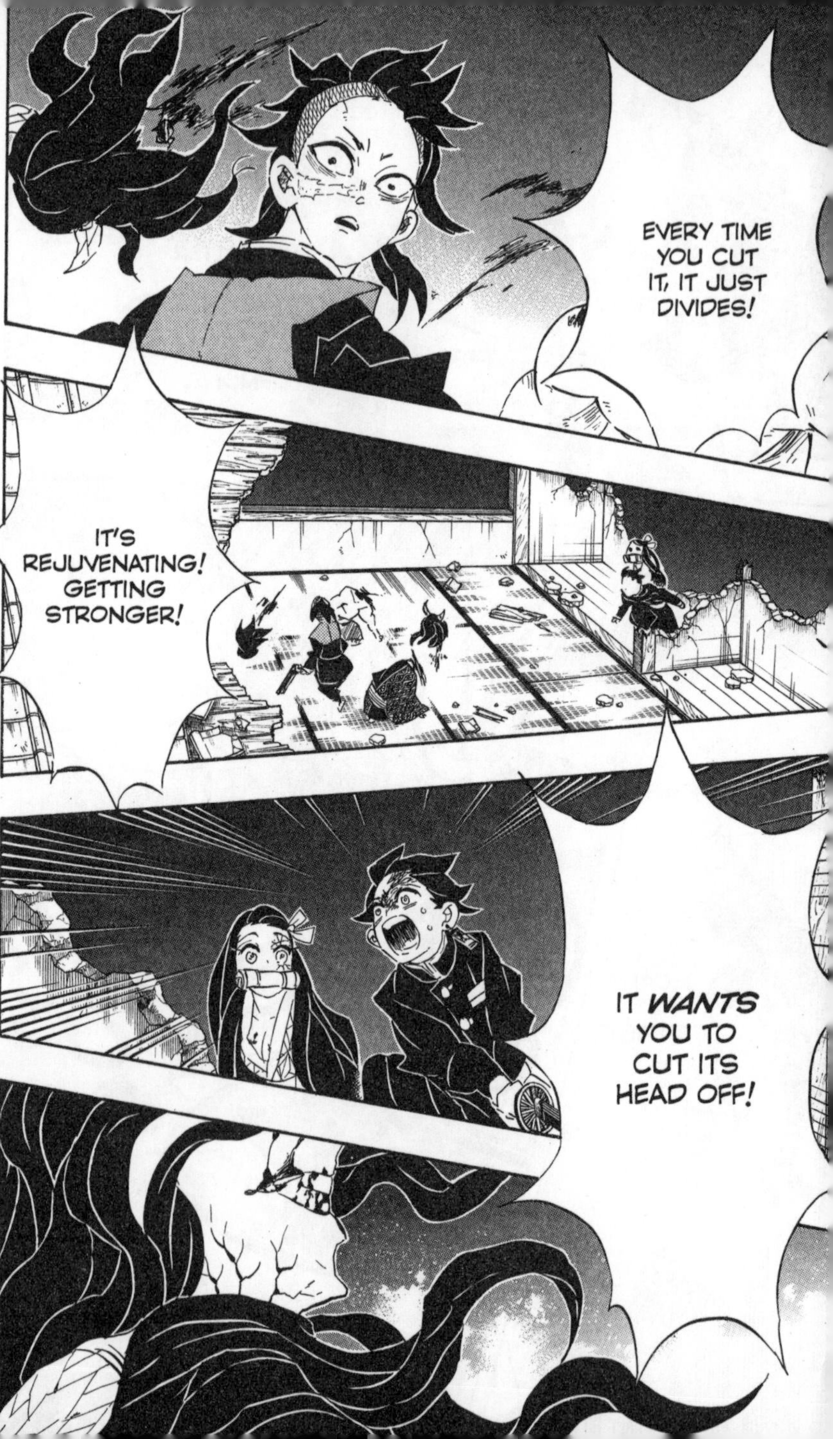
EVERY TIME YOU CUT IT, IT JUST DIVIDES!
IT'S REJUVENATING! GETTING STRONGER!
IT *WANTS* YOU TO CUT ITS HEAD OFF!

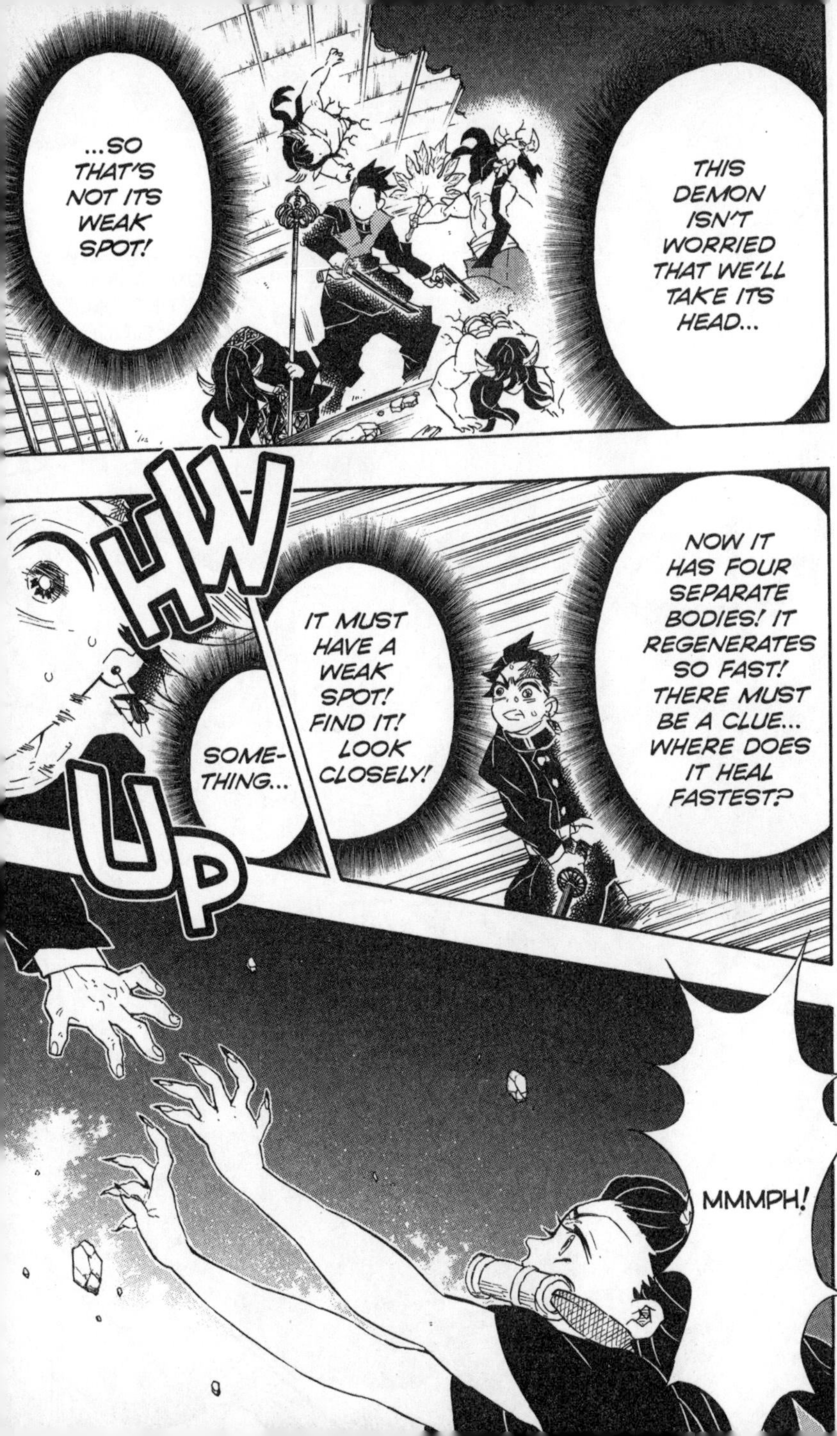
THIS DEMON ISN'T WORRIED THAT WE'LL TAKE ITS HEAD...
...SO THAT'S NOT ITS WEAK SPOT!
NOW IT HAS FOUR SEPARATE BODIES! IT REGENERATES SO FAST! THERE MUST BE A CLUE... WHERE DOES IT HEAL FASTEST?
IT MUST HAVE A WEAK SPOT! FIND IT! LOOK CLOSELY!
SOME-THING...
HWUP
MMMPH!

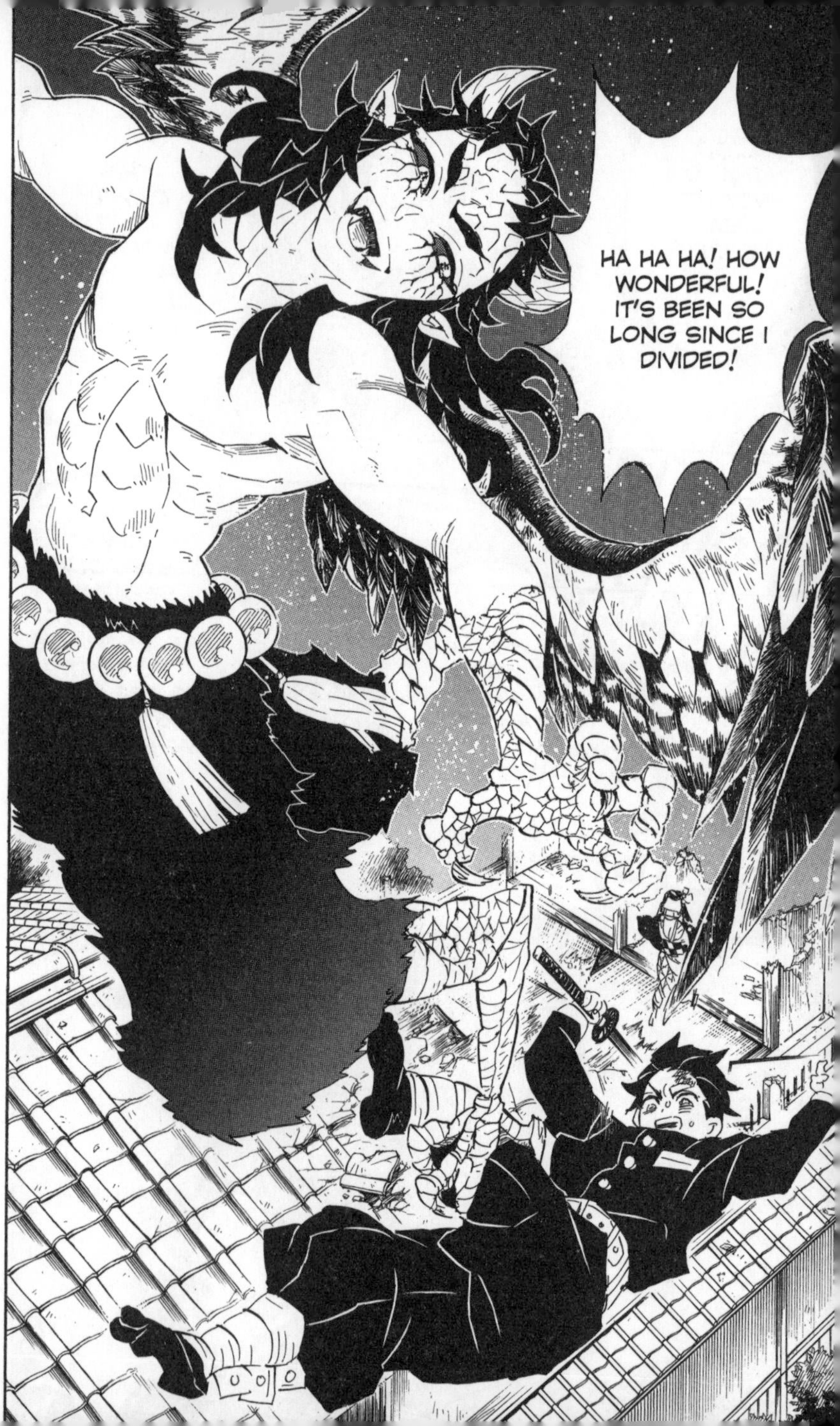
HA HA HA! HOW WONDERFUL! IT'S BEEN SO LONG SINCE I DIVIDED!

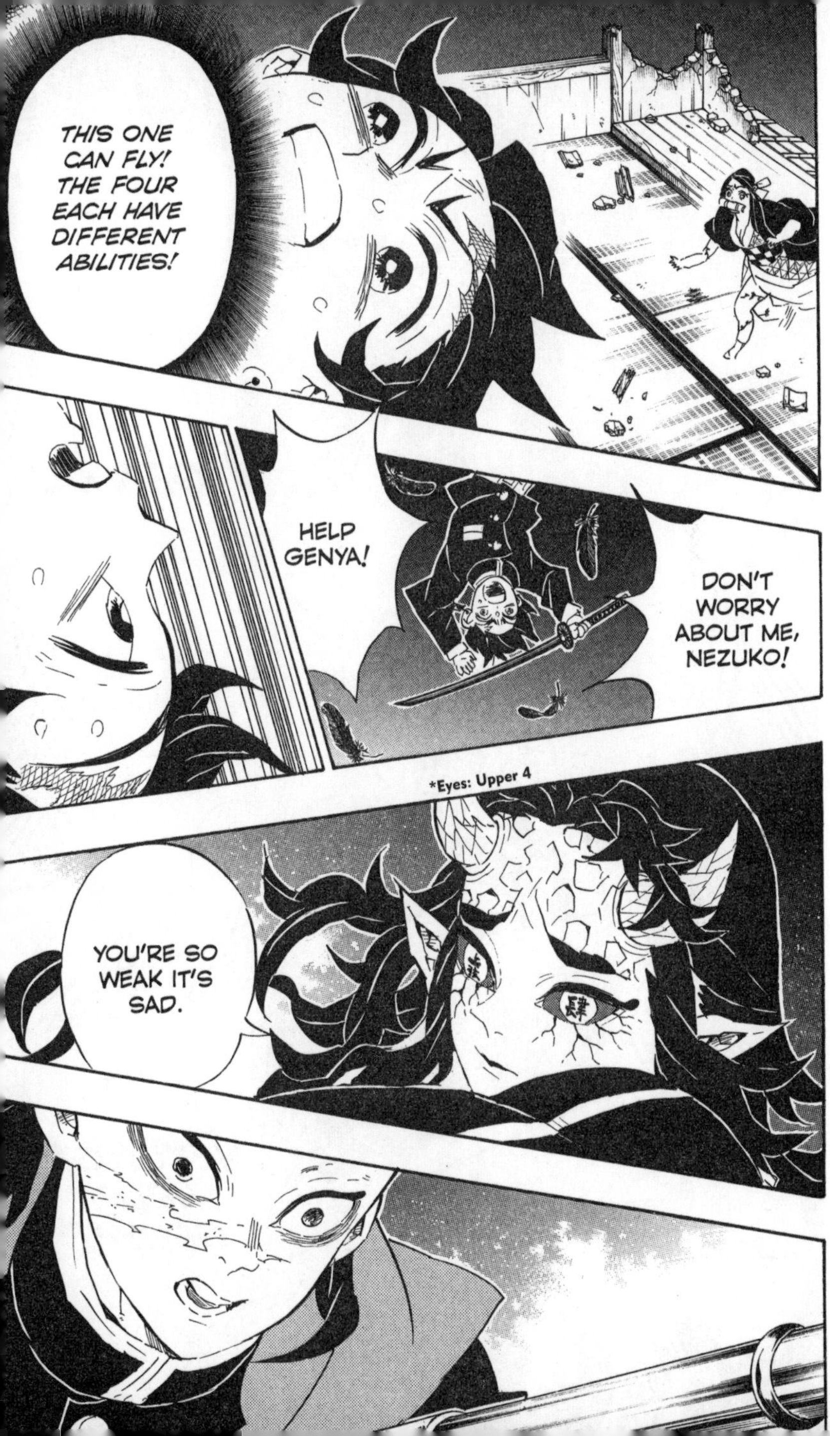
THIS ONE CAN FLY! THE FOUR EACH HAVE DIFFERENT ABILITIES!
DON'T WORRY ABOUT ME, NEZUKO!
HELP GENYA!
*Eyes: Upper 4
YOU'RE SO WEAK IT'S SAD.

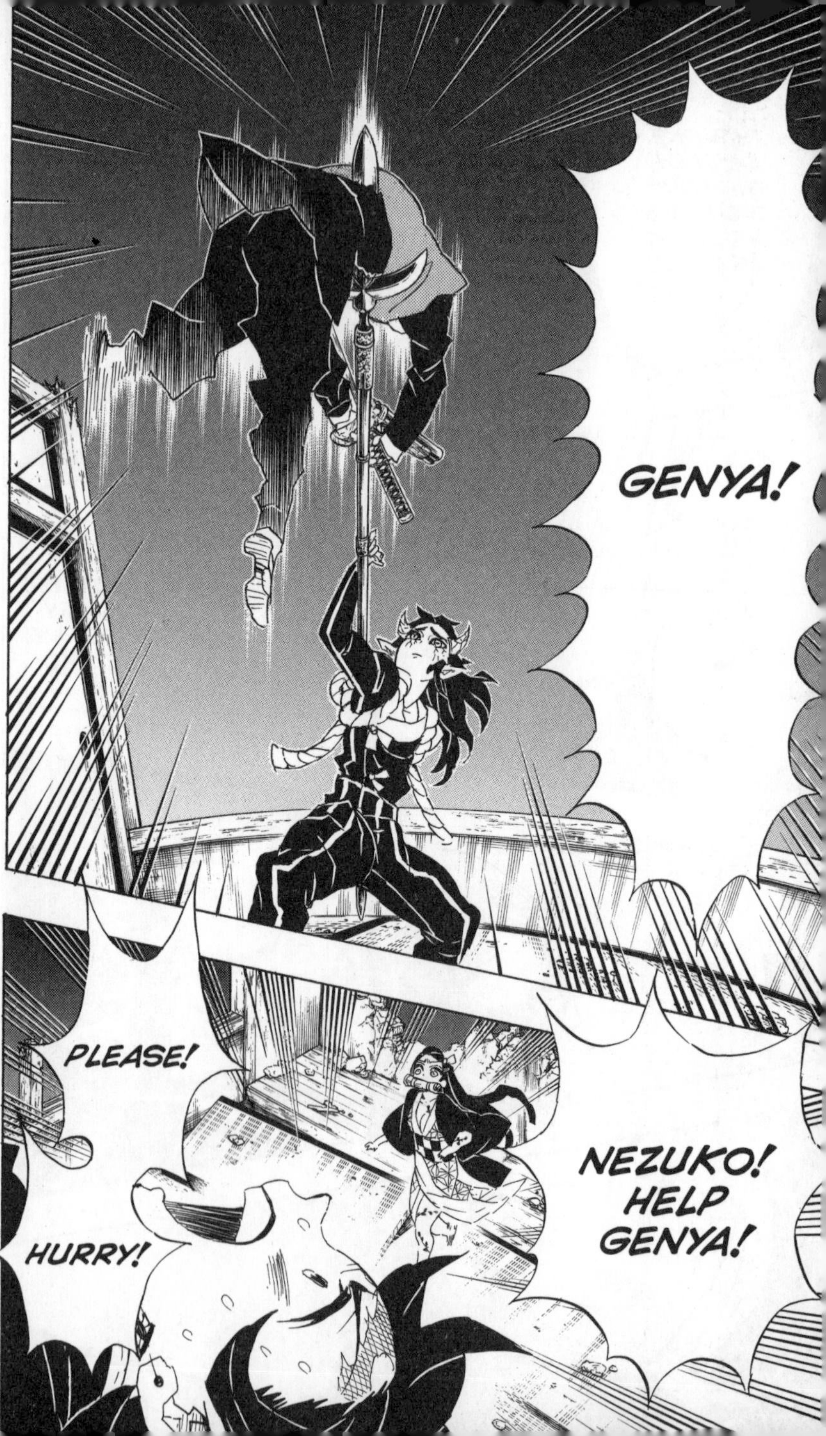
GENYA!
NEZUKO! HELP GENYA!
PLEASE!
HURRY!

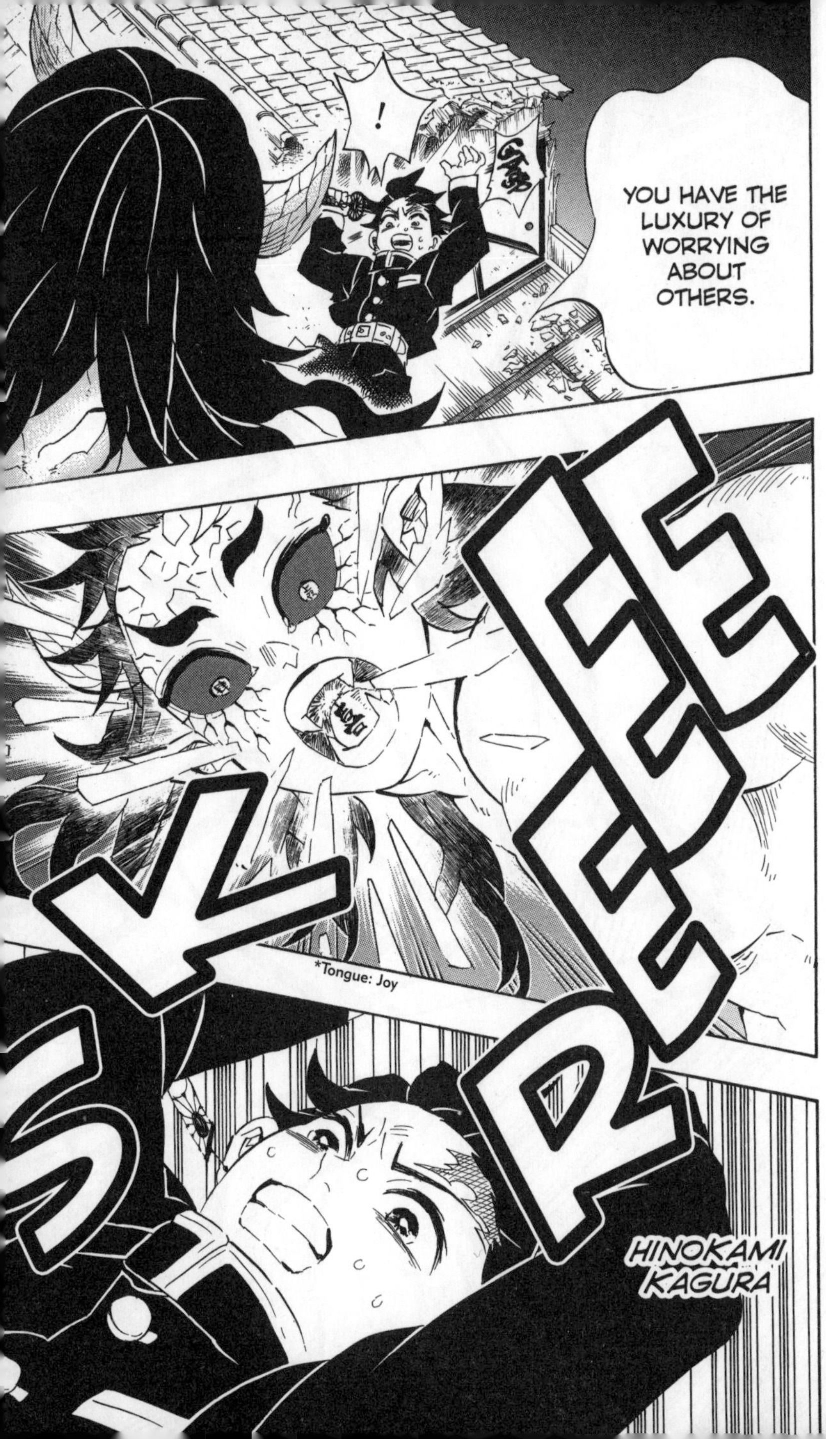
YOU HAVE THE LUXURY OF WORRYING ABOUT OTHERS.
!
SKREEE
*Tongue: Joy
HINOKAMI KAGURA

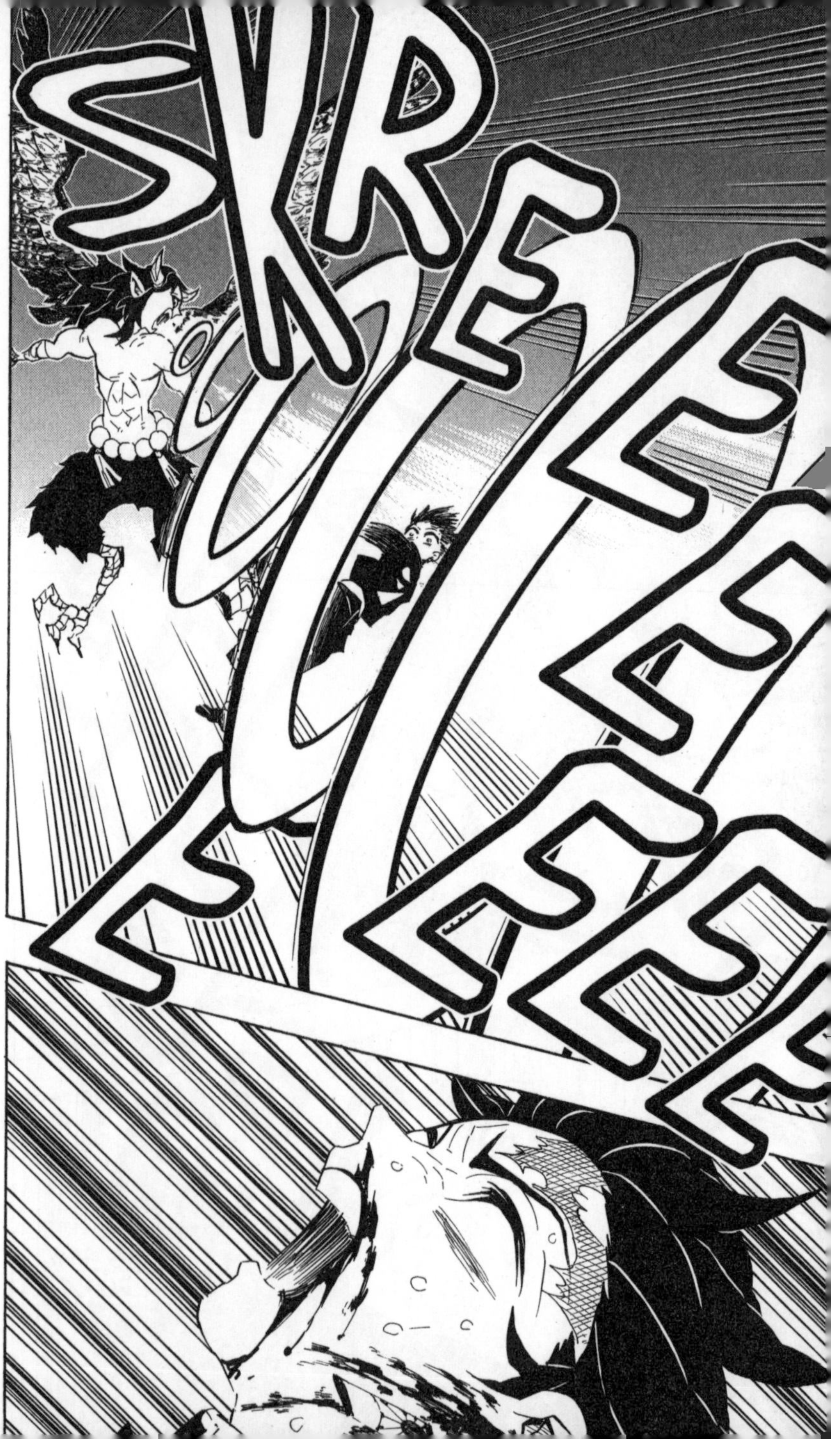
SKREEEE

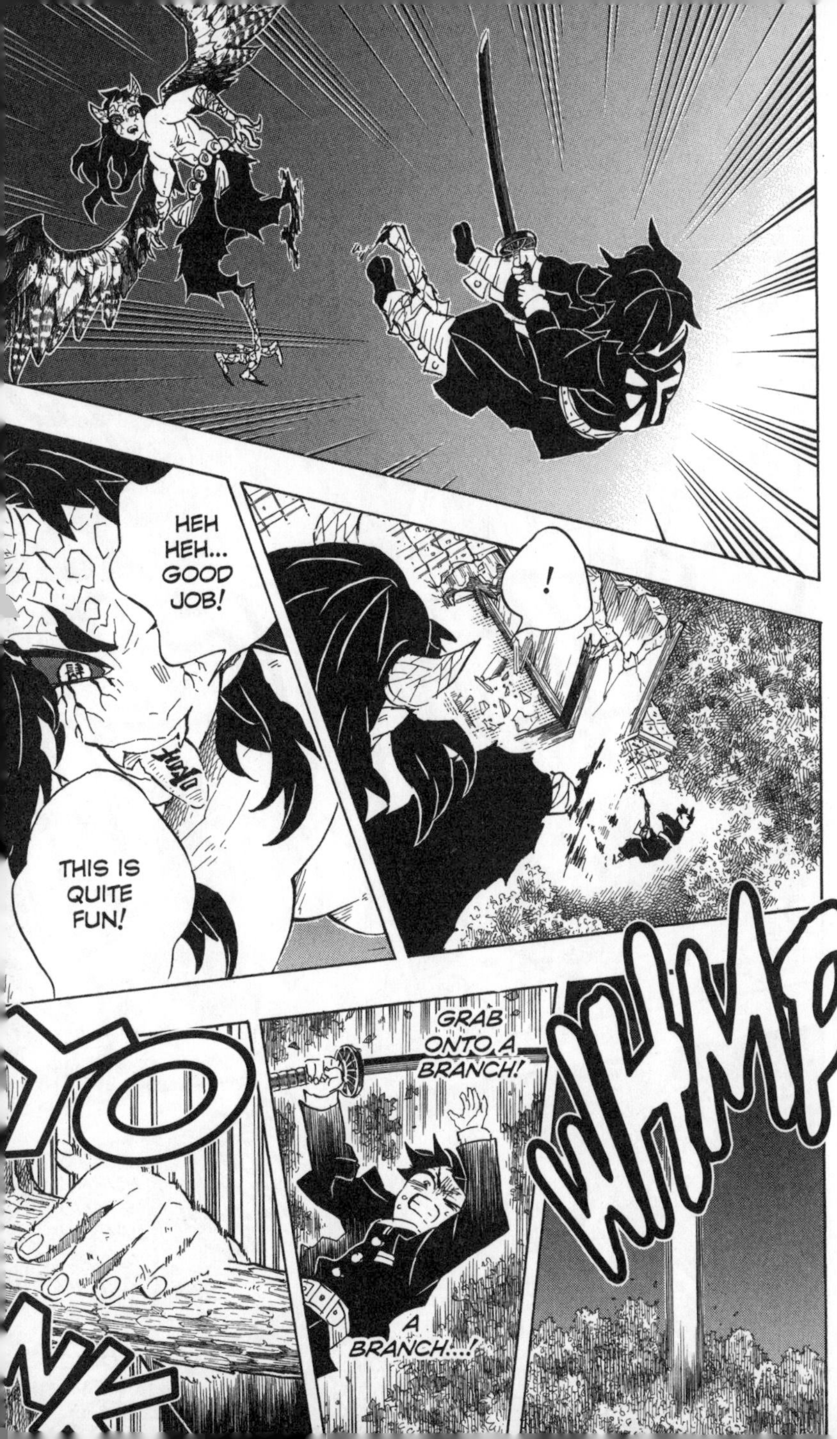
!
HEH HEH... GOOD JOB!
THIS IS QUITE FUN!
WHUMP
GRAB ONTO A BRANCH!
A BRANCH...!

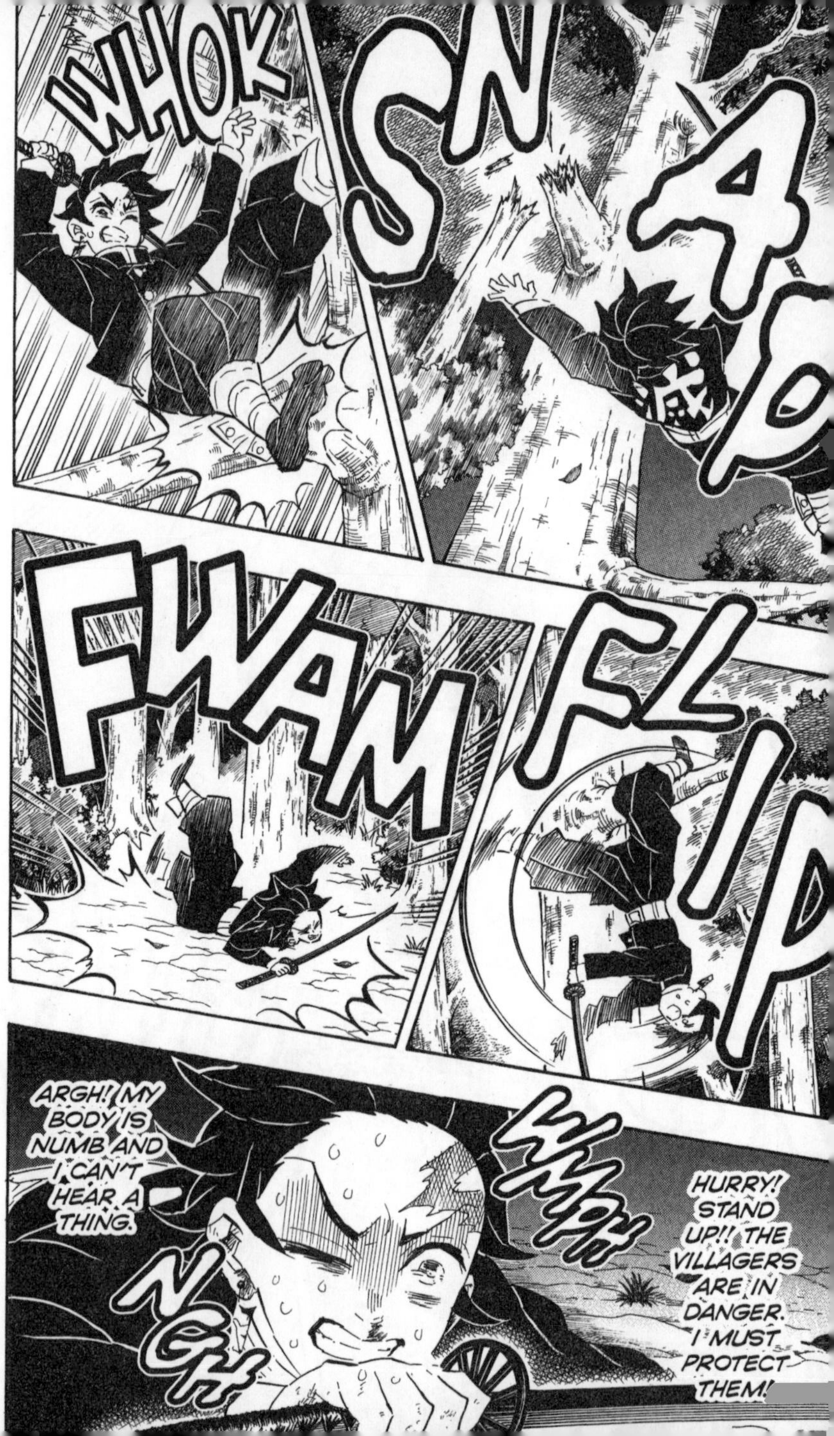
SNAP
WHOK
FLIP
FWAM
HURRY! STAND UP!! THE VILLAGERS ARE IN DANGER. I MUST PROTECT THEM!
WMPH
ARGH! MY BODY IS NUMB AND I CAN'T HEAR A THING.
NGH

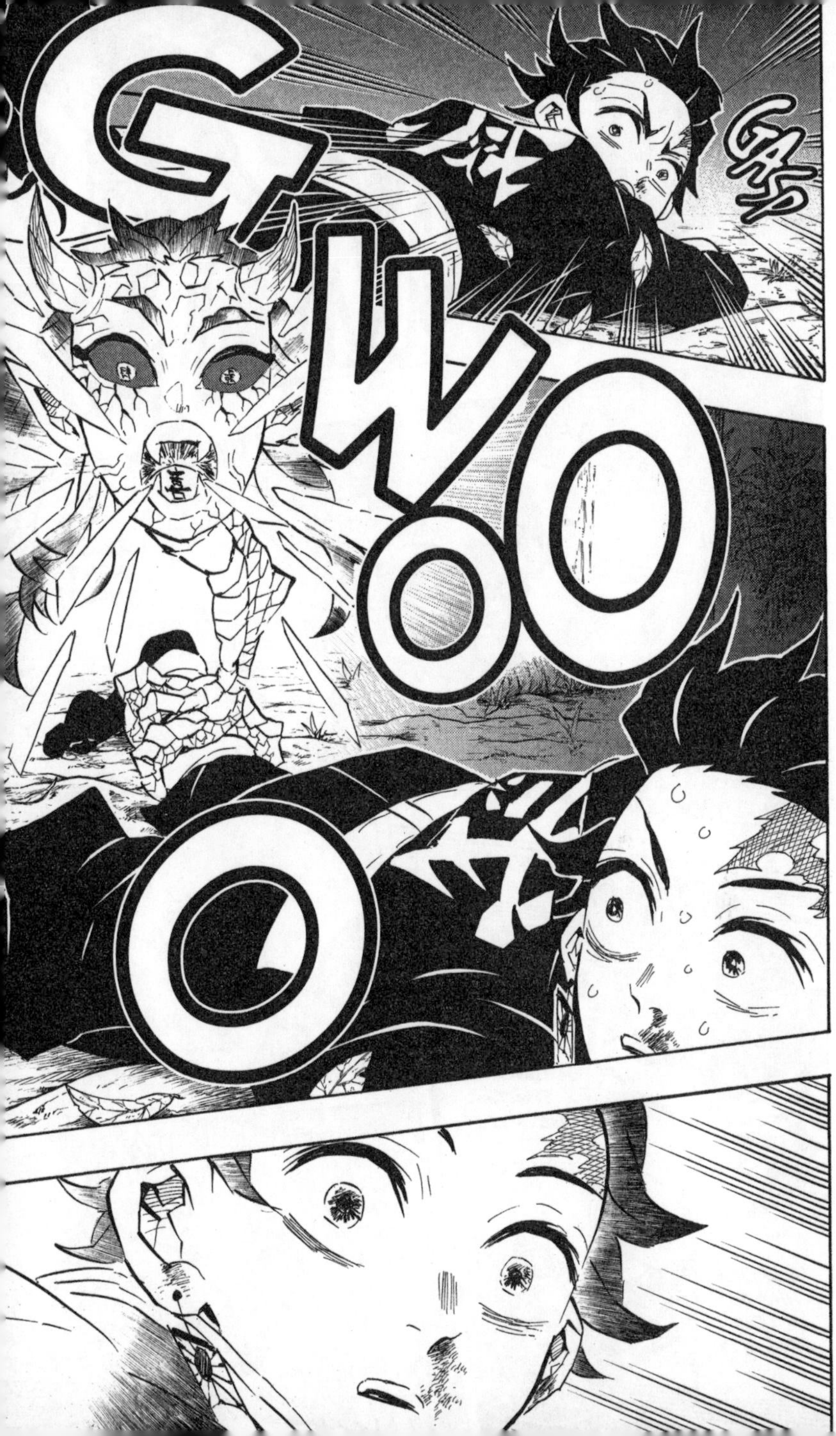
GASP
GWOOO
O

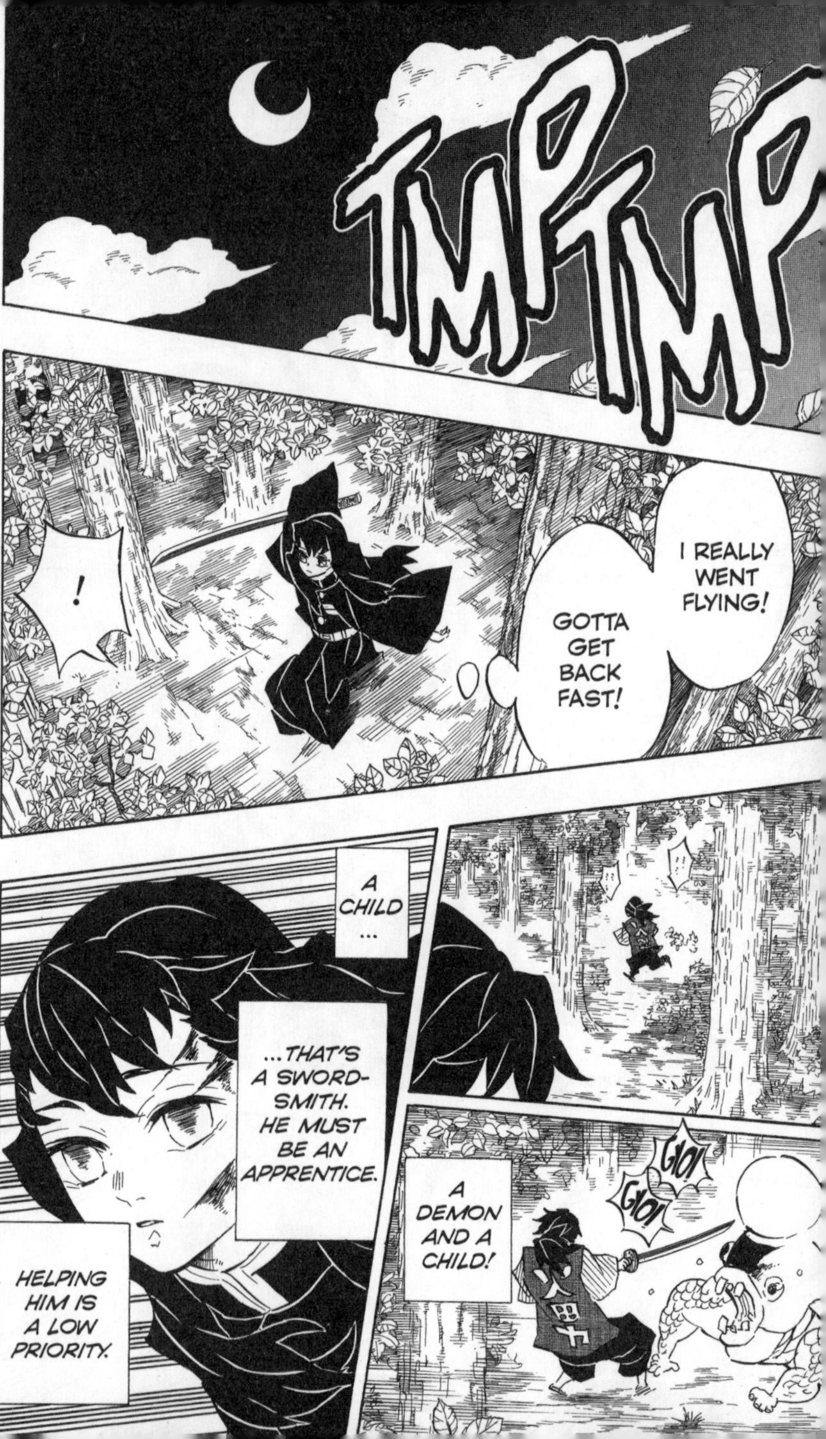
TMP TMP
I REALLY WENT FLYING!
GOTTA GET BACK FAST!
!
A CHILD ...
GYO! GYO!
A DEMON AND A CHILD!
...THAT'S A SWORD-SMITH. HE MUST BE AN APPRENTICE.
HELPING HIM IS A LOW PRIORITY.

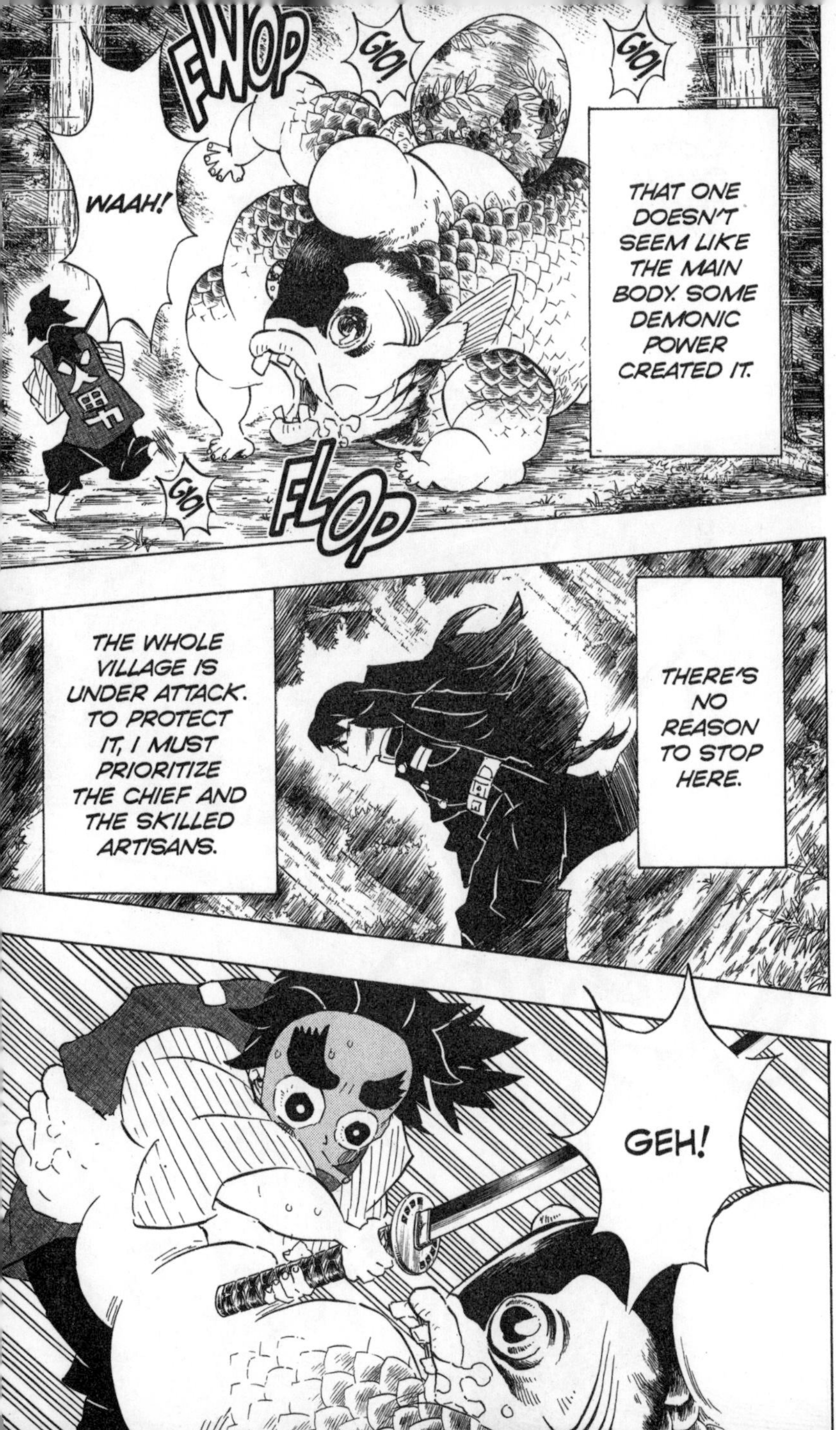
GYO!
THAT ONE DOESN'T SEEM LIKE THE MAIN BODY. SOME DEMONIC POWER CREATED IT.
GYO!
FWOP
WAAH!
FLOP
GYO!
THERE'S NO REASON TO STOP HERE.
THE WHOLE VILLAGE IS UNDER ATTACK. TO PROTECT IT, I MUST PRIORITIZE THE CHIEF AND THE SKILLED ARTISANS.
GEH!

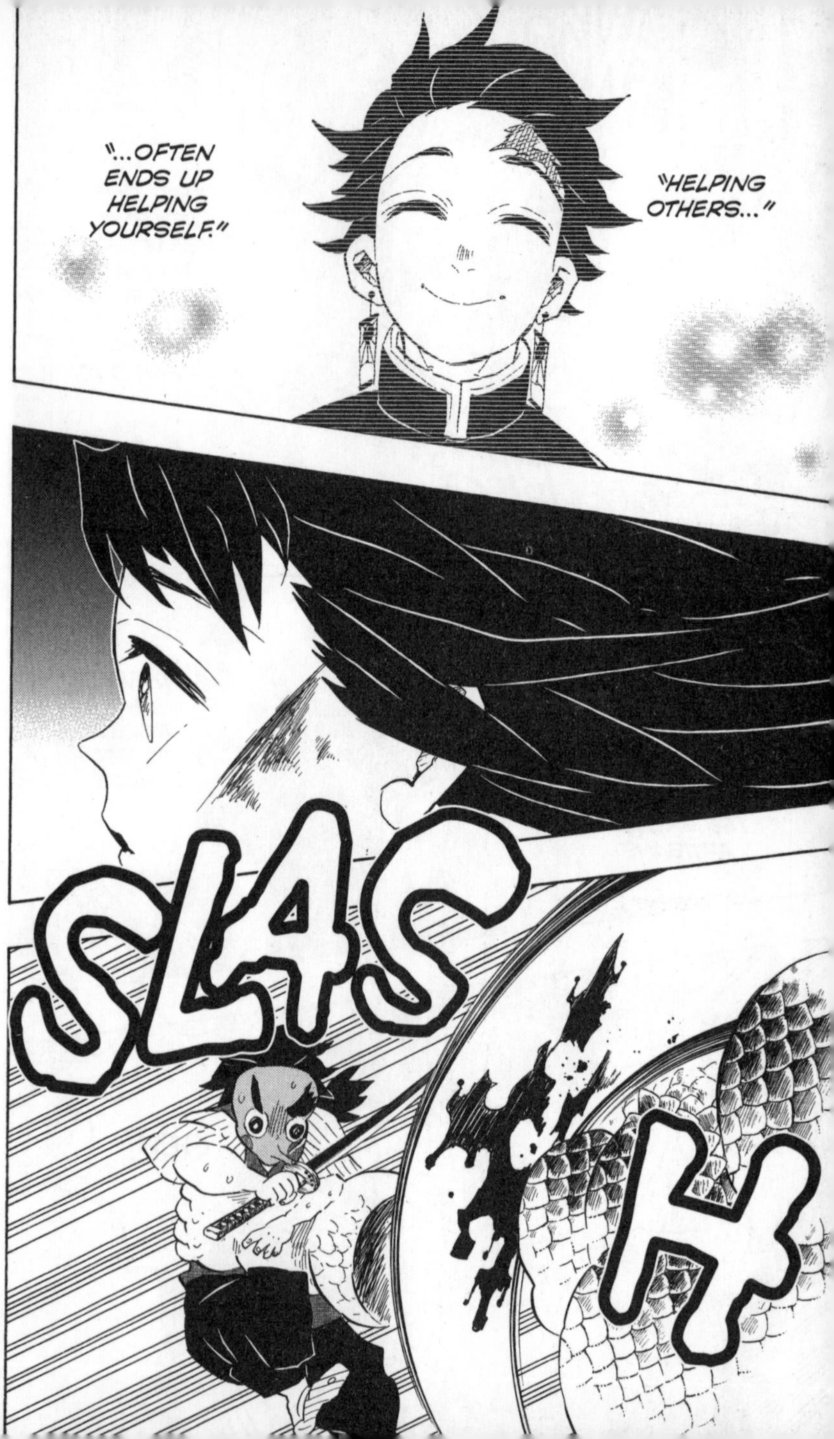
"HELPING OTHERS..."
"...OFTEN ENDS UP HELPING YOURSELF."
SLASH

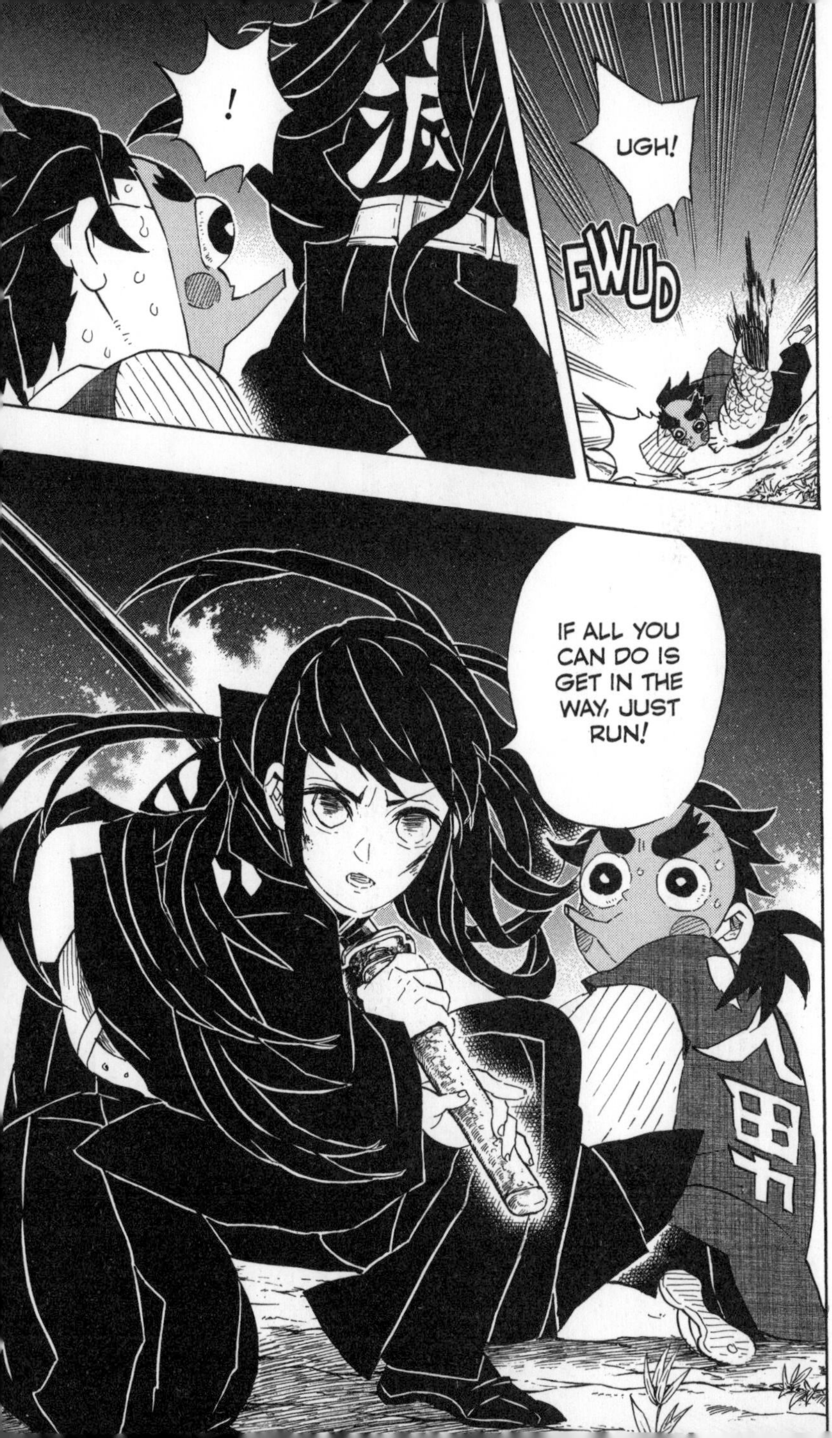
UGH!
FWUD
!
IF ALL YOU CAN DO IS GET IN THE WAY, JUST RUN!

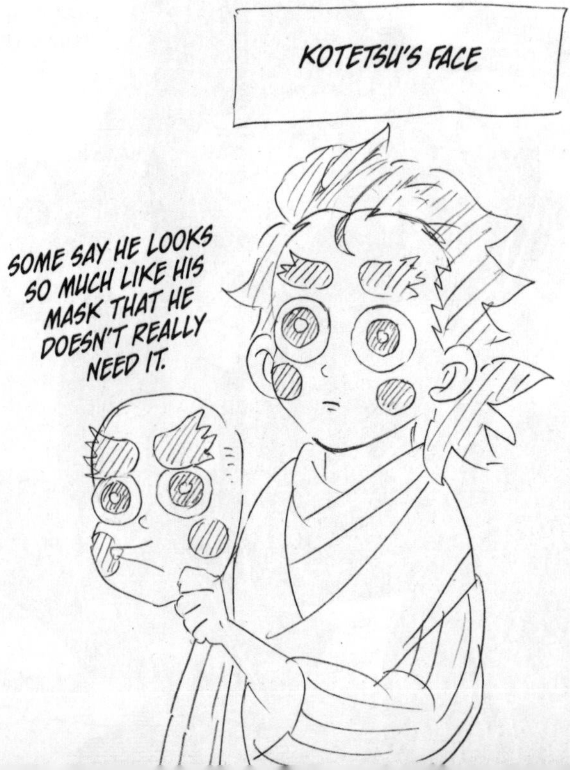
KOTETSU'S FACE
SOME SAY HE LOOKS SO MUCH LIKE HIS MASK THAT HE DOESN'T REALLY NEED IT.

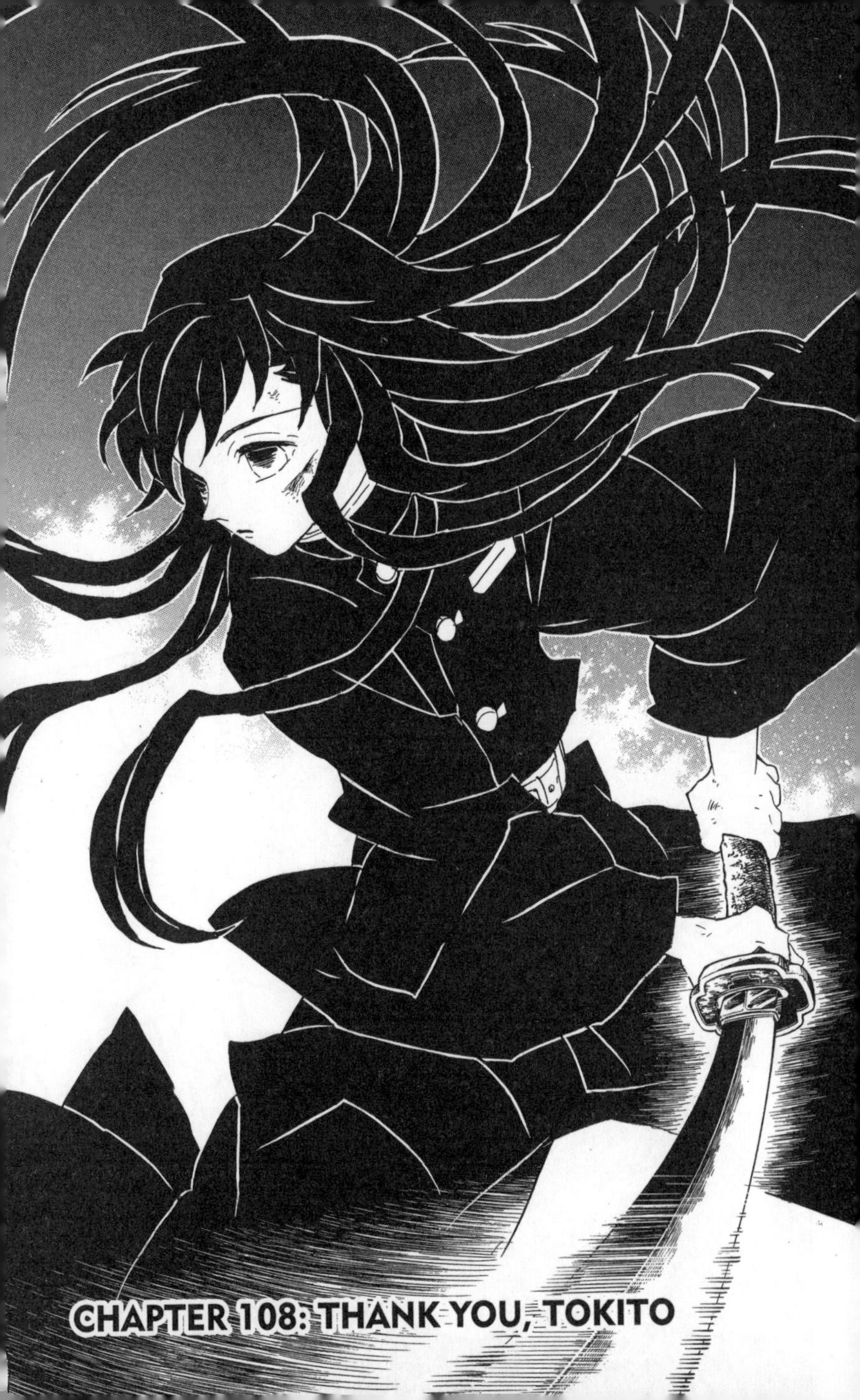

CHAPTER 108: THANK YOU, TOKITO

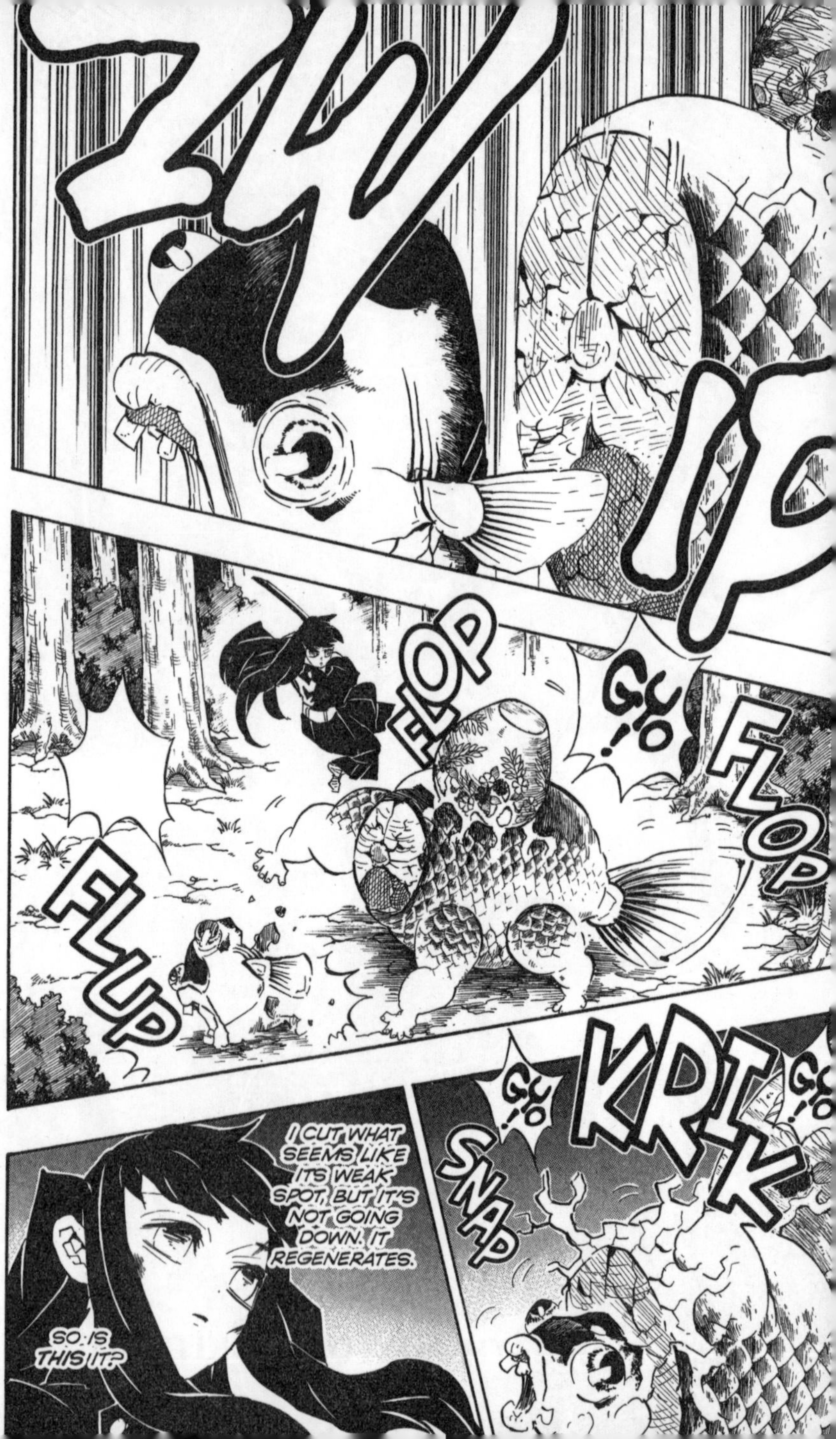
ZWIP
GYO!
FLOP
FLOP
FLUP
GYO!
KRIK
GYO!
SNAP
I CUT WHAT SEEMS LIKE ITS WEAK SPOT, BUT IT'S NOT GOING DOWN. IT REGENERATES.
SO IS THIS IT?

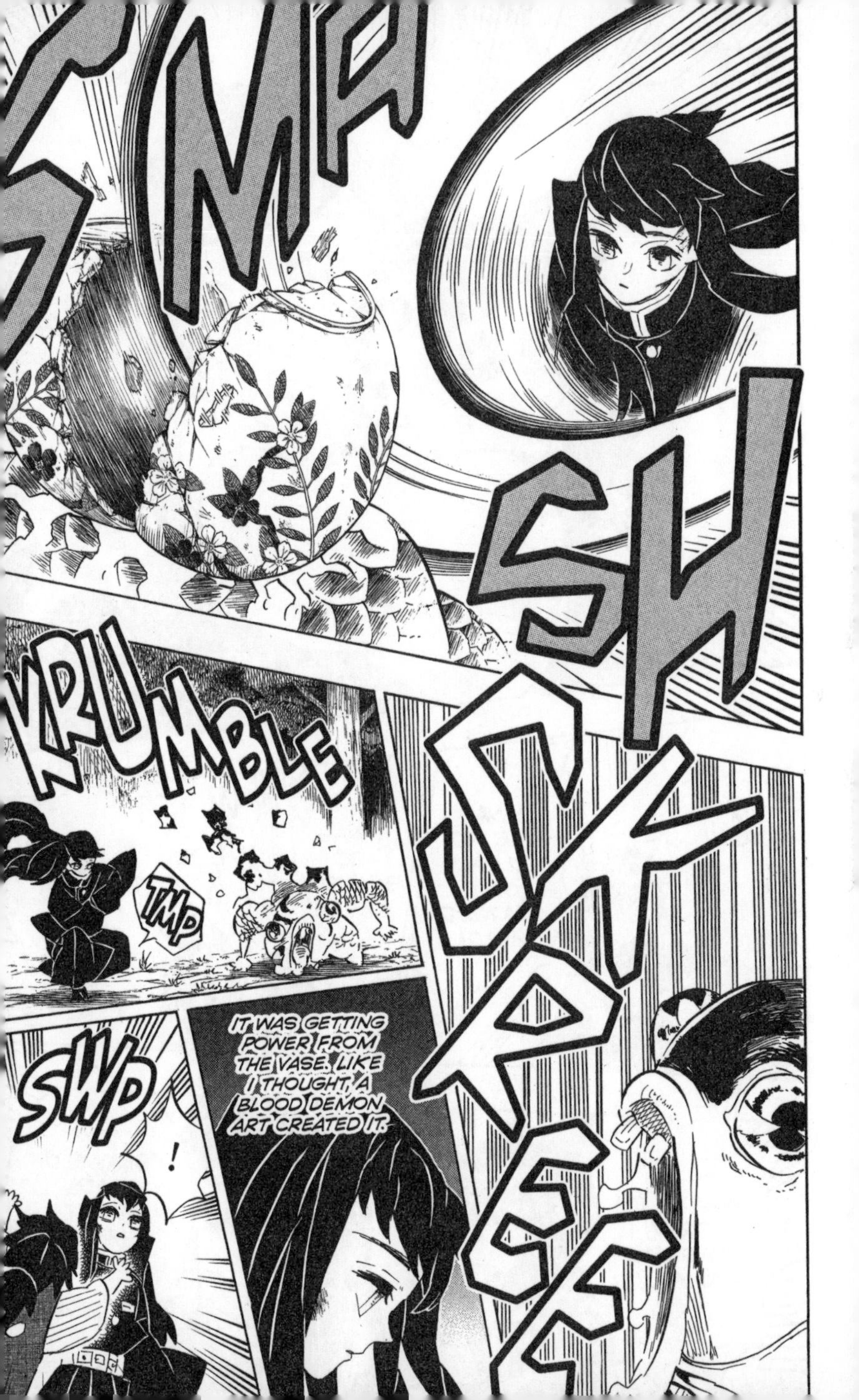
SMASH
KRUMBLE
TMP
IT WAS GETTING POWER FROM THE VASE. LIKE I THOUGHT, A BLOOD DEMON ART CREATED IT.
SWP
!

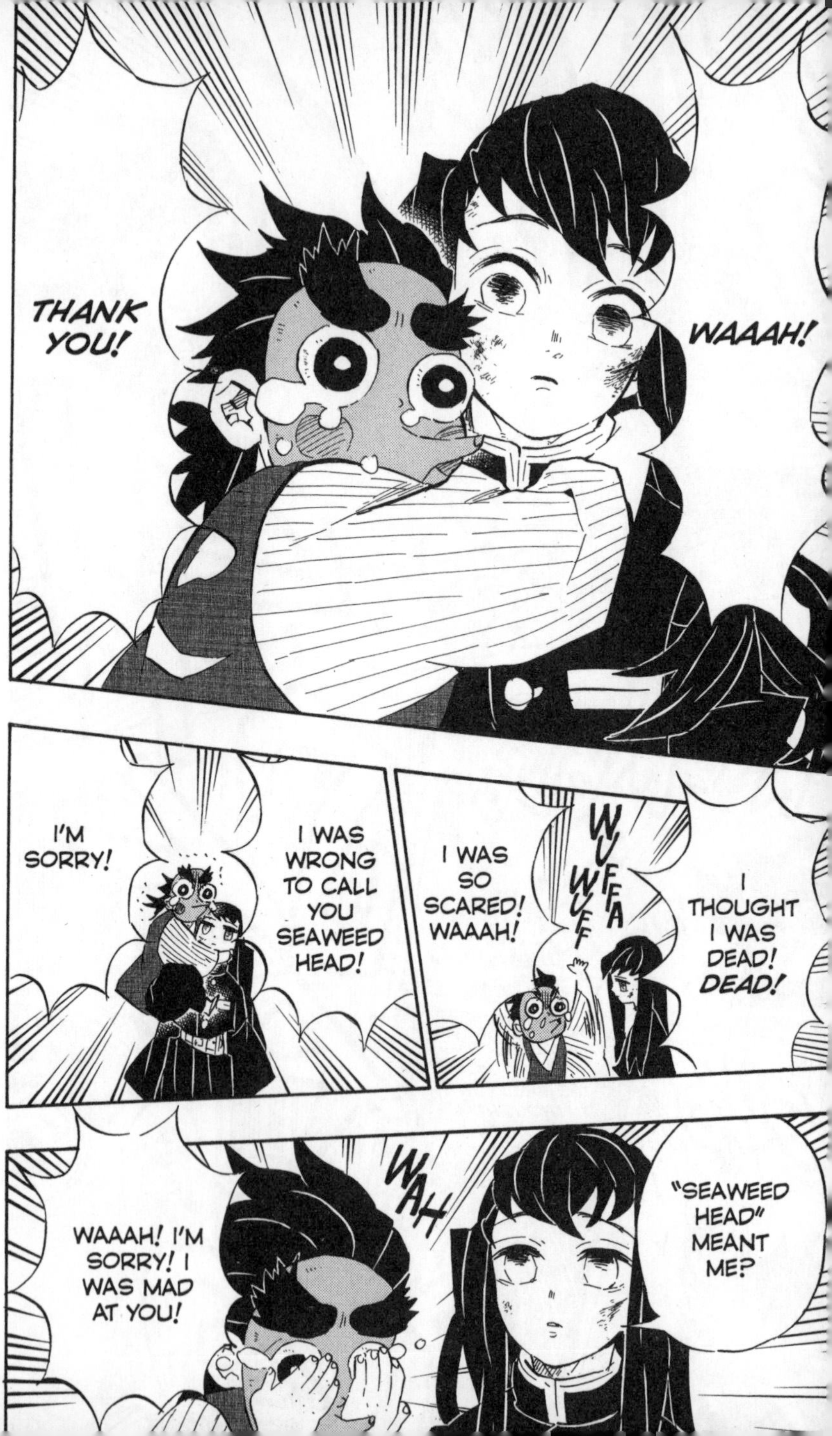
WAAAH!
THANK YOU!
I THOUGHT I WAS DEAD! DEAD!
WUFFA
WUFF
I WAS SO SCARED! WAAAH!
I WAS WRONG TO CALL YOU SEAWEED HEAD!
I'M SORRY!
"SEAWEED HEAD" MEANT ME?
WAH
WAAAH! I'M SORRY! I WAS MAD AT YOU!

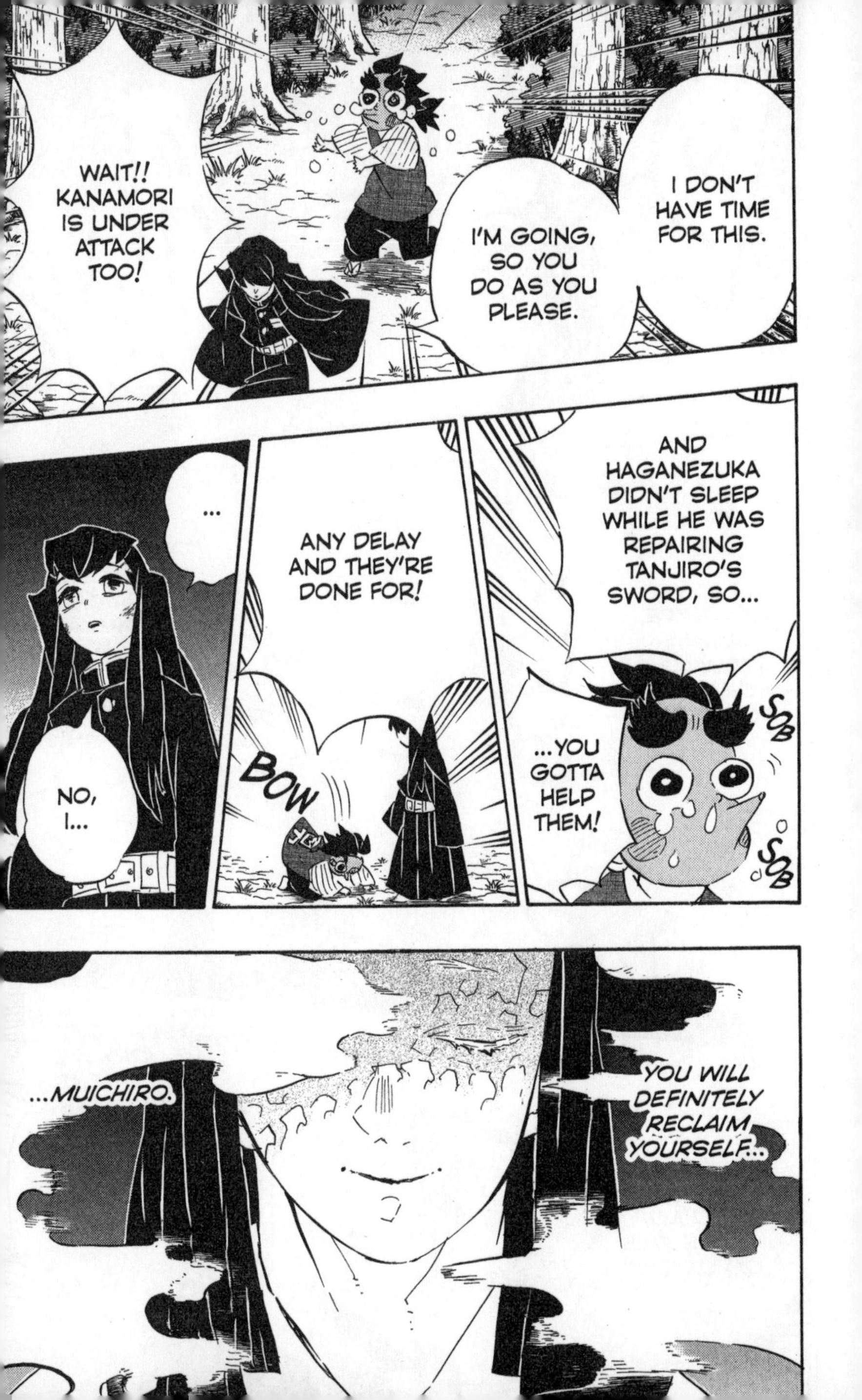
I DON'T HAVE TIME FOR THIS.
I'M GOING, SO YOU DO AS YOU PLEASE.
WAIT!! KANAMORI IS UNDER ATTACK TOO!
AND HAGANEZUKA DIDN'T SLEEP WHILE HE WAS REPAIRING TANJIRO'S SWORD, SO...
SOB
...YOU GOTTA HELP THEM!
SOB
ANY DELAY AND THEY'RE DONE FOR!
BOW
...
NO, I...
YOU WILL DEFINITELY RECLAIM YOURSELF...
...MUICHIRO.

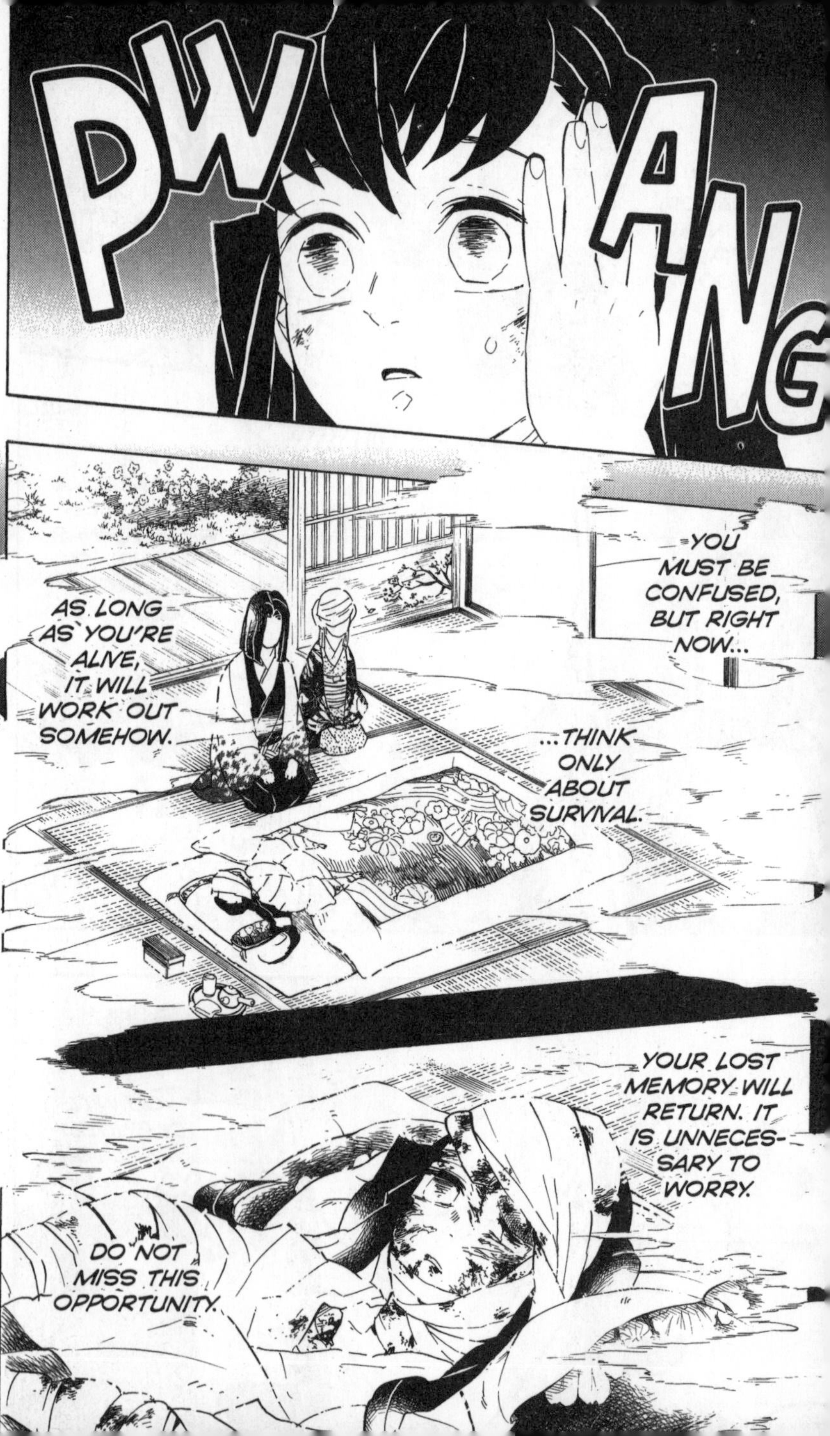
PWANG
YOU MUST BE CONFUSED, BUT RIGHT NOW...
...THINK ONLY ABOUT SURVIVAL.
AS LONG AS YOU'RE ALIVE, IT WILL WORK OUT SOMEHOW.
YOUR LOST MEMORY WILL RETURN. IT IS UNNECES-SARY TO WORRY.
DO NOT MISS THIS OPPORTUNITY.

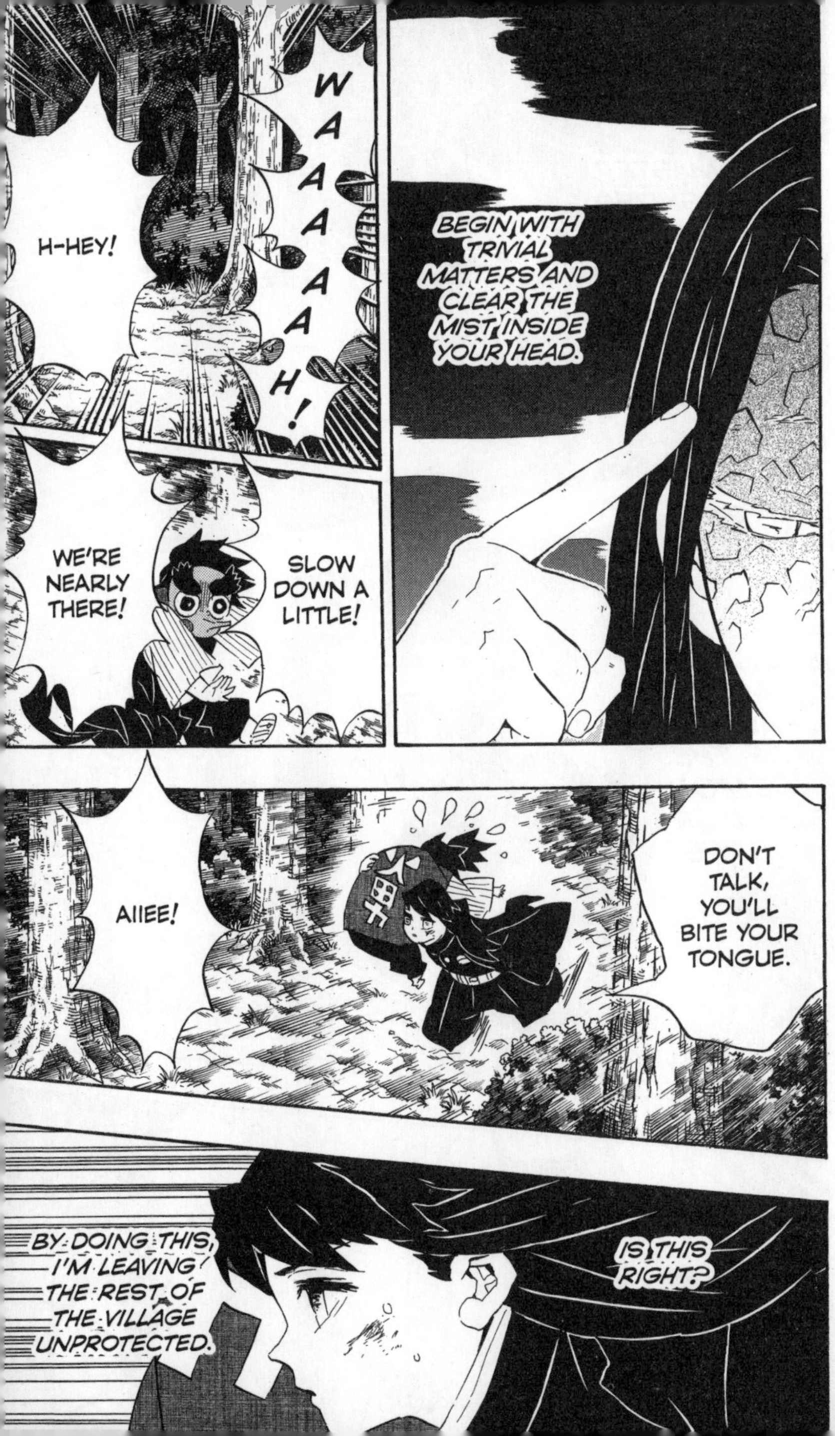
BEGIN WITH TRIVIAL MATTERS AND CLEAR THE MIST INSIDE YOUR HEAD.
WAAAAAH!
H-HEY!
SLOW DOWN A LITTLE!
WE'RE NEARLY THERE!
DON'T TALK, YOU'LL BITE YOUR TONGUE.
AIIEE!
IS THIS RIGHT?
BY DOING THIS, I'M LEAVING THE REST OF THE VILLAGE UNPROTECTED.

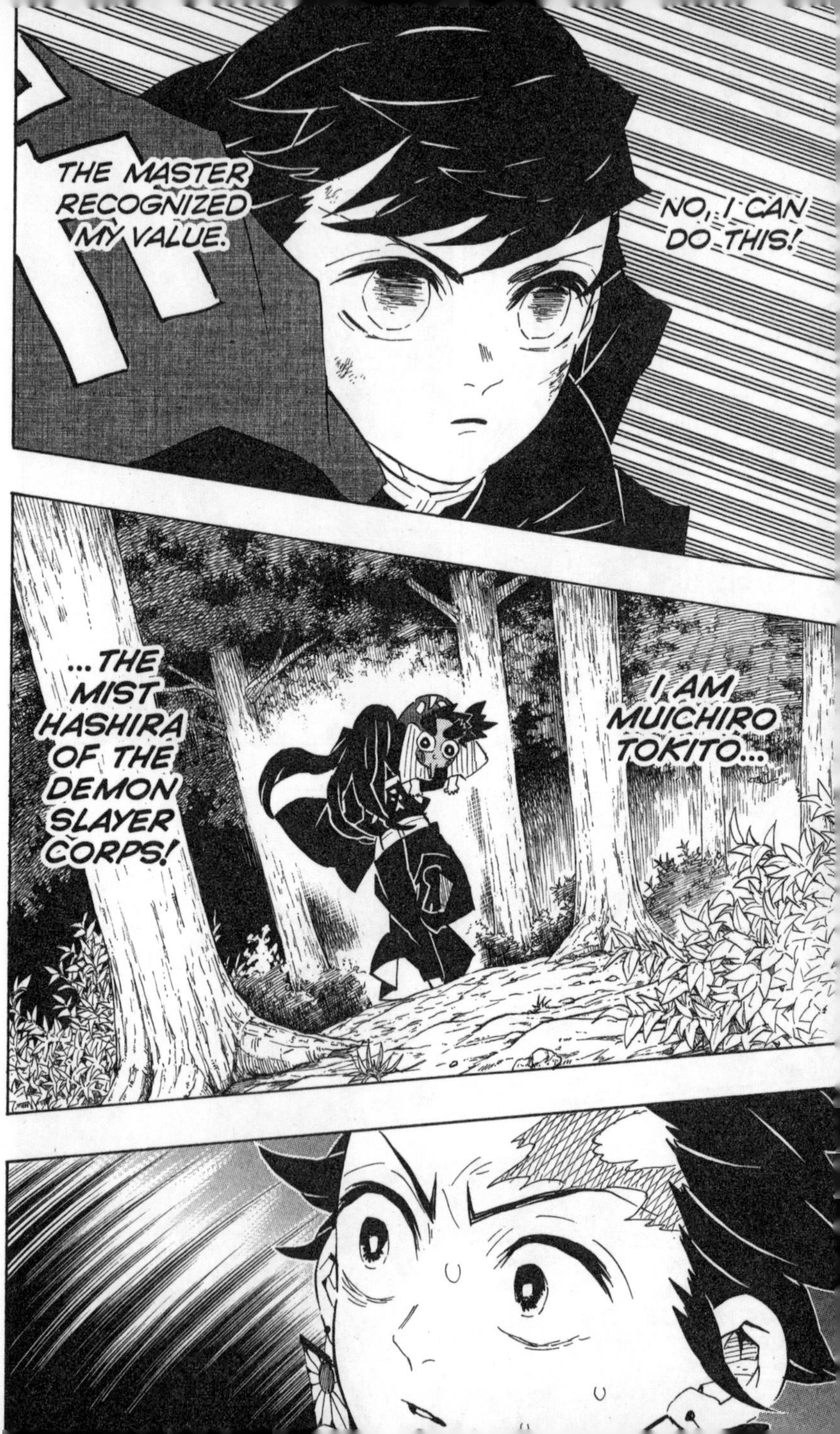
NO, I CAN DO THIS!
THE MASTER RECOGNIZED MY VALUE.
I AM MUICHIRO TOKITO...
...THE MIST HASHIRA OF THE DEMON SLAYER CORPS!

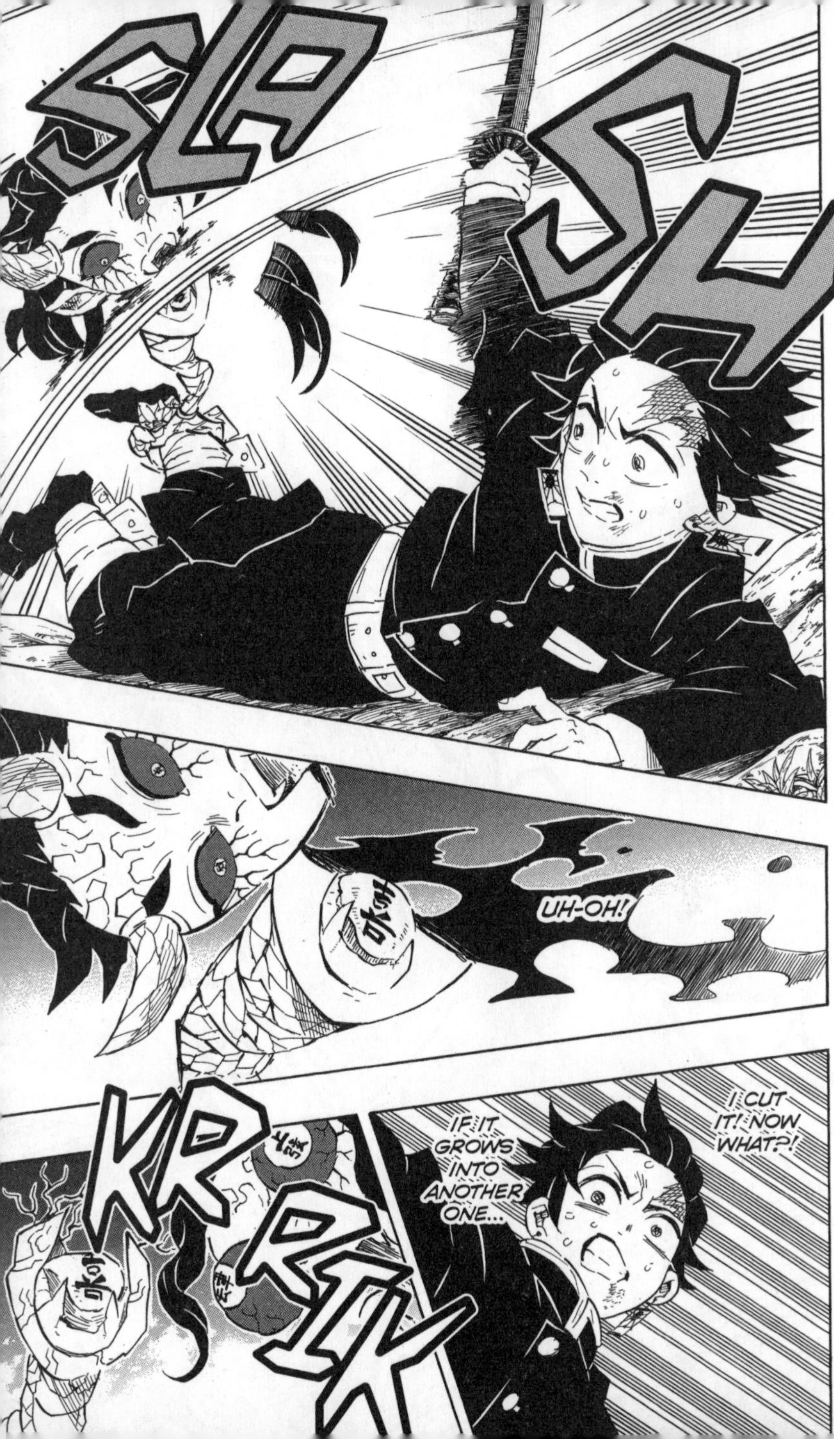
SLASH
UH-OH!
I CUT IT! NOW WHAT?!
IF IT GROWS INTO ANOTHER ONE...
KRRIK

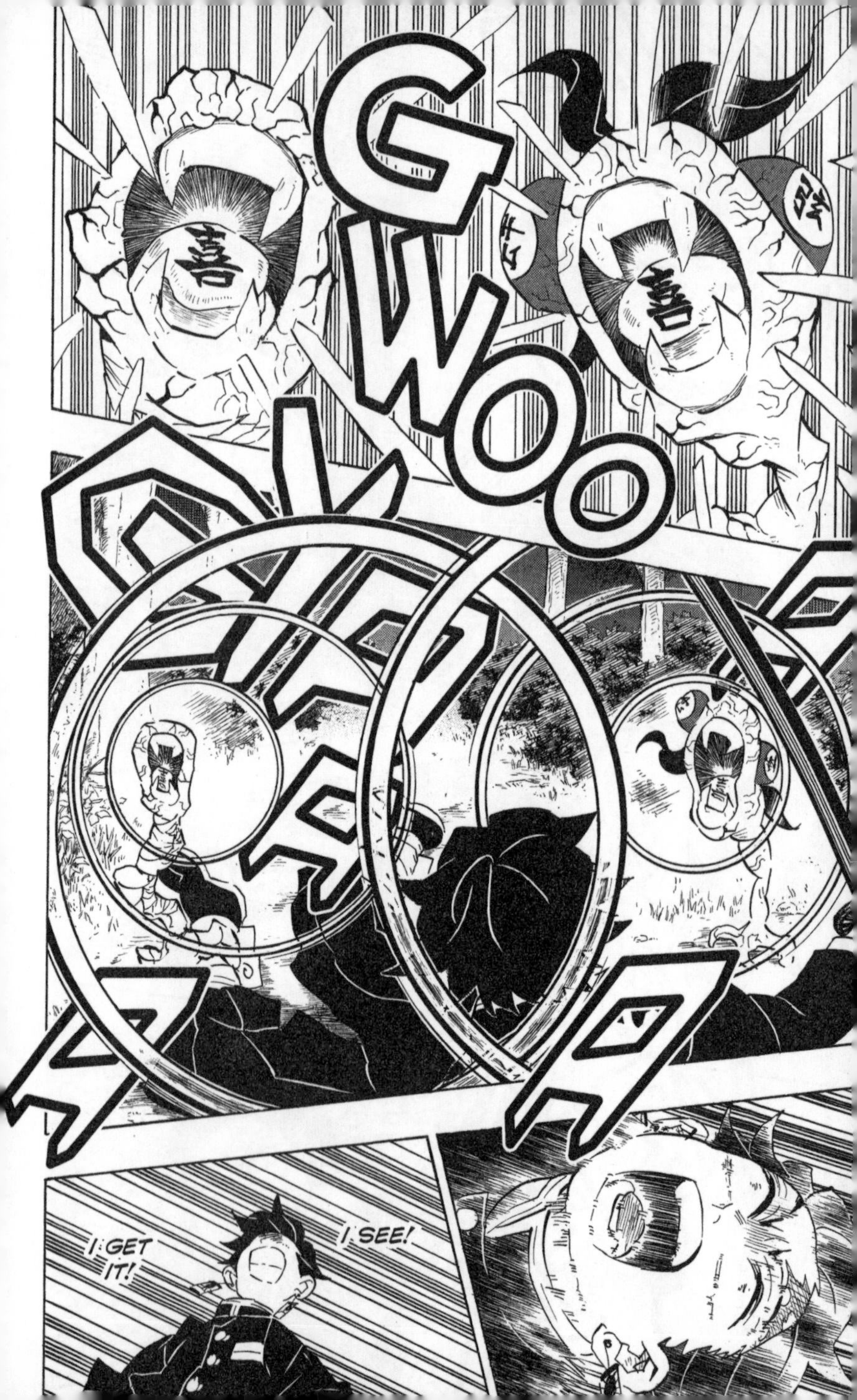
GWOO
I SEE!
I GET IT!

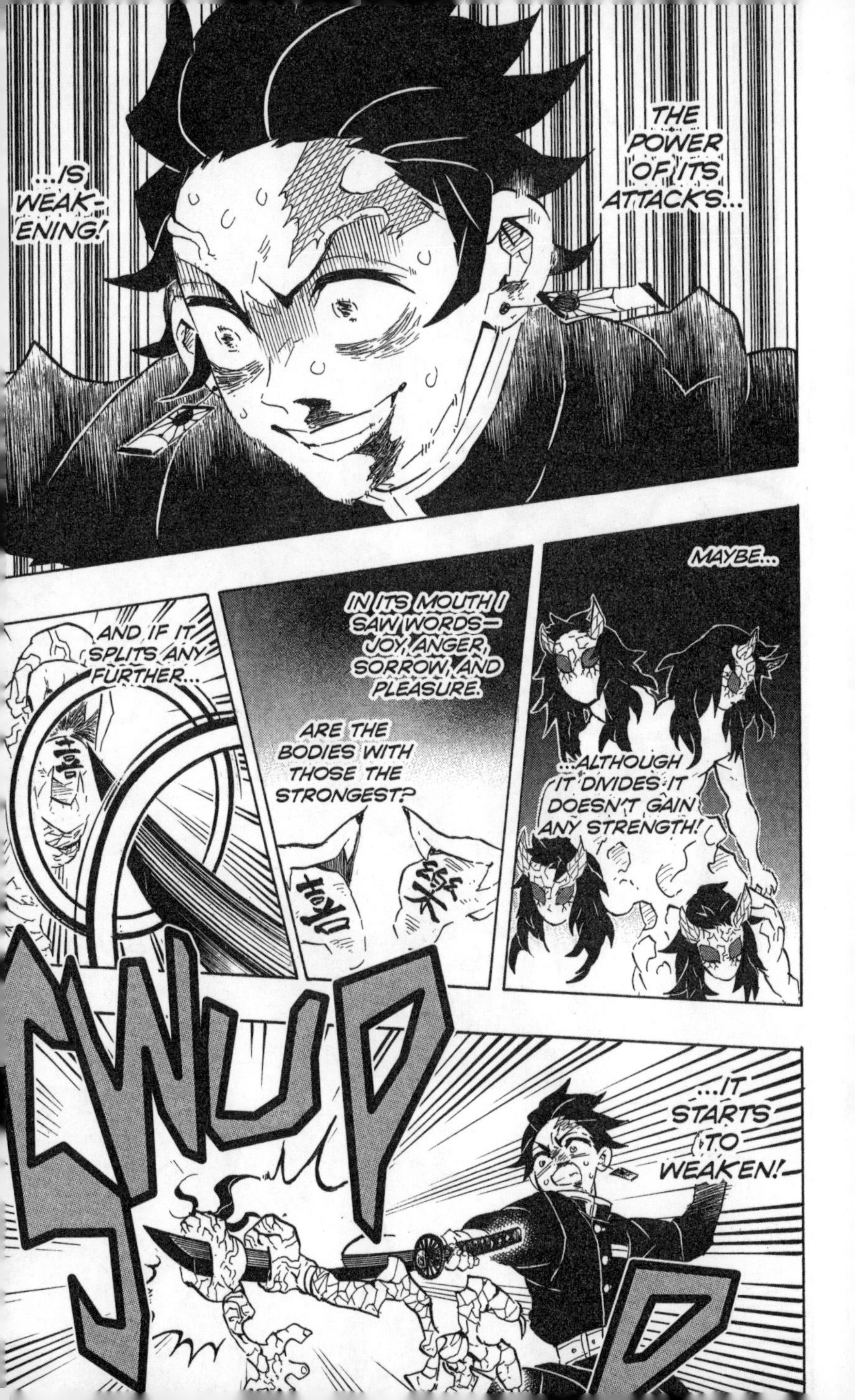
THE POWER OF ITS ATTACKS...
...IS WEAK-ENING!
MAYBE...
...ALTHOUGH IT DIVIDES IT DOESN'T GAIN ANY STRENGTH!
IN ITS MOUTH I SAW WORDS—JOY, ANGER, SORROW, AND PLEASURE.
ARE THE BODIES WITH THOSE THE STRONGEST?
AND IF IT SPLITS ANY FURTHER...
...IT STARTS TO WEAKEN!

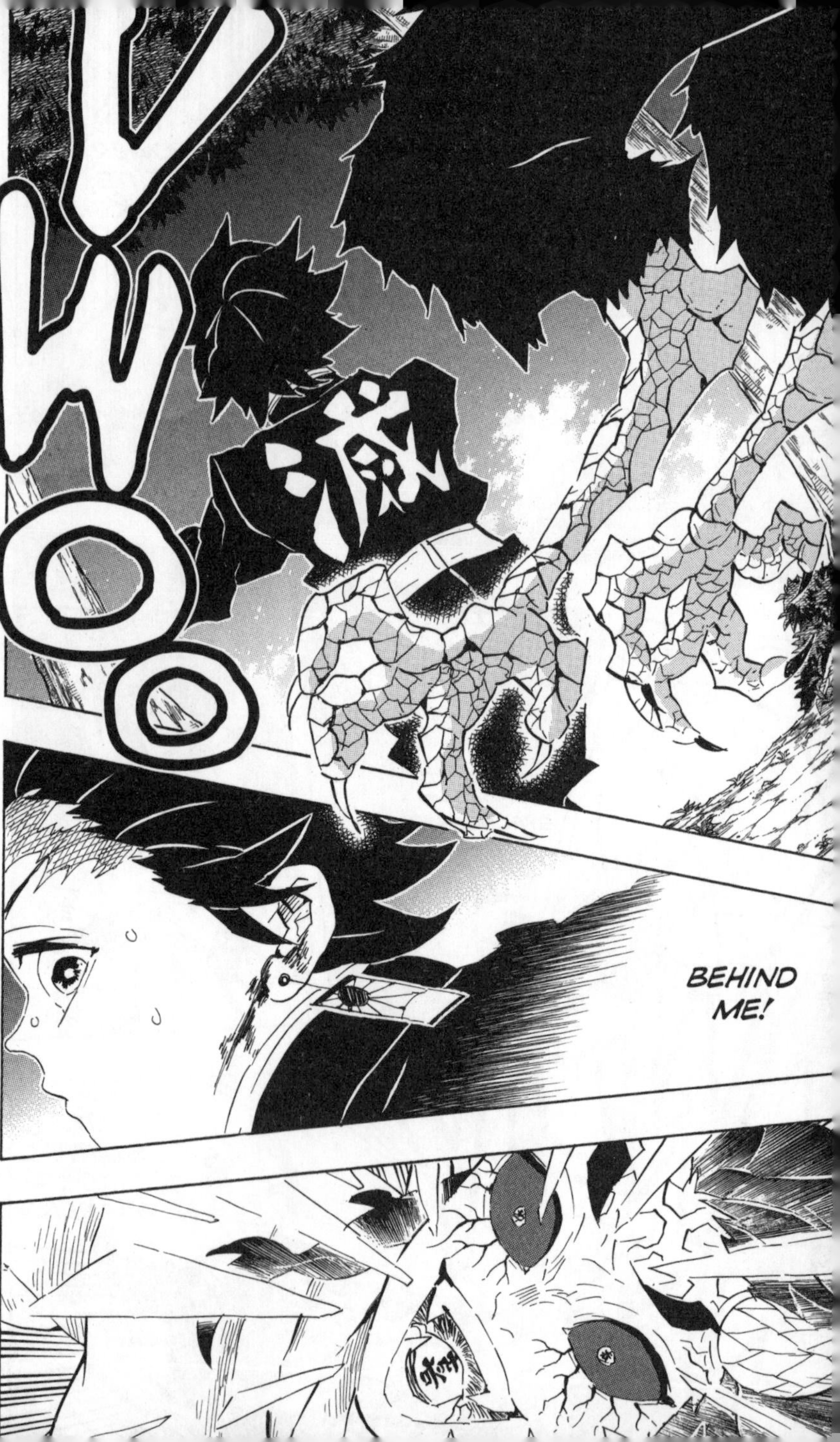
BEHIND ME!

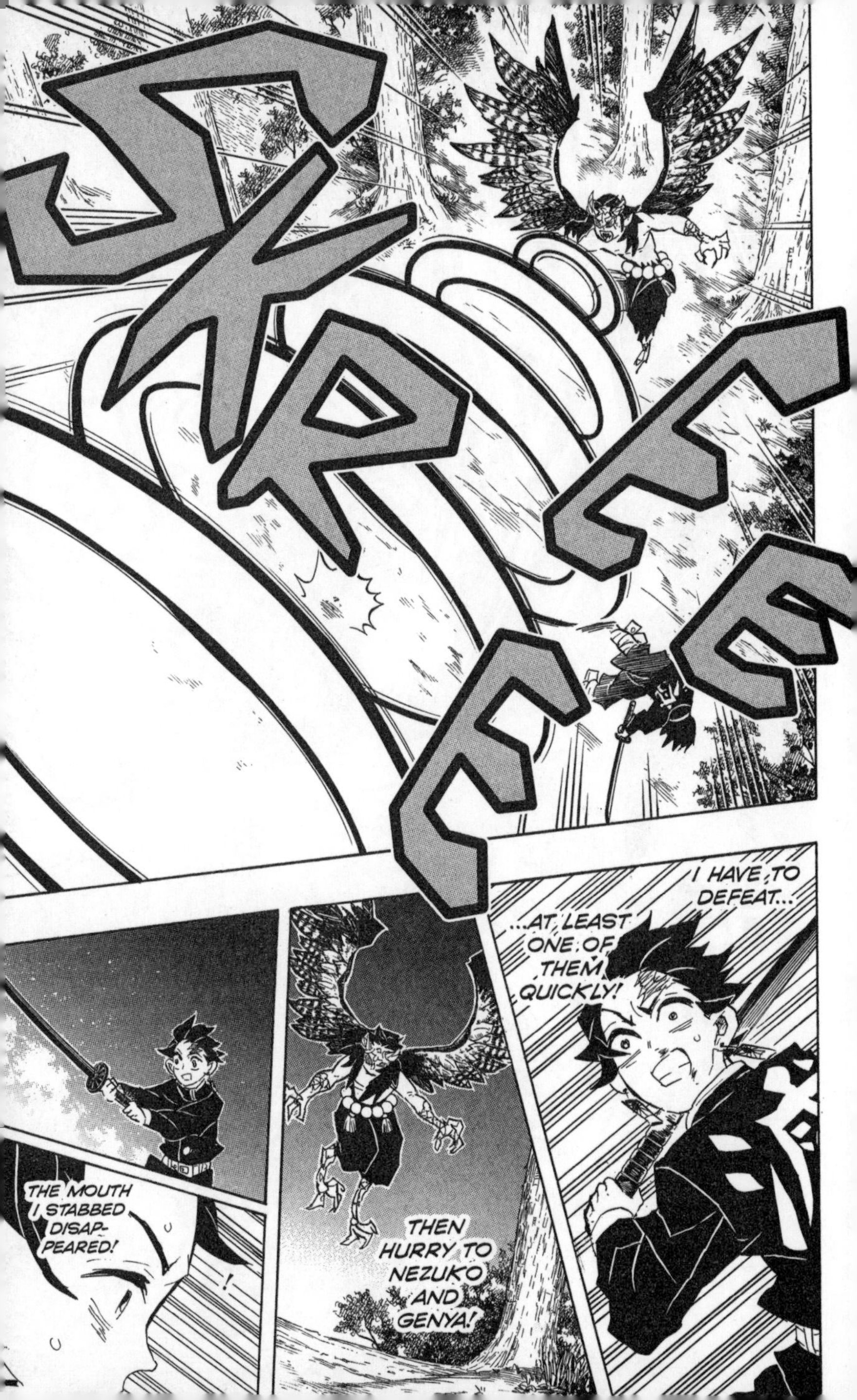
SKREEE
I HAVE TO DEFEAT...
...AT LEAST ONE OF THEM QUICKLY!
THEN HURRY TO NEZUKO AND GENYA!
THE MOUTH I STABBED DISAPPEARED!
!

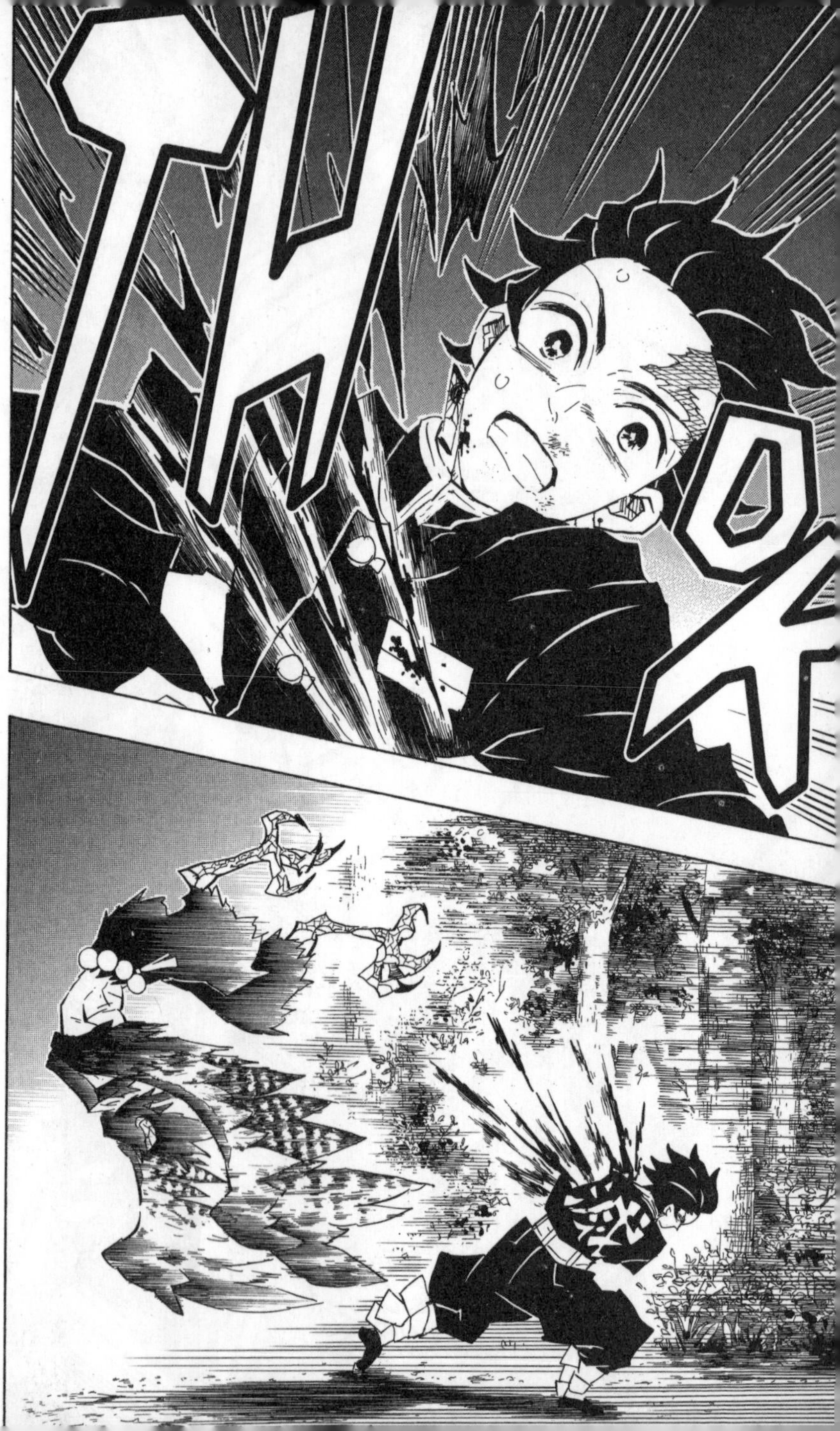

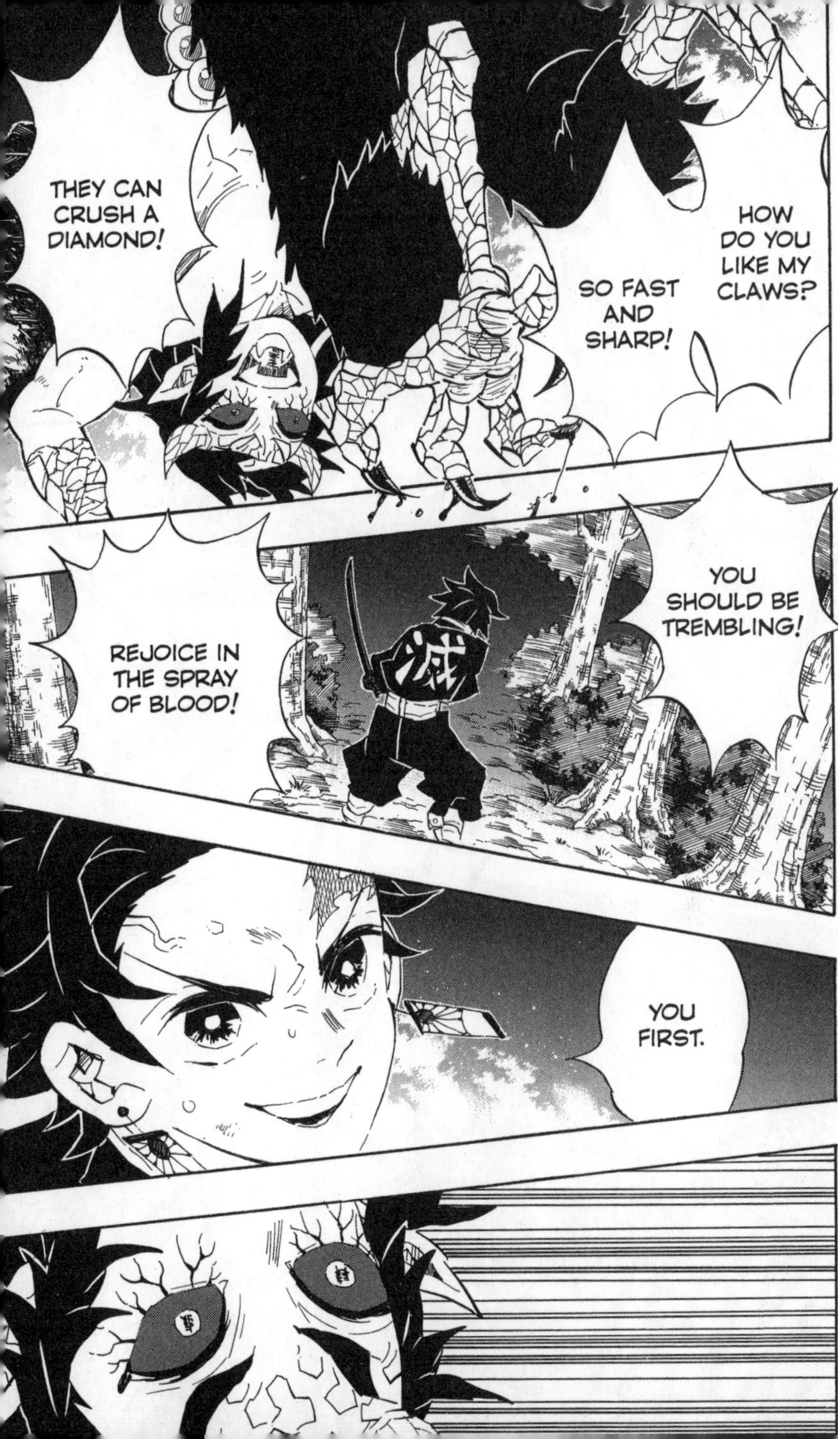
HOW DO YOU LIKE MY CLAWS?
SO FAST AND SHARP!
THEY CAN CRUSH A DIAMOND!
YOU SHOULD BE TREMBLING!
REJOICE IN THE SPRAY OF BLOOD!
YOU FIRST.

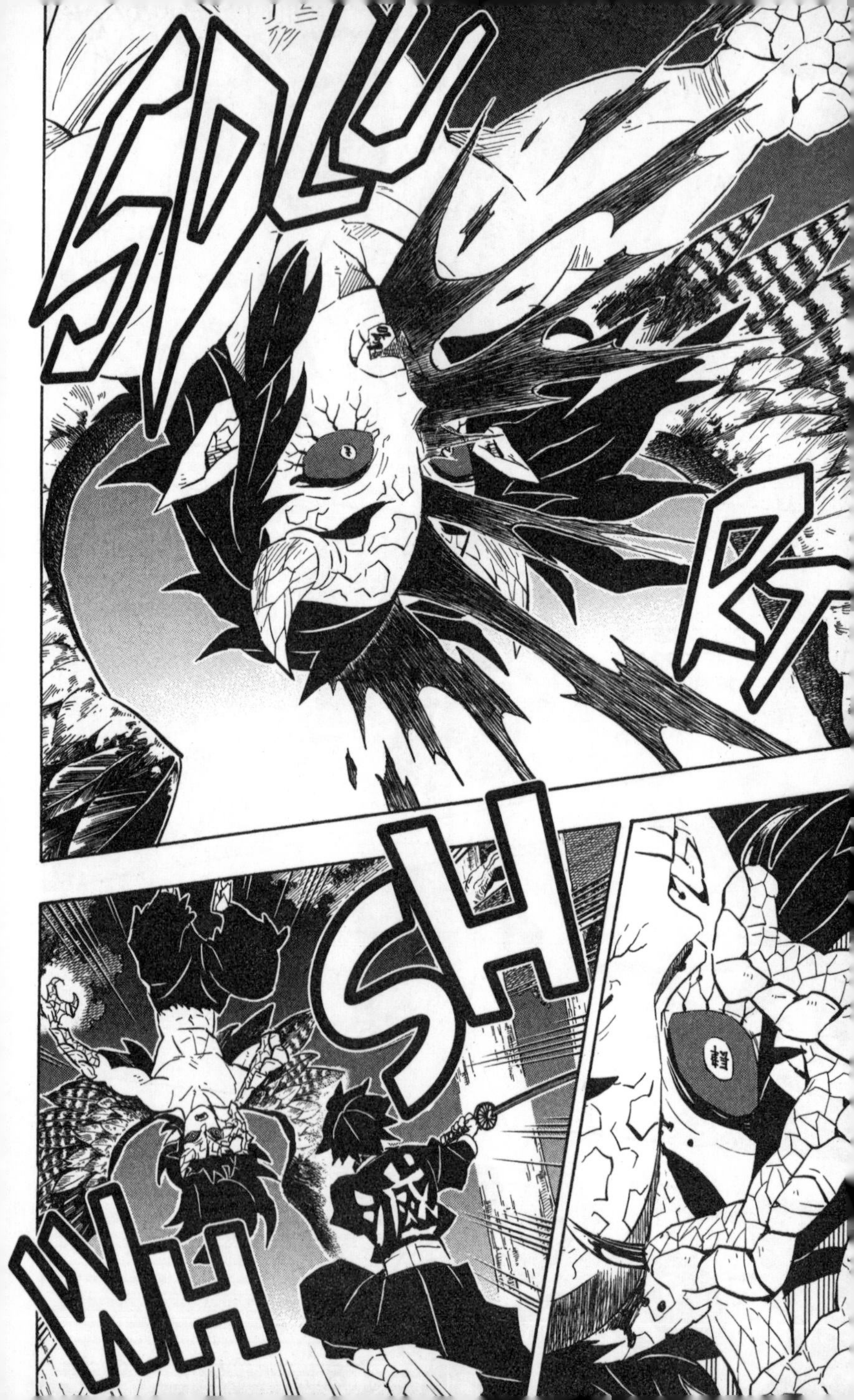
SPLU
RT
SH
WH

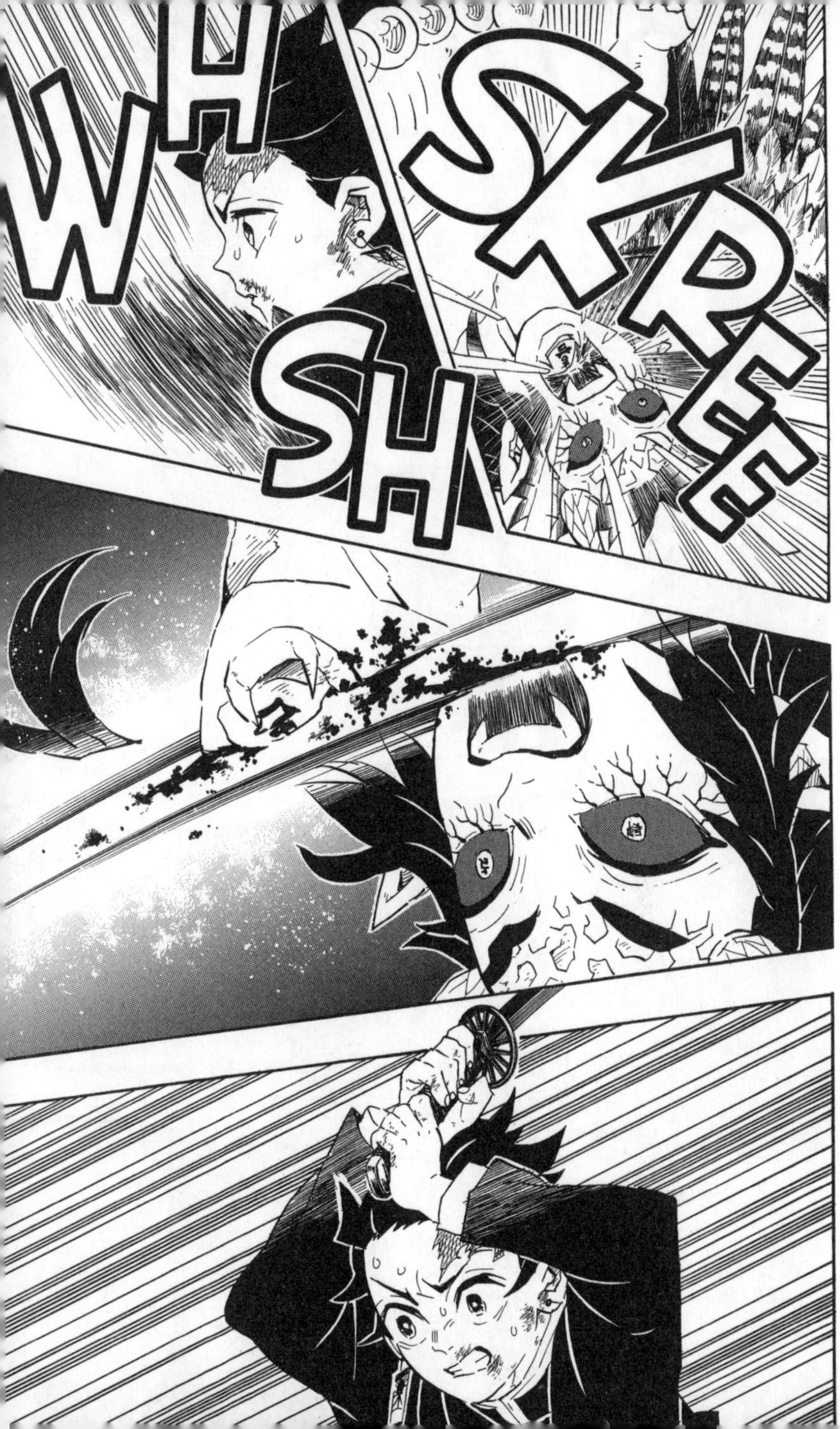
SKREEE
WHSH

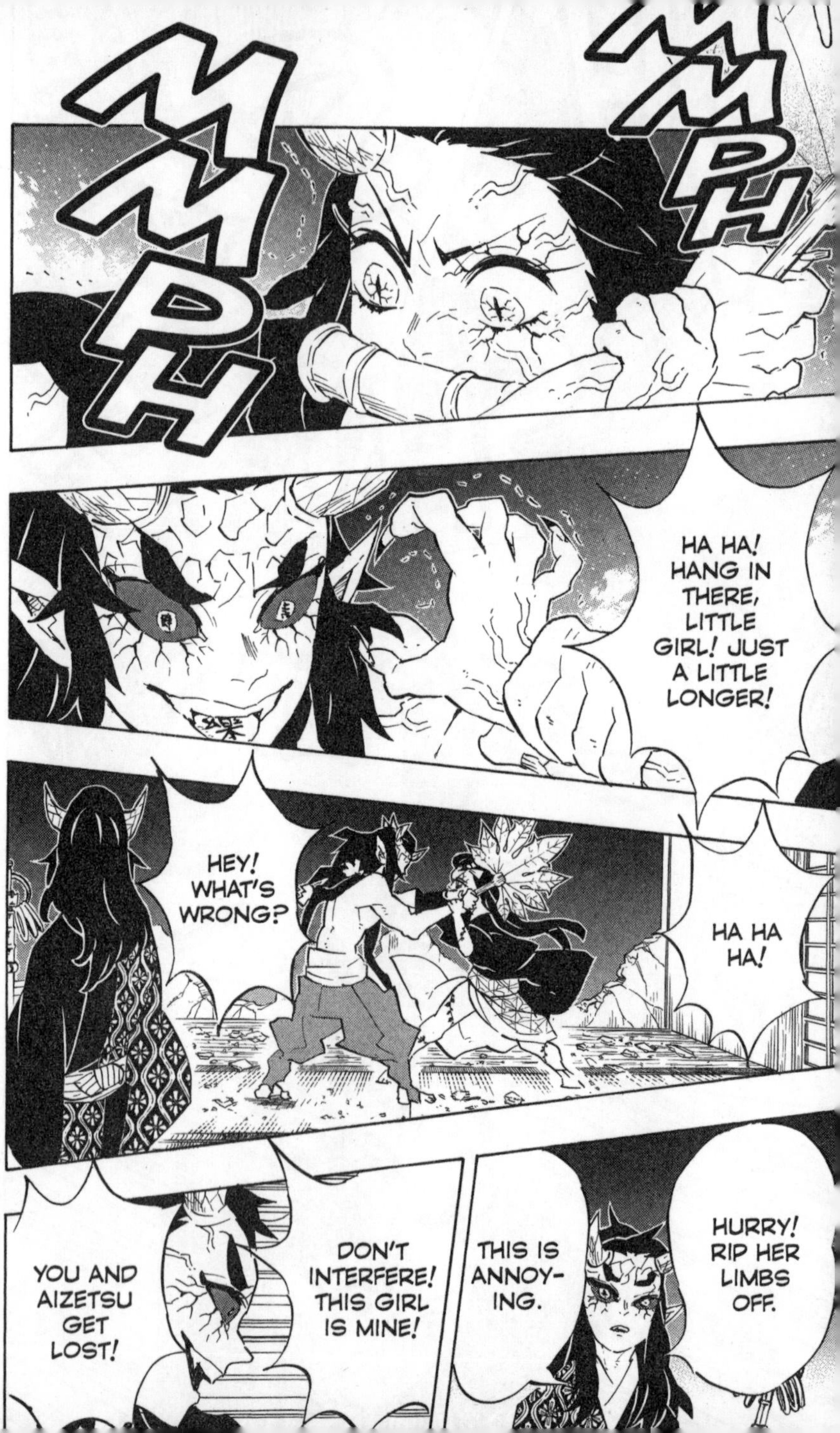
MMPH
MMPH
HA HA! HANG IN THERE, LITTLE GIRL! JUST A LITTLE LONGER!
HA HA HA!
HEY! WHAT'S WRONG?
HURRY! RIP HER LIMBS OFF.
THIS IS ANNOY-ING.
DON'T INTERFERE! THIS GIRL IS MINE!
YOU AND AIZETSU GET LOST!

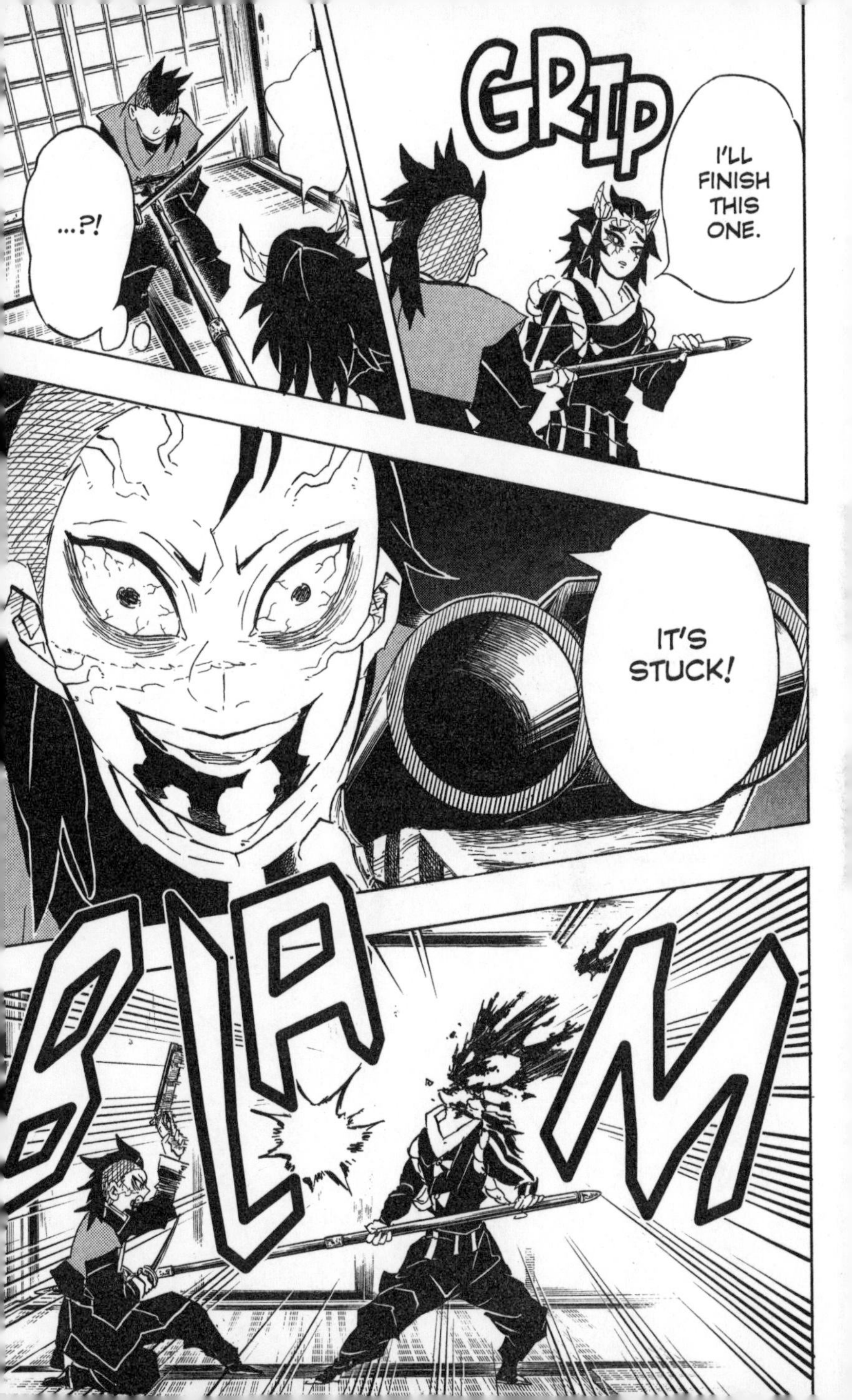
GRIP
I'LL FINISH THIS ONE.
...?!
IT'S STUCK!
BLAM

HIMEJIMA GOES TWEET

Stone Hashira Himejima
27 yrs. old
Virgo
Hobby: Shakuhachi

...

Once, when he played
for too long, his
grandmother hit him
with a broom.

Shakuha-
chi (flute)

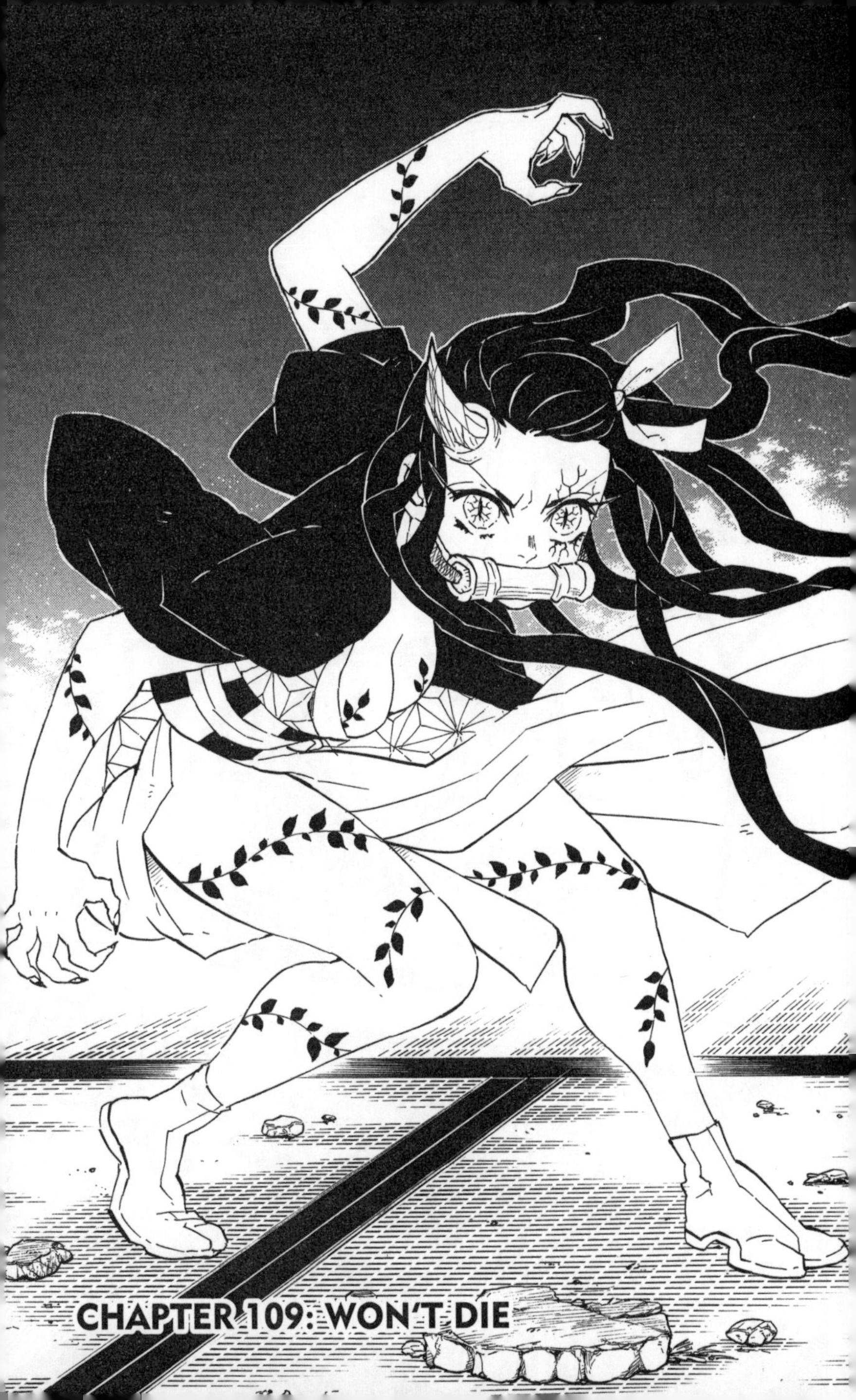
CHAPTER 109: WON'T DIE

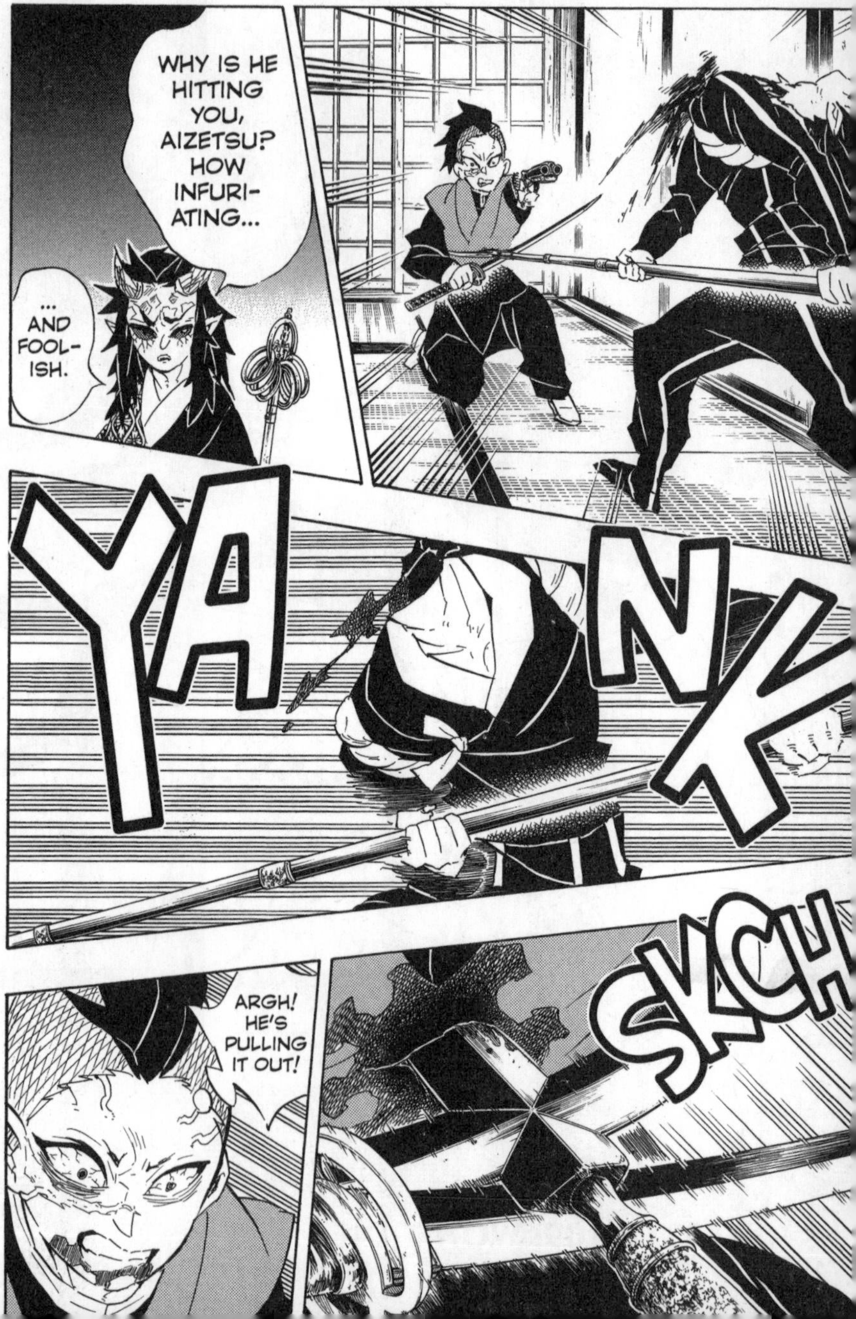
WHY IS HE HITTING YOU, AIZETSU? HOW INFURI-ATING...
... AND FOOL-ISH.
YANK
SKCH
ARGH! HE'S PULLING IT OUT!

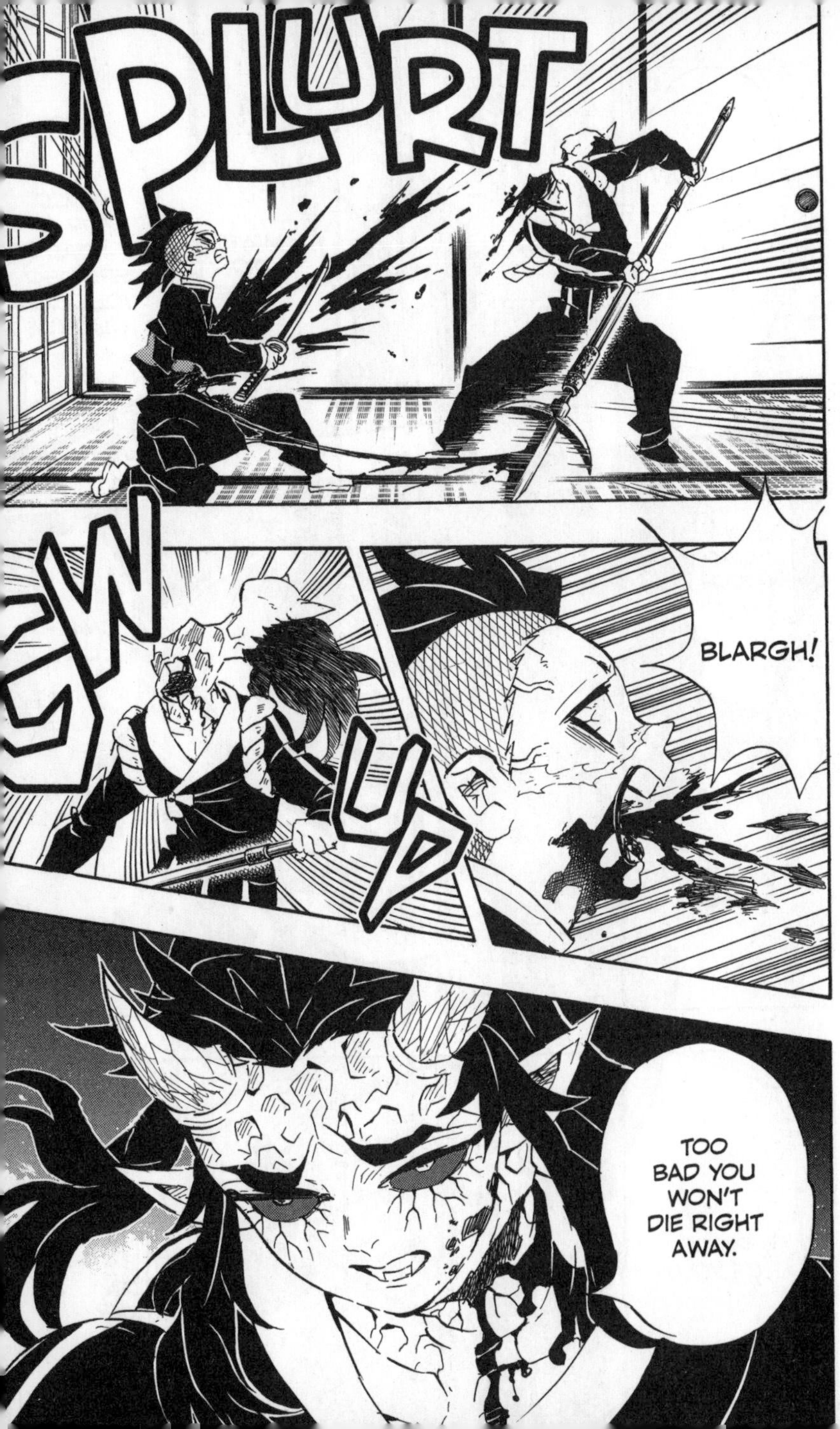
SPLURT
BLARGH!
TOO BAD YOU WON'T DIE RIGHT AWAY.

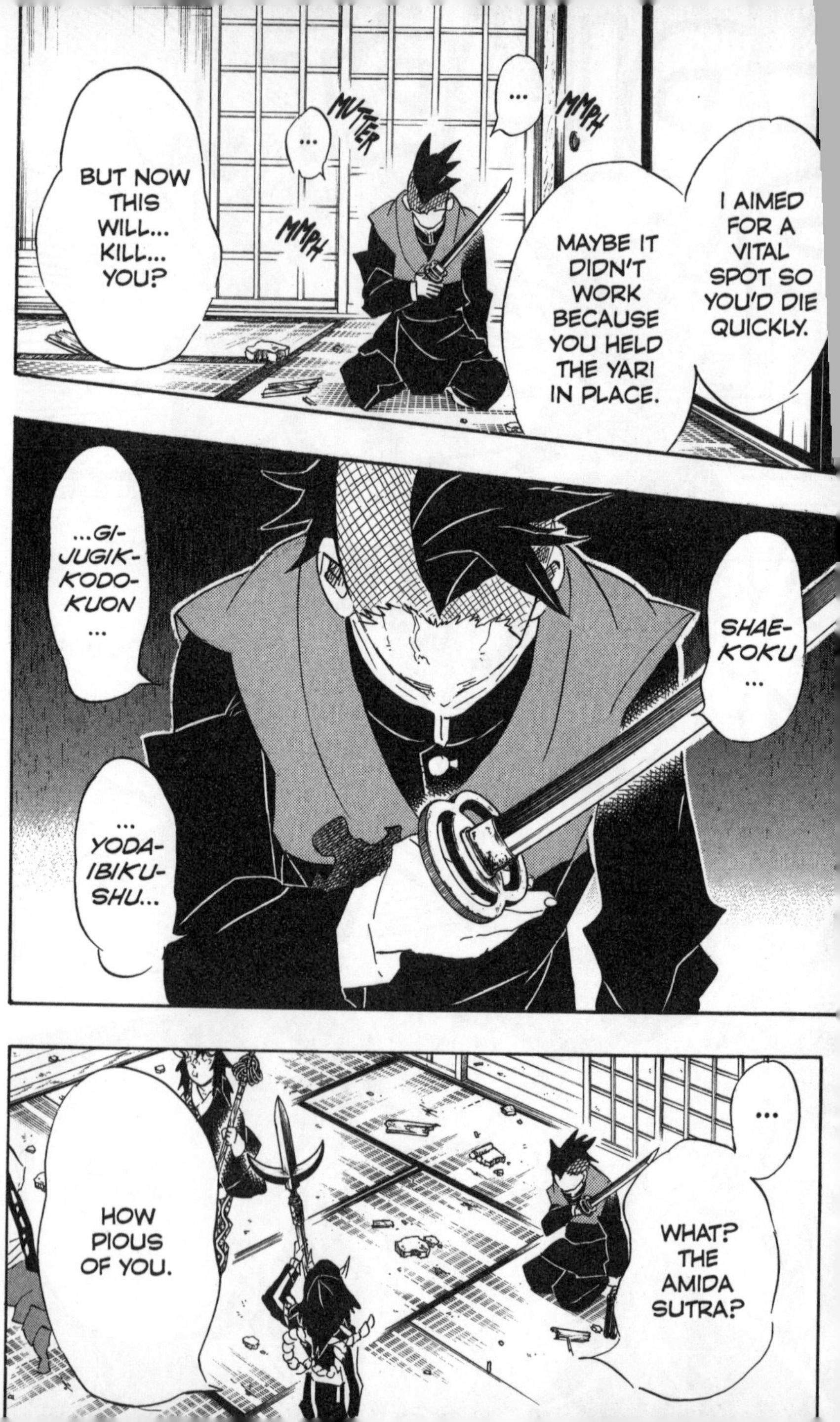
I AIMED FOR A VITAL SPOT SO YOU'D DIE QUICKLY.
MAYBE IT DIDN'T WORK BECAUSE YOU HELD THE YARI IN PLACE.
MMPH
...
MUTTER
...
MMPH
BUT NOW THIS WILL... KILL... YOU?
SHAE-KOKU ...
...GI-JUGIK-KODO-KUON ...
... YODA-IBIKU-SHU...
...
WHAT? THE AMIDA SUTRA?
HOW PIOUS OF YOU.

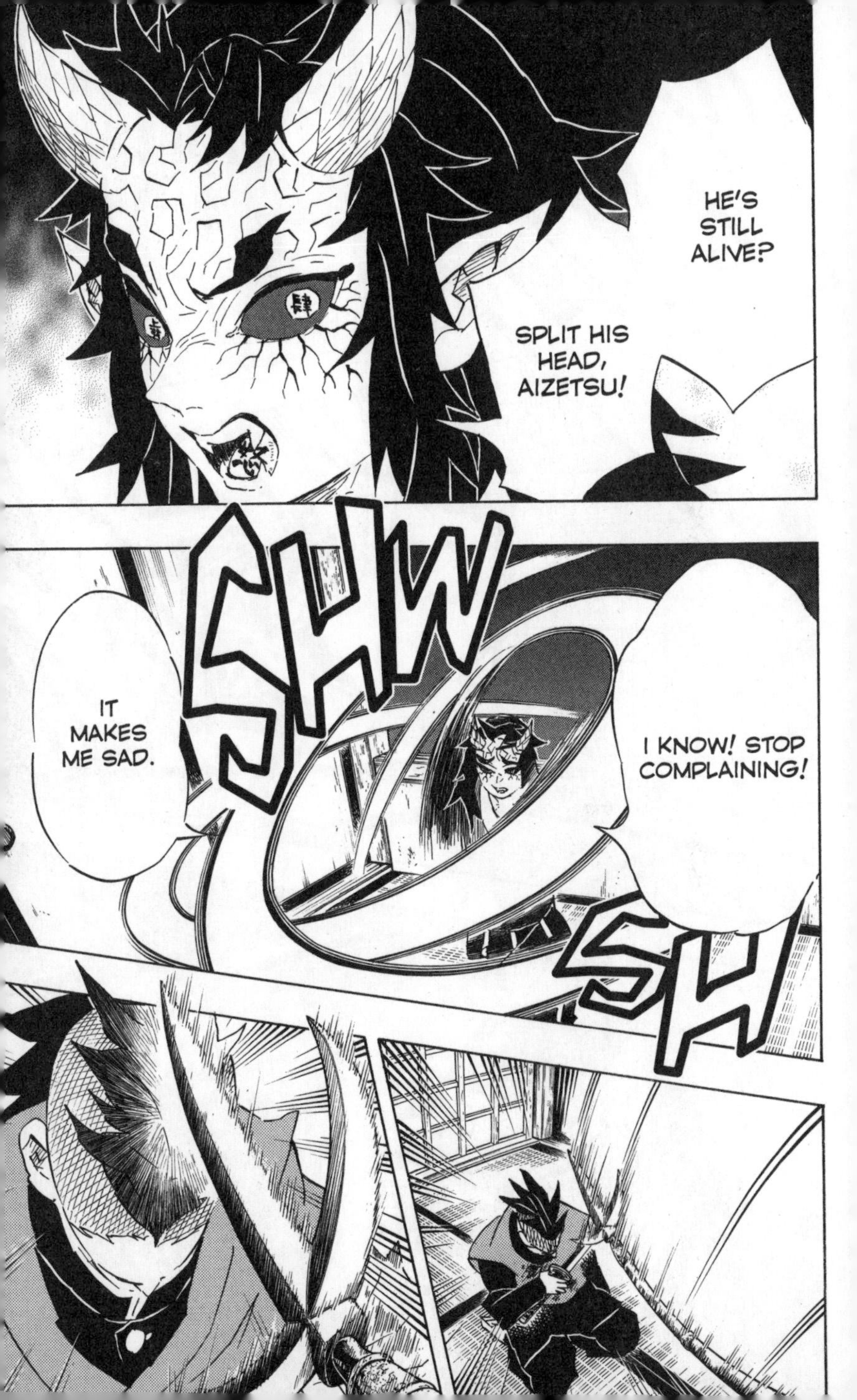
HE'S STILL ALIVE?
SPLIT HIS HEAD, AIZETSU!
I KNOW! STOP COMPLAINING!
IT MAKES ME SAD.
SHW
SH

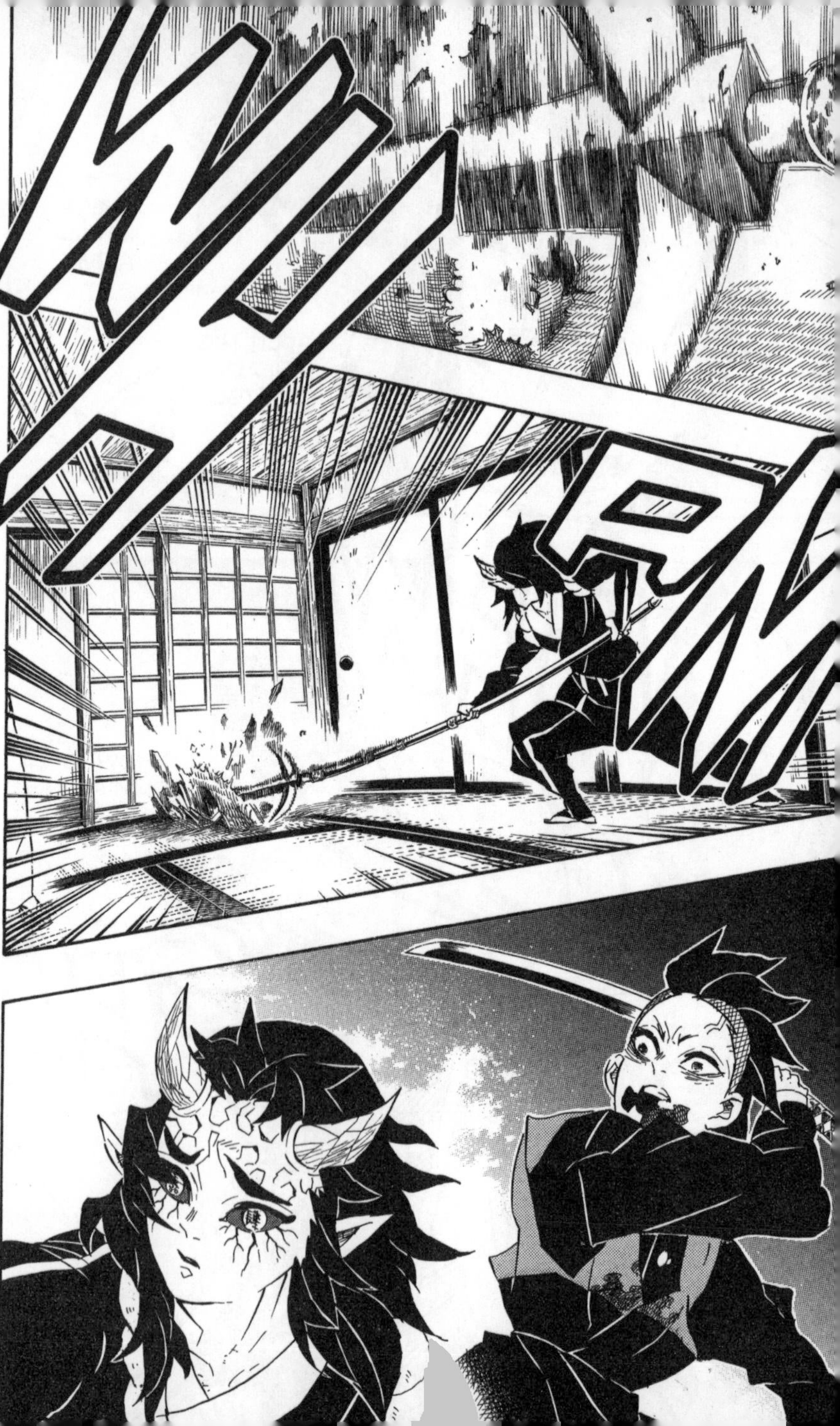

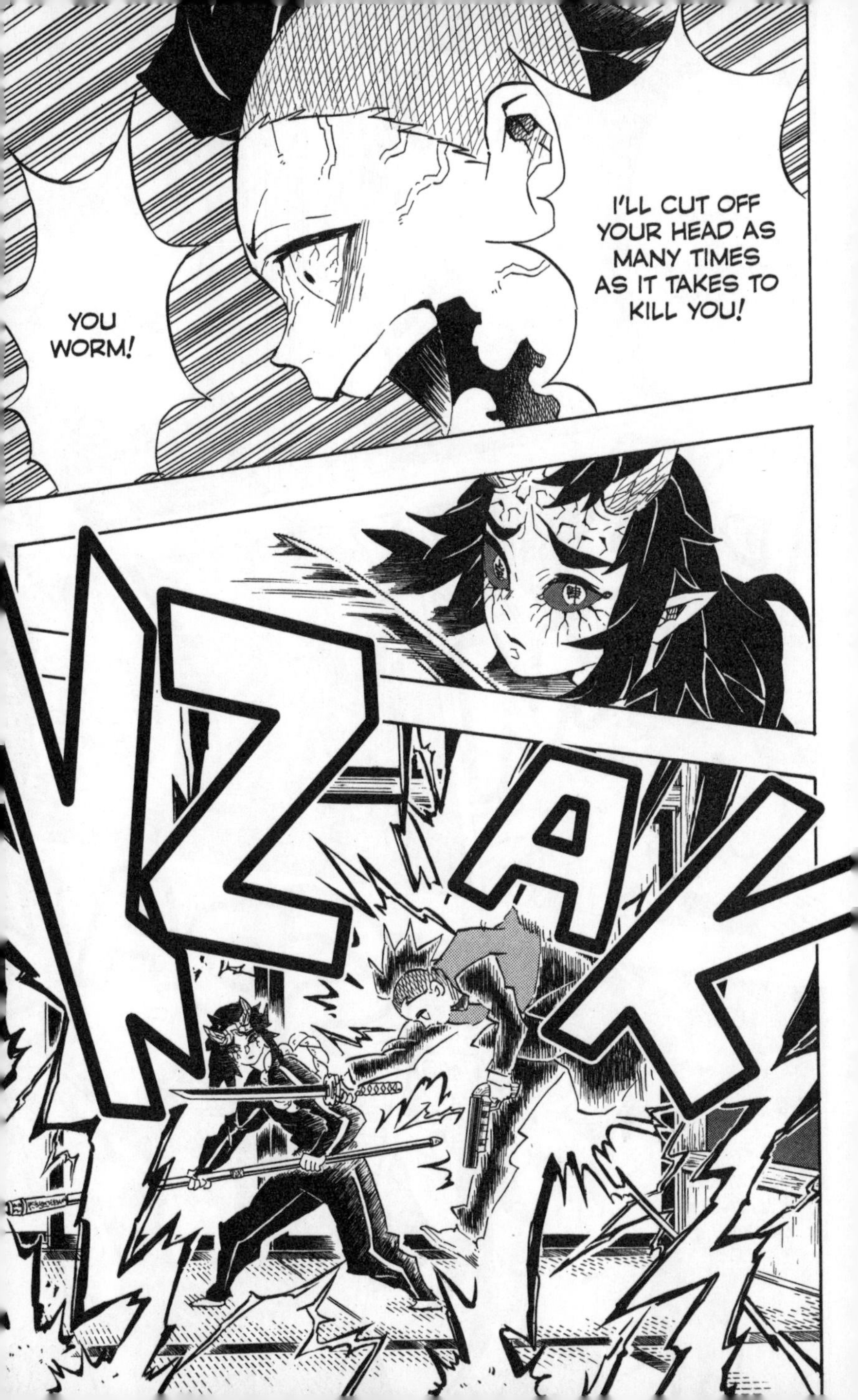
I'LL CUT OFF YOUR HEAD AS MANY TIMES AS IT TAKES TO KILL YOU!
YOU WORM!
KZAK

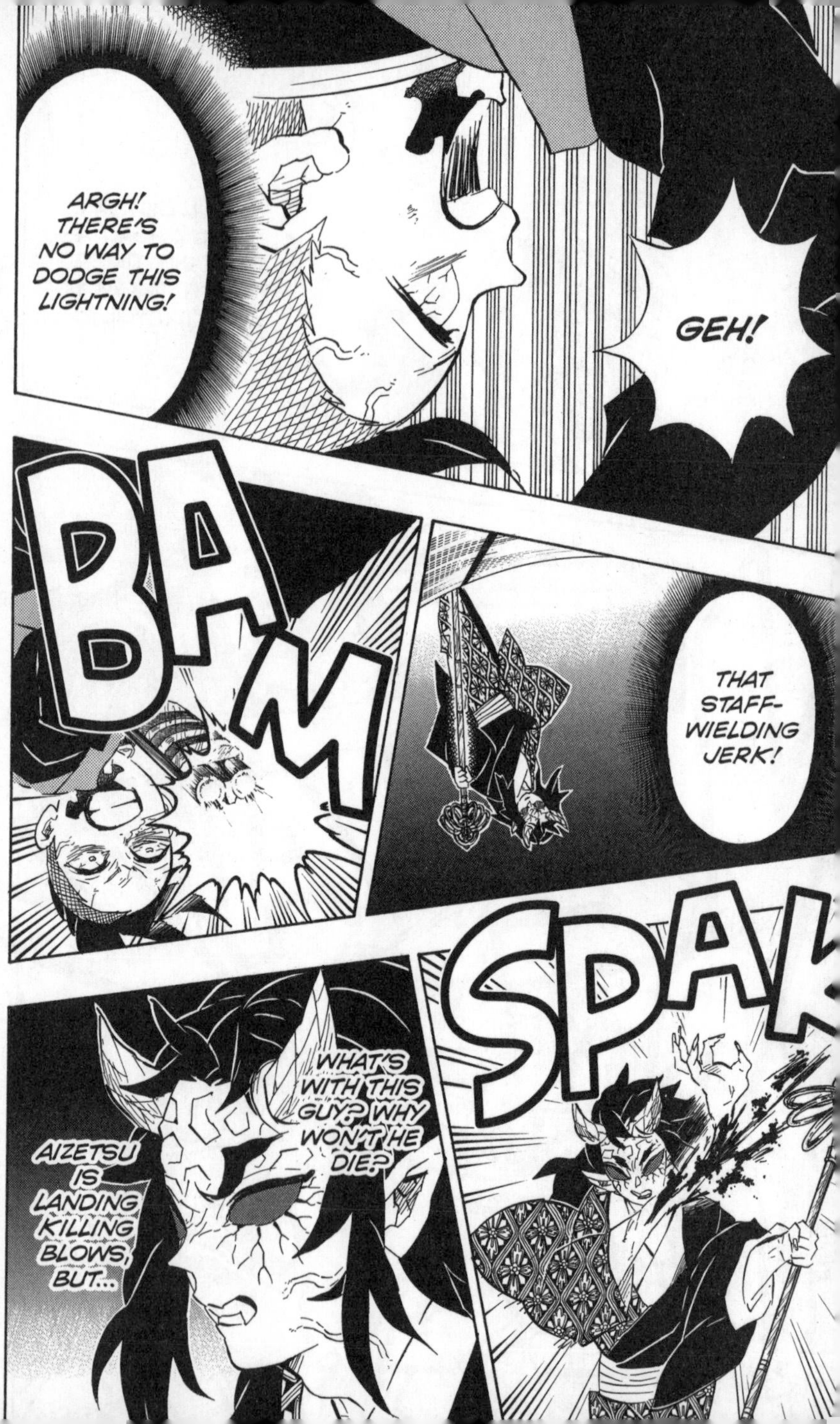
GEH!
ARGH! THERE'S NO WAY TO DODGE THIS LIGHTNING!
THAT STAFF-WIELDING JERK!
BAM
SPAK
WHAT'S WITH THIS GUY? WHY WON'T HE DIE?
AIZETSU IS LANDING KILLING BLOWS, BUT...

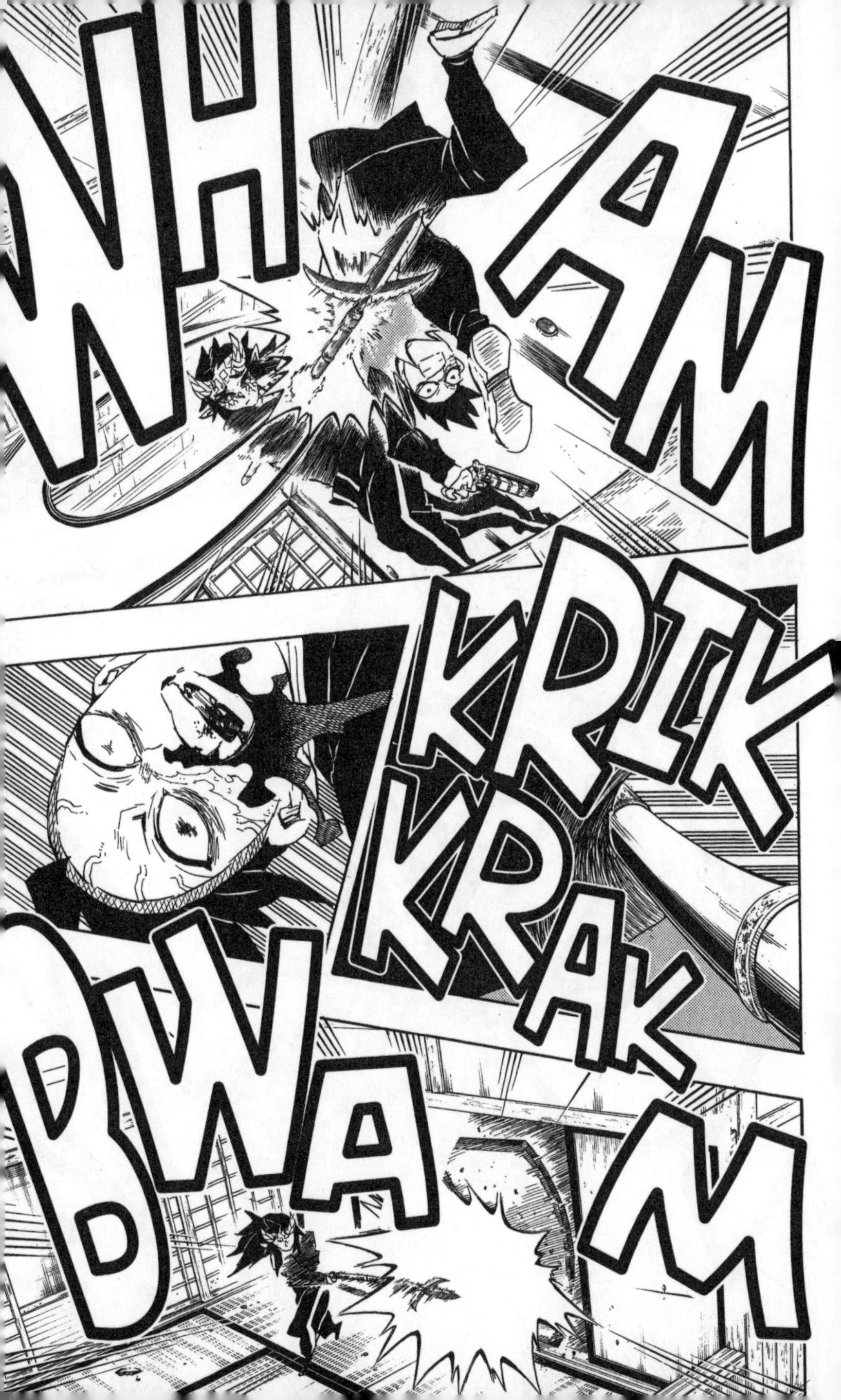
WHAM
KRIK KRAK
DWAM

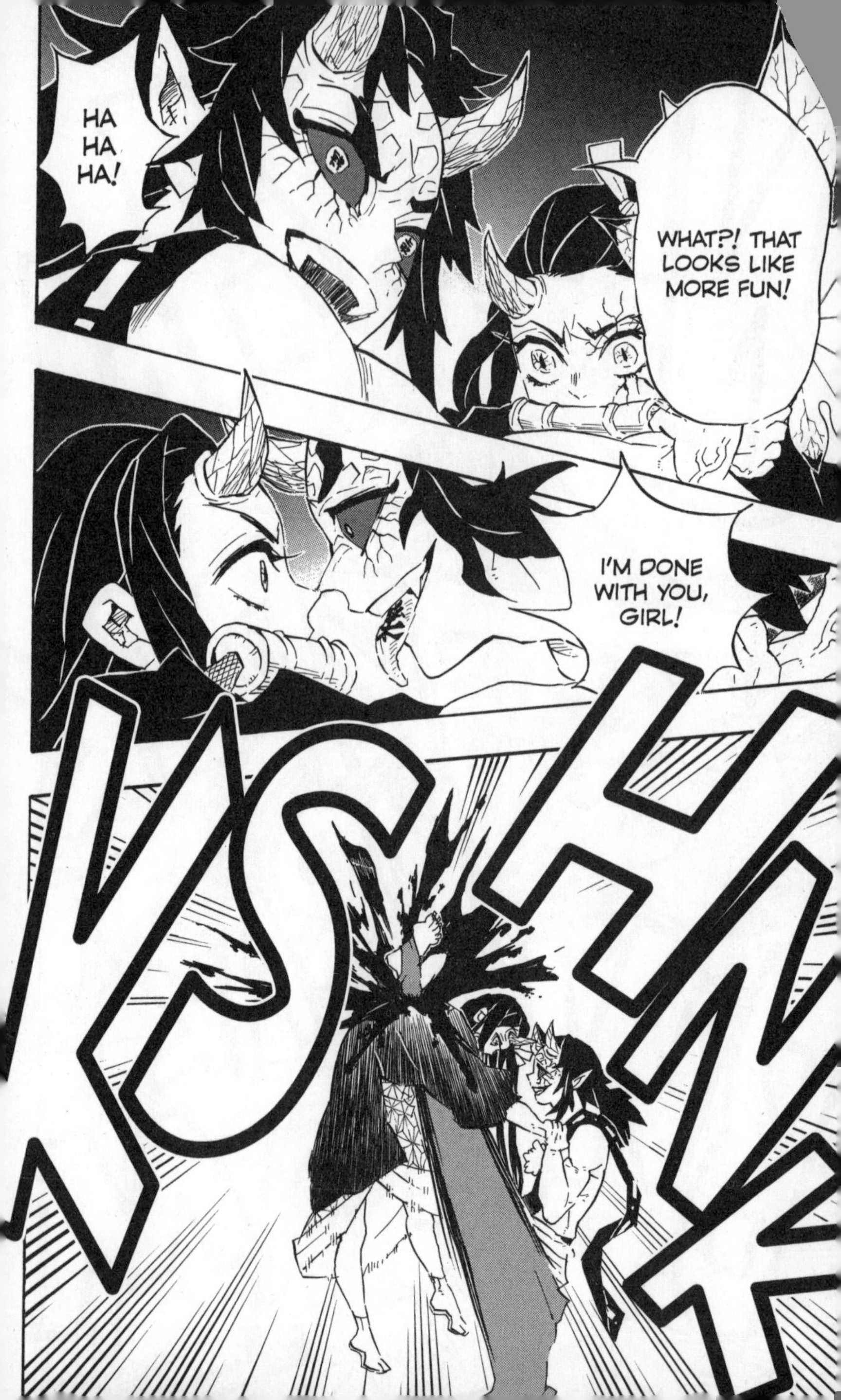
WHAT?! THAT LOOKS LIKE MORE FUN!
HA HA HA!
I'M DONE WITH YOU, GIRL!

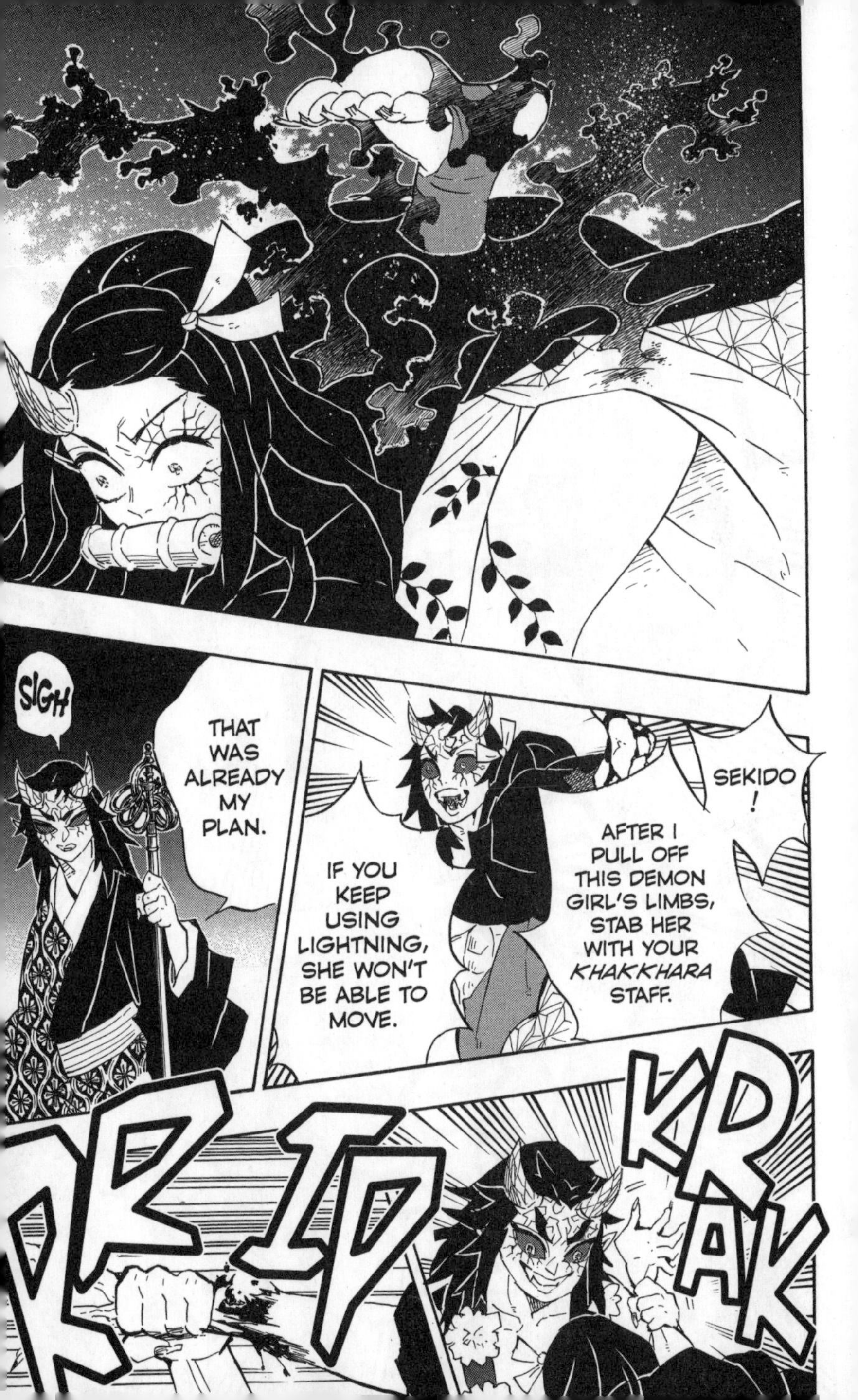
SEKIDO!
AFTER I PULL OFF THIS DEMON GIRL'S LIMBS, STAB HER WITH YOUR *KHAKKHARA* STAFF.
IF YOU KEEP USING LIGHTNING, SHE WON'T BE ABLE TO MOVE.
SIGH
THAT WAS ALREADY MY PLAN.
KRAK
RIP

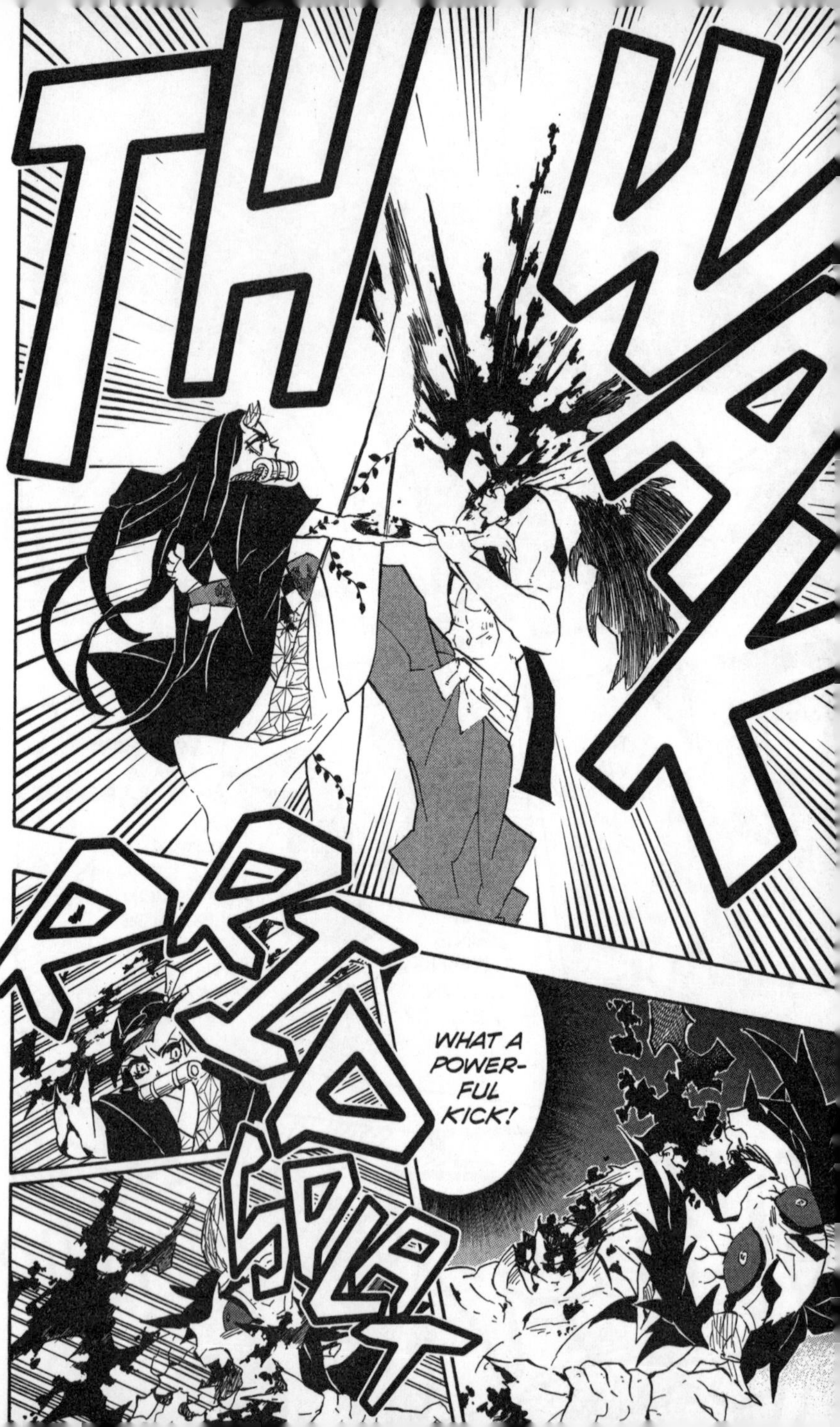
THWACK
WHAT A POWERFUL KICK!
SPLAT

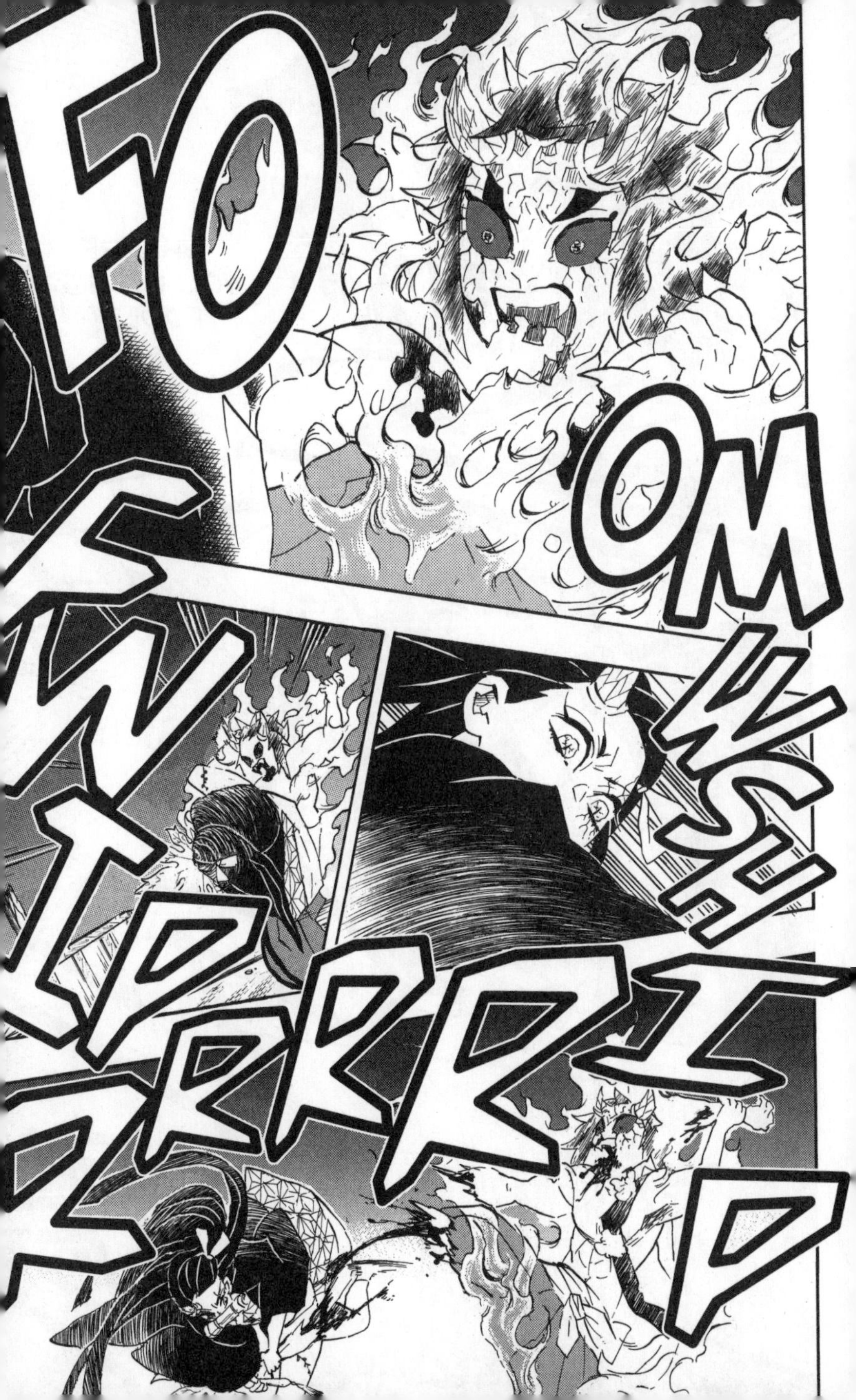
FOOM
WSH

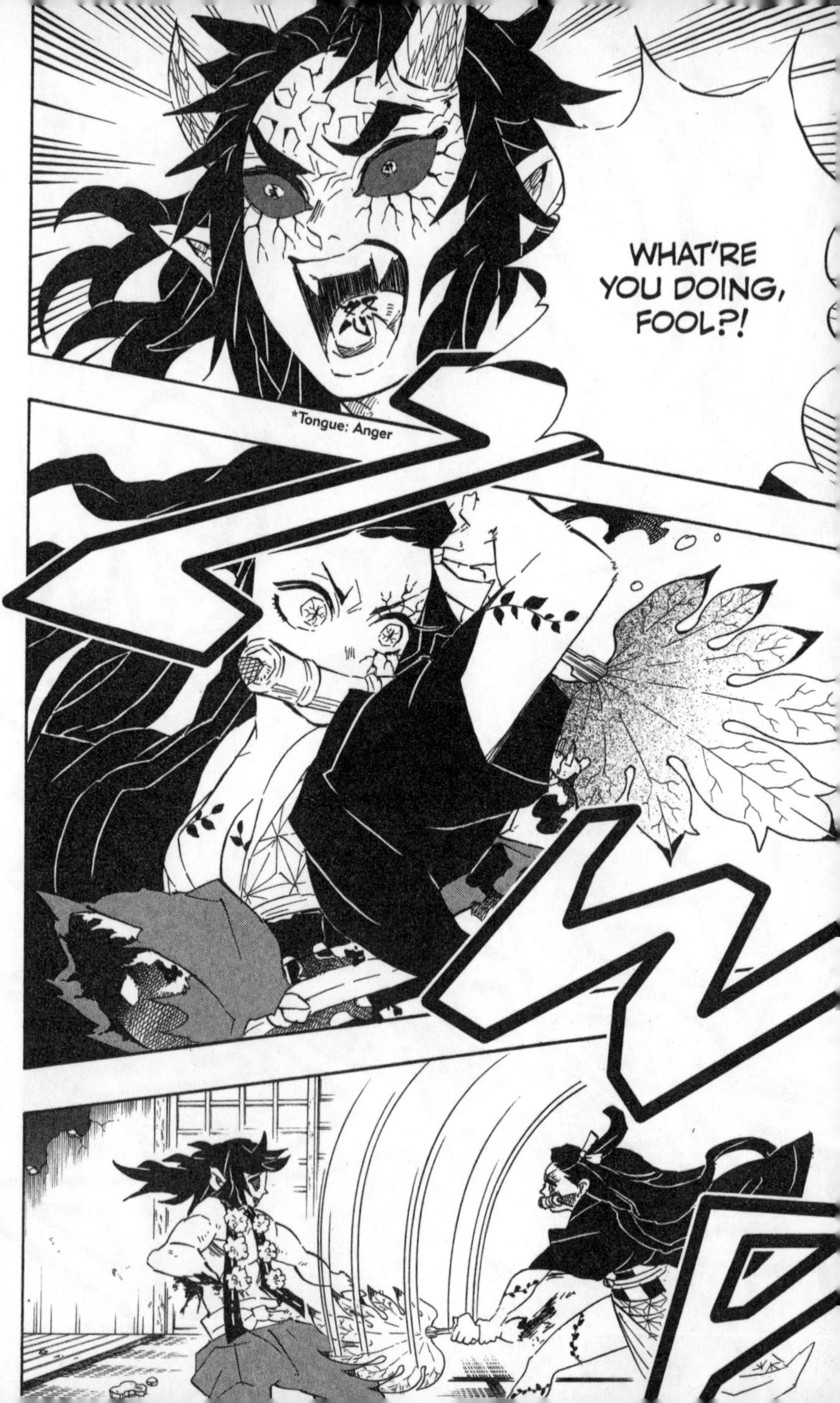
WHAT'RE YOU DOING, FOOL?!
*Tongue: Anger

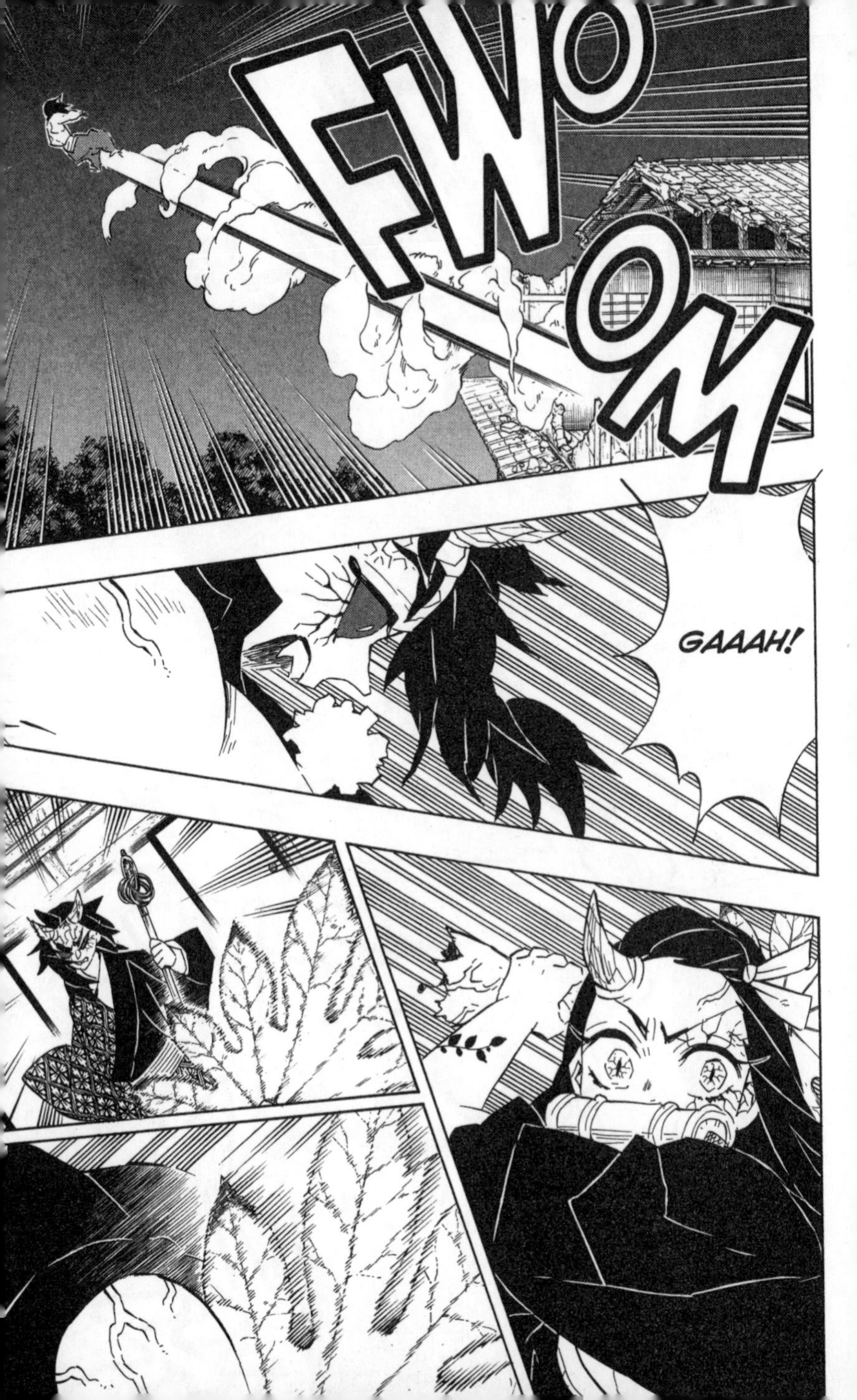
FWOOM
GAAAH!

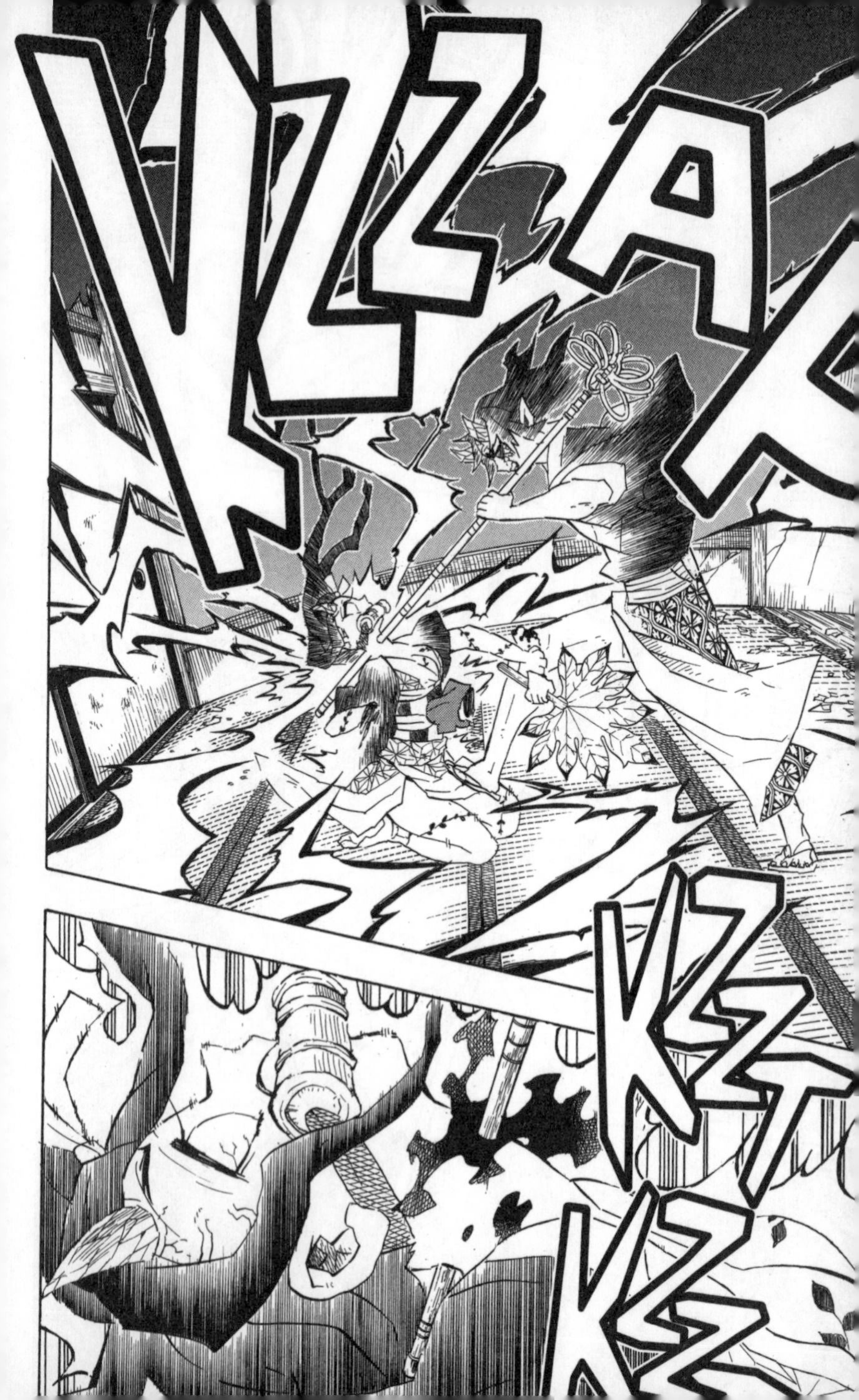
VZZA
KZZT
KZZ

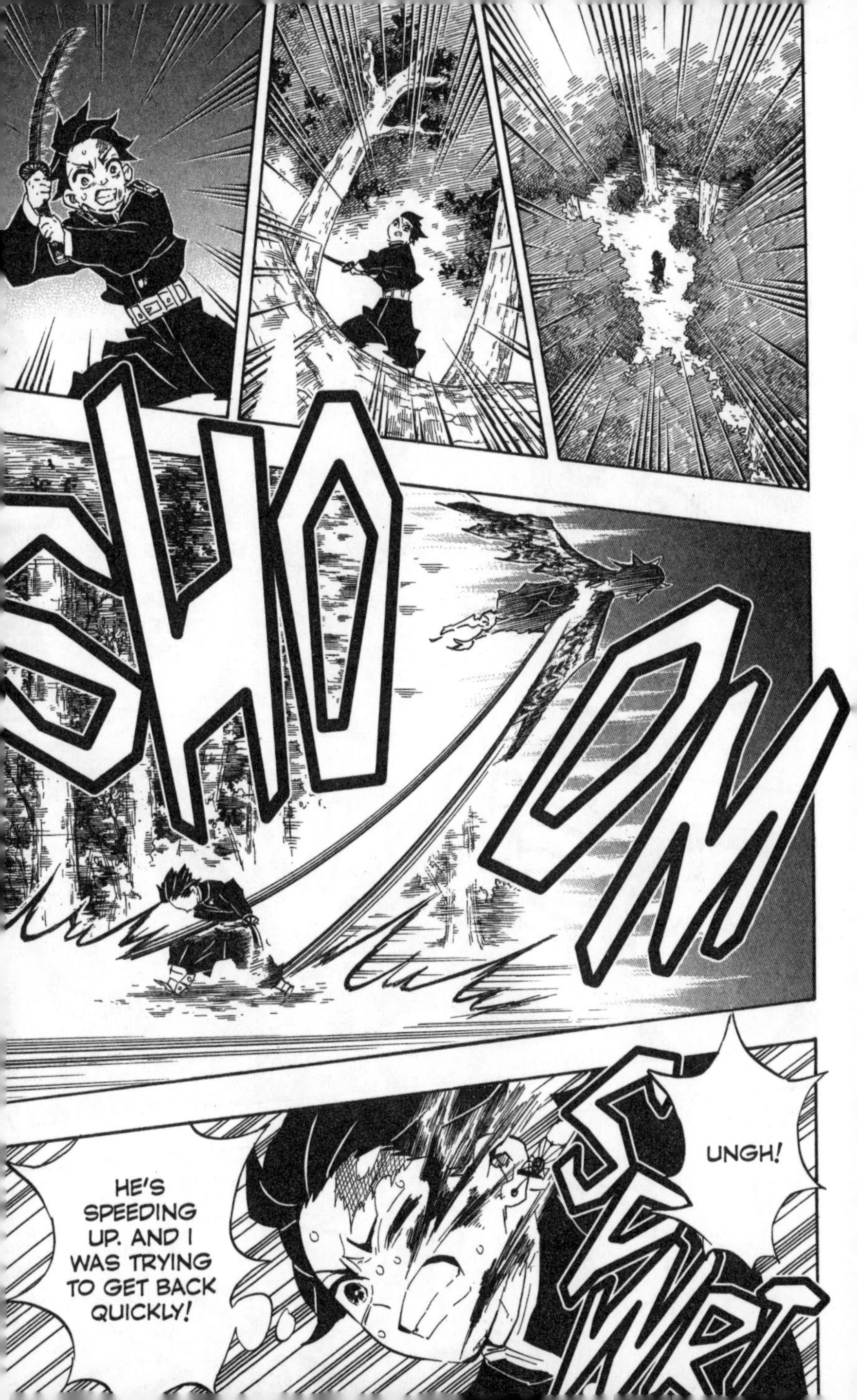
SHOOM
UNGH!
HE'S SPEEDING UP. AND I WAS TRYING TO GET BACK QUICKLY!

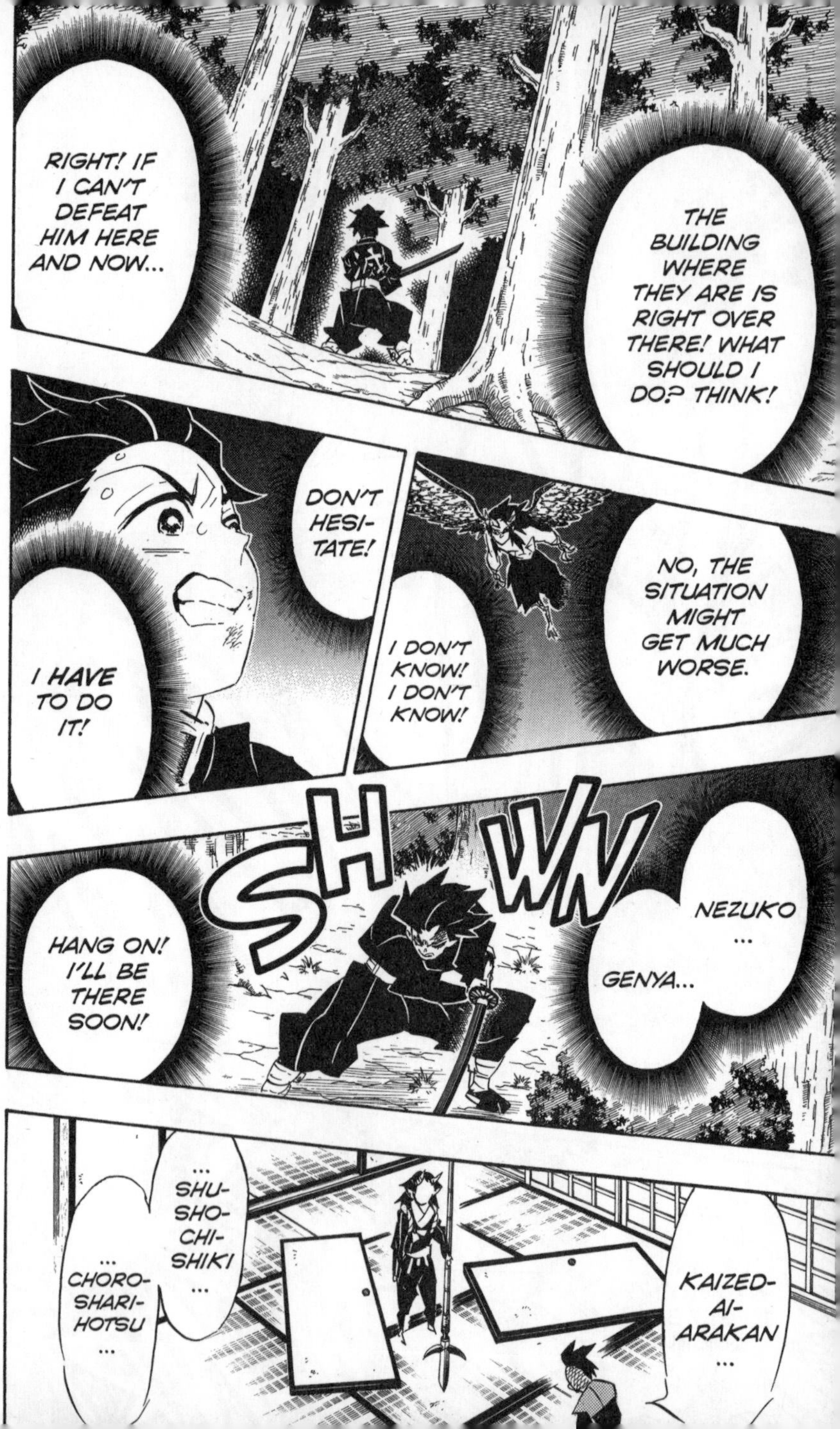
THE BUILDING WHERE THEY ARE IS RIGHT OVER THERE! WHAT SHOULD I DO? THINK!
RIGHT! IF I CAN'T DEFEAT HIM HERE AND NOW...
NO, THE SITUATION MIGHT GET MUCH WORSE.
I DON'T KNOW! I DON'T KNOW!
DON'T HESI-TATE!
I HAVE TO DO IT!
NEZUKO ... GENYA...
SHWN
HANG ON! I'LL BE THERE SOON!
KAIZED-AI-ARAKAN ...
... SHU-SHO-CHI-SHIKI ...
... CHORO-SHARI-HOTSU ...

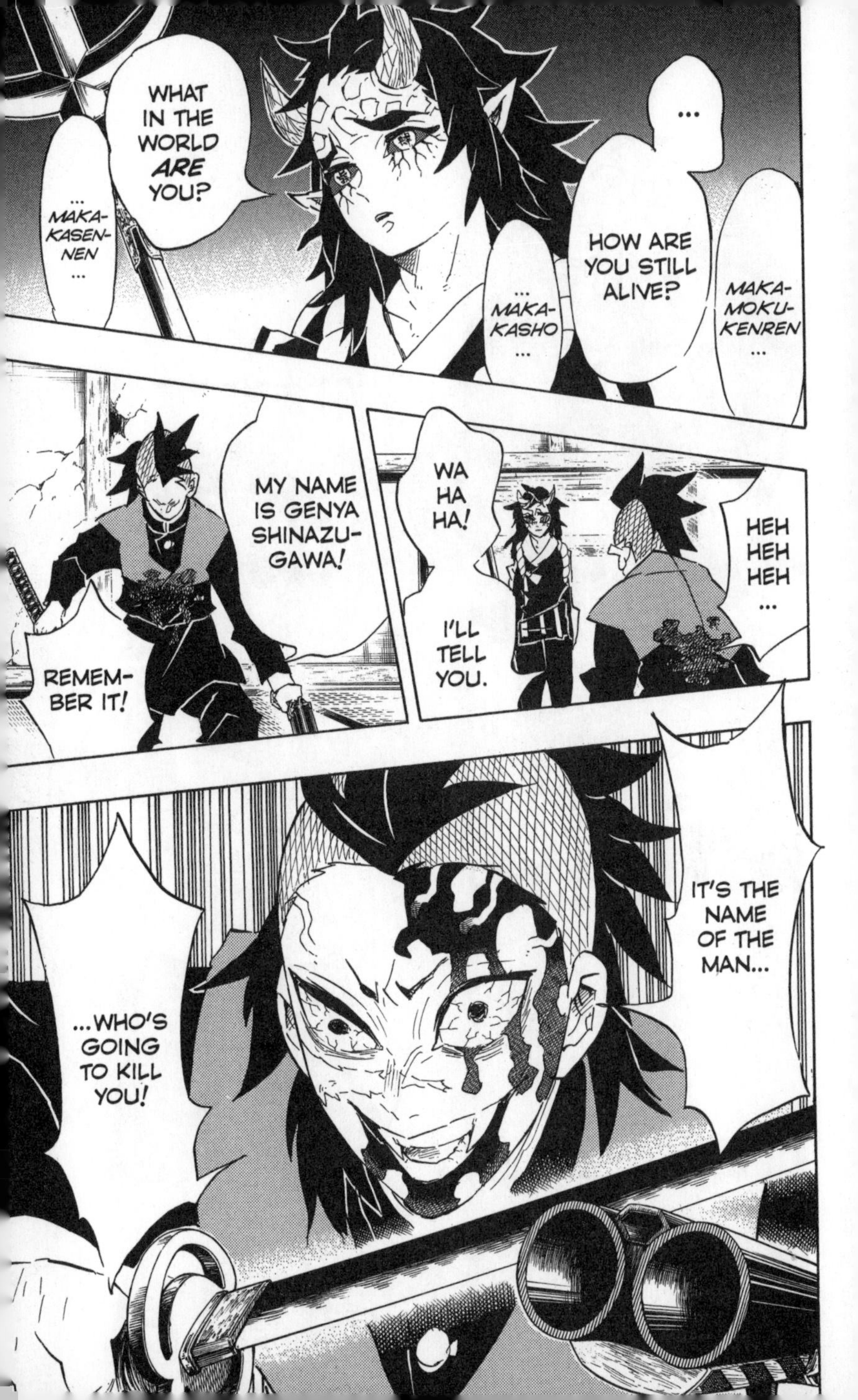
...
MAKA-MOKU-KENREN ...
HOW ARE YOU STILL ALIVE?
... MAKA-KASHO ...
WHAT IN THE WORLD *ARE* YOU?
... MAKA-KASEN-NEN ...
HEH HEH HEH ...
WA HA HA!
I'LL TELL YOU.
MY NAME IS GENYA SHINAZU-GAWA!
REMEM-BER IT!
IT'S THE NAME OF THE MAN...
...WHO'S GOING TO KILL YOU!

From *Weekly Shonen Jump,* issue No. 36-37, 2018

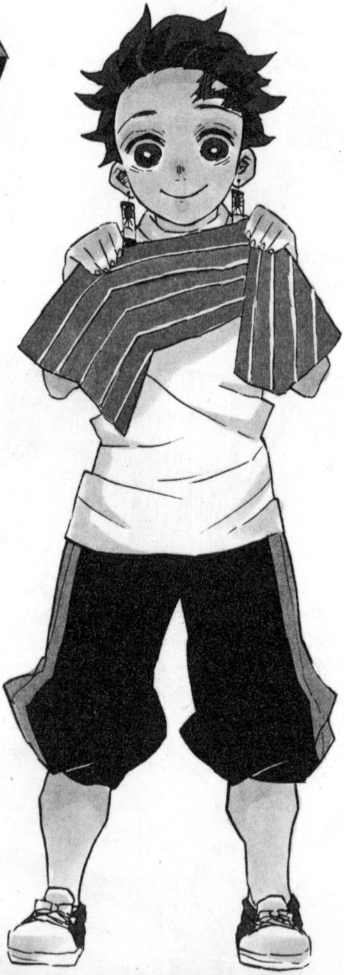

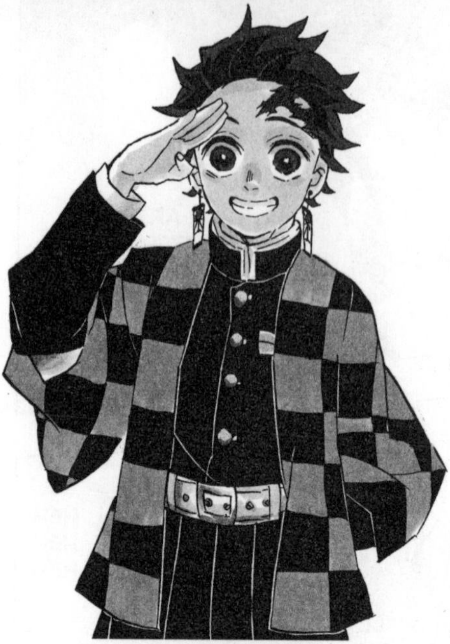

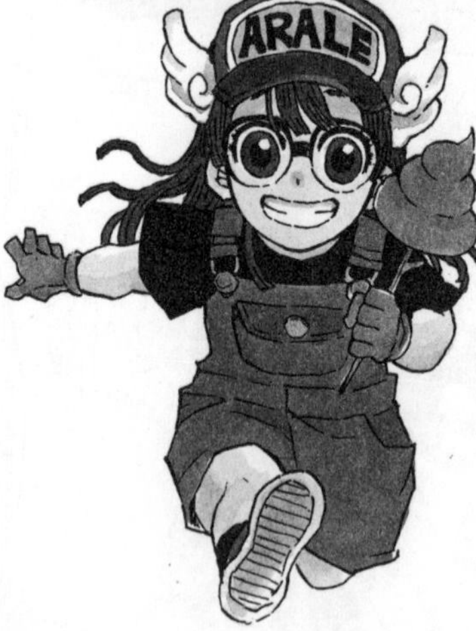
ARALE

From *Weekly Shonen Jump,* issue No. 33, 2018

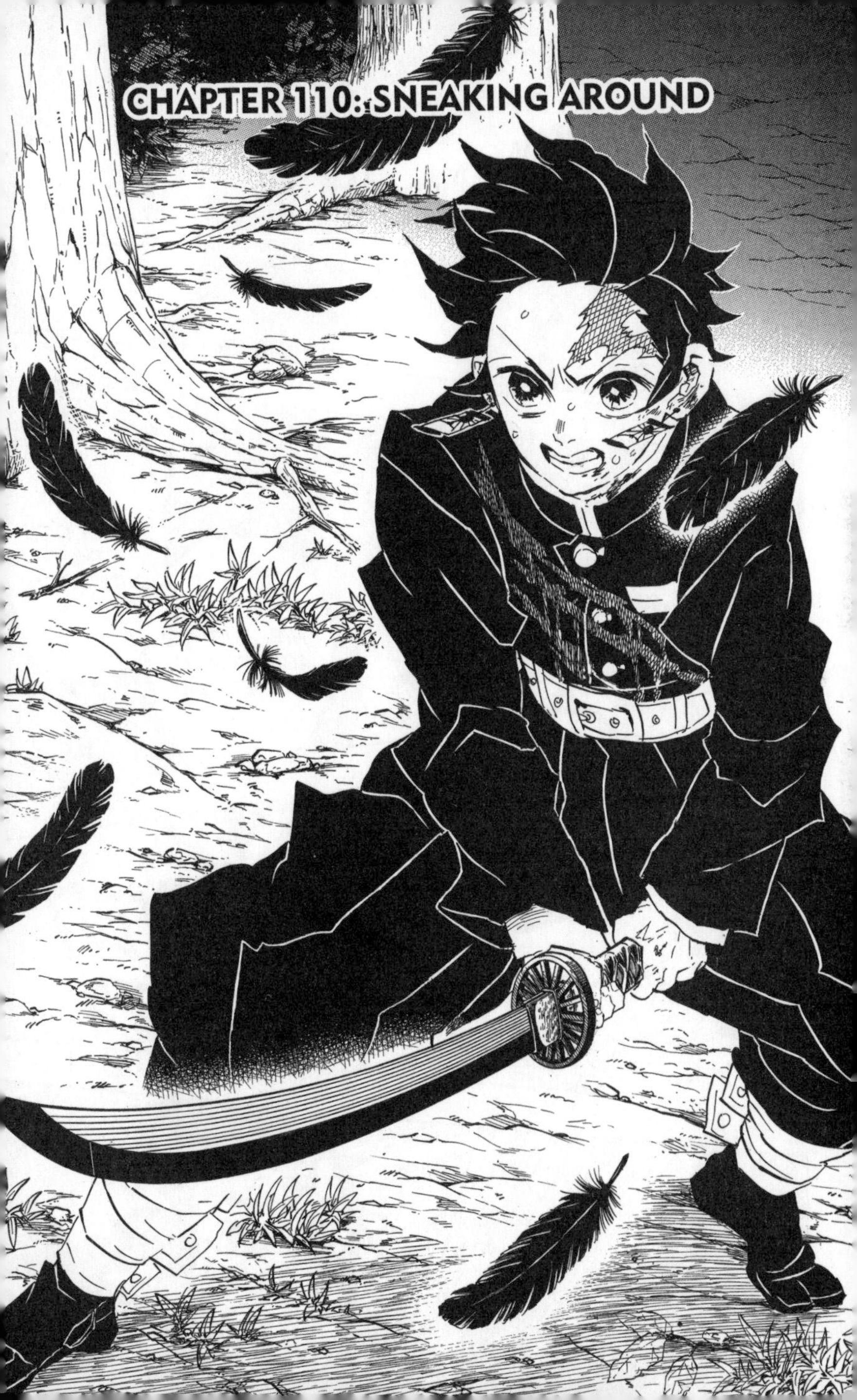
CHAPTER 110: SNEAKING AROUND

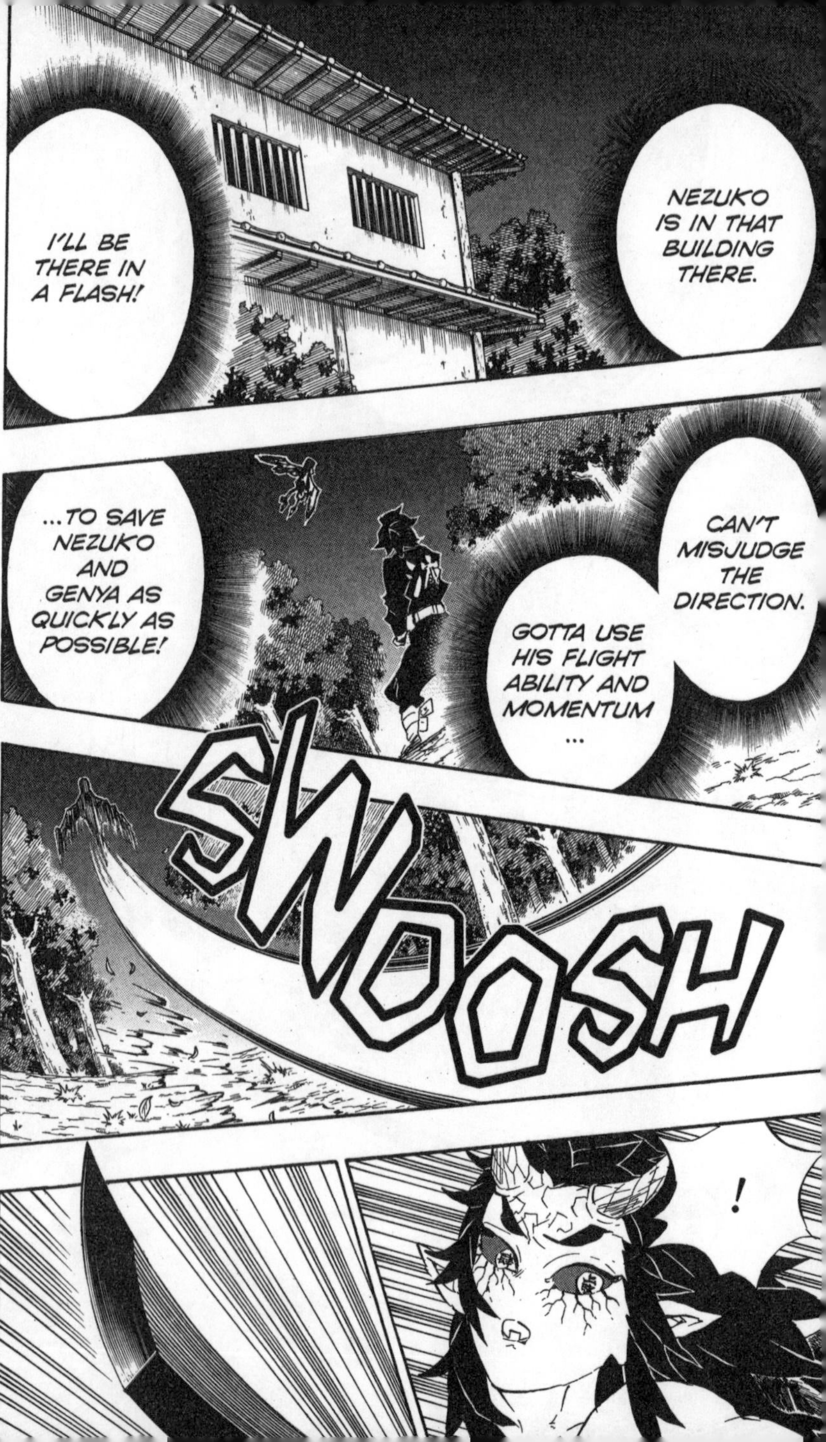
NEZUKO IS IN THAT BUILDING THERE.
I'LL BE THERE IN A FLASH!
CAN'T MISJUDGE THE DIRECTION.
GOTTA USE HIS FLIGHT ABILITY AND MOMENTUM ...
...TO SAVE NEZUKO AND GENYA AS QUICKLY AS POSSIBLE!
SWOOSH
!

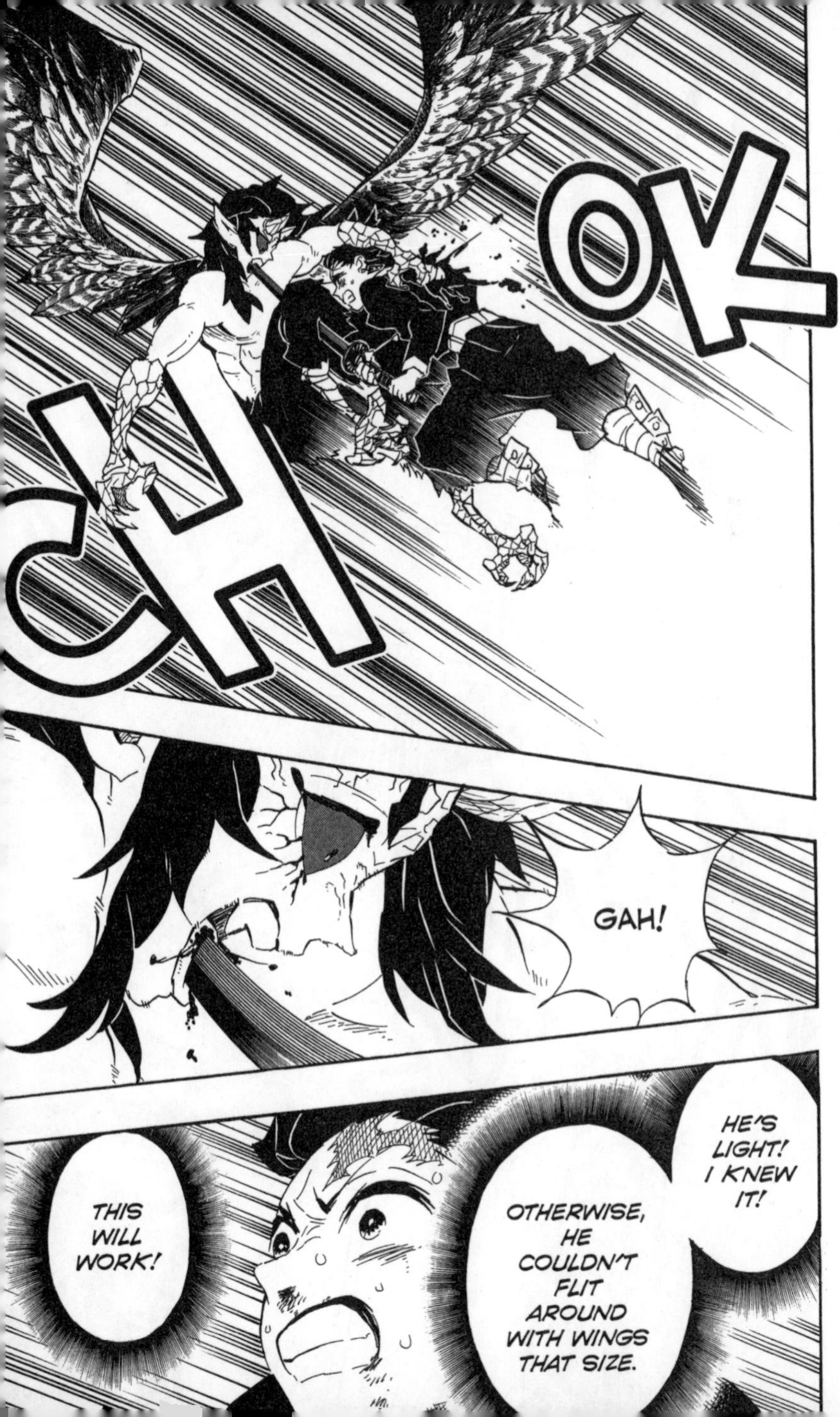
CHOK
GAH!
HE'S LIGHT! I KNEW IT!
OTHERWISE, HE COULDN'T FLIT AROUND WITH WINGS THAT SIZE.
THIS WILL WORK!

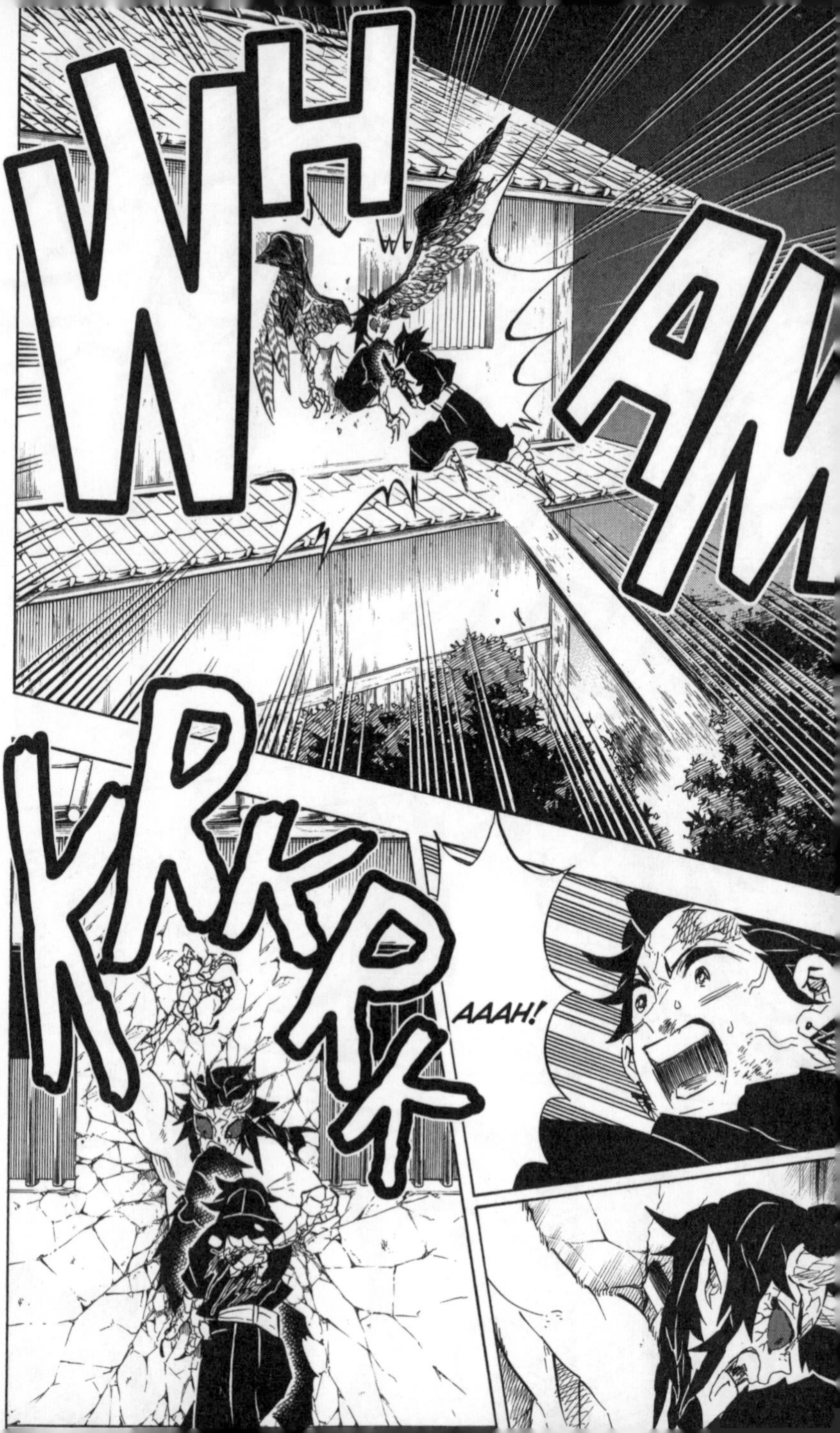
WHAM
KRAK
AAAH!

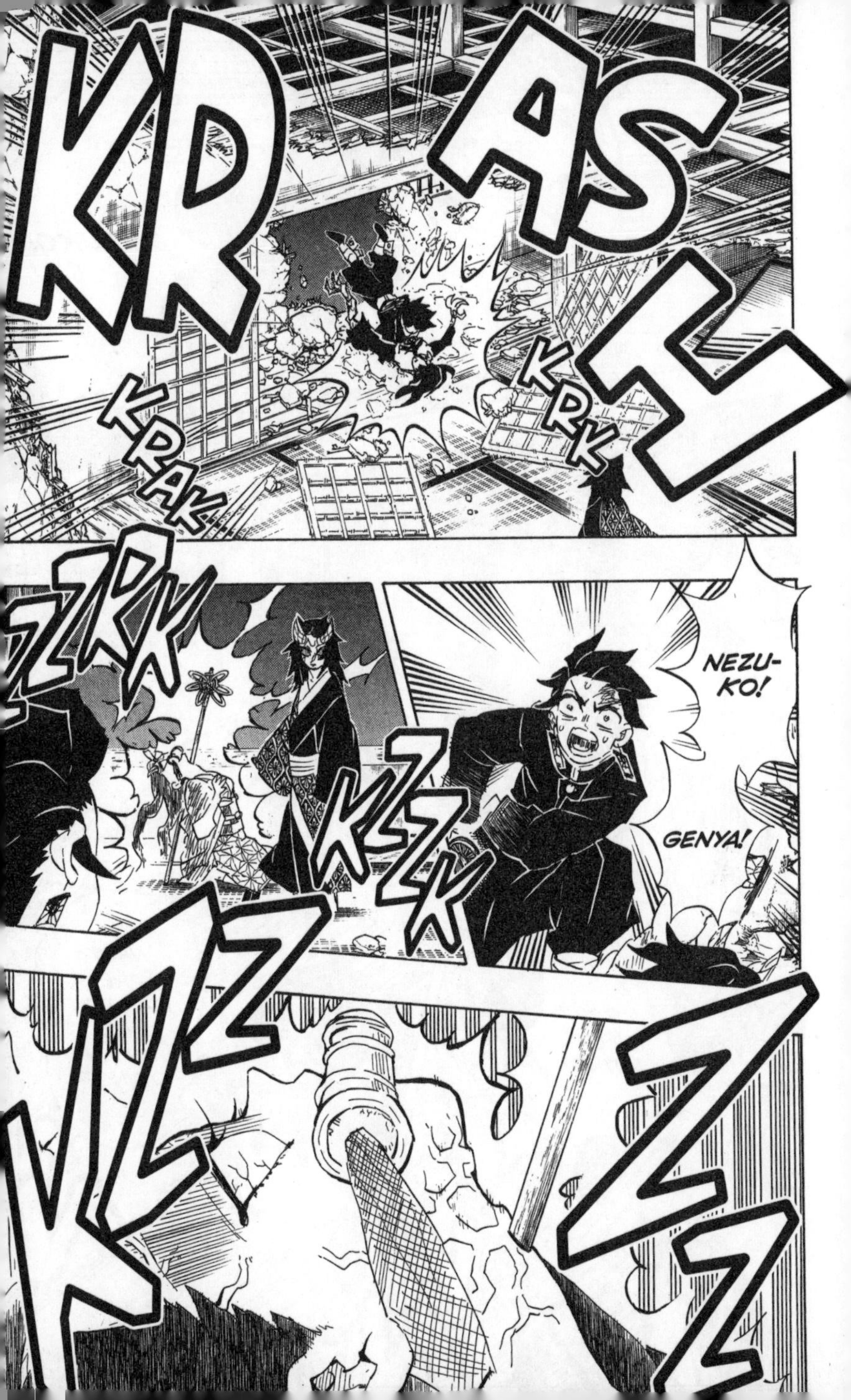
KRASH
KRK
KRAK
NEZU-
KO!
GENYA!

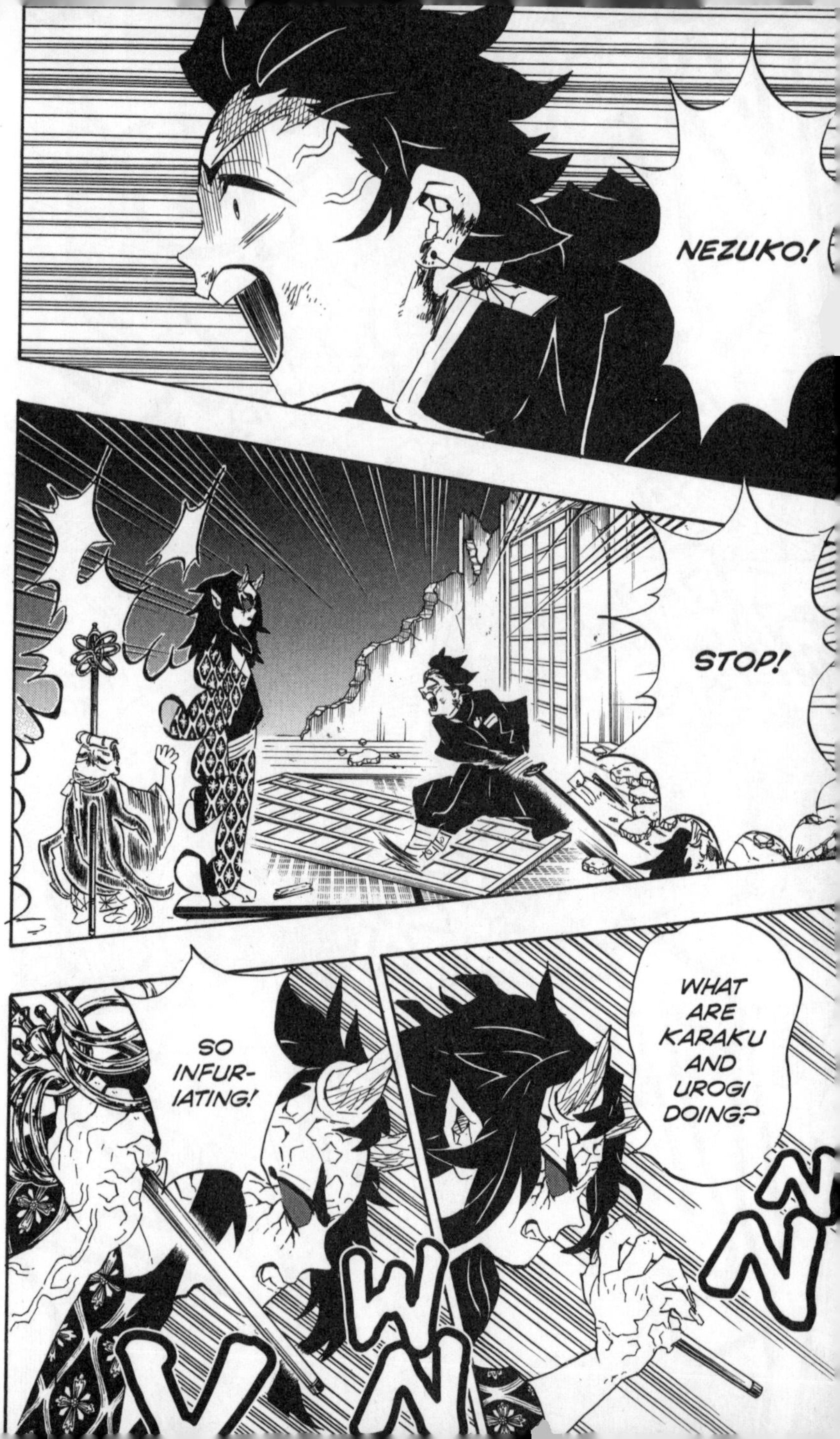
NEZUKO!
STOP!
WHAT ARE KARAKU AND UROGI DOING?
SO INFURIATING!

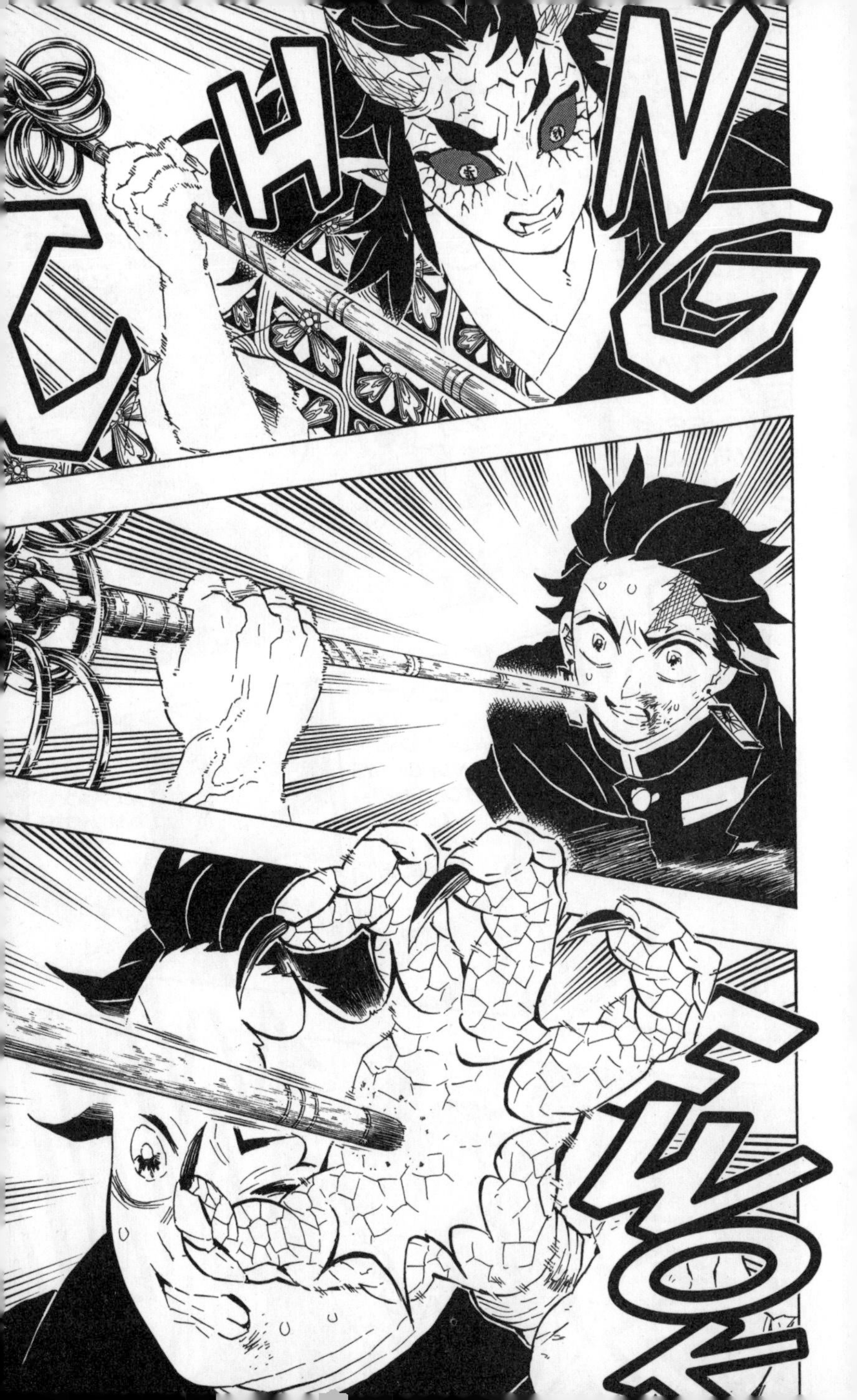

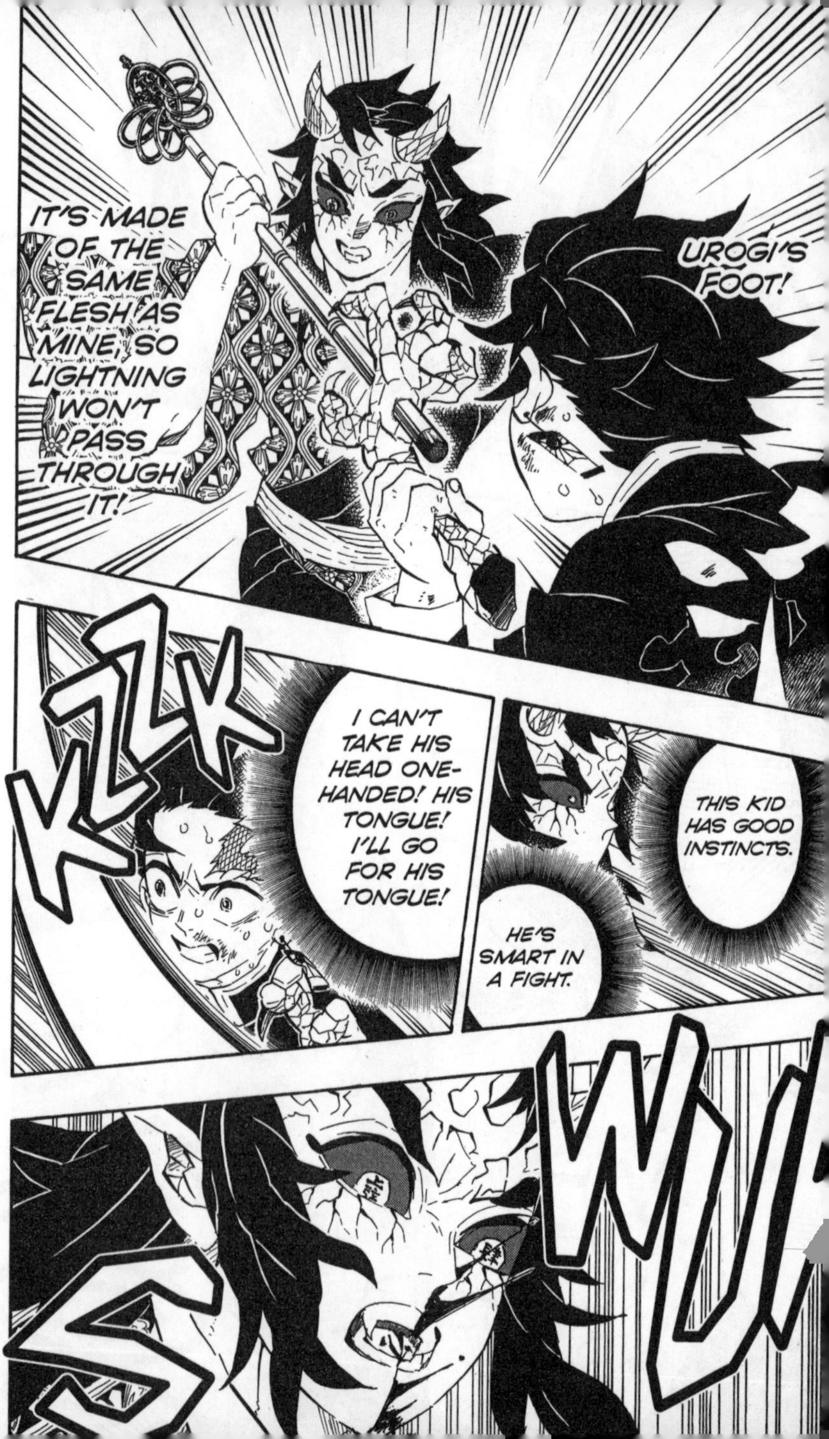
UROGI'S FOOT!
IT'S MADE OF THE SAME FLESH AS MINE, SO LIGHTNING WON'T PASS THROUGH IT!
THIS KID HAS GOOD INSTINCTS.
HE'S SMART IN A FIGHT.
I CAN'T TAKE HIS HEAD ONE-HANDED! HIS TONGUE! I'LL GO FOR HIS TONGUE!
KZZK

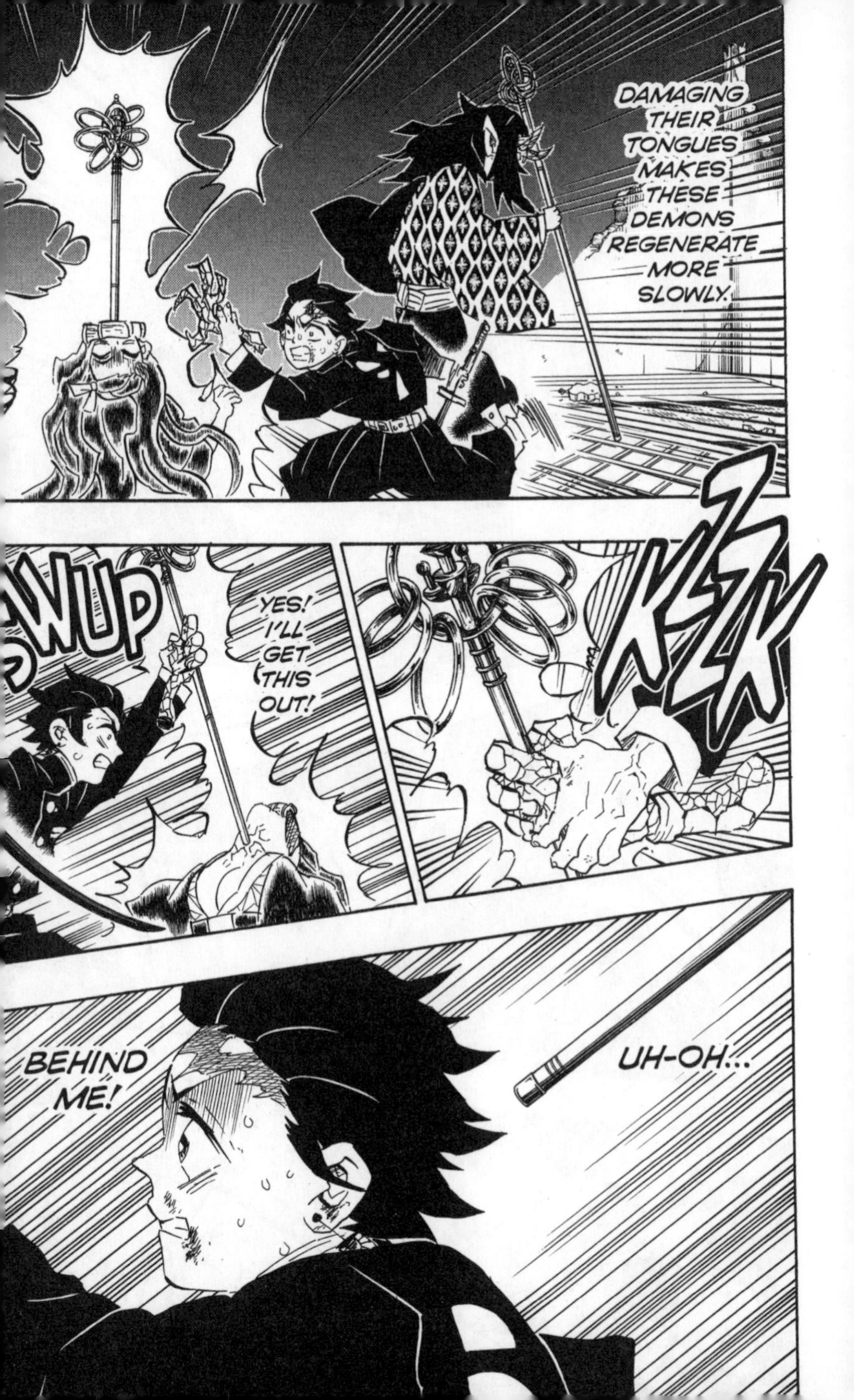
DAMAGING THEIR TONGUES MAKES THESE DEMONS REGENERATE MORE SLOWLY.
KZK
YES! I'LL GET THIS OUT!
SWUP
UH-OH...
BEHIND ME!

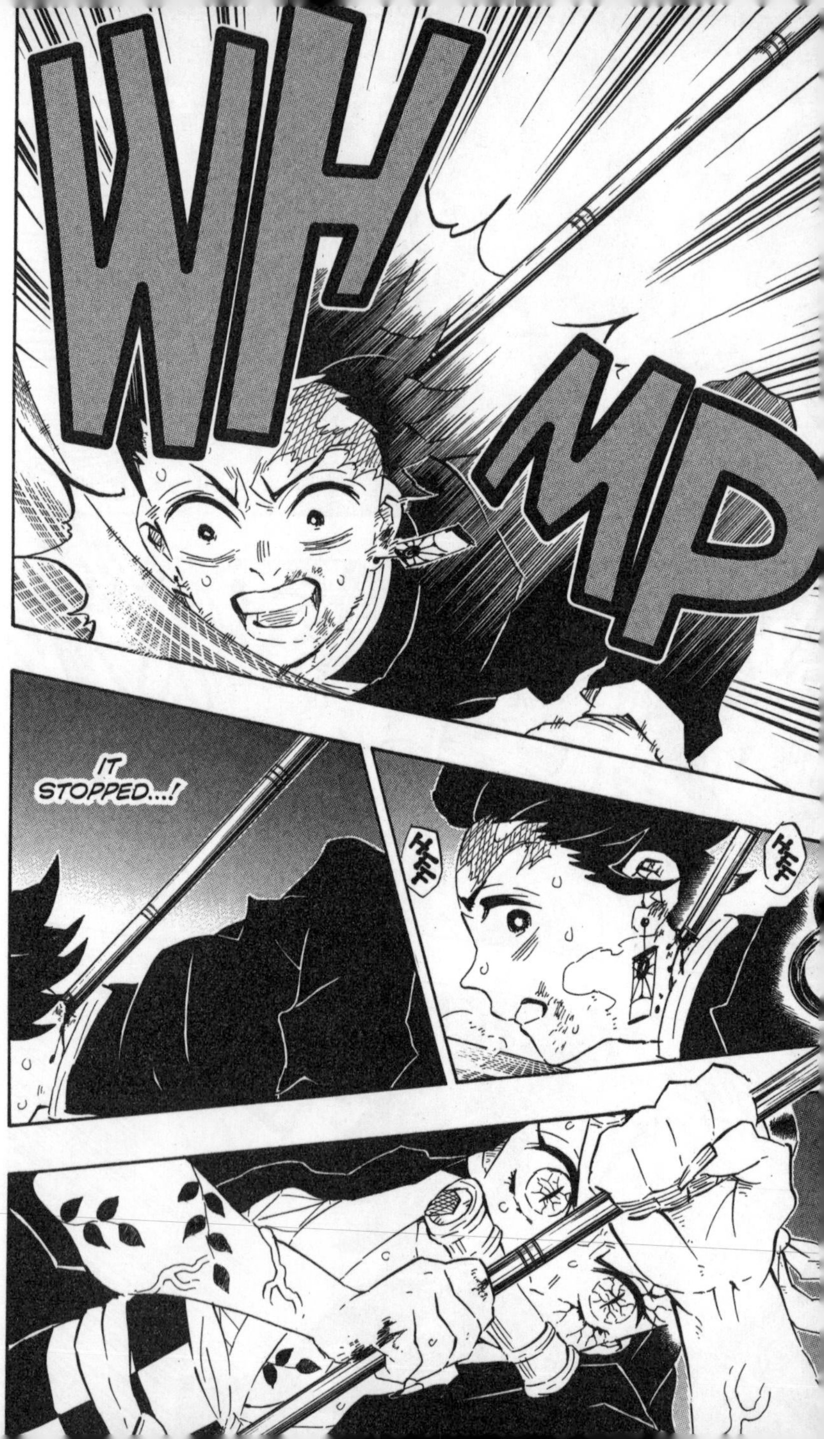
WHMP
HUFF
HUFF
IT STOPPED...!

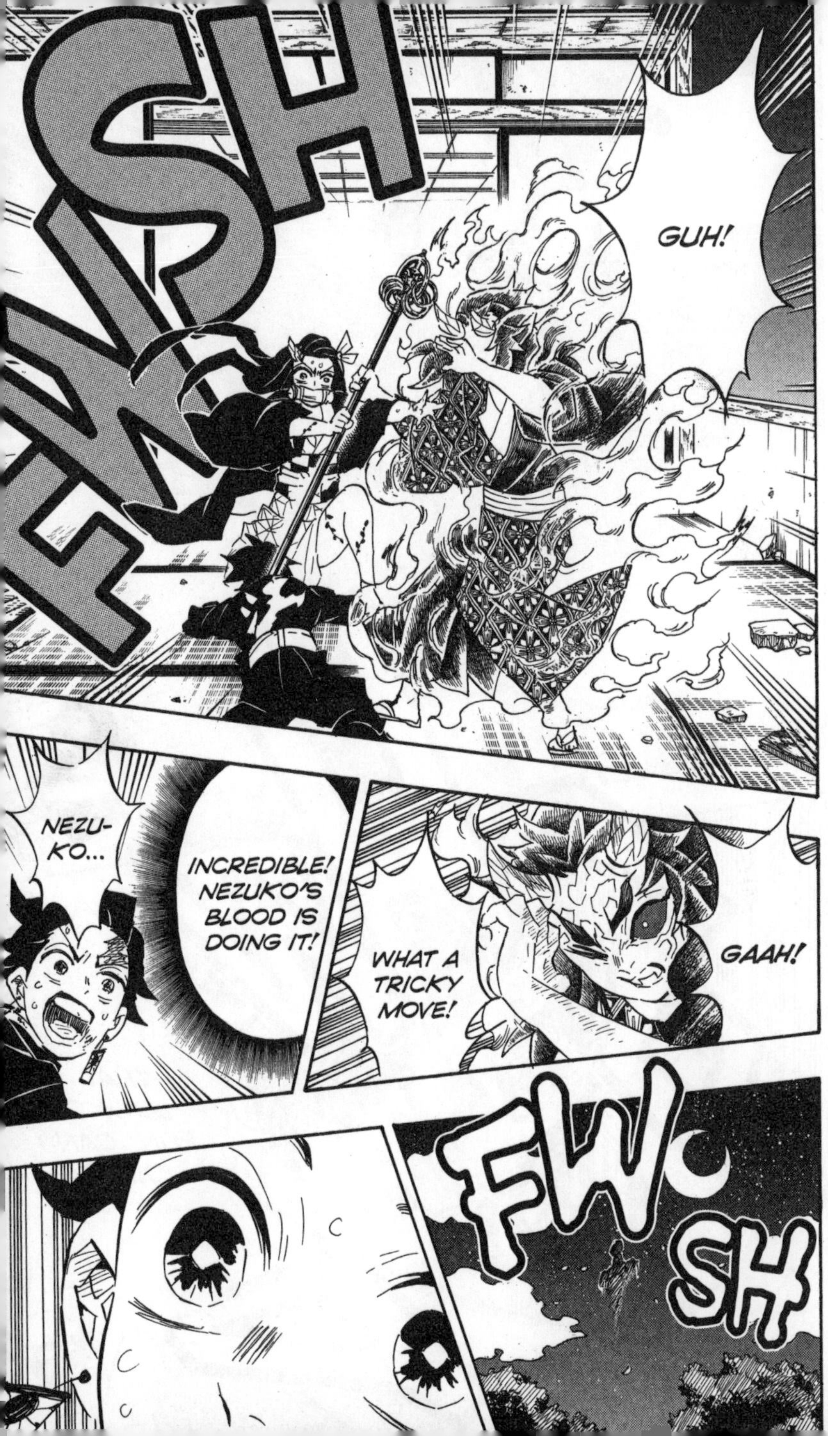
GUH!
GAAH!
WHAT A TRICKY MOVE!
INCREDIBLE! NEZUKO'S BLOOD IS DOING IT!
NEZU-KO...
FW
SH

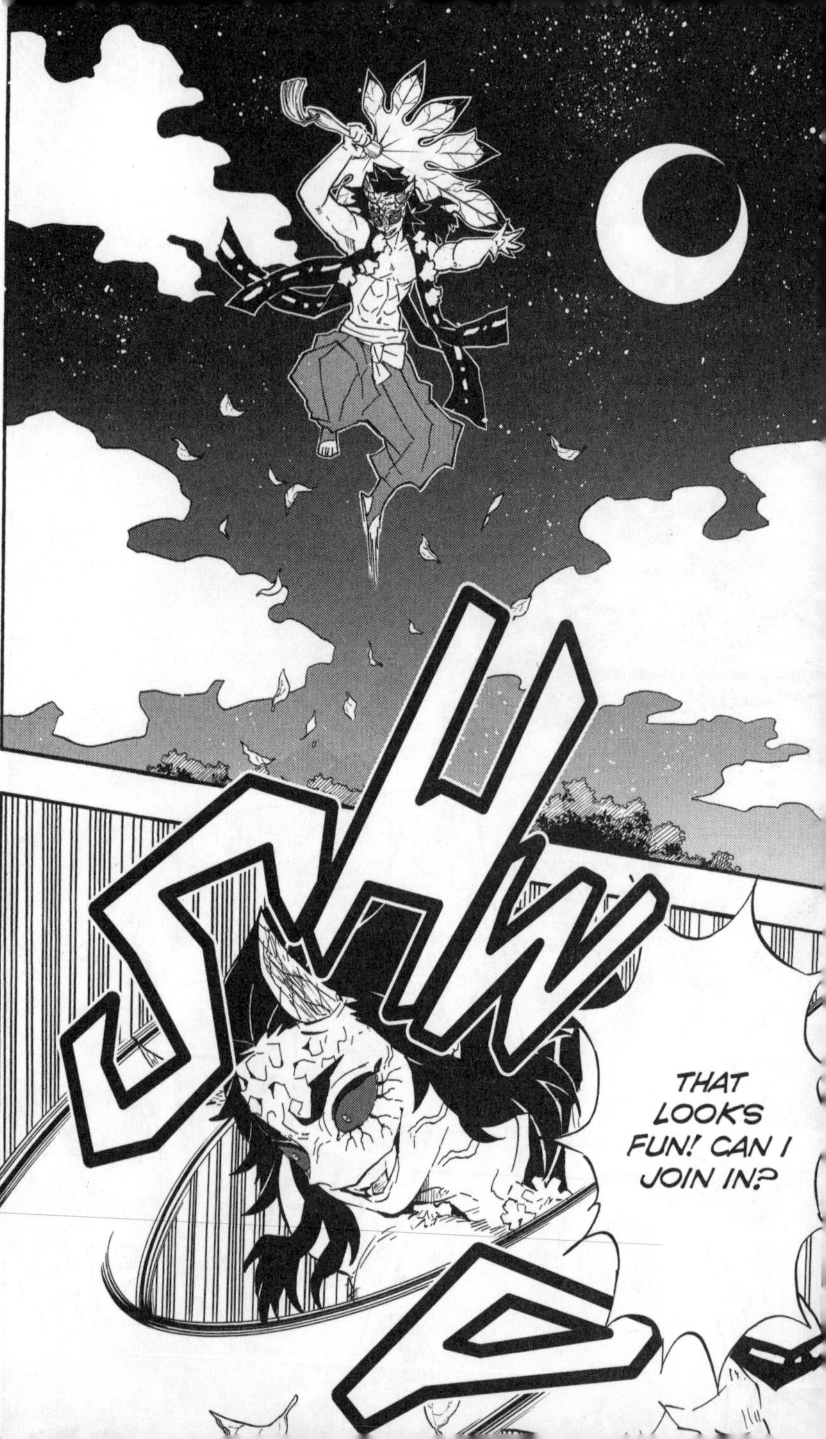
THAT LOOKS FUN! CAN I JOIN IN?

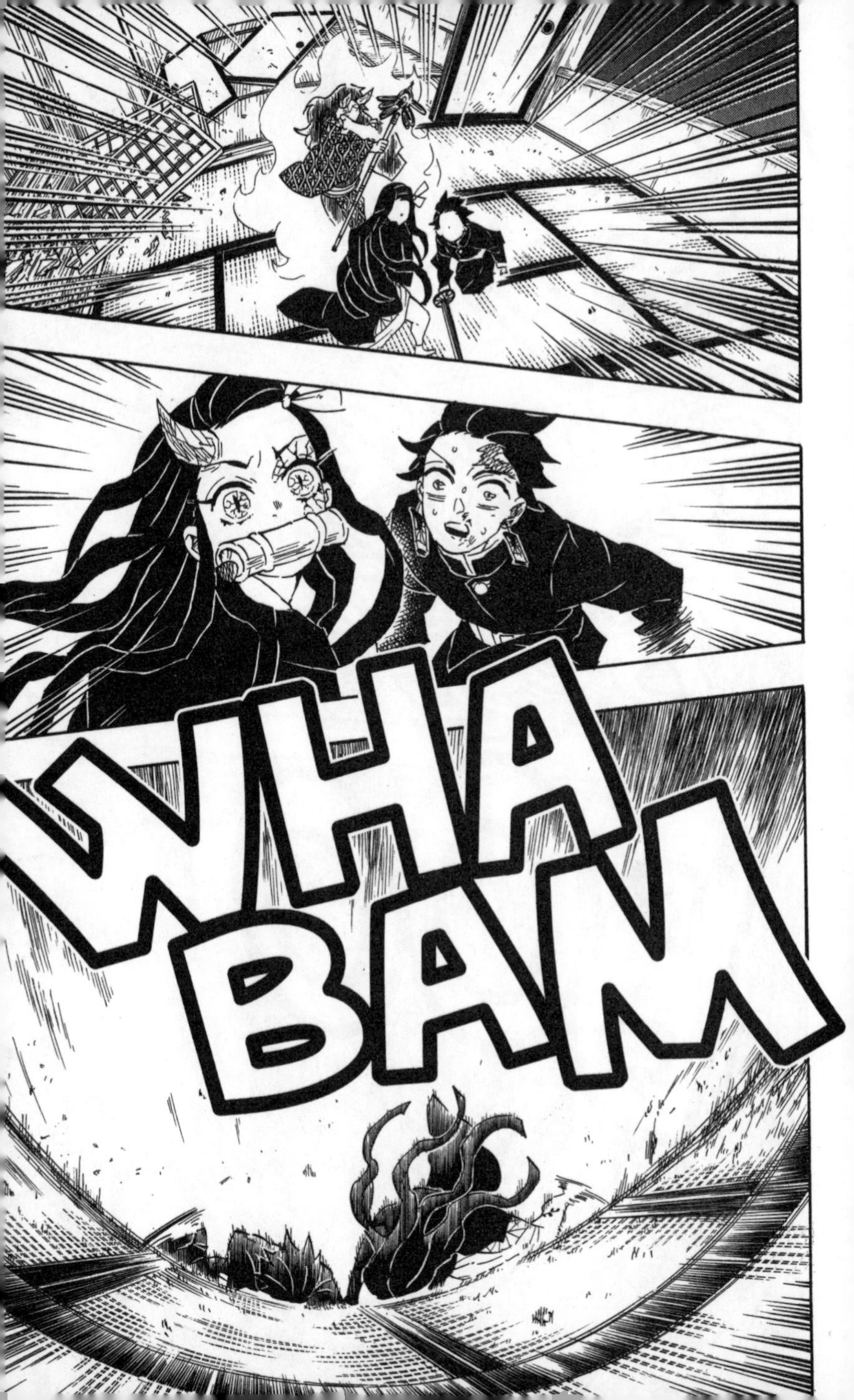
WHABAM

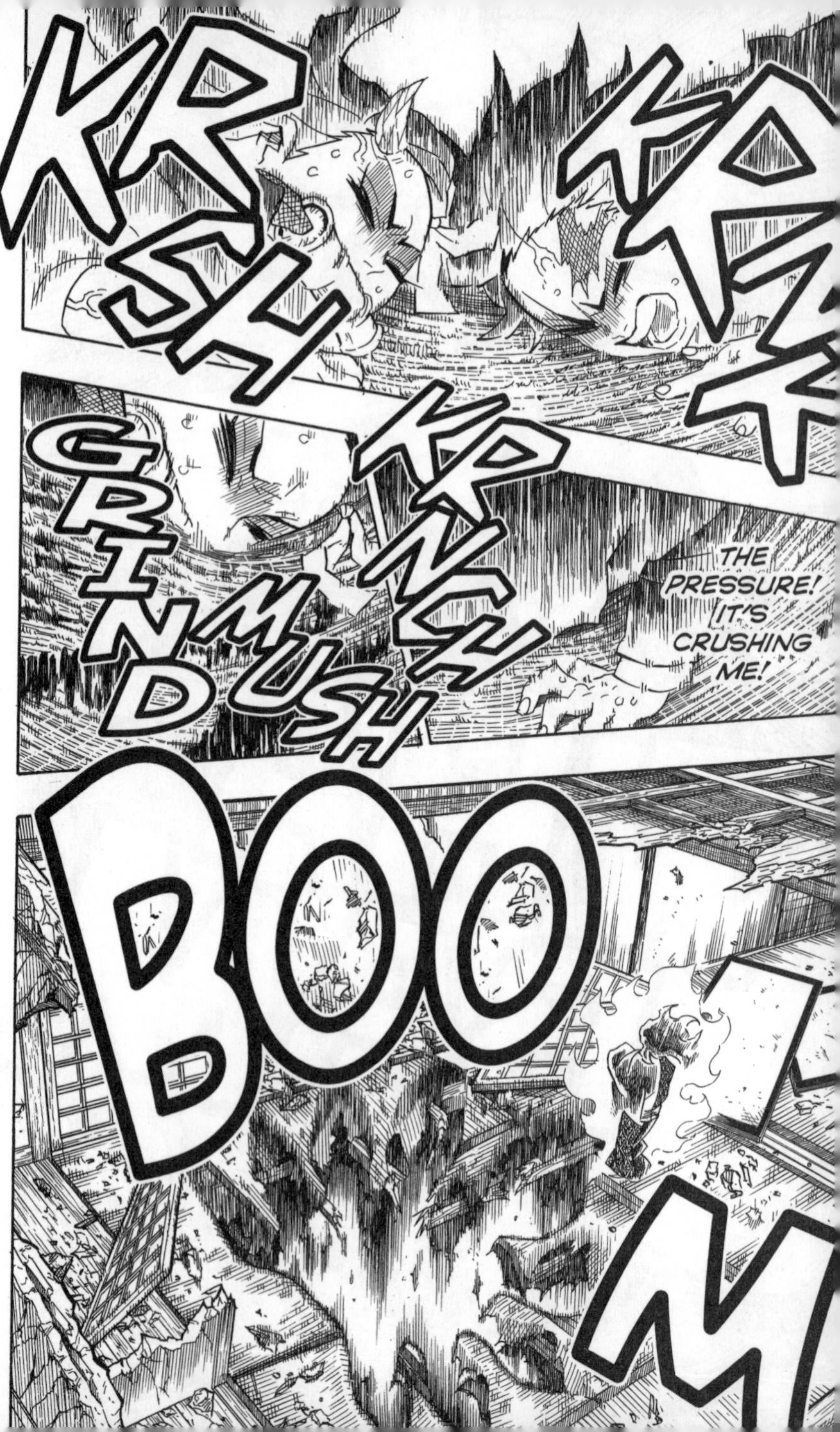
KRSH
THE PRESSURE! IT'S CRUSHING ME!
KRNCH
MUSH
GRIND
BOOM

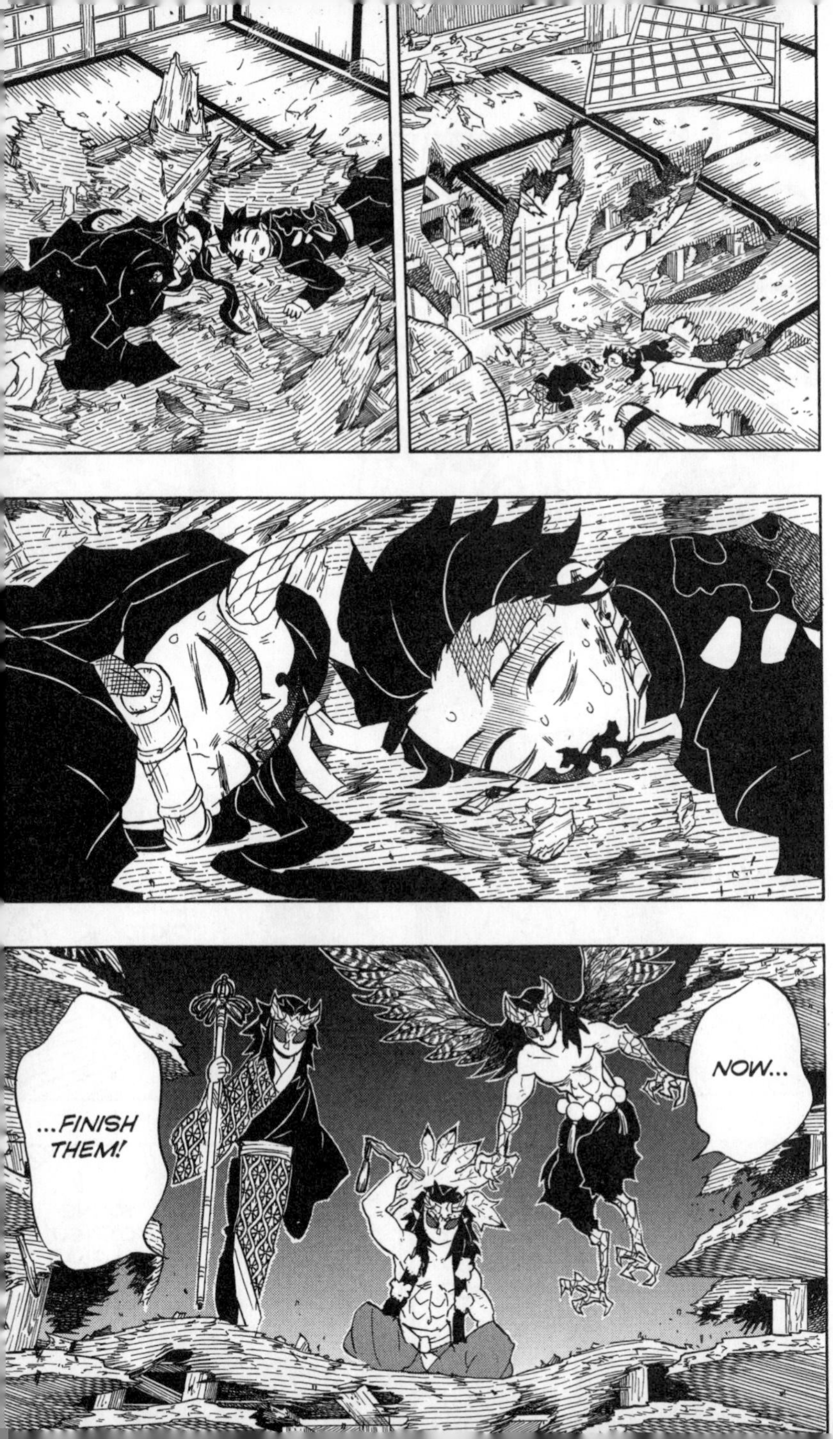
NOW...
...FINISH THEM!

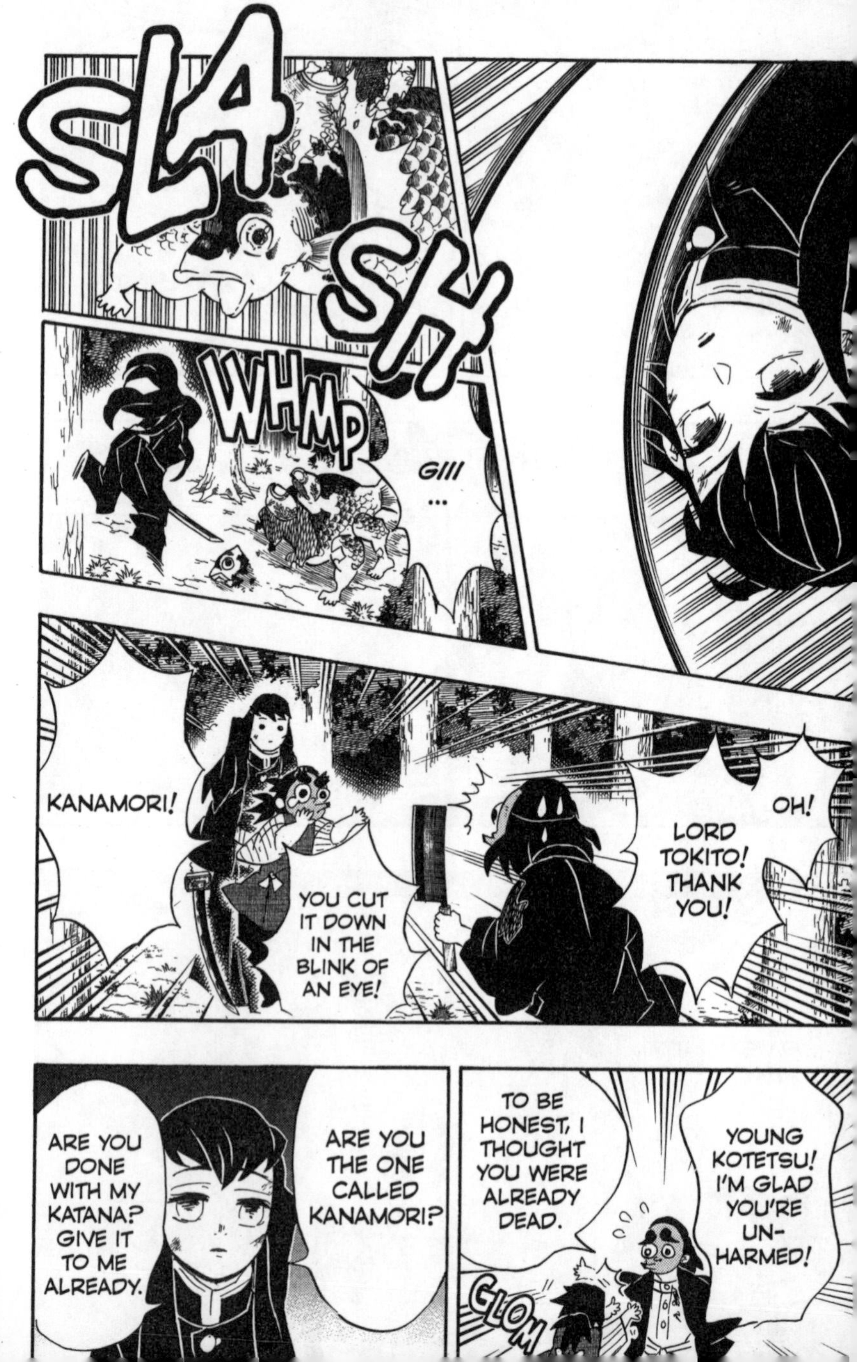
SLASH
WHMP
GIII ...
OH!
LORD TOKITO! THANK YOU!
YOU CUT IT DOWN IN THE BLINK OF AN EYE!
KANAMORI!
YOUNG KOTETSU! I'M GLAD YOU'RE UN-HARMED!
TO BE HONEST, I THOUGHT YOU WERE ALREADY DEAD.
GLOM
ARE YOU THE ONE CALLED KANAMORI?
ARE YOU DONE WITH MY KATANA? GIVE IT TO ME ALREADY.

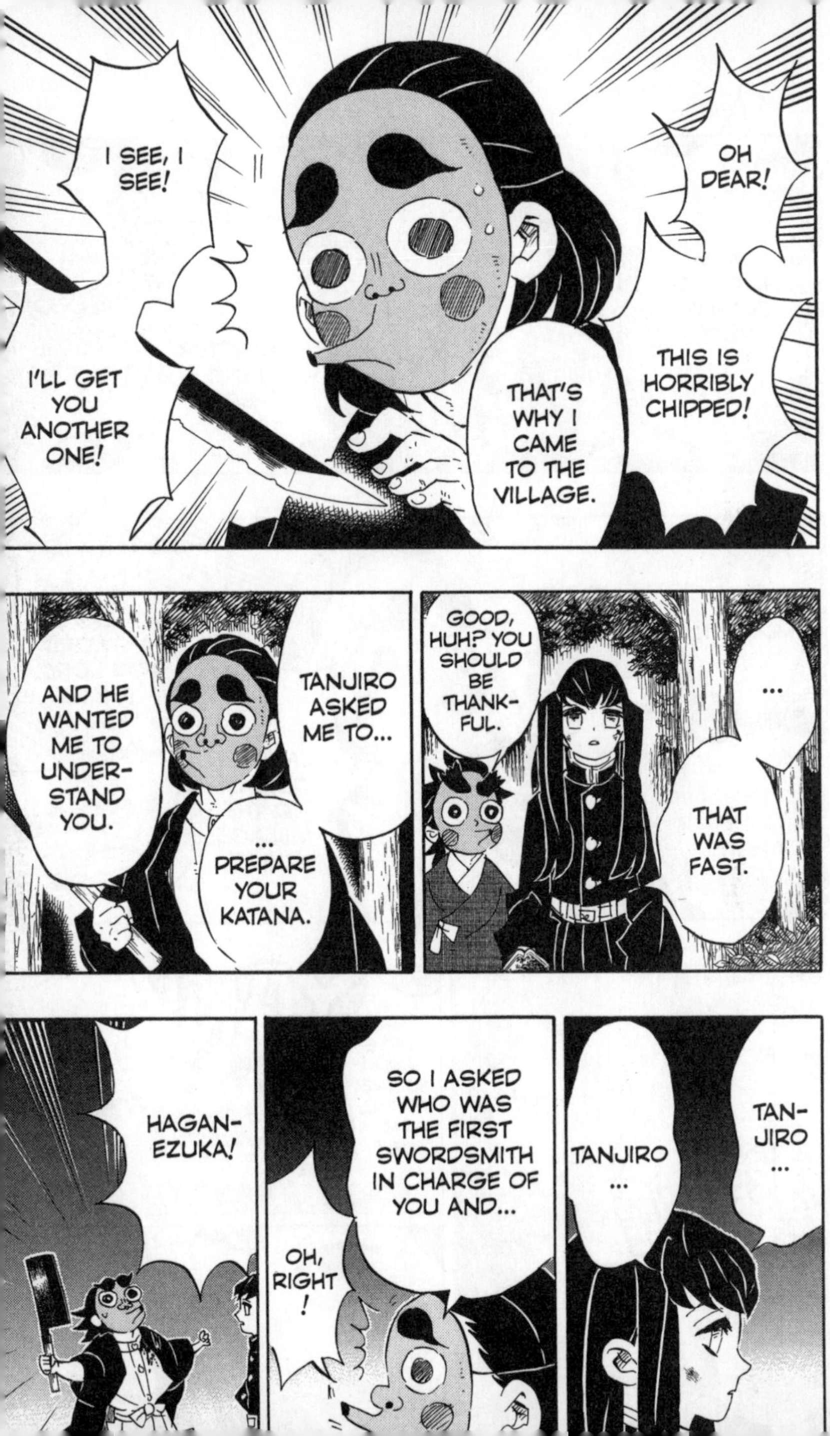
OH DEAR!
THIS IS HORRIBLY CHIPPED!
THAT'S WHY I CAME TO THE VILLAGE.
I SEE, I SEE!
I'LL GET YOU ANOTHER ONE!
...
THAT WAS FAST.
GOOD, HUH? YOU SHOULD BE THANK-FUL.
TANJIRO ASKED ME TO...
AND HE WANTED ME TO UNDER-STAND YOU.
... PREPARE YOUR KATANA.
TAN-JIRO ...
TANJIRO ...
SO I ASKED WHO WAS THE FIRST SWORDSMITH IN CHARGE OF YOU AND...
OH, RIGHT!
HAGAN-EZUKA!

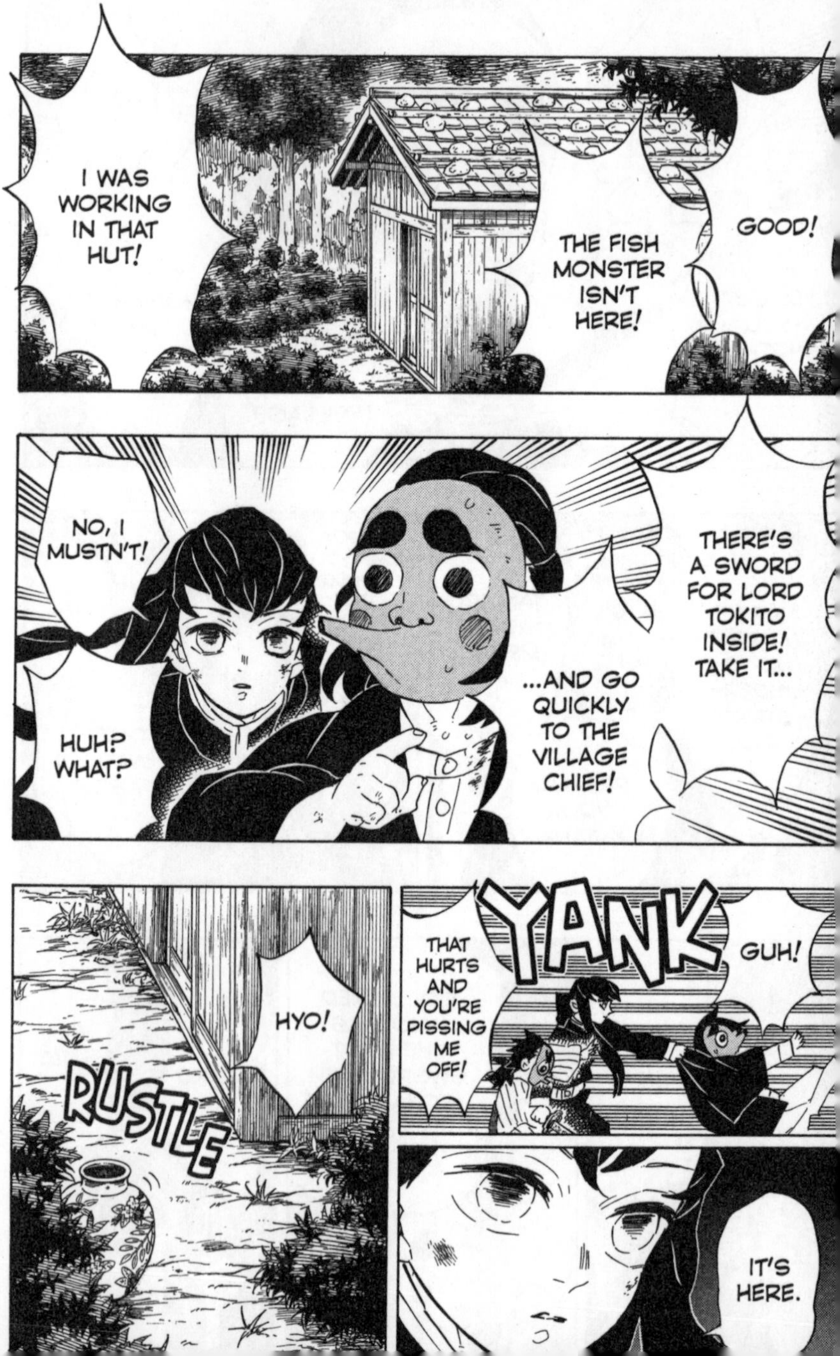
GOOD!
THE FISH MONSTER ISN'T HERE!
I WAS WORKING IN THAT HUT!
THERE'S A SWORD FOR LORD TOKITO INSIDE! TAKE IT...
...AND GO QUICKLY TO THE VILLAGE CHIEF!
NO, I MUSTN'T!
HUH? WHAT?
YANK
GUH!
THAT HURTS AND YOU'RE PISSING ME OFF!
IT'S HERE.
HYO!
RUSTLE

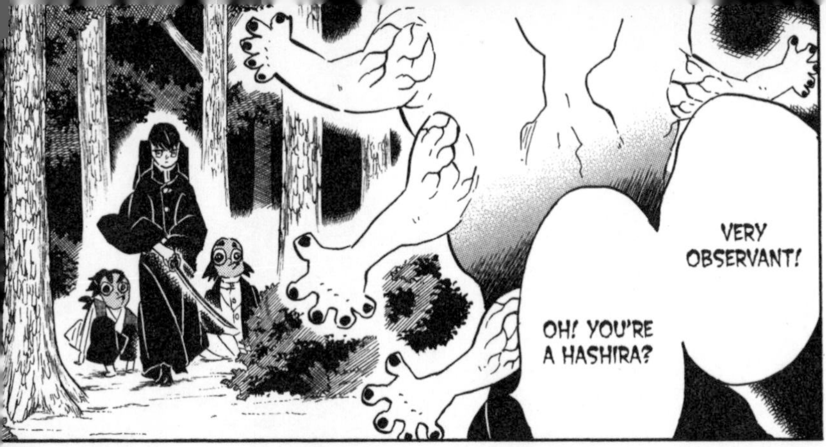
VERY OBSERVANT!
OH! YOU'RE A HASHIRA?

*Upper 5

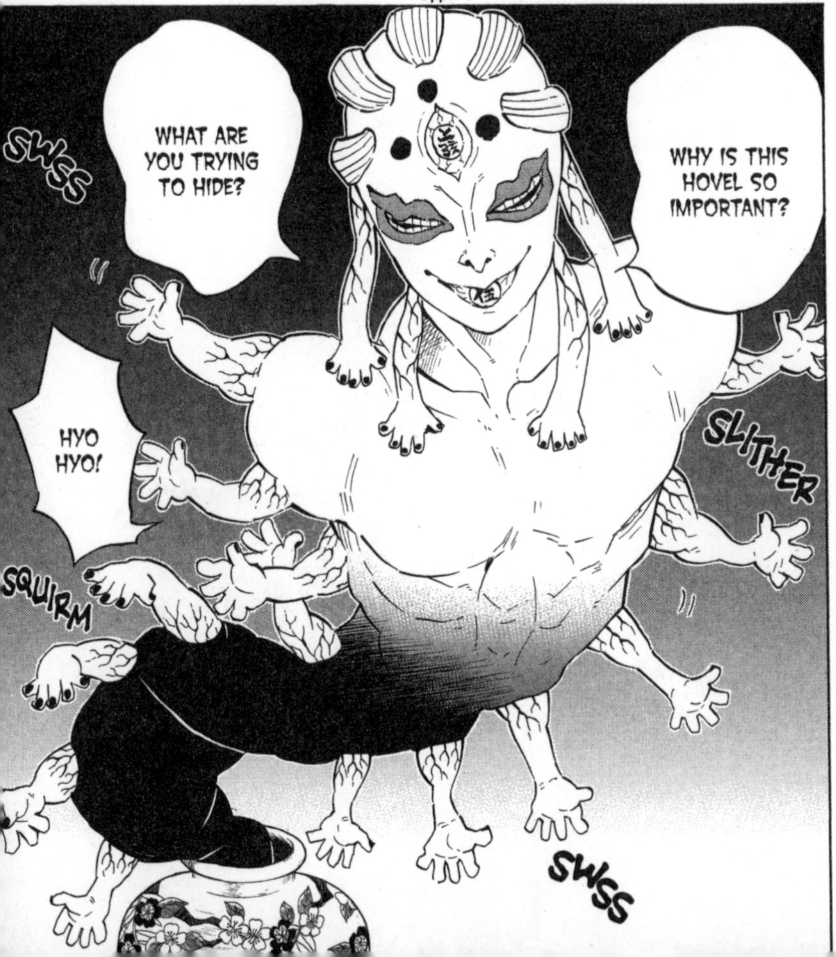
WHY IS THIS HOVEL SO IMPORTANT?
SLITHER
WHAT ARE YOU TRYING TO HIDE?
SWSS
HYO HYO!
SQUIRM
SWSS

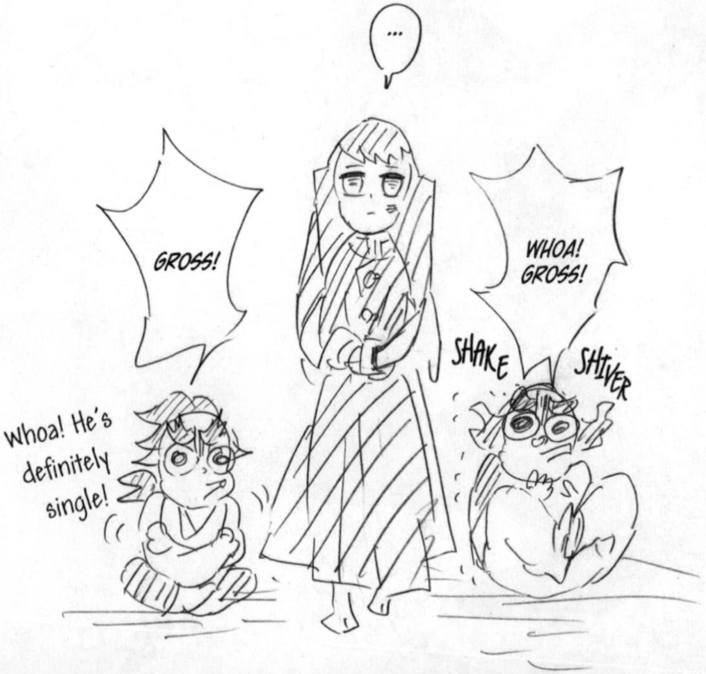
...
WHOA! GROSS!
SHIVER
SHAKE
GROSS!
Whoa! He's definitely single!

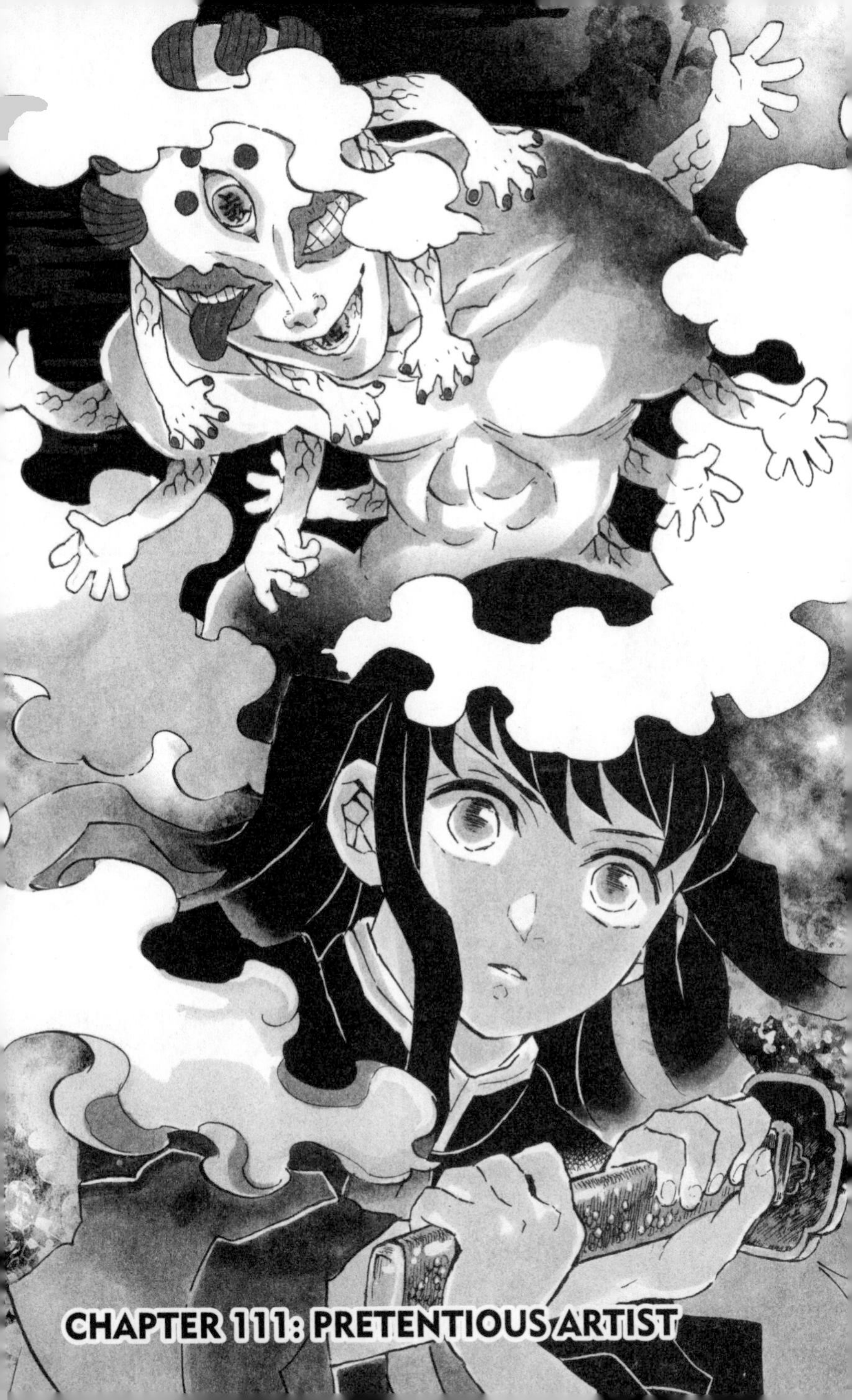
CHAPTER 111: PRETENTIOUS ARTIST

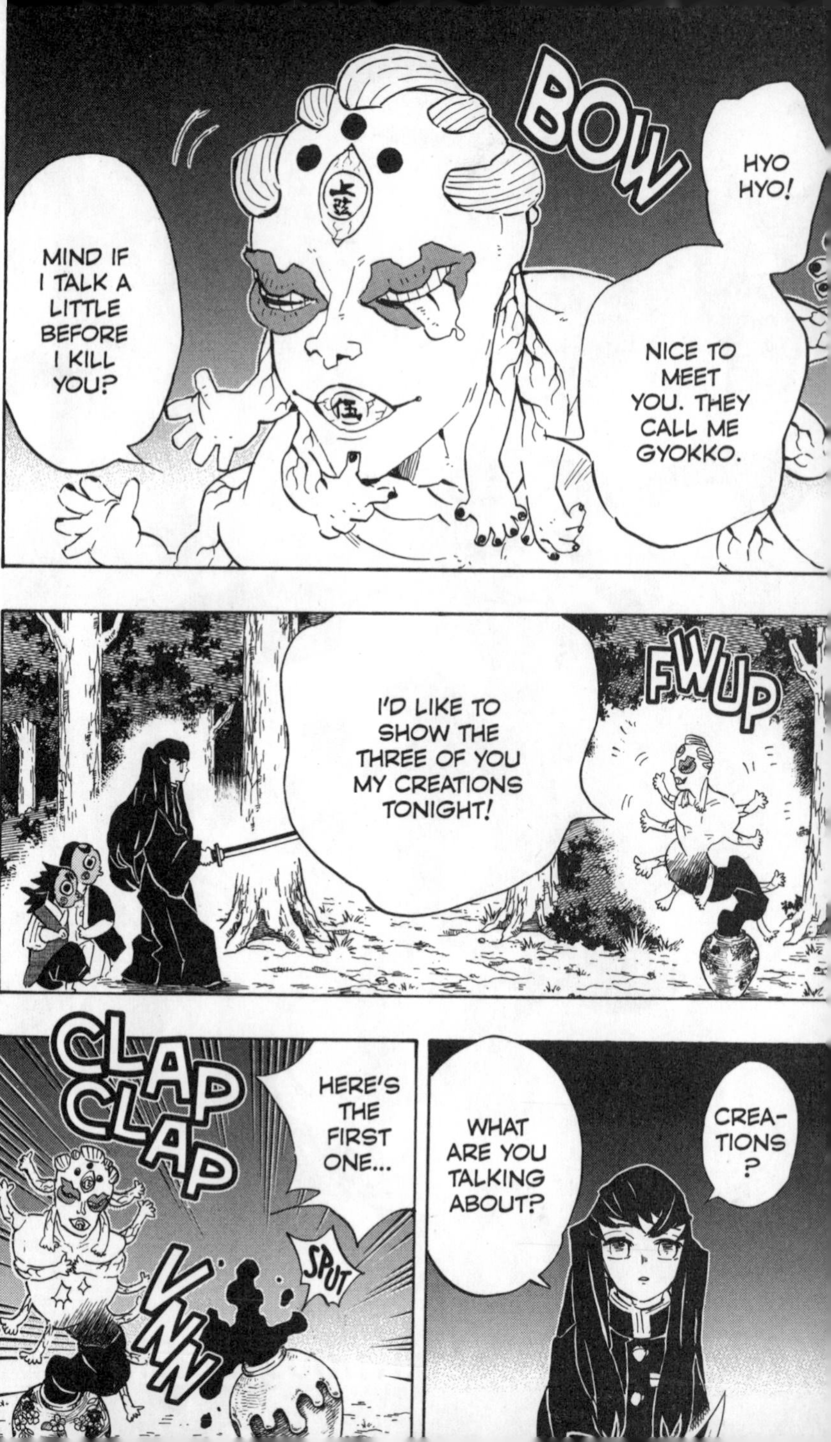
HYO HYO!
BOW
NICE TO MEET YOU. THEY CALL ME GYOKKO.
MIND IF I TALK A LITTLE BEFORE I KILL YOU?
FWUP
I'D LIKE TO SHOW THE THREE OF YOU MY CREATIONS TONIGHT!
CREA-TIONS?
WHAT ARE YOU TALKING ABOUT?
HERE'S THE FIRST ONE...
CLAP CLAP
SPUT
VNN

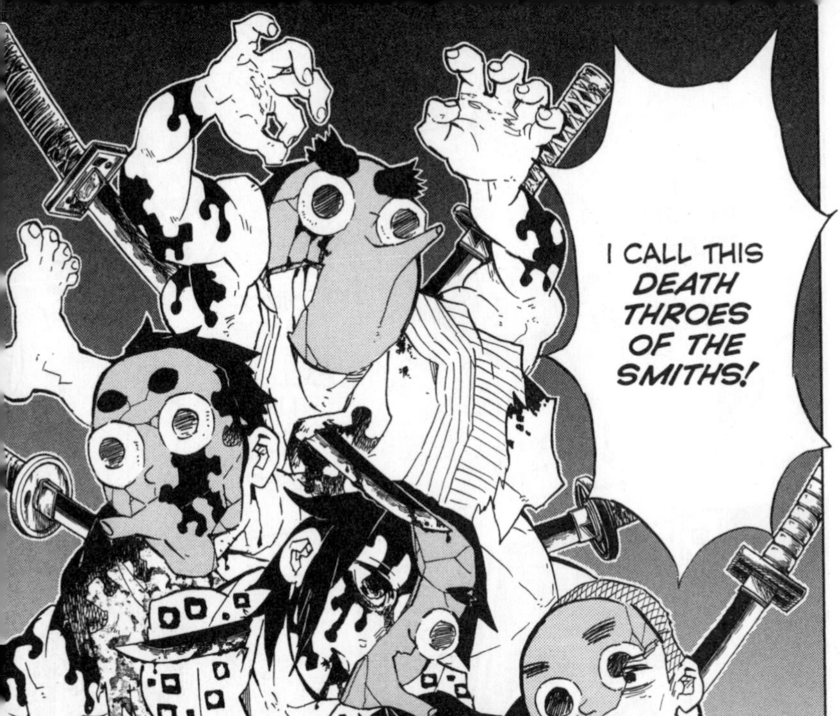
I CALL THIS DEATH THROES OF THE SMITHS!
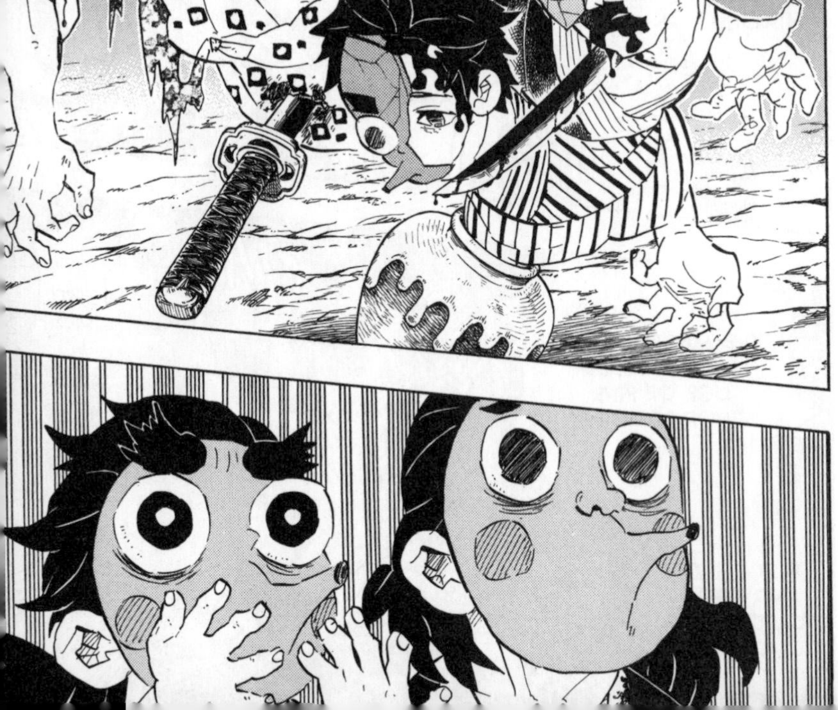

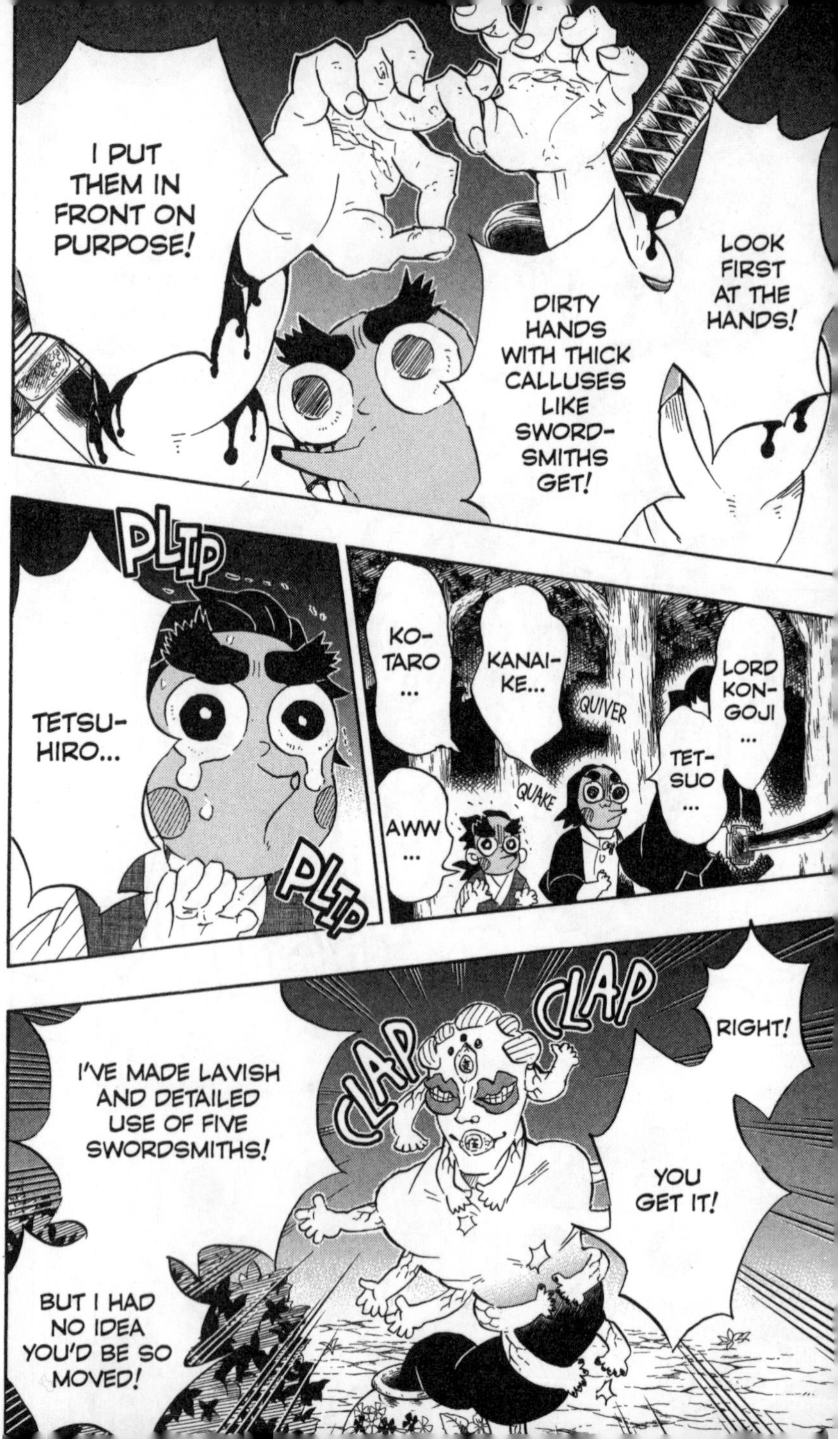
LOOK FIRST AT THE HANDS!
DIRTY HANDS WITH THICK CALLUSES LIKE SWORD-SMITHS GET!
I PUT THEM IN FRONT ON PURPOSE!
LORD KON-GOJI ...
KANAI-KE...
QUIVER
TET-SUO ...
KO-TARO ...
QUAKE
AWW ...
PLIP
TETSU-HIRO...
PLIP
RIGHT!
CLAP
CLAP
YOU GET IT!
I'VE MADE LAVISH AND DETAILED USE OF FIVE SWORDSMITHS!
BUT I HAD NO IDEA YOU'D BE SO MOVED!

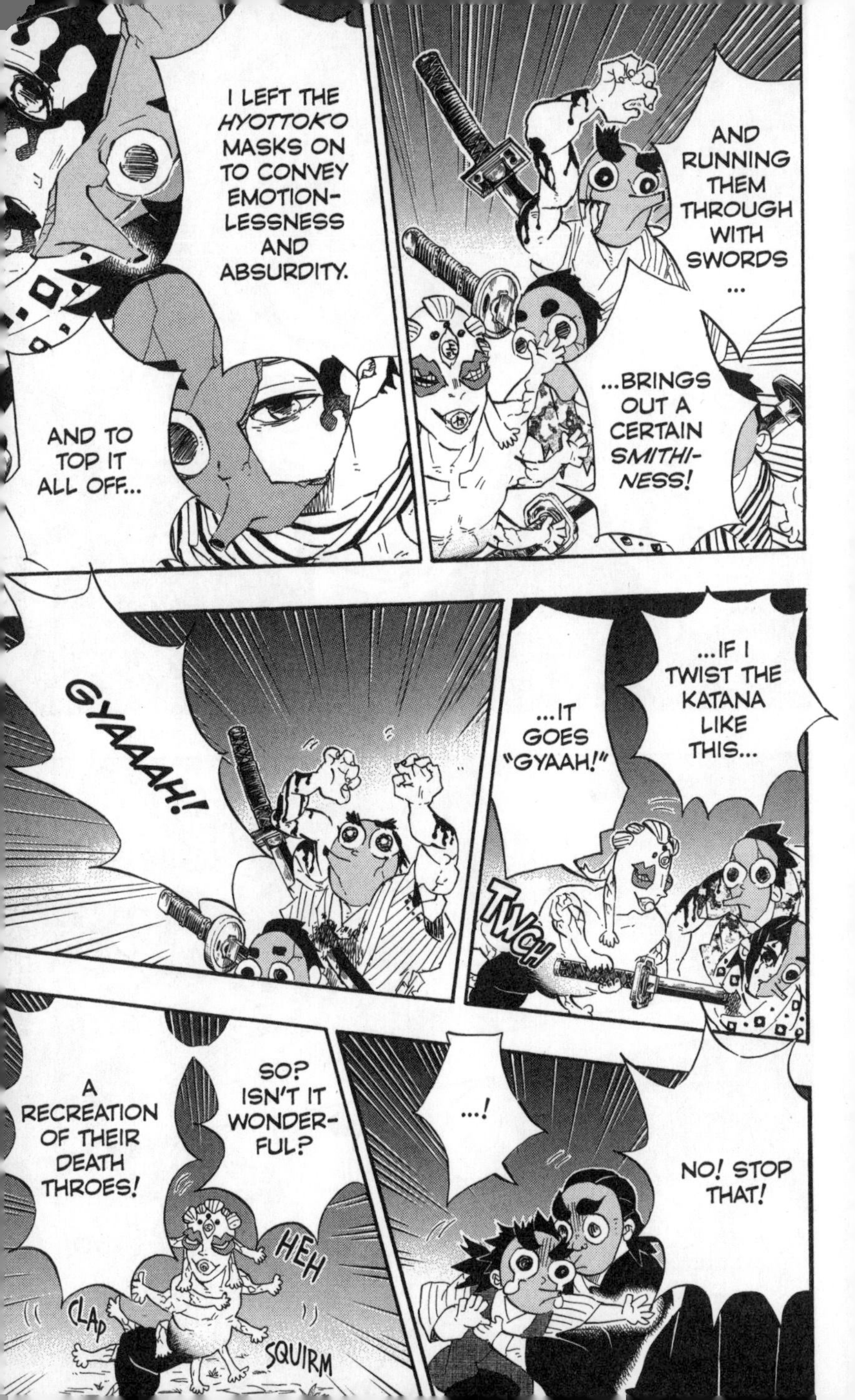
AND RUNNING THEM THROUGH WITH SWORDS ...
...BRINGS OUT A CERTAIN SMITHI-NESS!
I LEFT THE HYOTTOKO MASKS ON TO CONVEY EMOTION-LESSNESS AND ABSURDITY.
AND TO TOP IT ALL OFF...
...IF I TWIST THE KATANA LIKE THIS...
...IT GOES "GYAAH!"
TWCH
GYAAAH!
...!
NO! STOP THAT!
SO? ISN'T IT WONDER-FUL?
A RECREATION OF THEIR DEATH THROES!
HEH
CLAP
SQUIRM

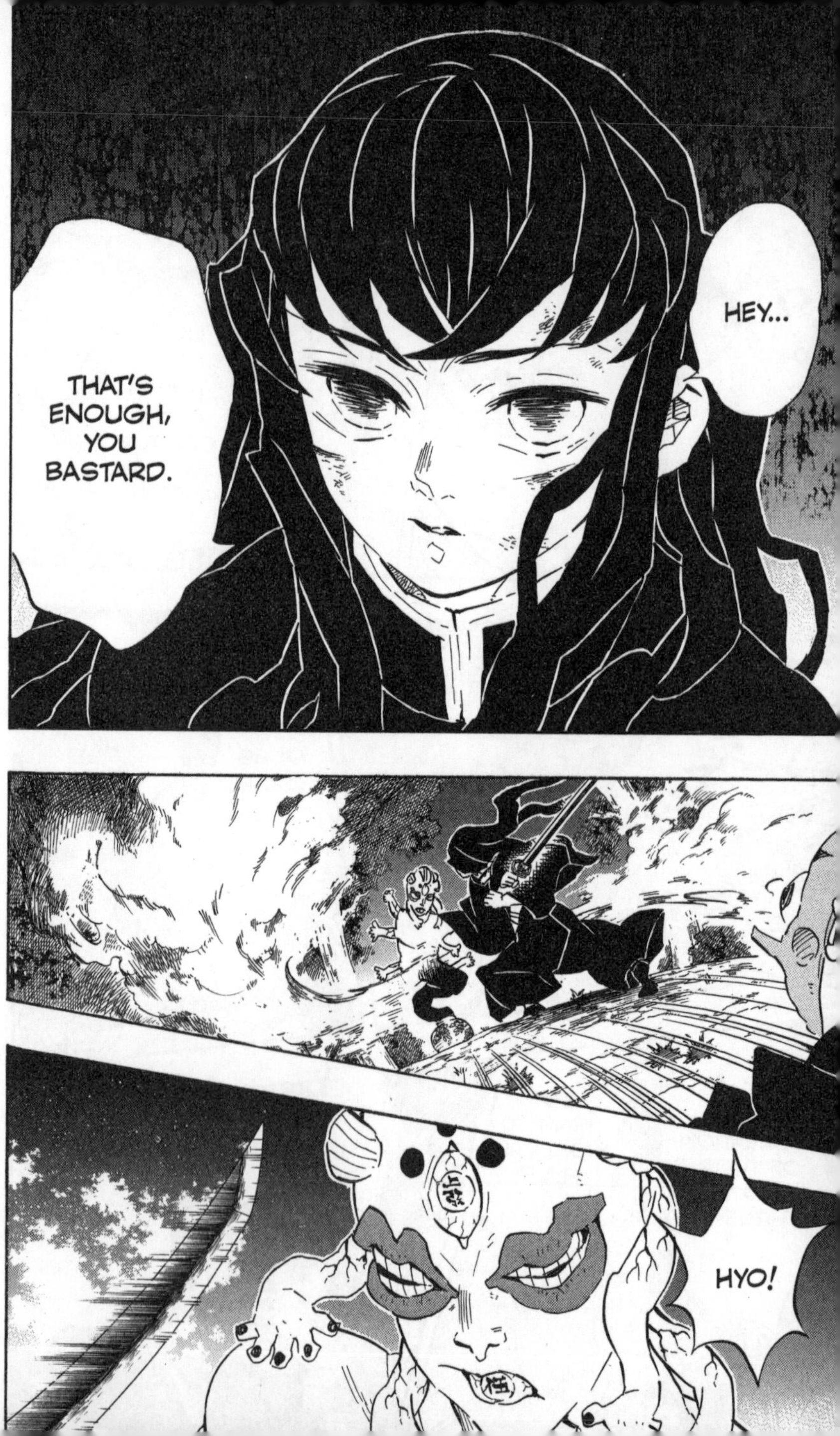
HEY...
THAT'S ENOUGH, YOU BASTARD.
HYO!

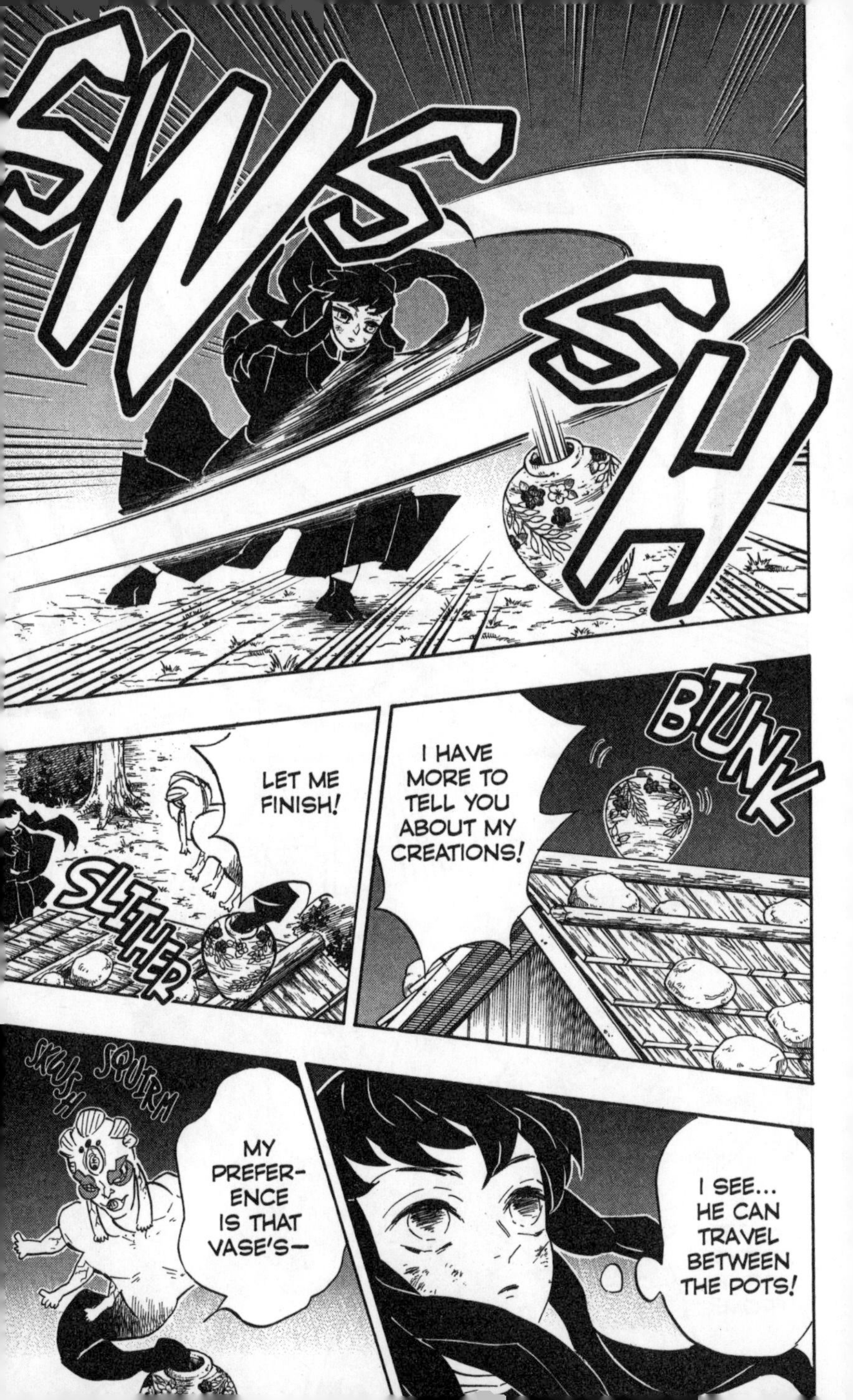

SWSSH
BTUNK
I HAVE MORE TO TELL YOU ABOUT MY CREATIONS!
LET ME FINISH!
SLITHER
I SEE... HE CAN TRAVEL BETWEEN THE POTS!
SQUIRM
SKUSH
MY PREFER-ENCE IS THAT VASE'S—

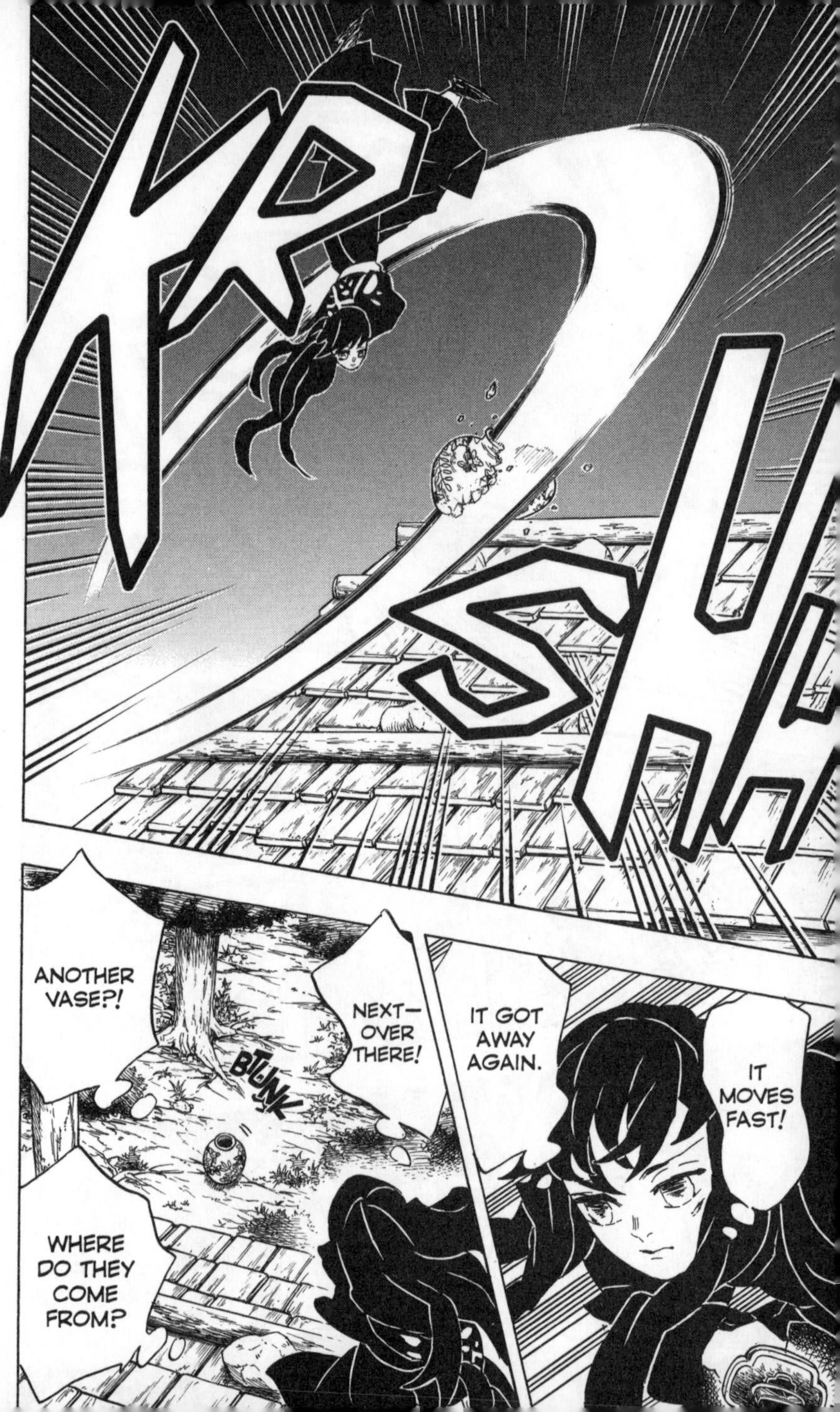
KRSHH
IT MOVES FAST!
IT GOT AWAY AGAIN.
NEXT— OVER THERE!
ANOTHER VASE?!
BTUNK
WHERE DO THEY COME FROM?

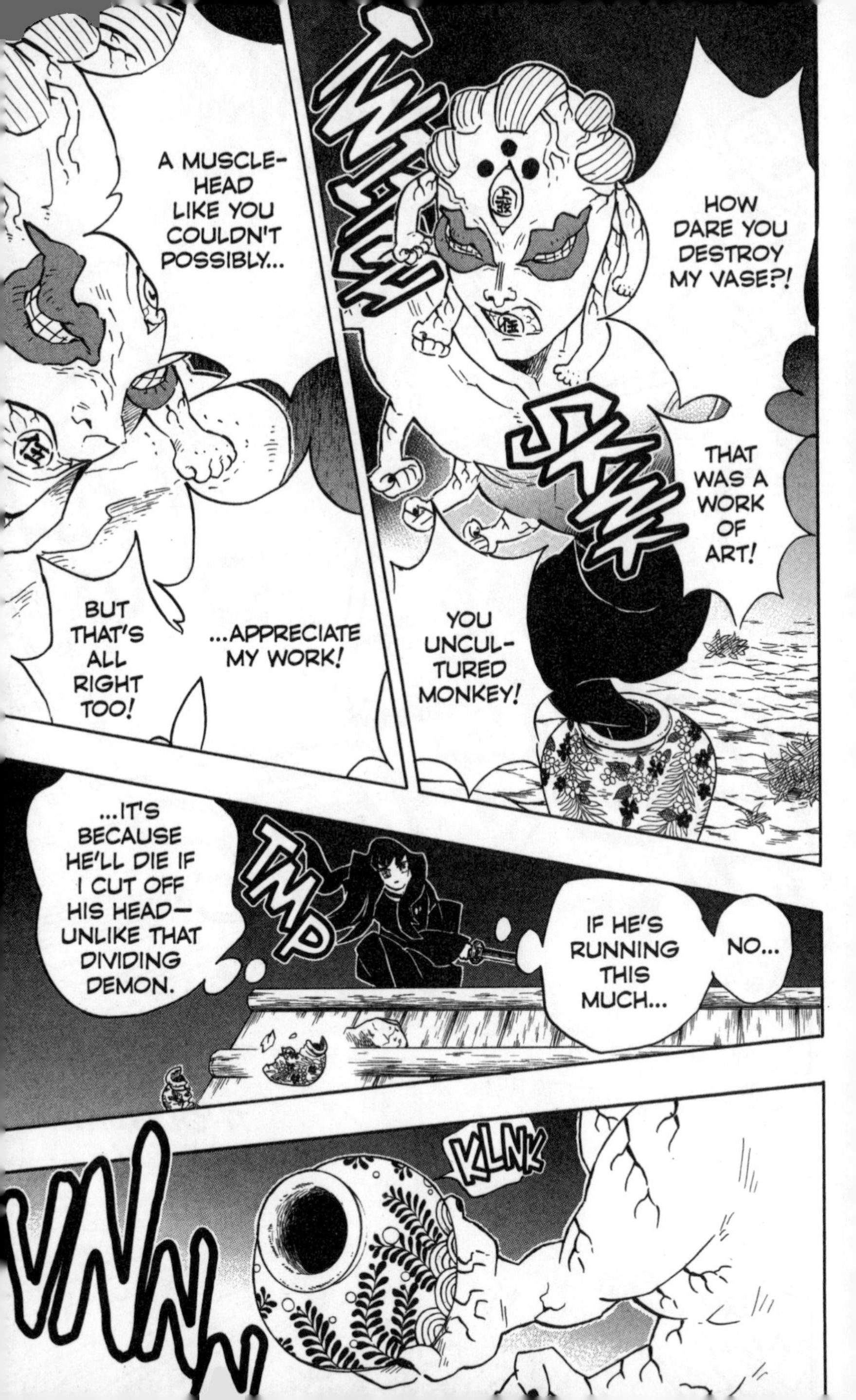
HOW DARE YOU DESTROY MY VASE?!
THAT WAS A WORK OF ART!
YOU UNCUL-TURED MONKEY!
A MUSCLE-HEAD LIKE YOU COULDN'T POSSIBLY...
...APPRECIATE MY WORK!
BUT THAT'S ALL RIGHT TOO!
NO...
IF HE'S RUNNING THIS MUCH...
TMP
...IT'S BECAUSE HE'LL DIE IF I CUT OFF HIS HEAD—UNLIKE THAT DIVIDING DEMON.
KLINK

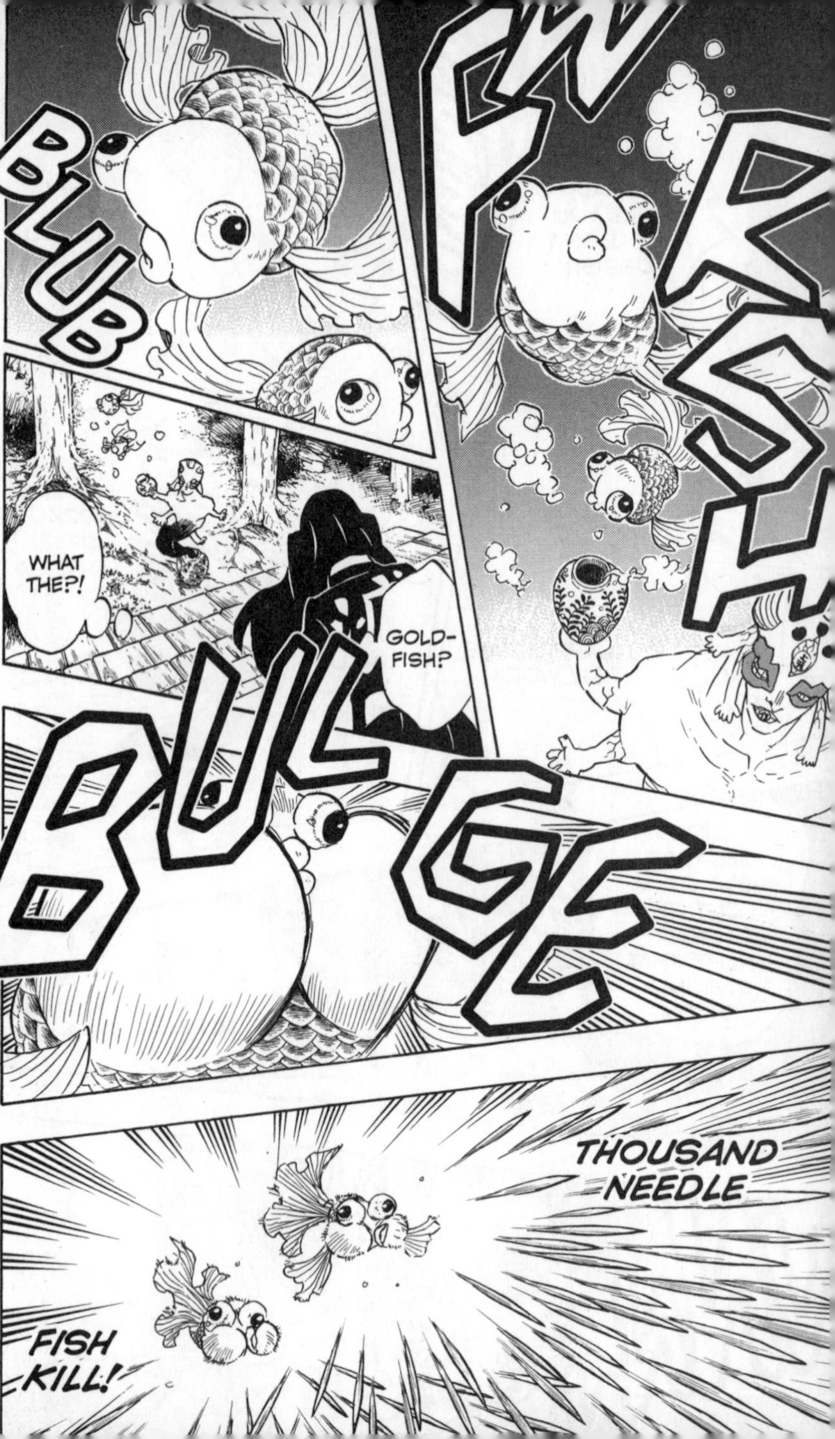
BLUB
WHAT THE?!
GOLD-FISH?
BULGE
THOUSAND NEEDLE
FISH KILL!

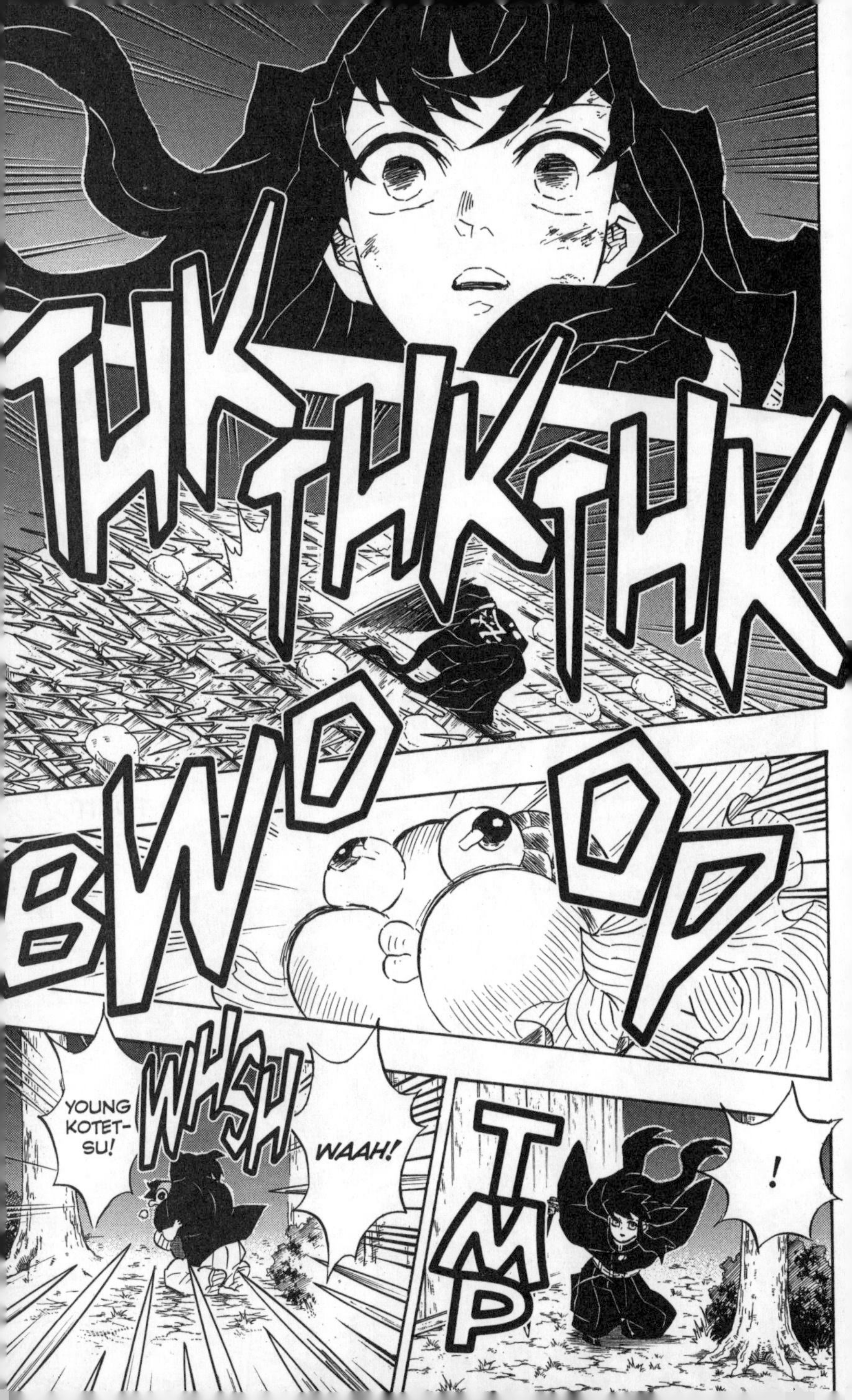

THKTHKTHK
BWOOP
!
TMP
WHSH
WAAH!
YOUNG KOTET-SU!

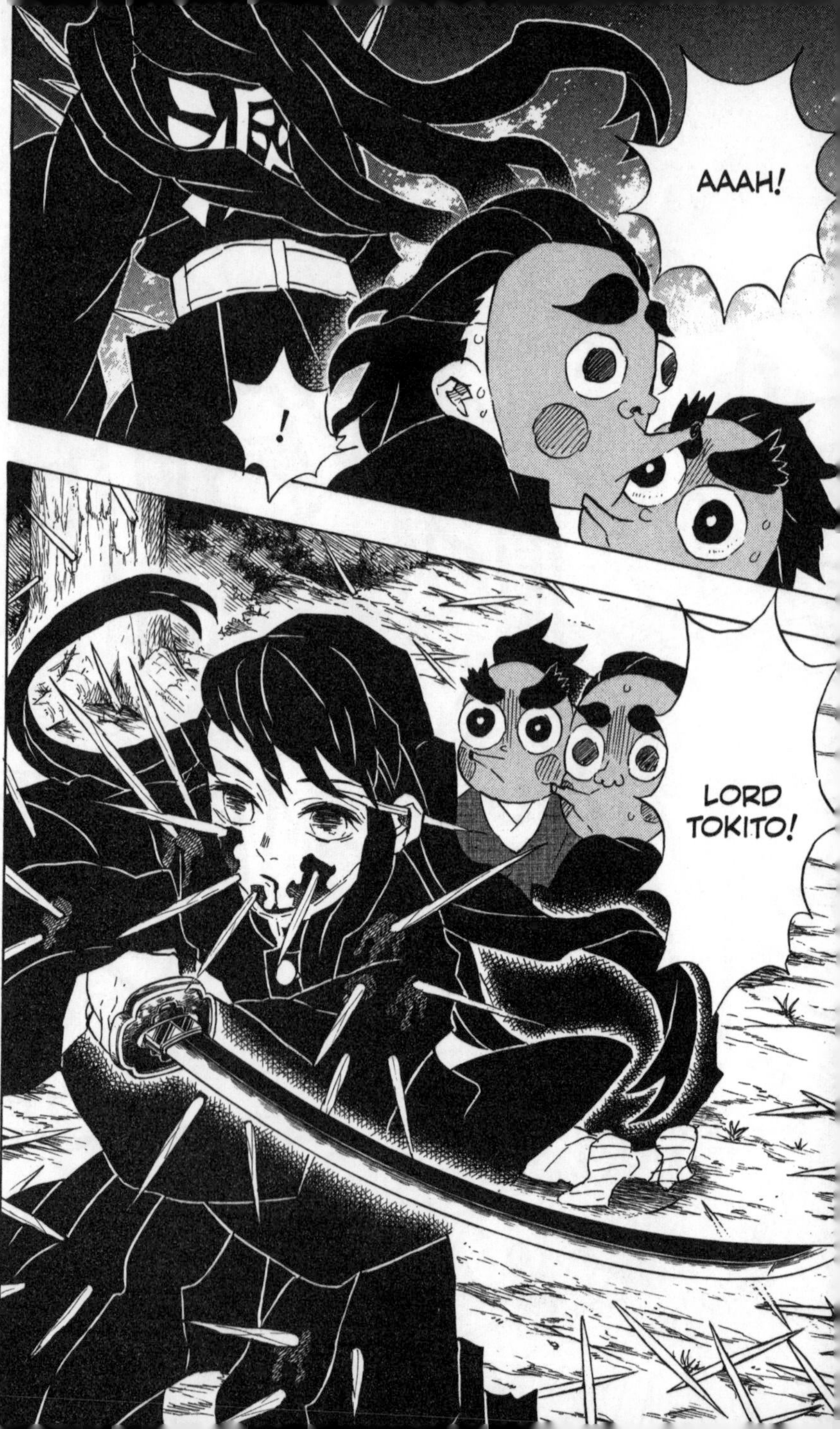
AAAH!
!
LORD TOKITO!

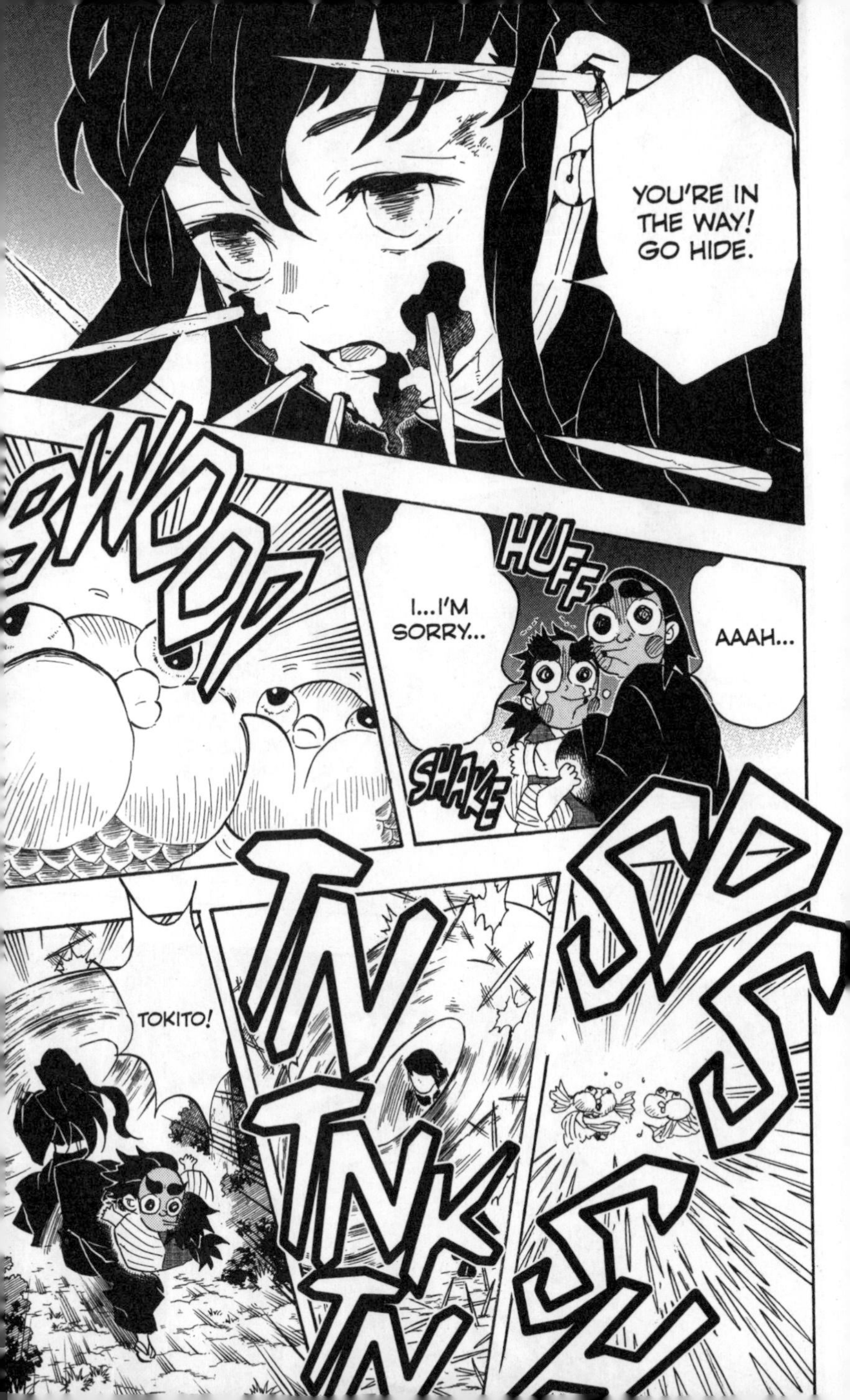
YOU'RE IN THE WAY! GO HIDE.
AAAH...
HUFF
I...I'M SORRY...
SHAKE
SWOOP
TINK
TINK
TOKITO!

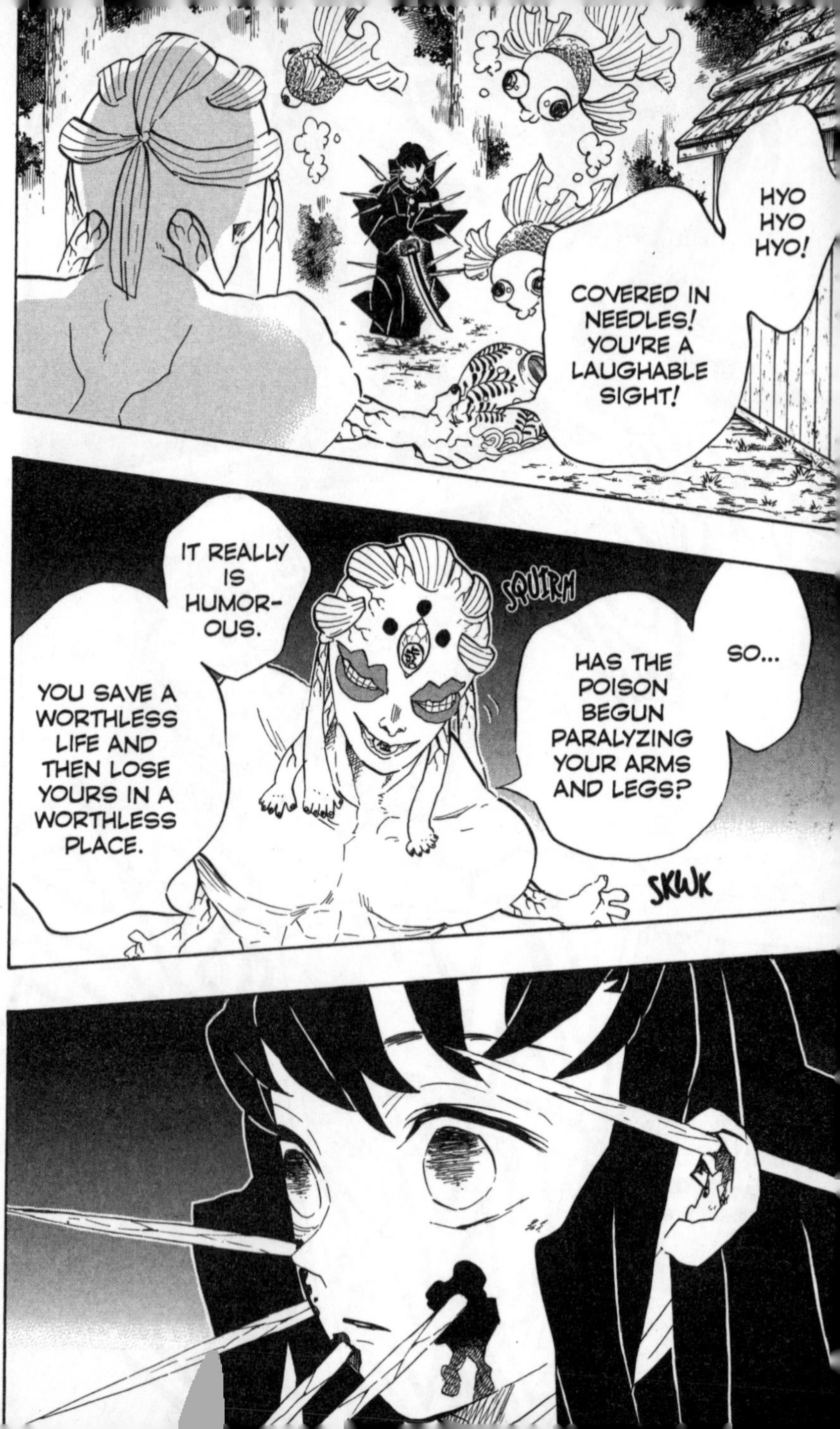
HYO HYO HYO!
COVERED IN NEEDLES! YOU'RE A LAUGHABLE SIGHT!
SO...
HAS THE POISON BEGUN PARALYZING YOUR ARMS AND LEGS?
SQUIRM
IT REALLY IS HUMOR-OUS.
YOU SAVE A WORTHLESS LIFE AND THEN LOSE YOURS IN A WORTHLESS PLACE.
SKWK

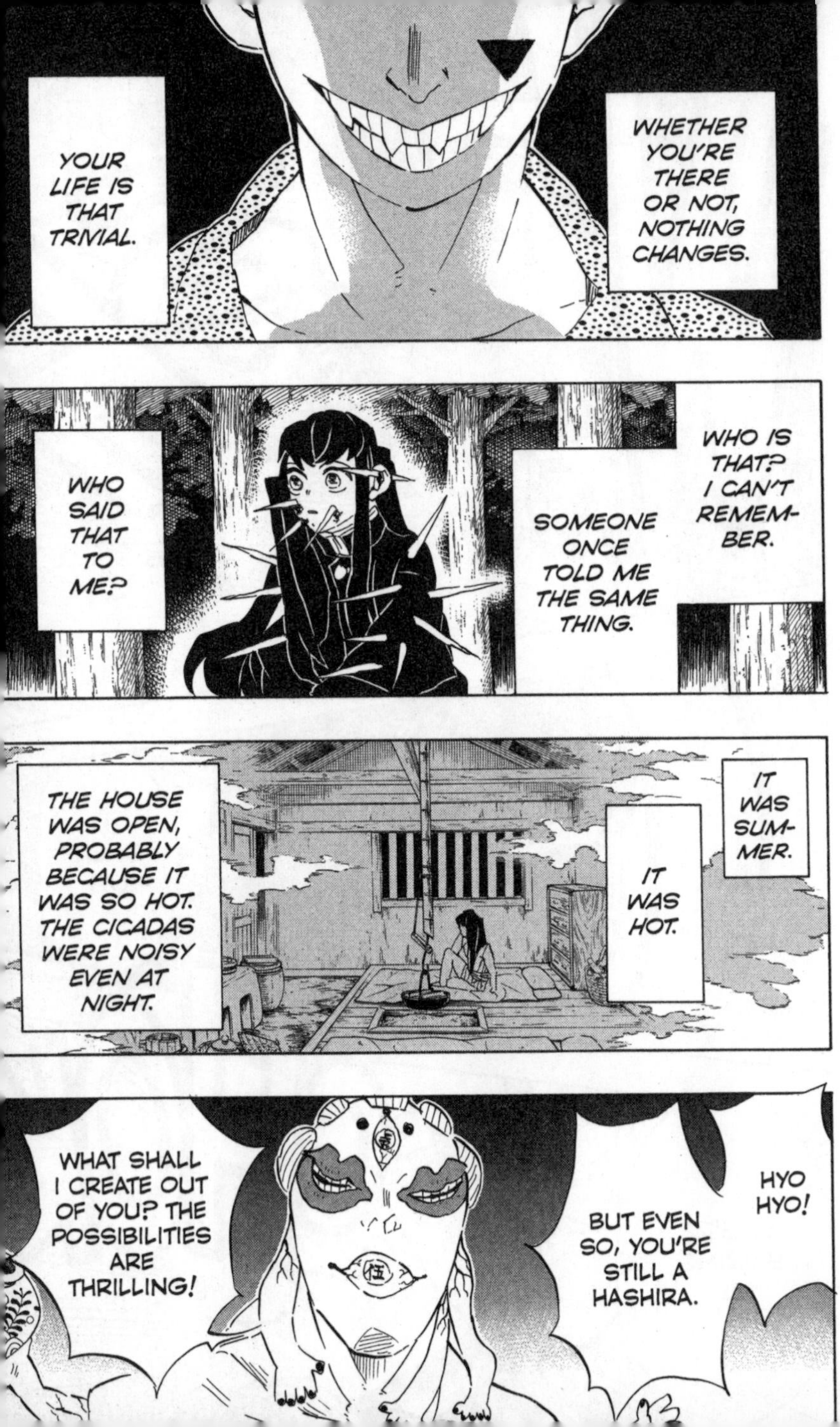
WHETHER YOU'RE THERE OR NOT, NOTHING CHANGES.
YOUR LIFE IS THAT TRIVIAL.
WHO IS THAT? I CAN'T REMEMBER.
SOMEONE ONCE TOLD ME THE SAME THING.
WHO SAID THAT TO ME?
IT WAS SUMMER.
IT WAS HOT.
THE HOUSE WAS OPEN, PROBABLY BECAUSE IT WAS SO HOT. THE CICADAS WERE NOISY EVEN AT NIGHT.
HYO HYO!
BUT EVEN SO, YOU'RE STILL A HASHIRA.
WHAT SHALL I CREATE OUT OF YOU? THE POSSIBILITIES ARE THRILLING!

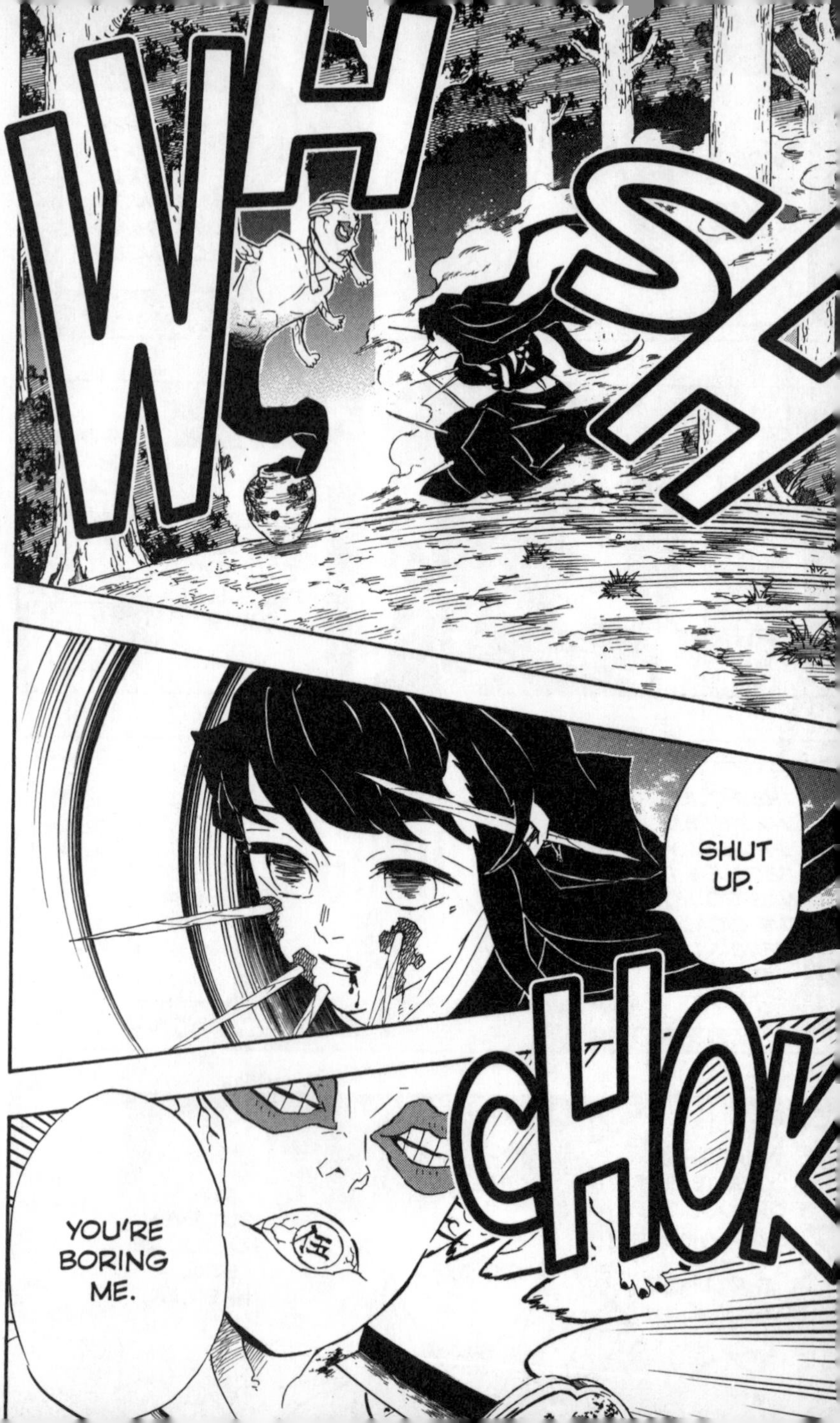
WHS
SHUT UP.
CHOK
YOU'RE BORING ME.

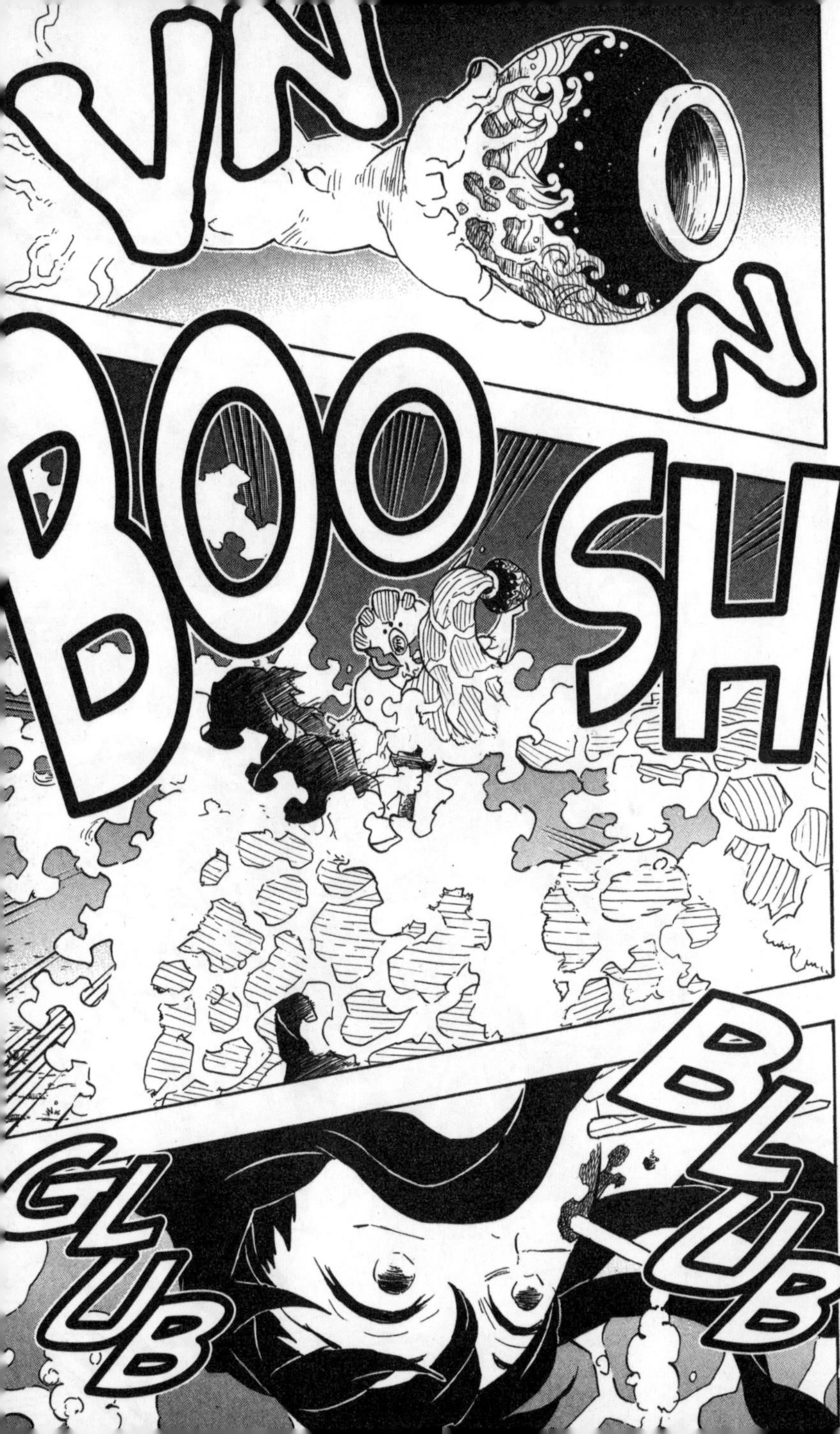
BOOSH
BLUB
GLUB

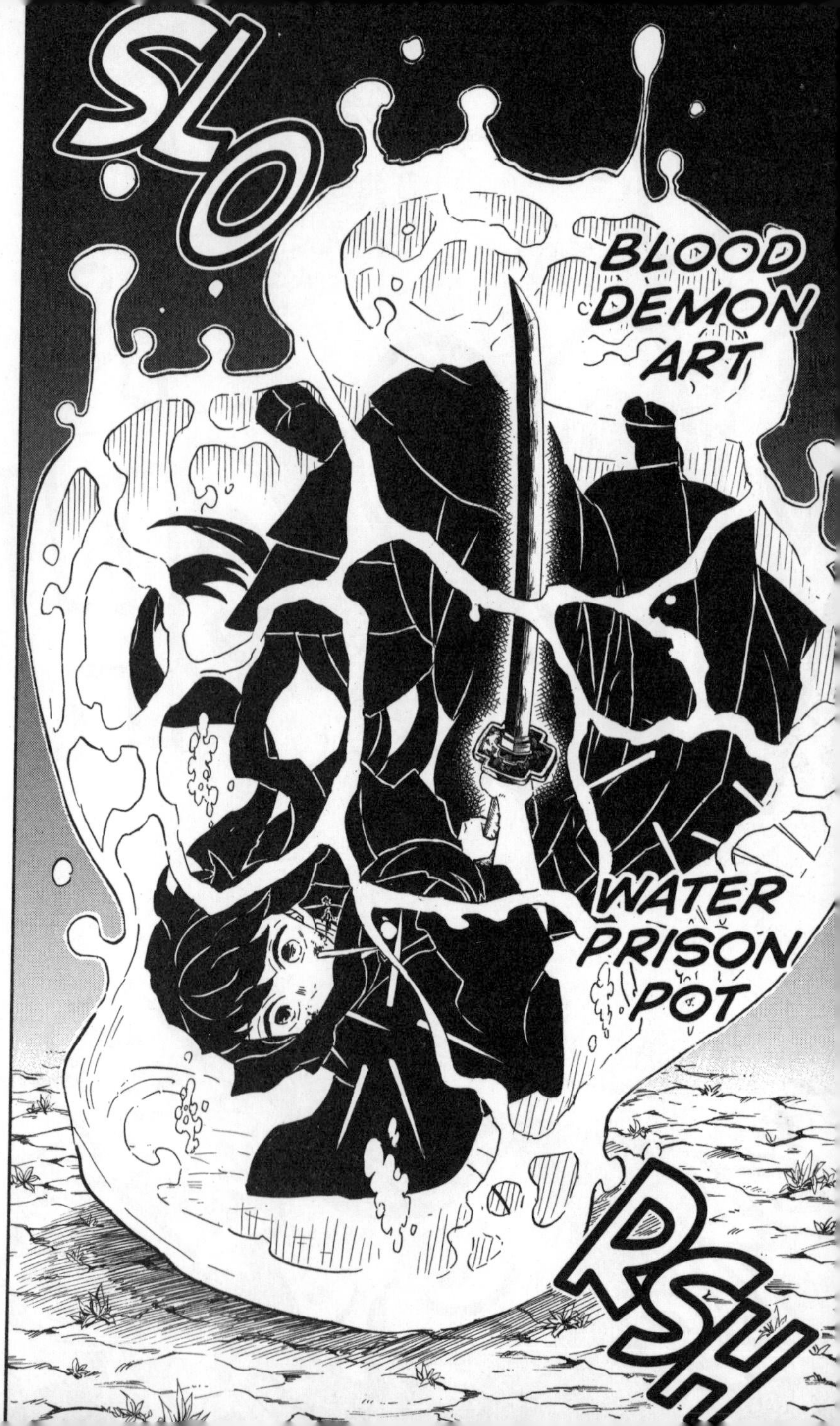
SLO
BLOOD DEMON ART
WATER PRISON POT
RSH

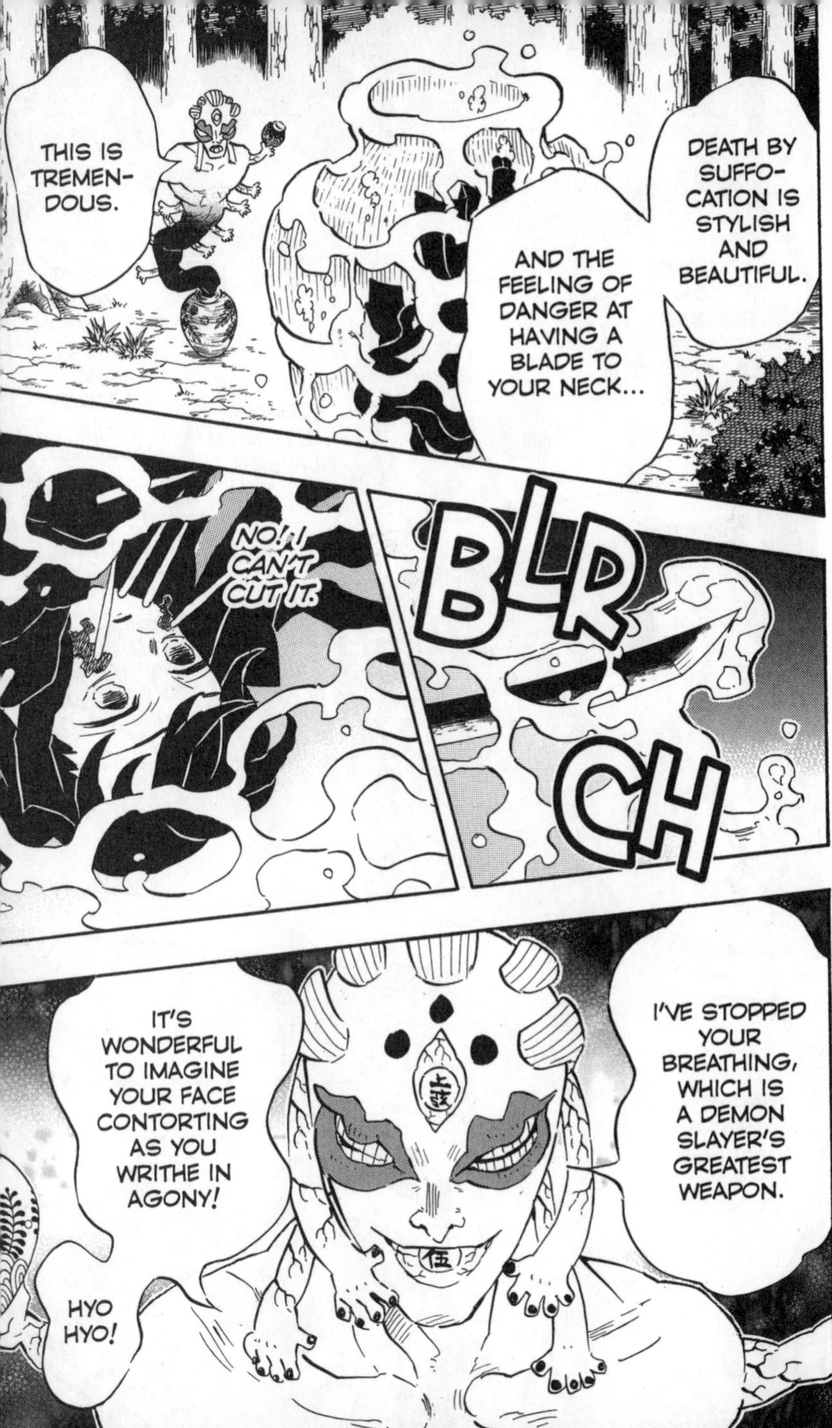
DEATH BY SUFFOCATION IS STYLISH AND BEAUTIFUL.
AND THE FEELING OF DANGER AT HAVING A BLADE TO YOUR NECK...
THIS IS TREMENDOUS.
BLRCH
NO! I CAN'T CUT IT.
I'VE STOPPED YOUR BREATHING, WHICH IS A DEMON SLAYER'S GREATEST WEAPON.
IT'S WONDERFUL TO IMAGINE YOUR FACE CONTORTING AS YOU WRITHE IN AGONY!
HYO HYO!

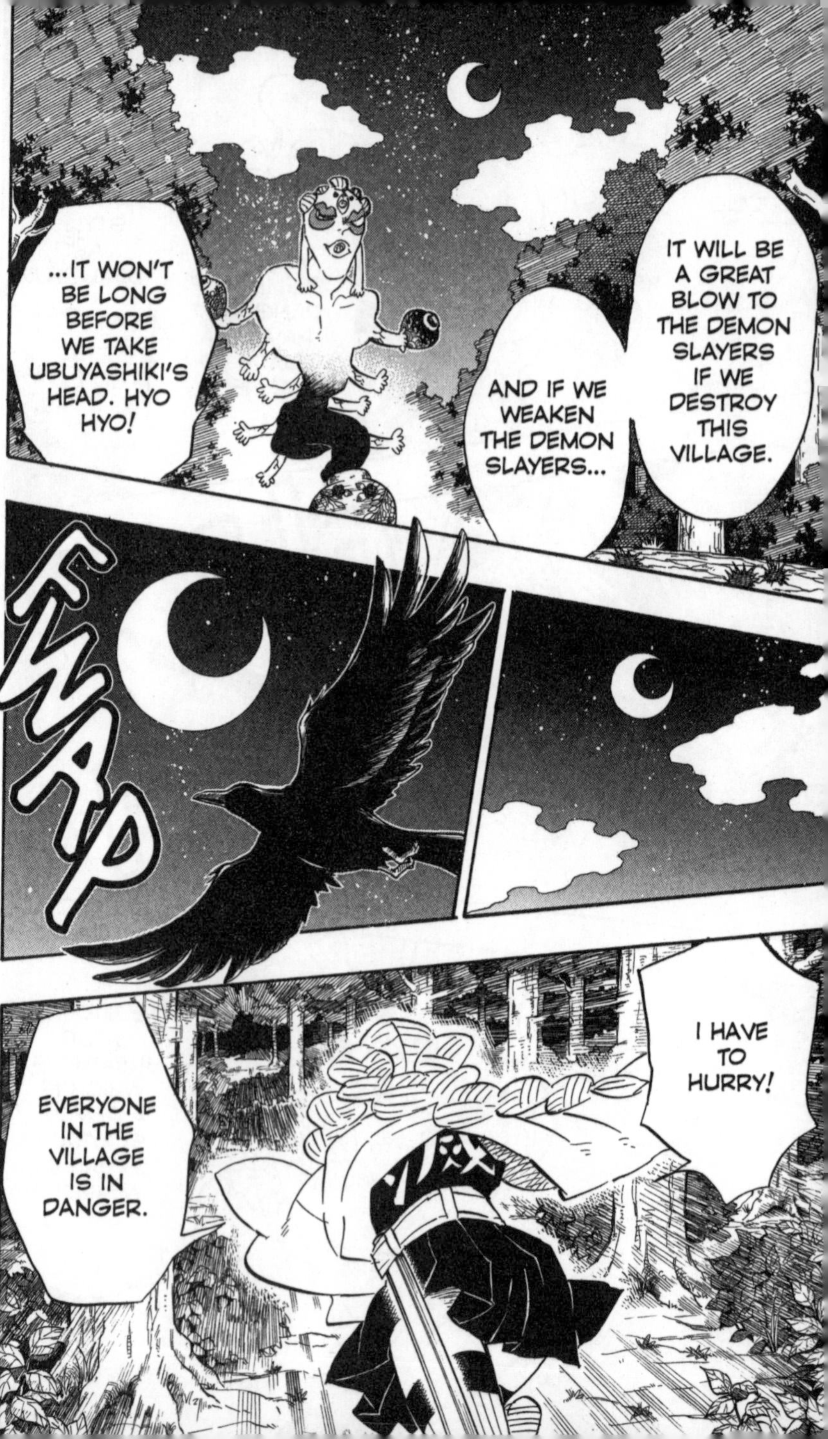
IT WILL BE A GREAT BLOW TO THE DEMON SLAYERS IF WE DESTROY THIS VILLAGE.
AND IF WE WEAKEN THE DEMON SLAYERS...
...IT WON'T BE LONG BEFORE WE TAKE UBUYASHIKI'S HEAD. HYO HYO!
FWAP
I HAVE TO HURRY!
EVERYONE IN THE VILLAGE IS IN DANGER.

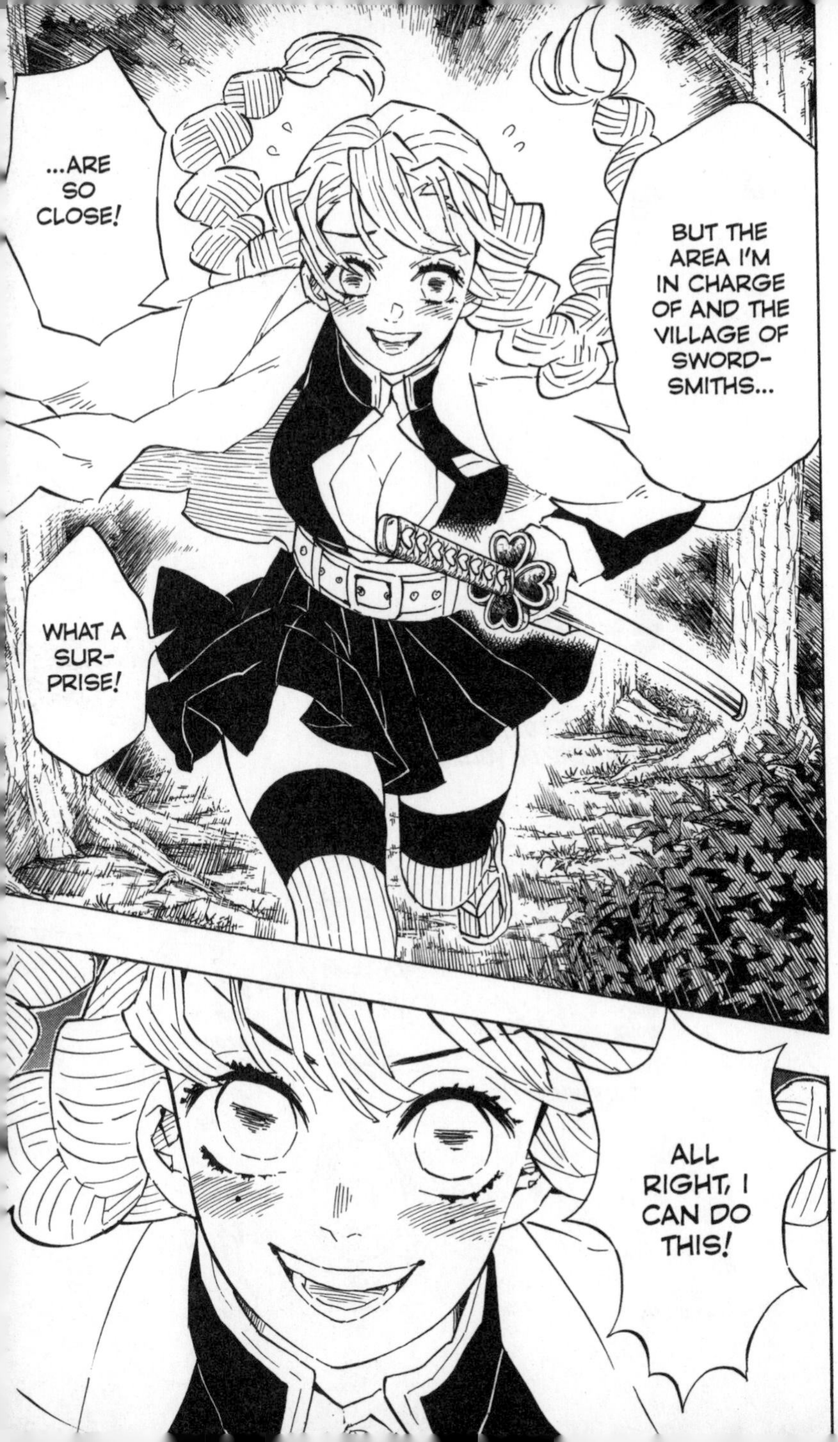
BUT THE AREA I'M IN CHARGE OF AND THE VILLAGE OF SWORD-SMITHS...
...ARE SO CLOSE!
WHAT A SUR-PRISE!
ALL RIGHT, I CAN DO THIS!

~APOLOGY 1~
AT THE END OF VOLUME 7
Sorry.
I got their names wrong. They're glaring at me.
Wrong
NAHO TAKADA
KIYO TERAUCHI
SUMI NAKAHARA
THAT'S WHAT IT SAID, BUT...
Cor-rect
SUMI NAKAHARA
KIYO TERAUCHI
NAHO TAKADA

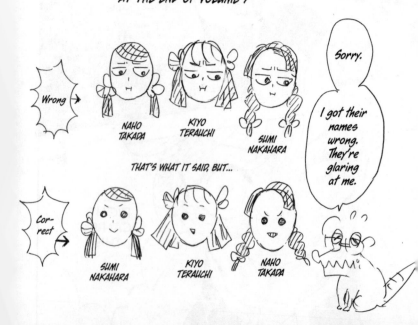

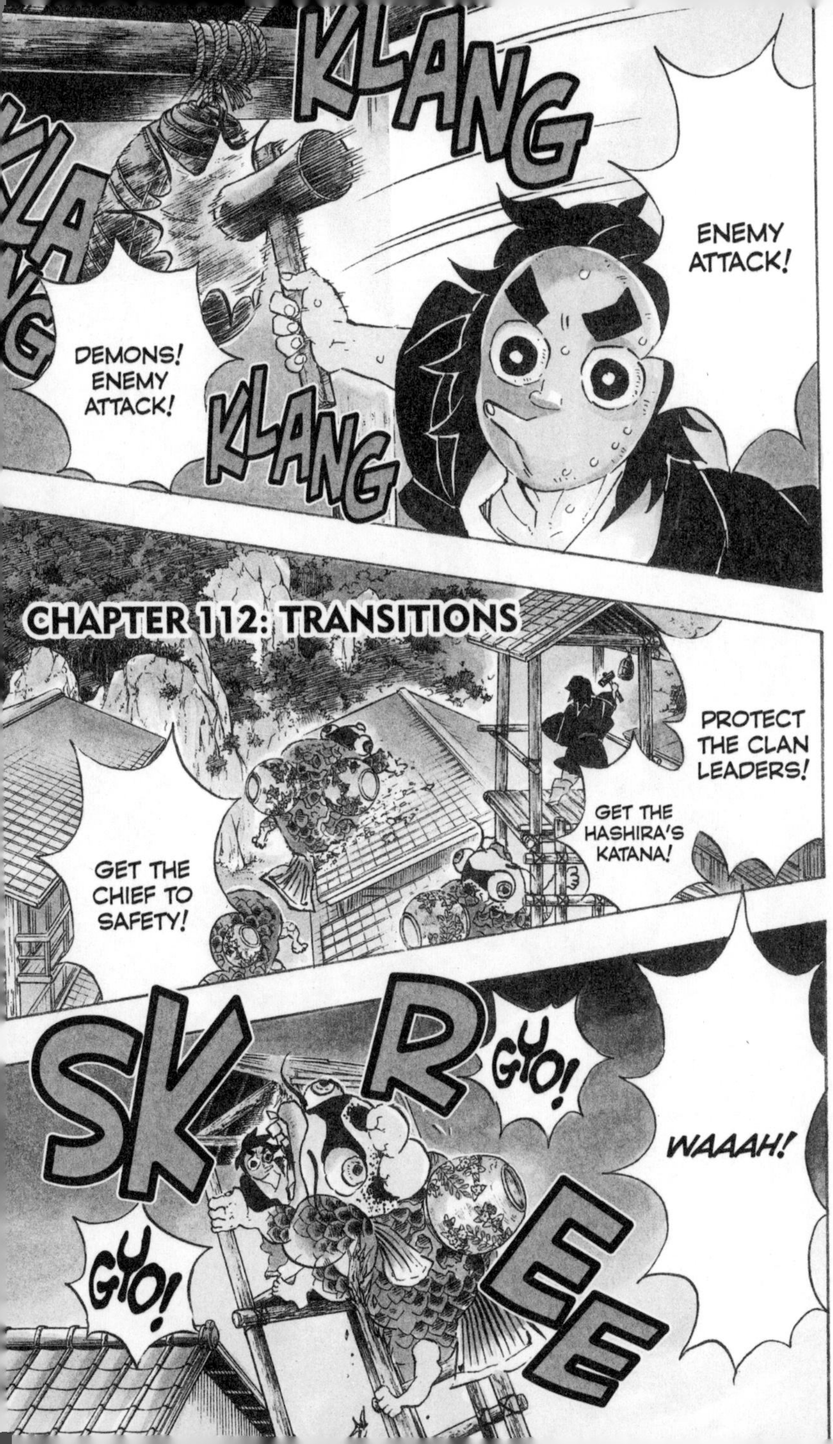
ENEMY ATTACK!
KLANG
KLANG
DEMONS! ENEMY ATTACK!
CHAPTER 112: TRANSITIONS
PROTECT THE CLAN LEADERS!
GET THE HASHIRA'S KATANA!
GET THE CHIEF TO SAFETY!
WAAAH!
UGYO!
SKREE
UGYO!

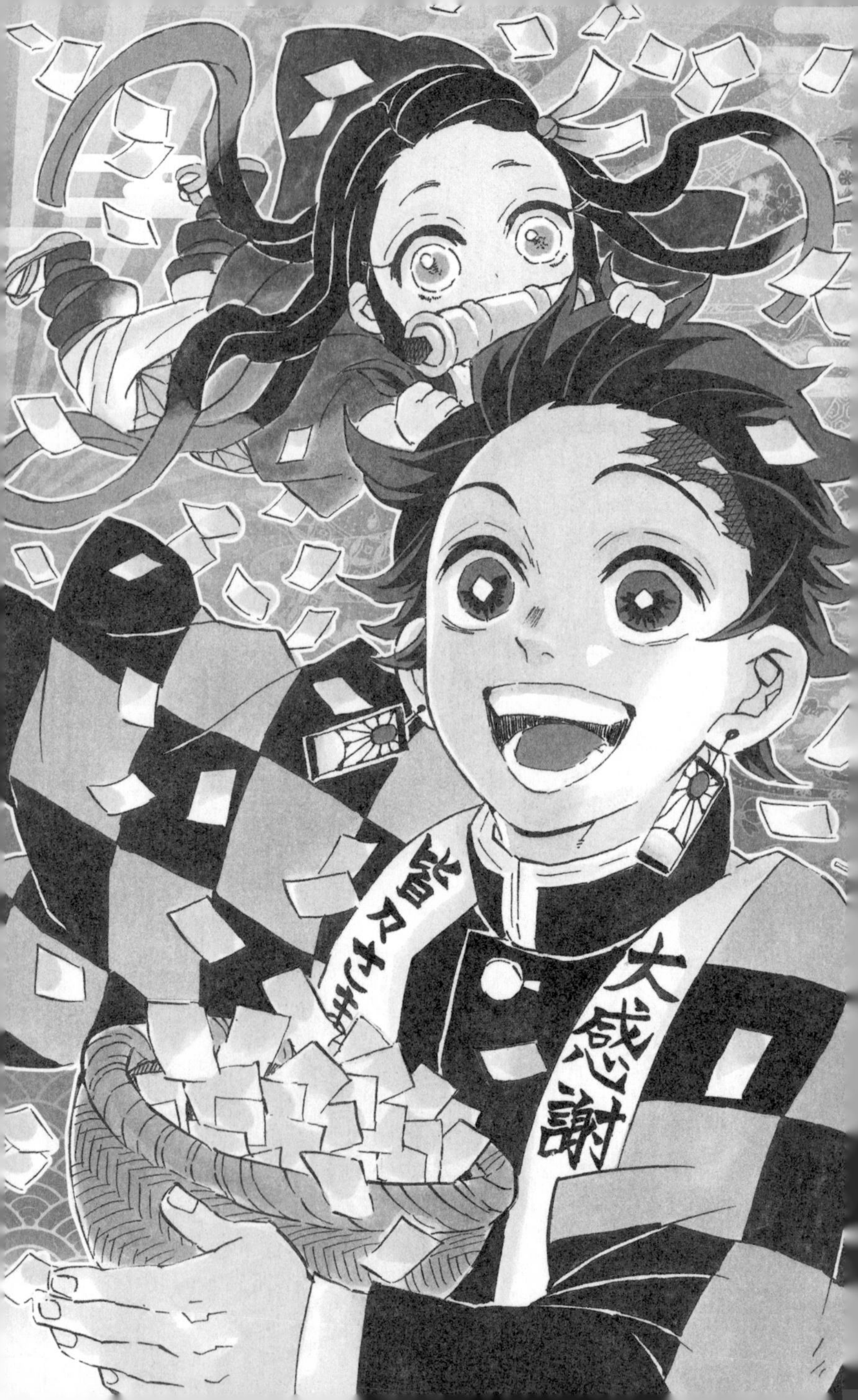
大感謝
皆々さま

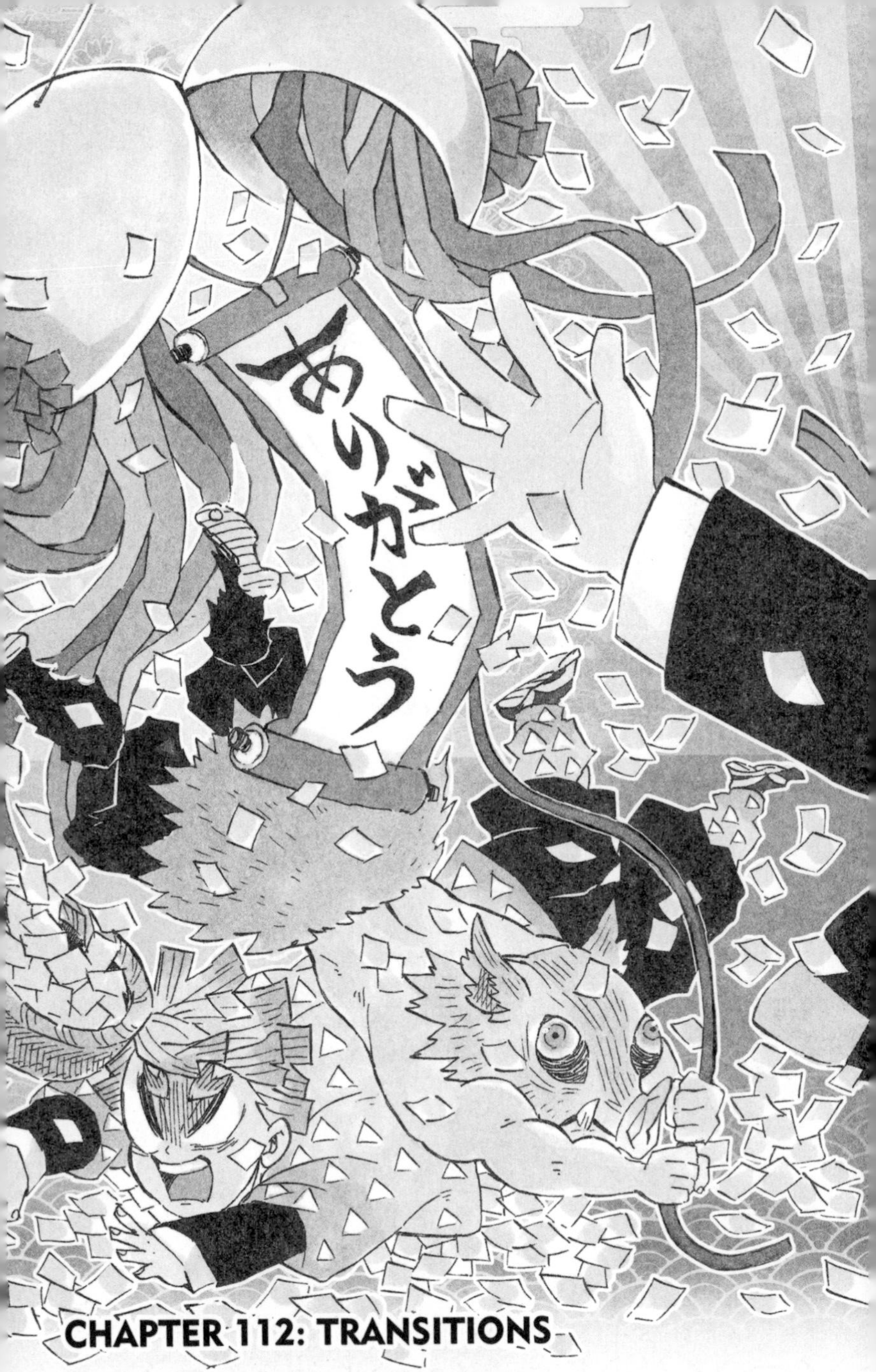
ありがとう

CHAPTER 112: TRANSITIONS

~APOLOGY 2~

In the magazine, the opening color pages announced the anime series. To the graphic novel readers, I apologize from the bottom of my heart for any misunderstanding caused by the gleeful two-page spread in the middle of the attack on the village. Even the words "Congrats on the anime!" are missing, so it just looks like Tanjiro and the others are allies of the demons. It's a deeply regrettable mistake on the part of the author. Please forgive me.

Upper Ranks are here. It's hard!

I'm very sorry!

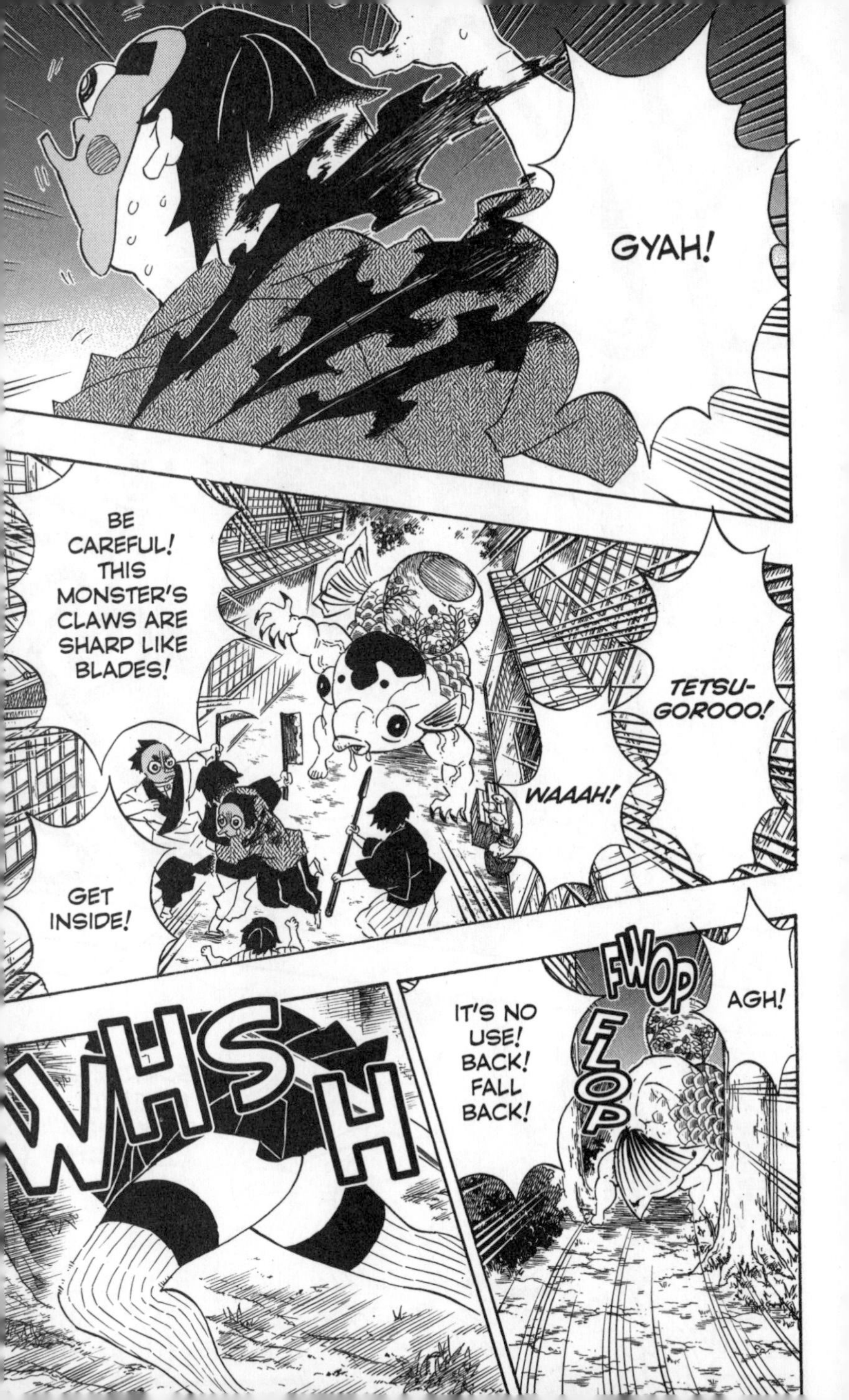
GYAH!
TETSU-GOROOO!
WAAAH!
BE CAREFUL! THIS MONSTER'S CLAWS ARE SHARP LIKE BLADES!
GET INSIDE!
AGH!
FWOP
FLOP
IT'S NO USE! BACK! FALL BACK!
WHSH

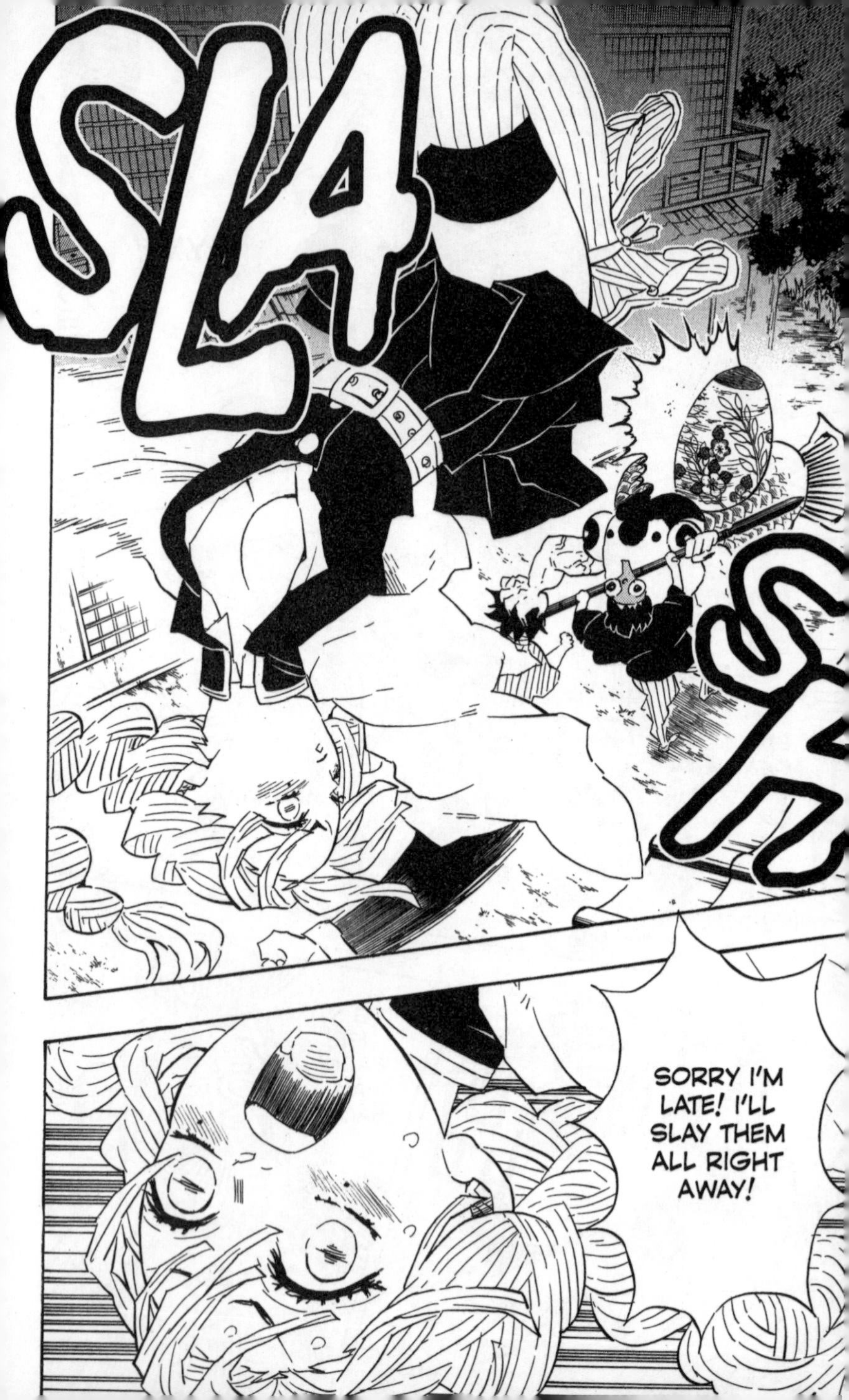
SLA
SORRY I'M LATE! I'LL SLAY THEM ALL RIGHT AWAY!

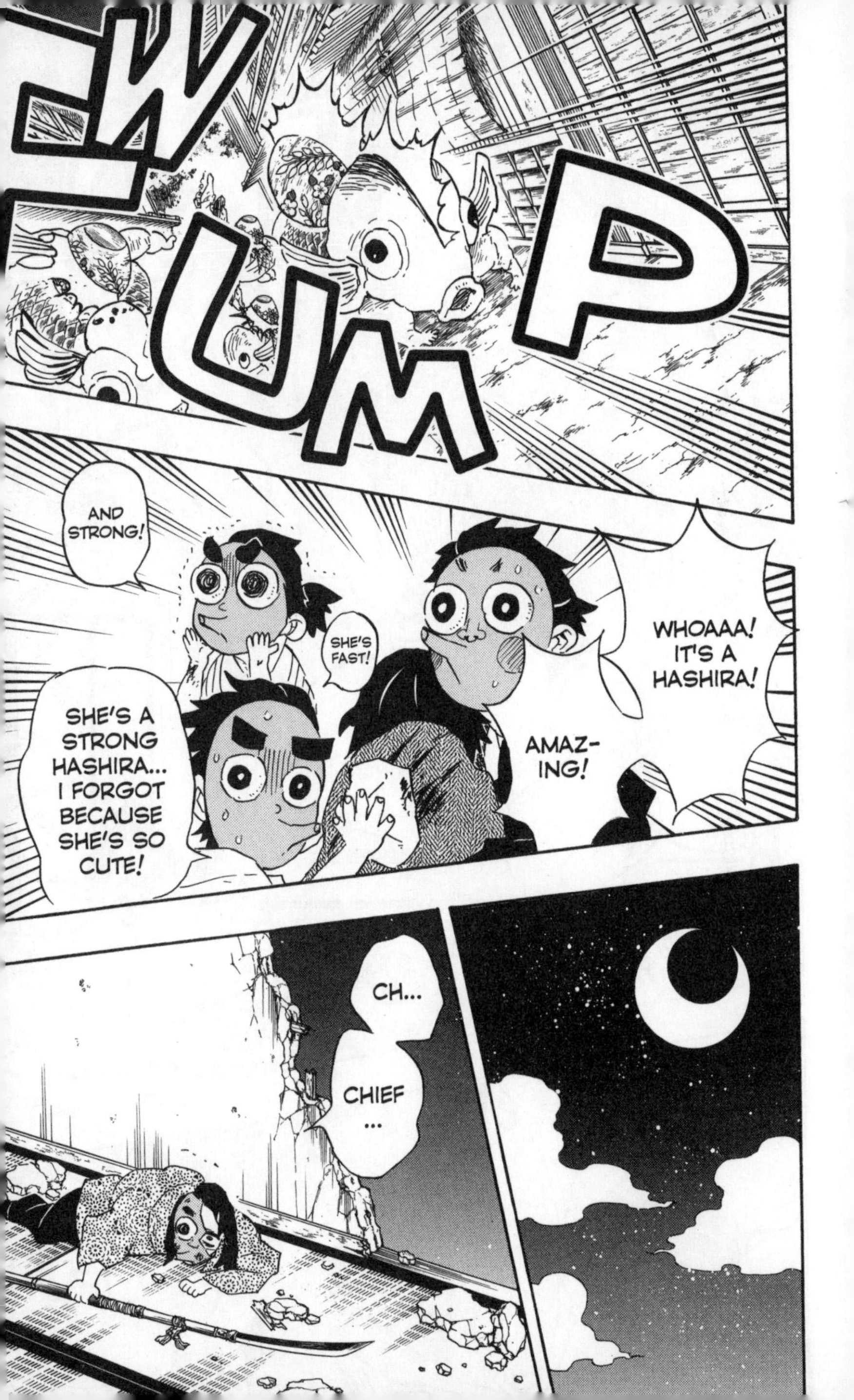
UMP
WHOAAA! IT'S A HASHIRA!
AMAZ-ING!
SHE'S FAST!
AND STRONG!
SHE'S A STRONG HASHIRA... I FORGOT BECAUSE SHE'S SO CUTE!
CH...
CHIEF ...

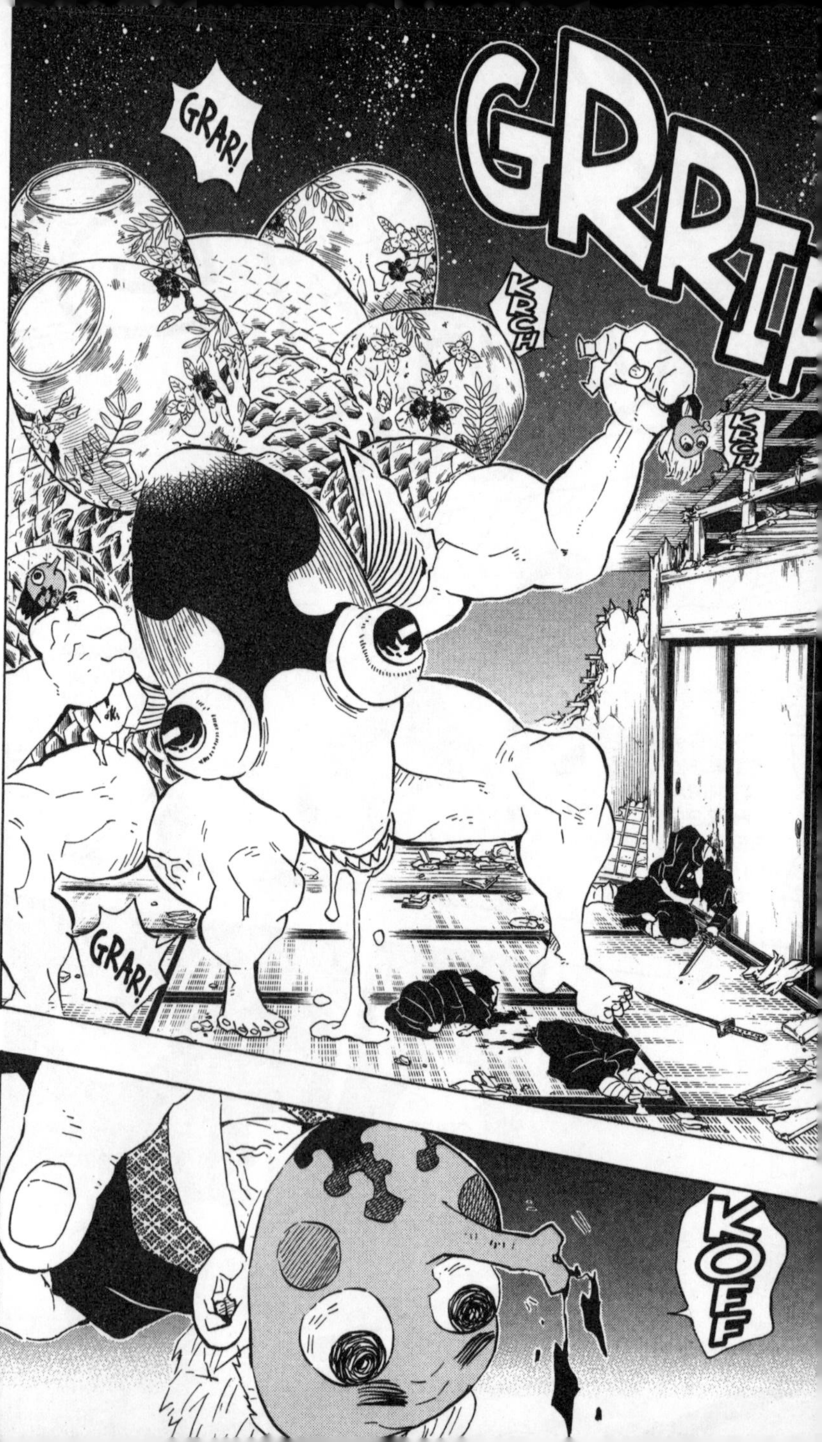
GRRIP
KRCH
KRCH
GRAR!
GRAR!
KOFF

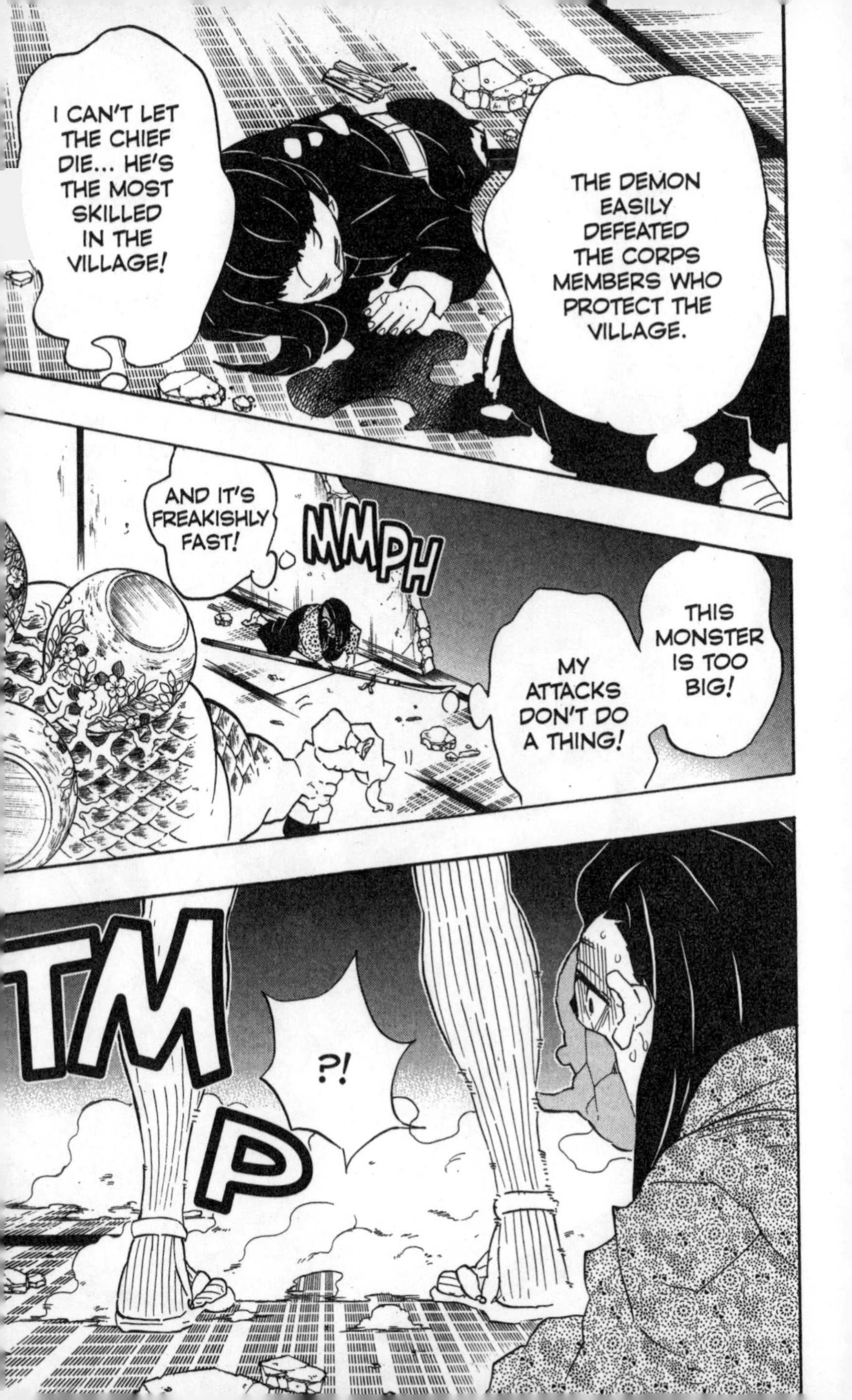
THE DEMON EASILY DEFEATED THE CORPS MEMBERS WHO PROTECT THE VILLAGE.
I CAN'T LET THE CHIEF DIE... HE'S THE MOST SKILLED IN THE VILLAGE!
THIS MONSTER IS TOO BIG!
MY ATTACKS DON'T DO A THING!
MMPH
AND IT'S FREAKISHLY FAST!
?!
TMP

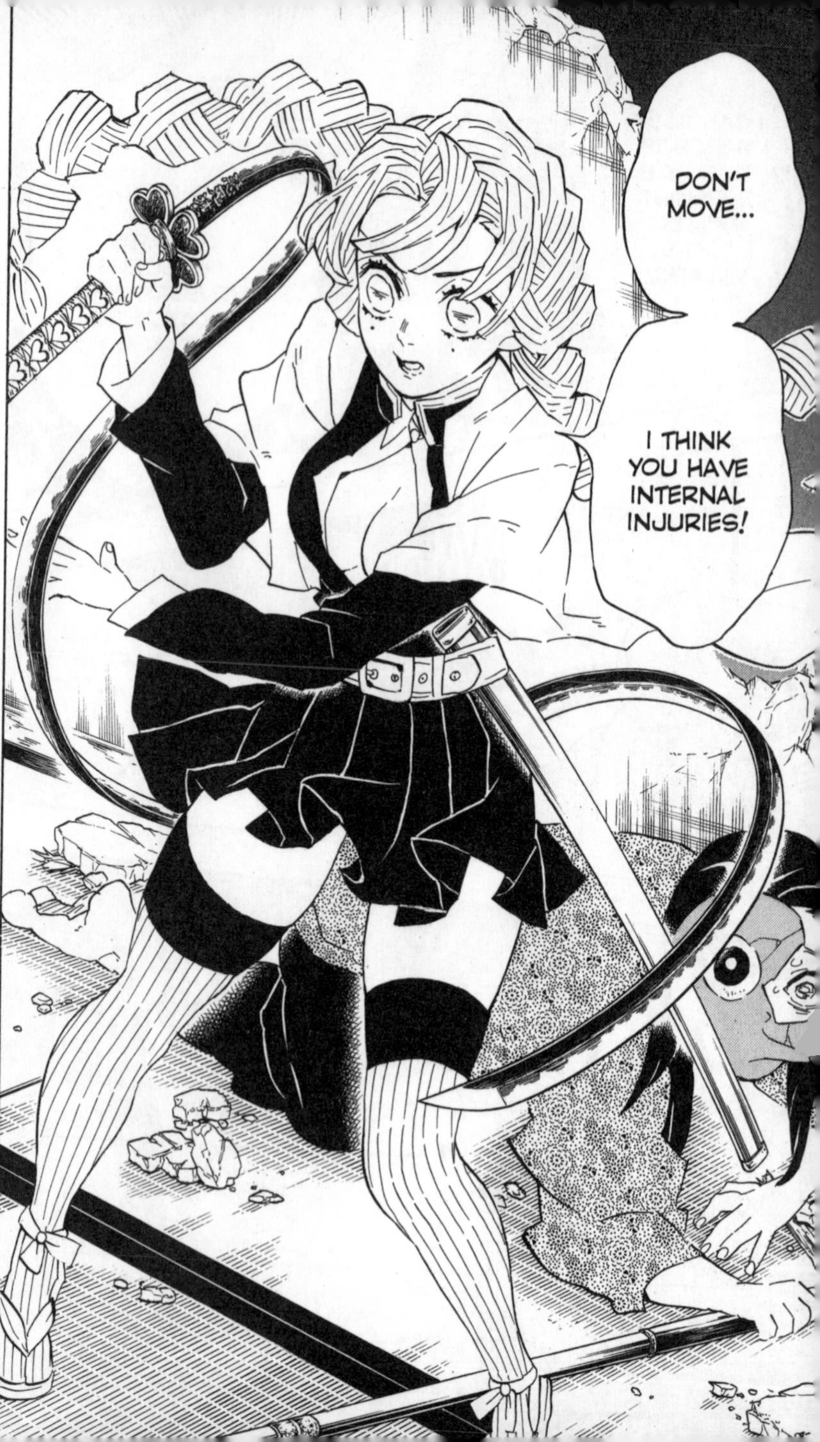
DON'T MOVE...
I THINK YOU HAVE INTERNAL INJURIES!

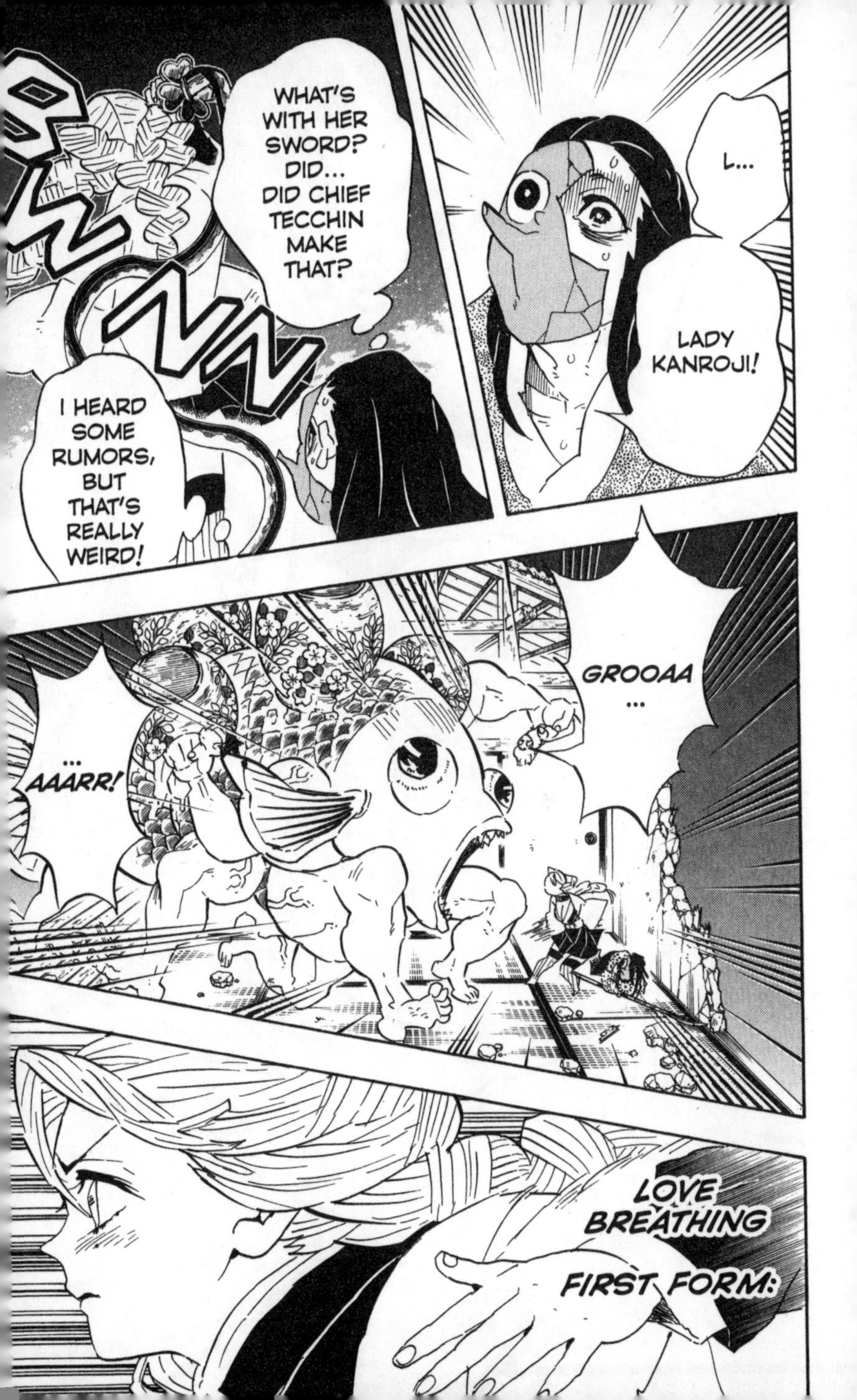
L...
LADY KANROJI!
WHAT'S WITH HER SWORD? DID... DID CHIEF TECCHIN MAKE THAT?
I HEARD SOME RUMORS, BUT THAT'S REALLY WEIRD!
GROOAA ...
... AAARR!
LOVE BREATHING
FIRST FORM:

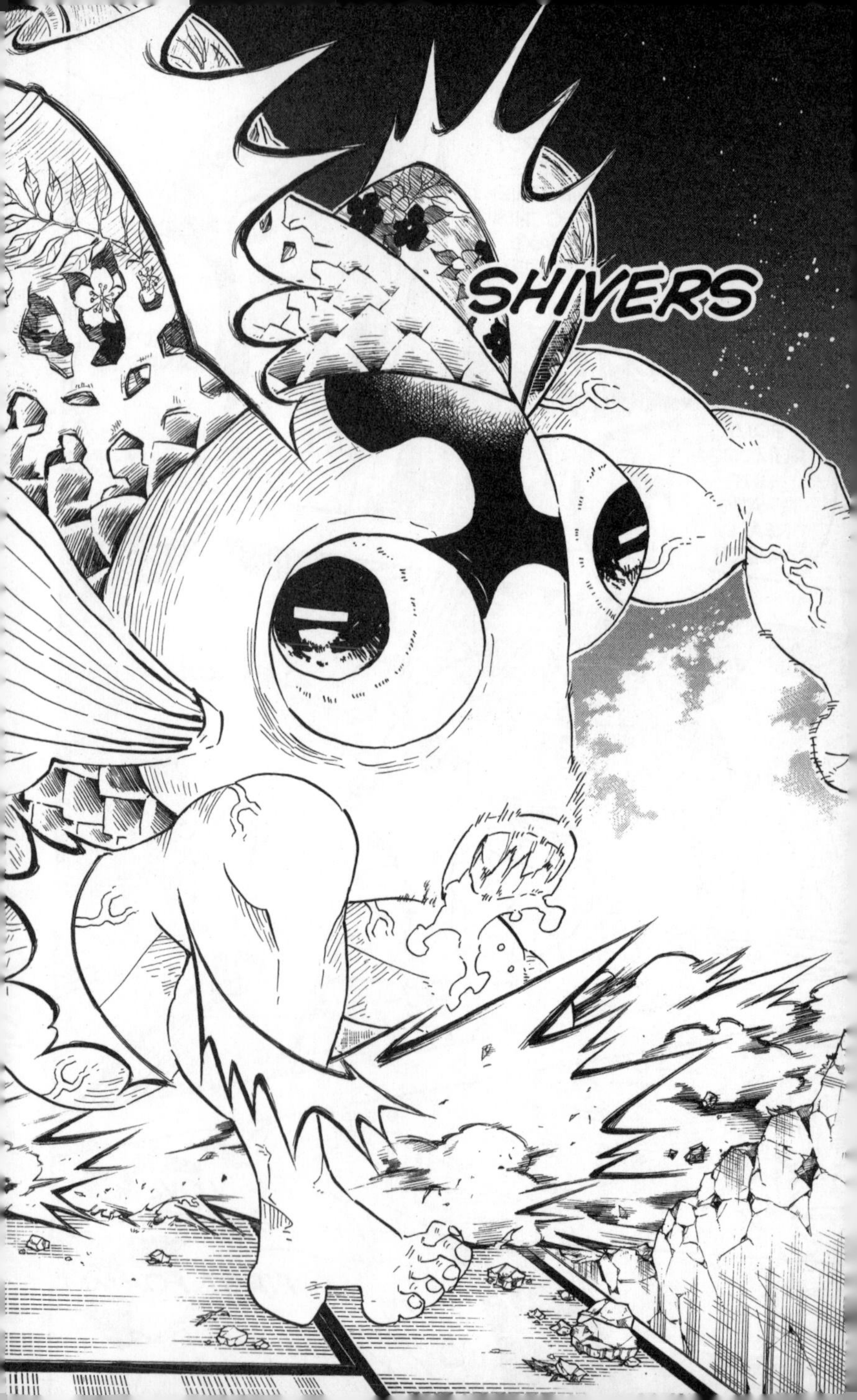
SHIVERS

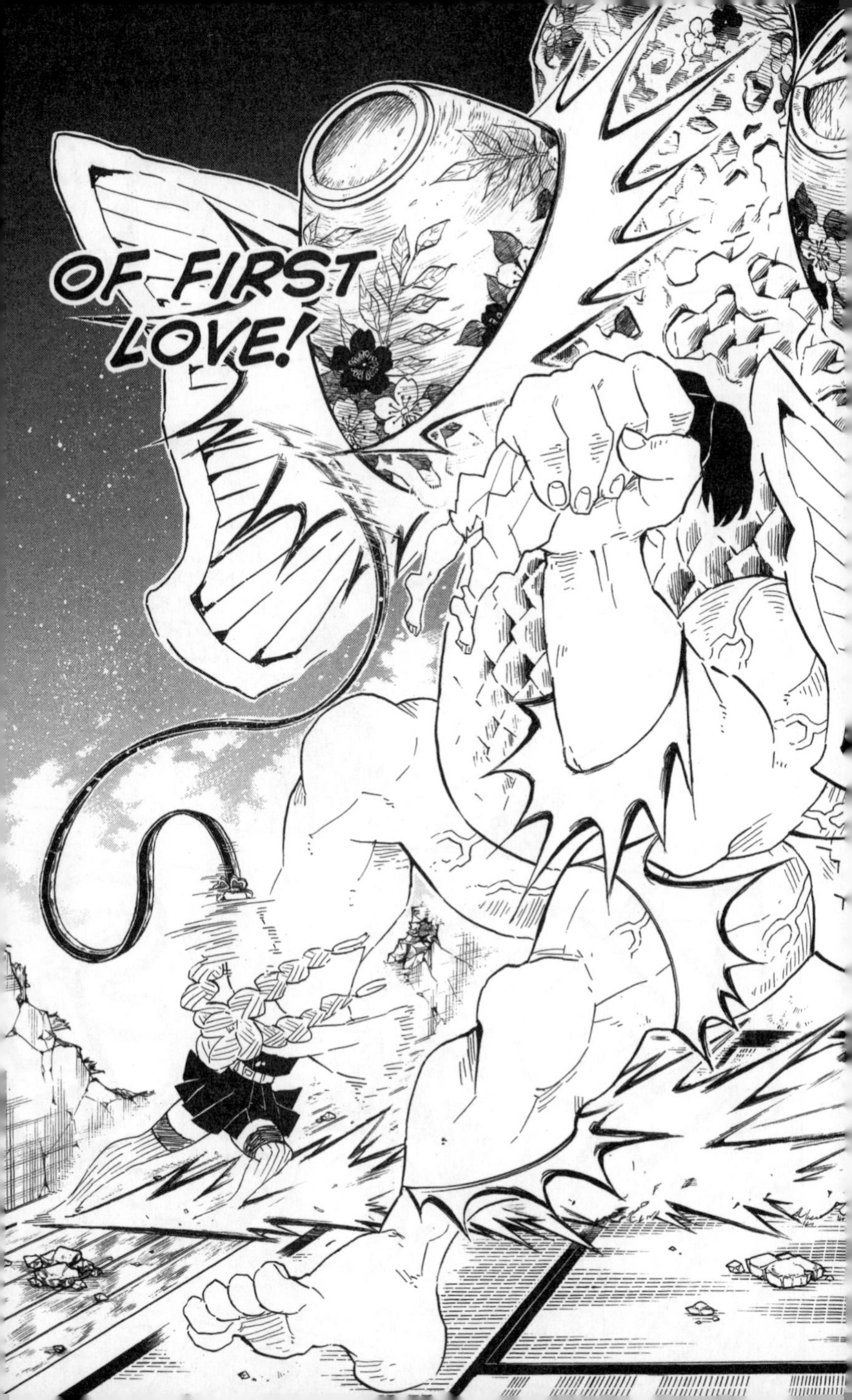
OF FIRST
LOVE!

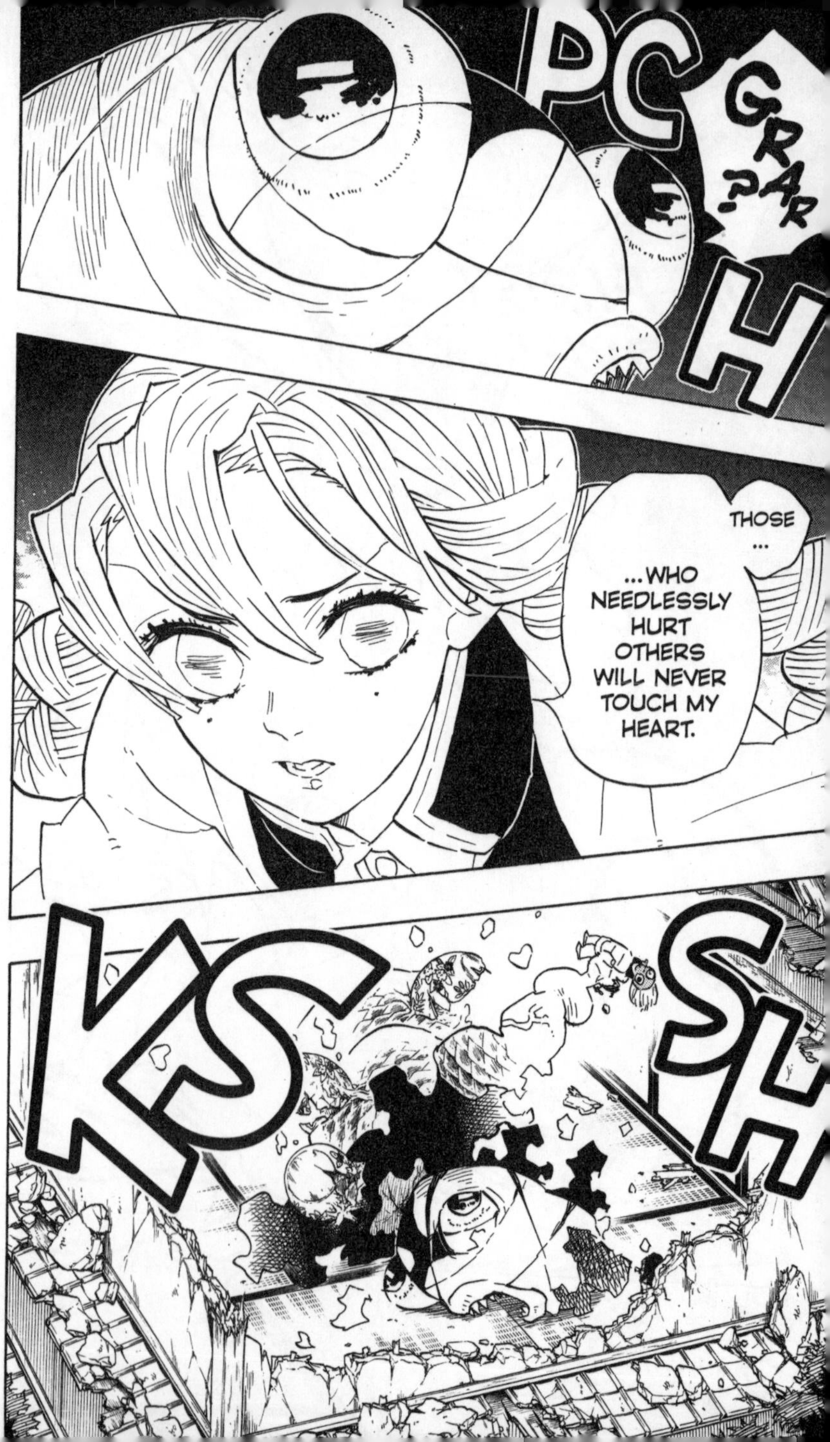
PC
GRAR
?
H
THOSE ...
...WHO NEEDLESSLY HURT OTHERS WILL NEVER TOUCH MY HEART.
KSSH

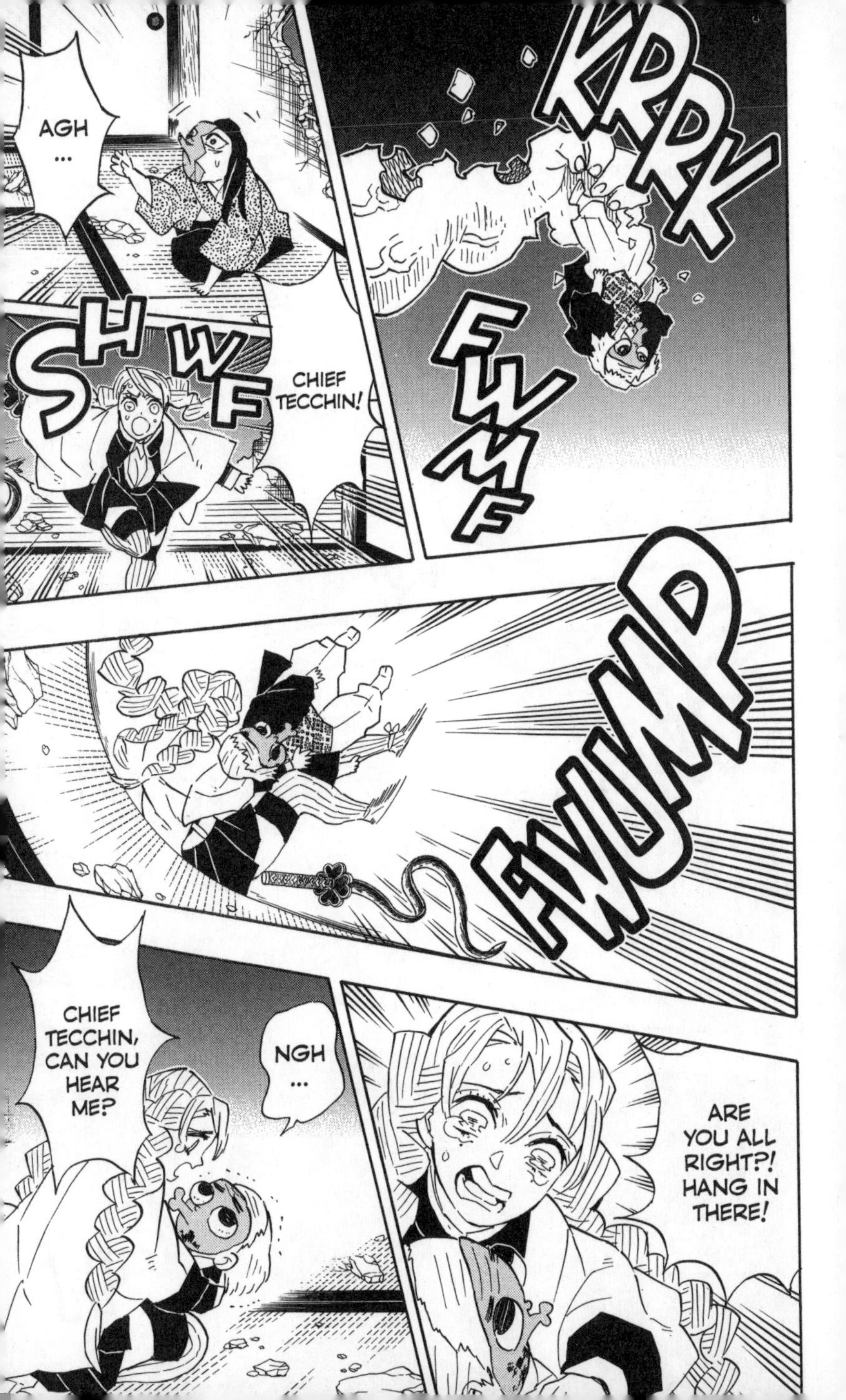
KRRK
FWMF
AGH ...
SHWF
CHIEF TECCHIN!
FWUMP
ARE YOU ALL RIGHT?! HANG IN THERE!
NGH ...
CHIEF TECCHIN, CAN YOU HEAR ME?

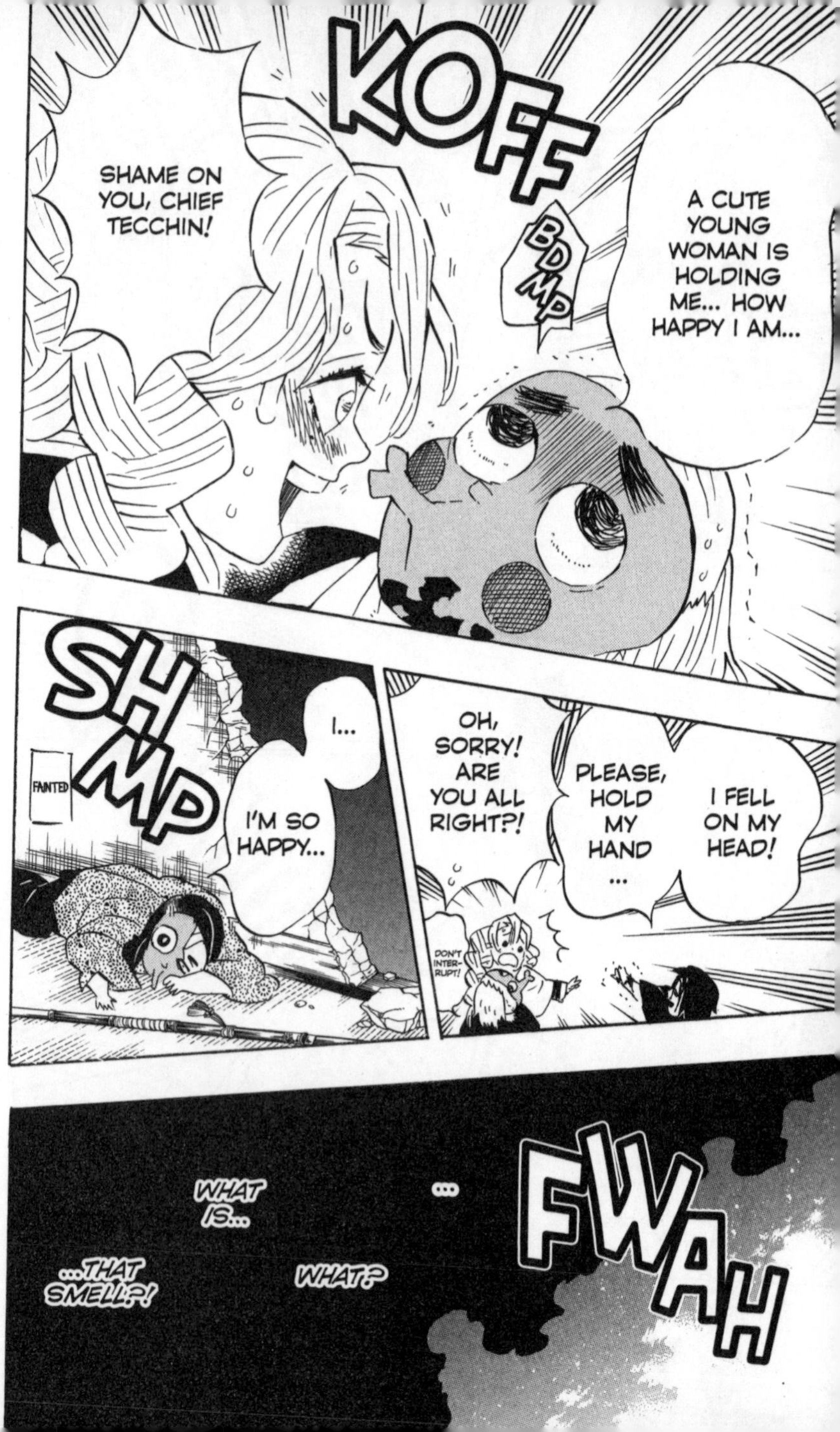
A CUTE YOUNG WOMAN IS HOLDING ME... HOW HAPPY I AM...
KOFF
BDMP
SHAME ON YOU, CHIEF TECCHIN!
I FELL ON MY HEAD!
PLEASE, HOLD MY HAND...
OH, SORRY! ARE YOU ALL RIGHT?!
DON'T INTER-RUPT!
I...
I'M SO HAPPY...
SHMP
FAINTED
FWAH
...
WHAT?
WHAT IS...
...THAT SMELL?!

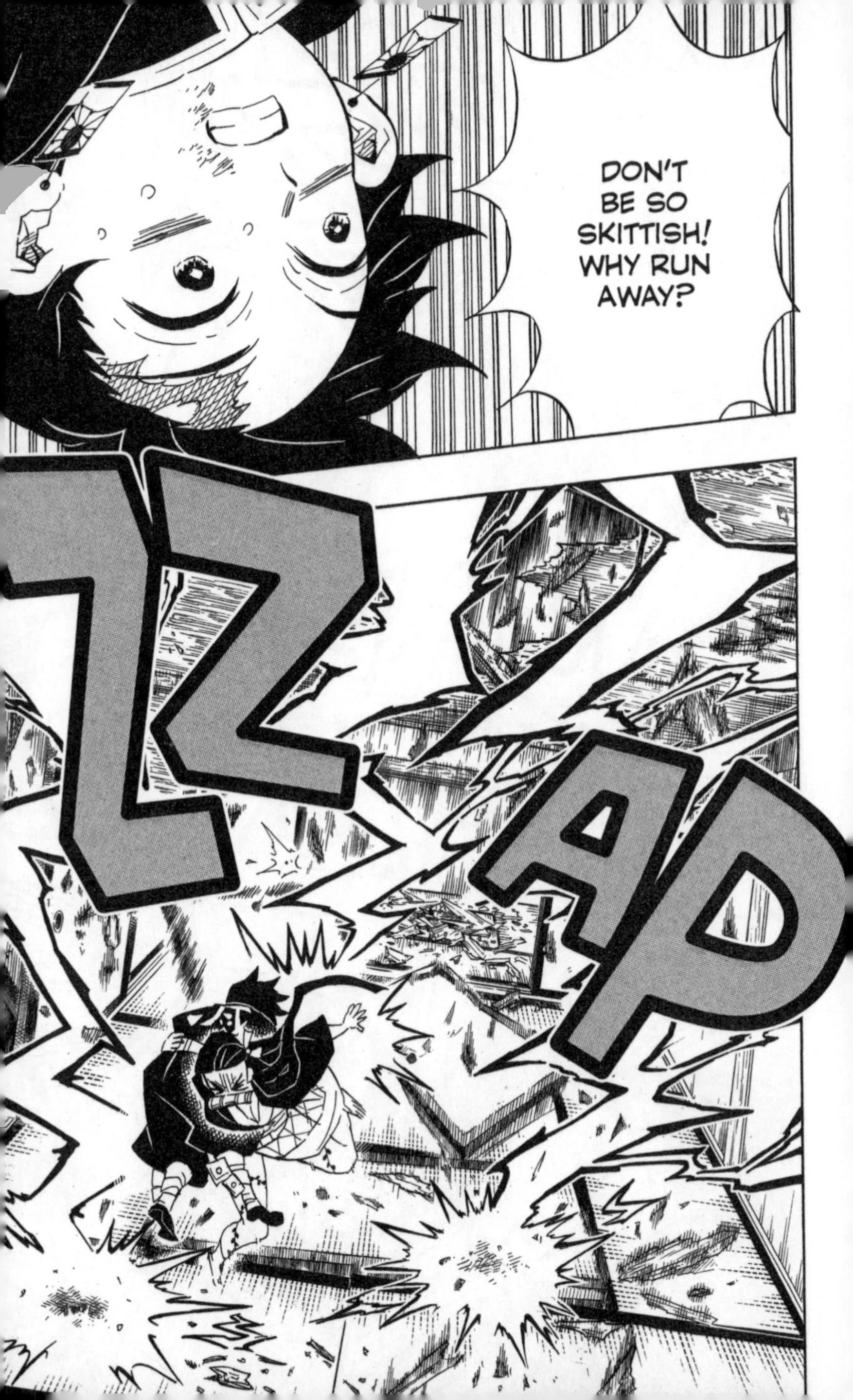
DON'T BE SO SKITTISH! WHY RUN AWAY?
ZZAP

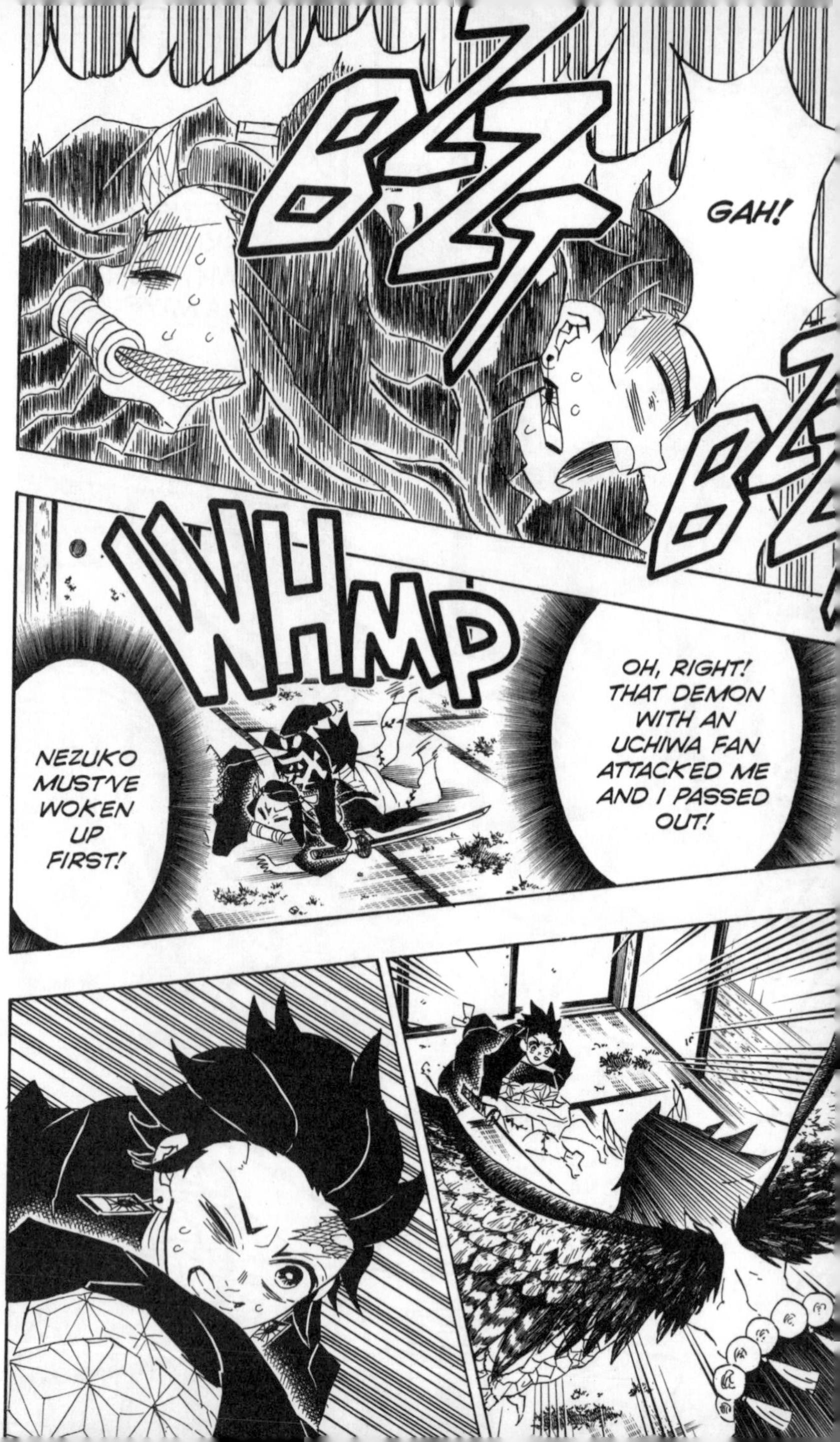
GAH!
BZT
WHMP
OH, RIGHT! THAT DEMON WITH AN UCHIWA FAN ATTACKED ME AND I PASSED OUT!
NEZUKO MUST'VE WOKEN UP FIRST!

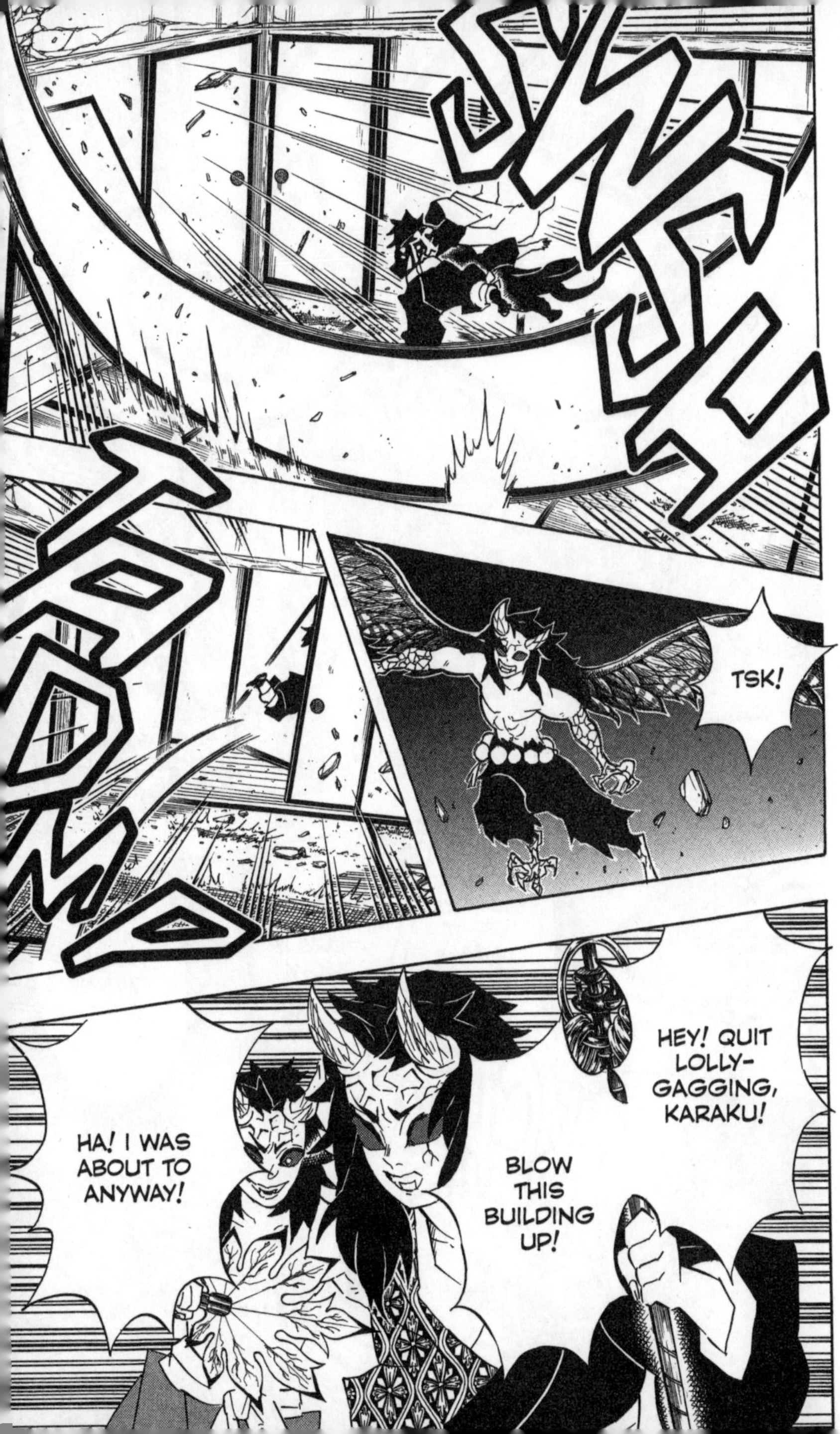
TSK!
HEY! QUIT LOLLY-GAGGING, KARAKU!
BLOW THIS BUILDING UP!
HA! I WAS ABOUT TO ANYWAY!

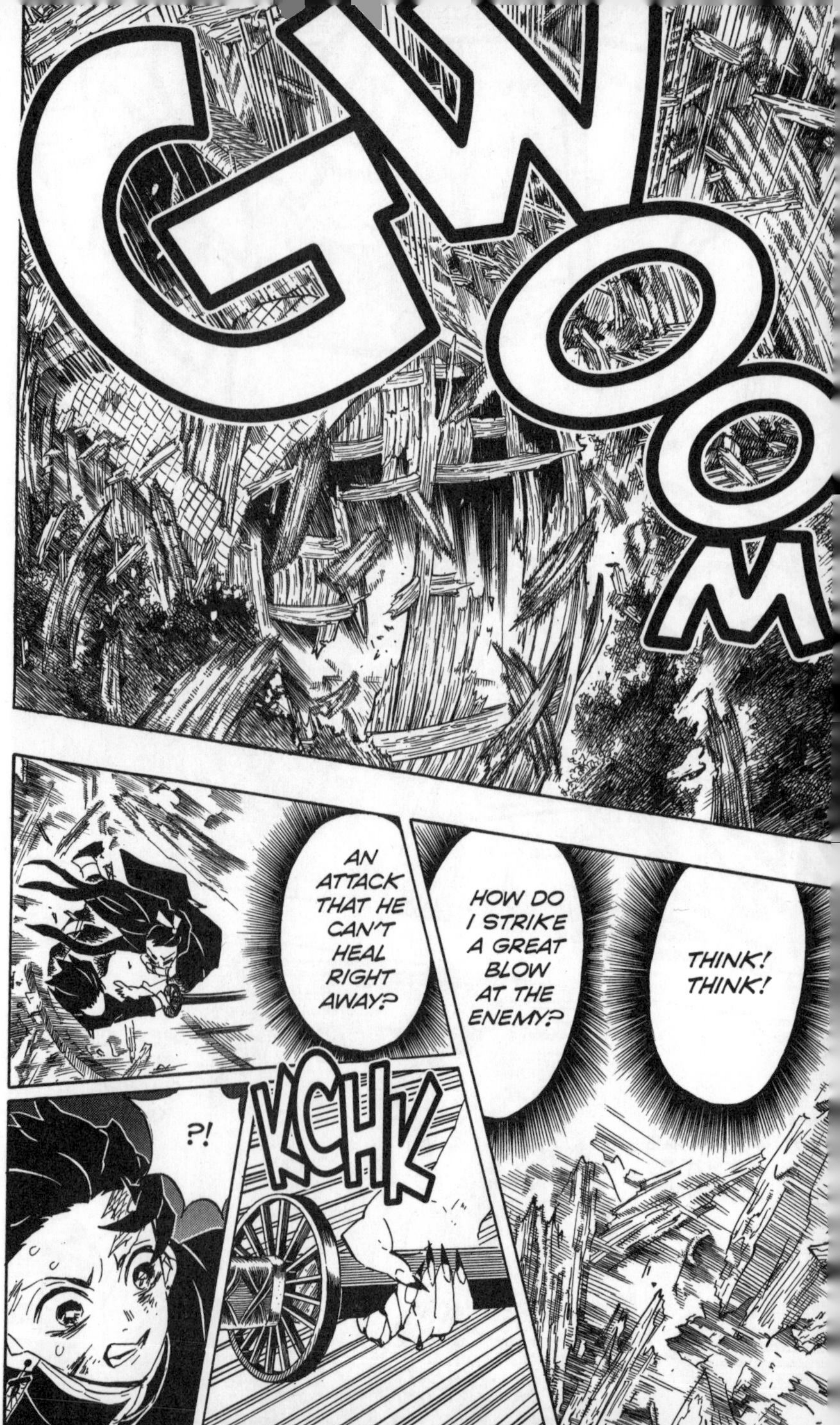
CWOOM
THINK! THINK!
HOW DO I STRIKE A GREAT BLOW AT THE ENEMY?
AN ATTACK THAT HE CAN'T HEAL RIGHT AWAY?
KCHK
?!

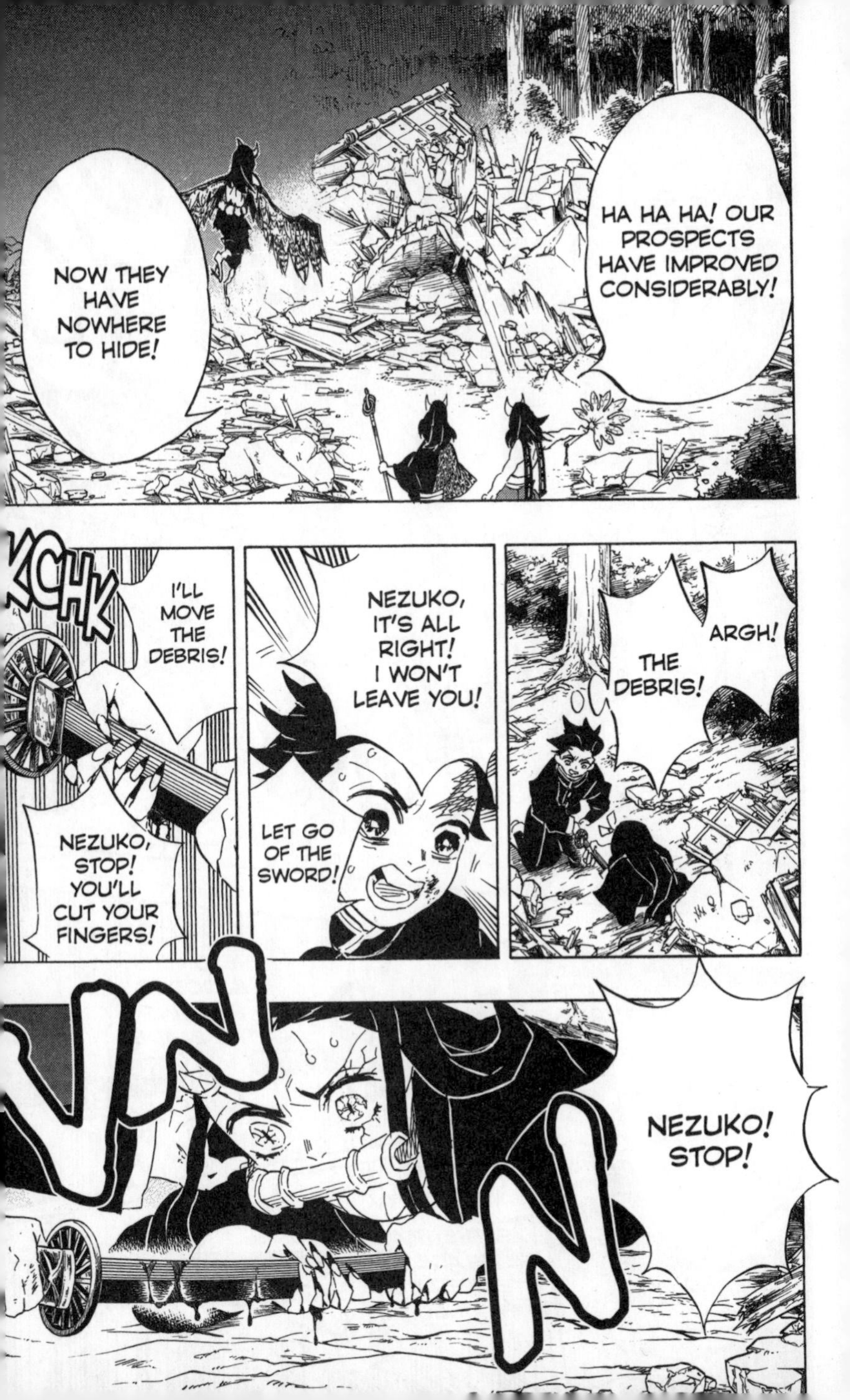
HA HA HA! OUR PROSPECTS HAVE IMPROVED CONSIDERABLY!
NOW THEY HAVE NOWHERE TO HIDE!
ARGH!
THE DEBRIS!
NEZUKO, IT'S ALL RIGHT! I WON'T LEAVE YOU!
LET GO OF THE SWORD!
I'LL MOVE THE DEBRIS!
NEZUKO, STOP! YOU'LL CUT YOUR FINGERS!
NEZUKO! STOP!

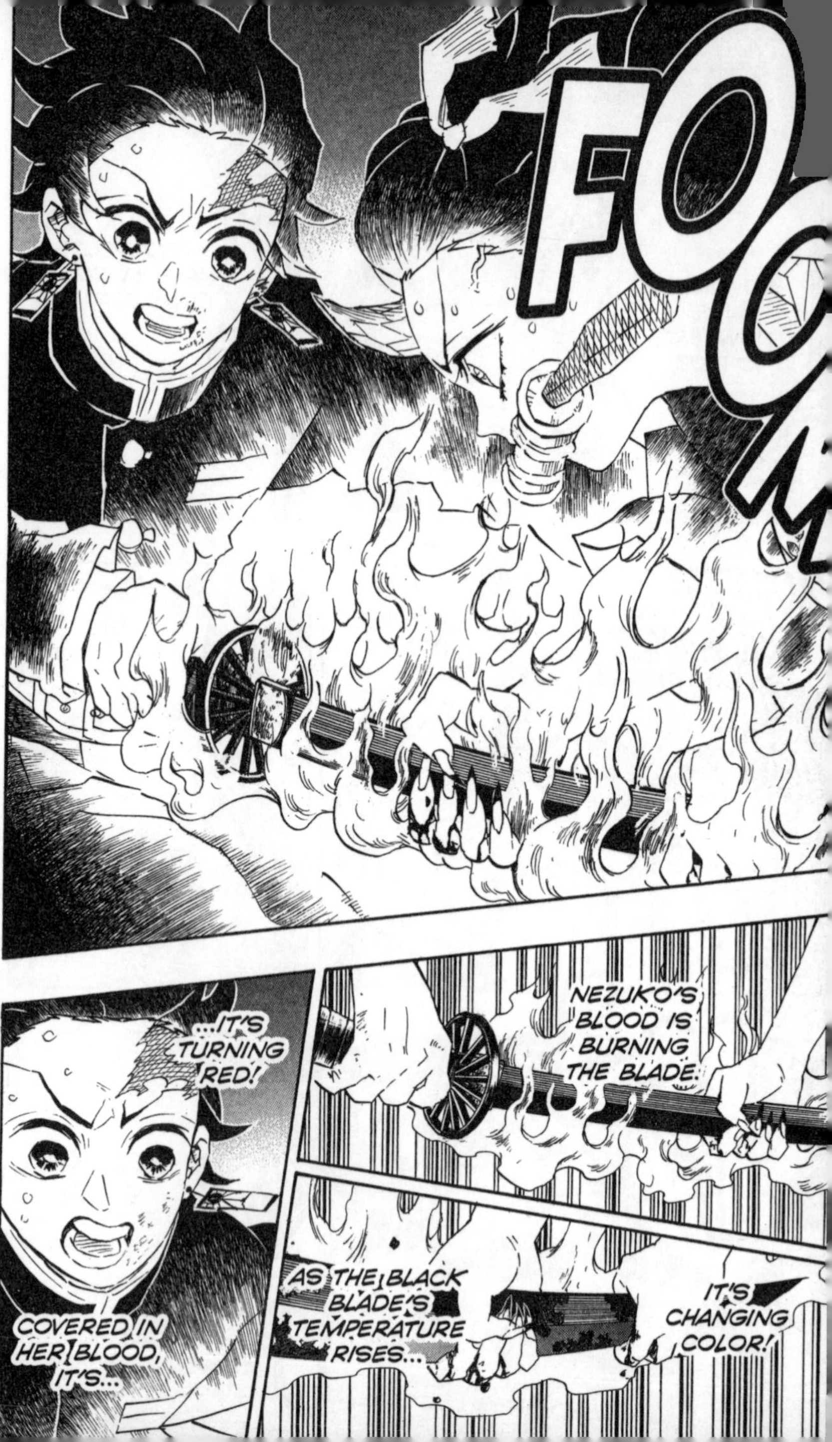
NEZUKO'S BLOOD IS BURNING THE BLADE.
IT'S CHANGING COLOR!
AS THE BLACK BLADE'S TEMPERATURE RISES...
...IT'S TURNING RED!
COVERED IN HER BLOOD, IT'S...

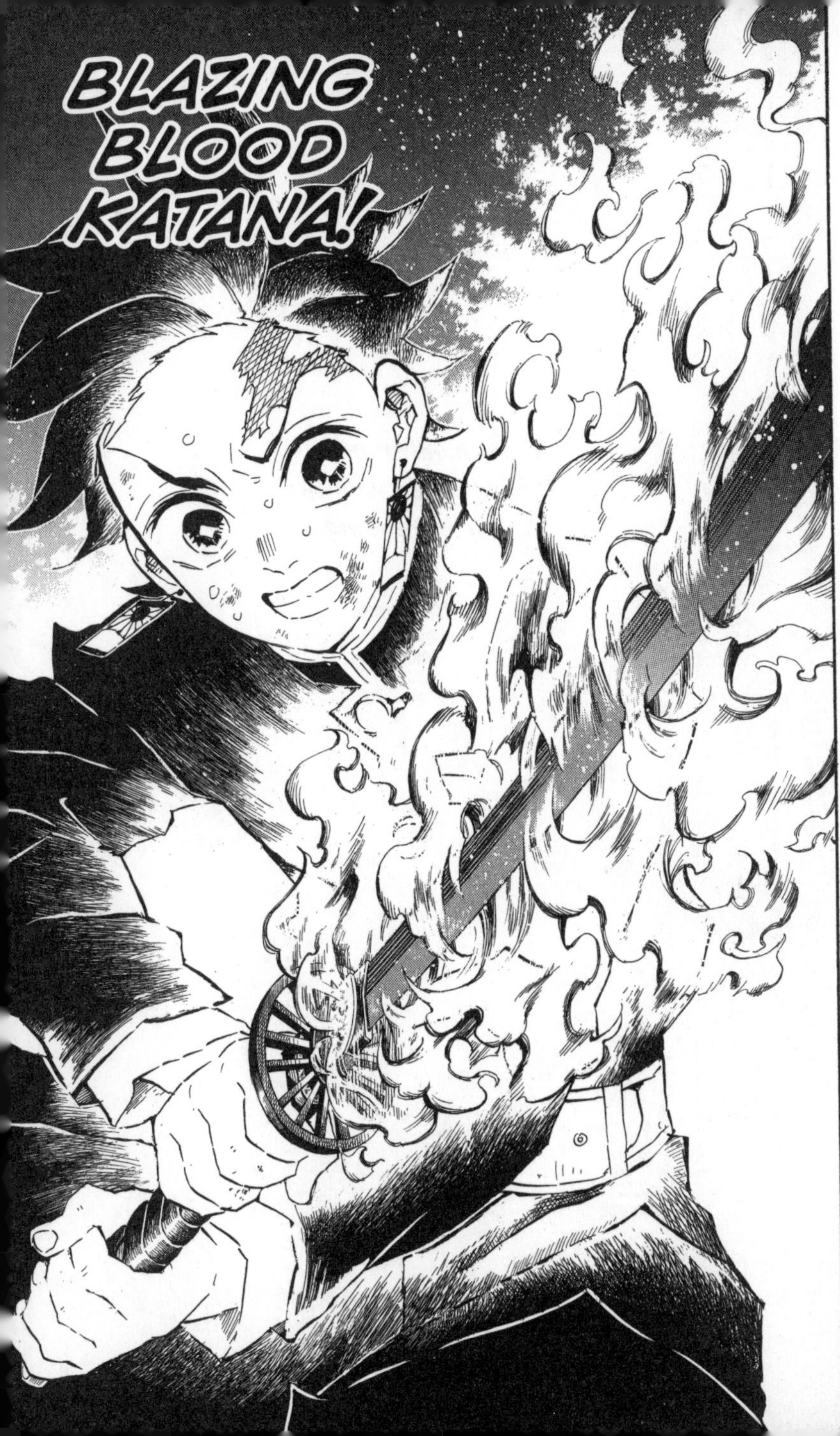
BLAZING BLOOD KATANA!

The number of Tanjiro's pen pals is rapidly increasing.

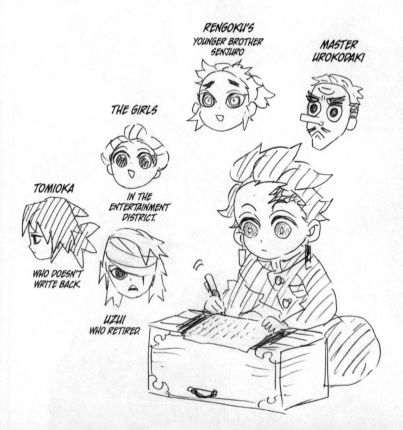

MASTER UROKODAKI
RENGOKU'S YOUNGER BROTHER SENJURO
THE GIRLS IN THE ENTERTAINMENT DISTRICT.
UZUI WHO RETIRED.
TOMIOKA WHO DOESN'T WRITE BACK.

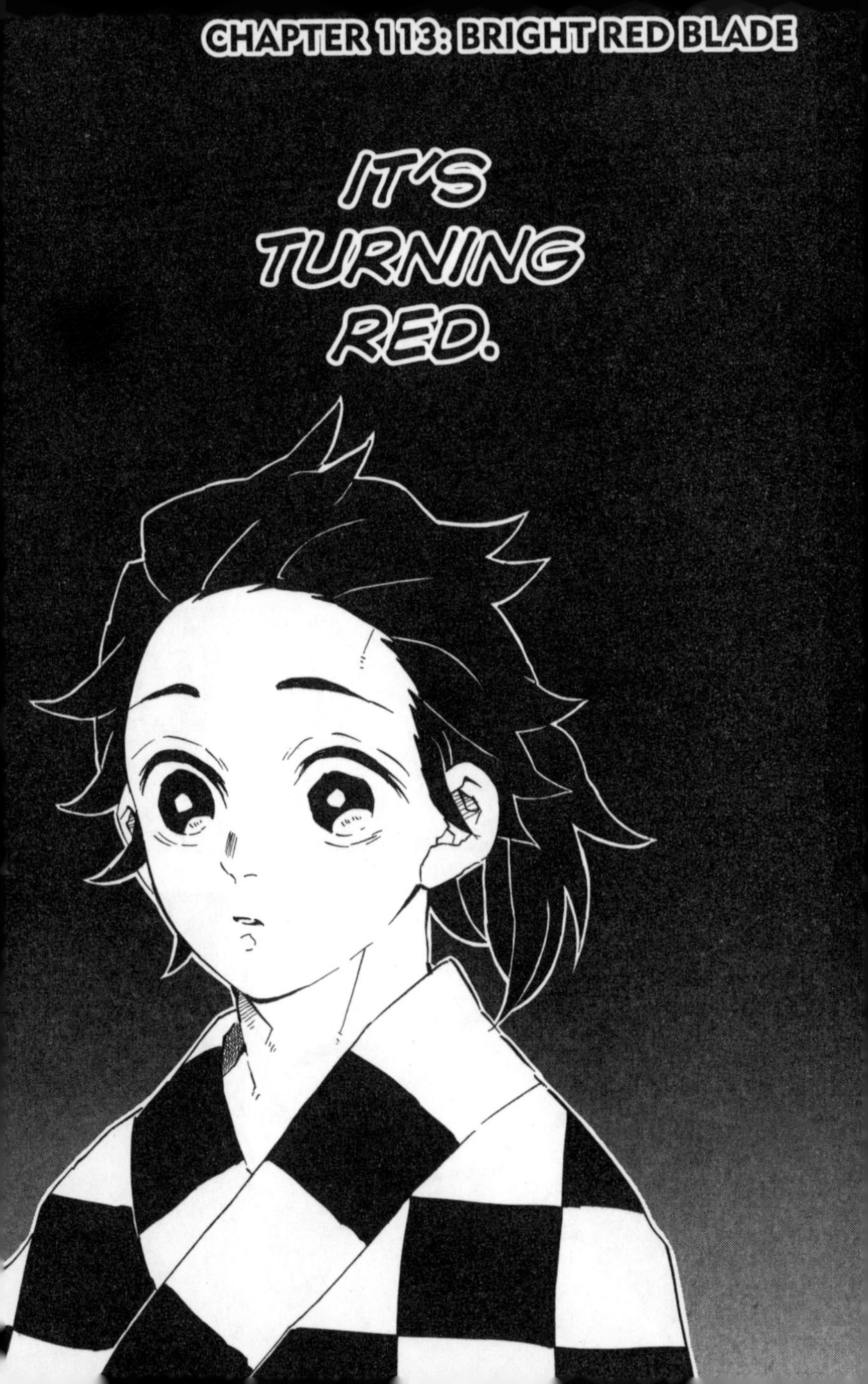
CHAPTER 113: BRIGHT RED BLADE
IT'S TURNING RED.

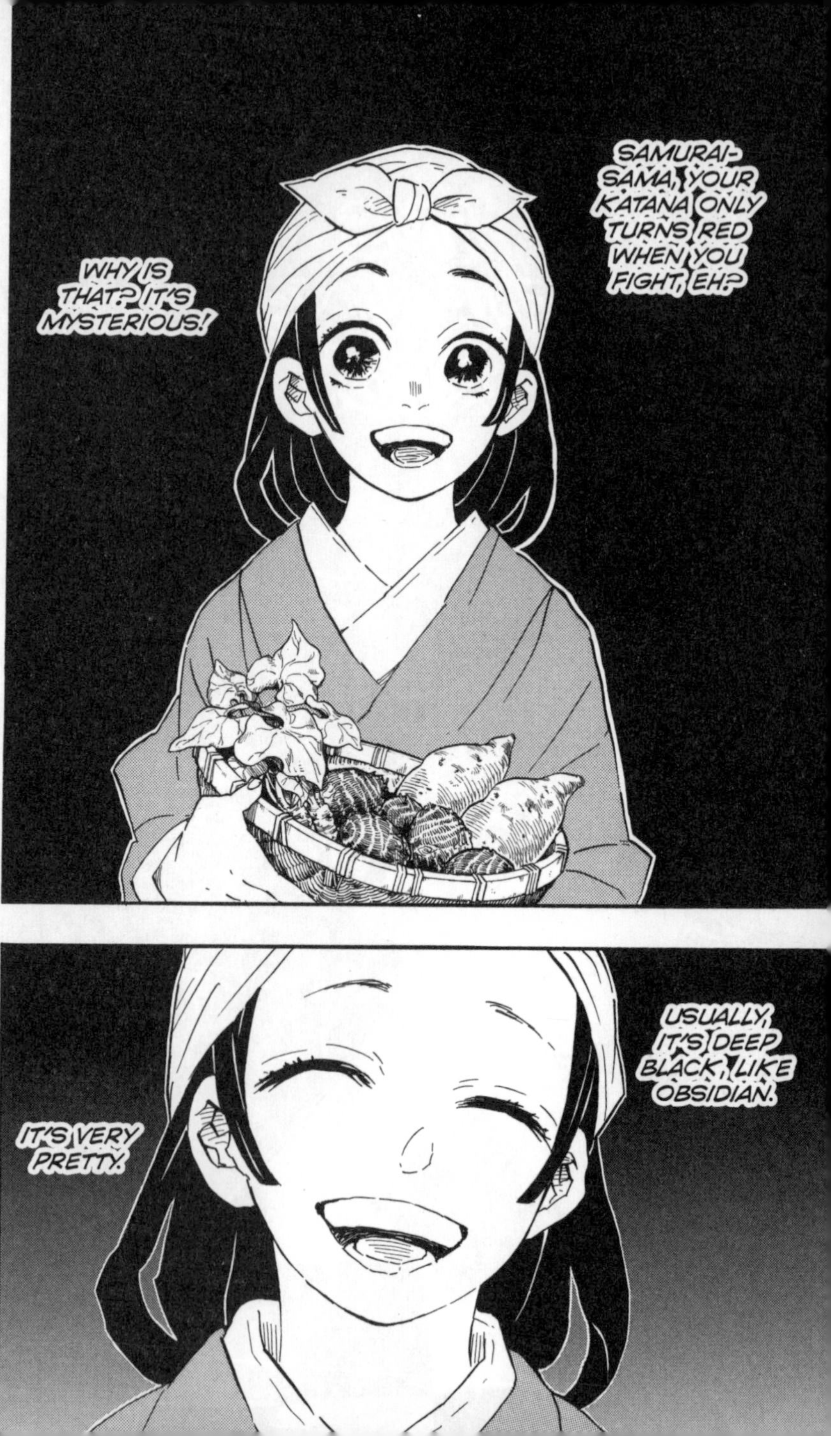
SAMURAI-SAMA, YOUR KATANA ONLY TURNS RED WHEN YOU FIGHT, EH?
WHY IS THAT? IT'S MYSTERIOUS!
USUALLY, IT'S DEEP BLACK, LIKE OBSIDIAN.
IT'S VERY PRETTY.

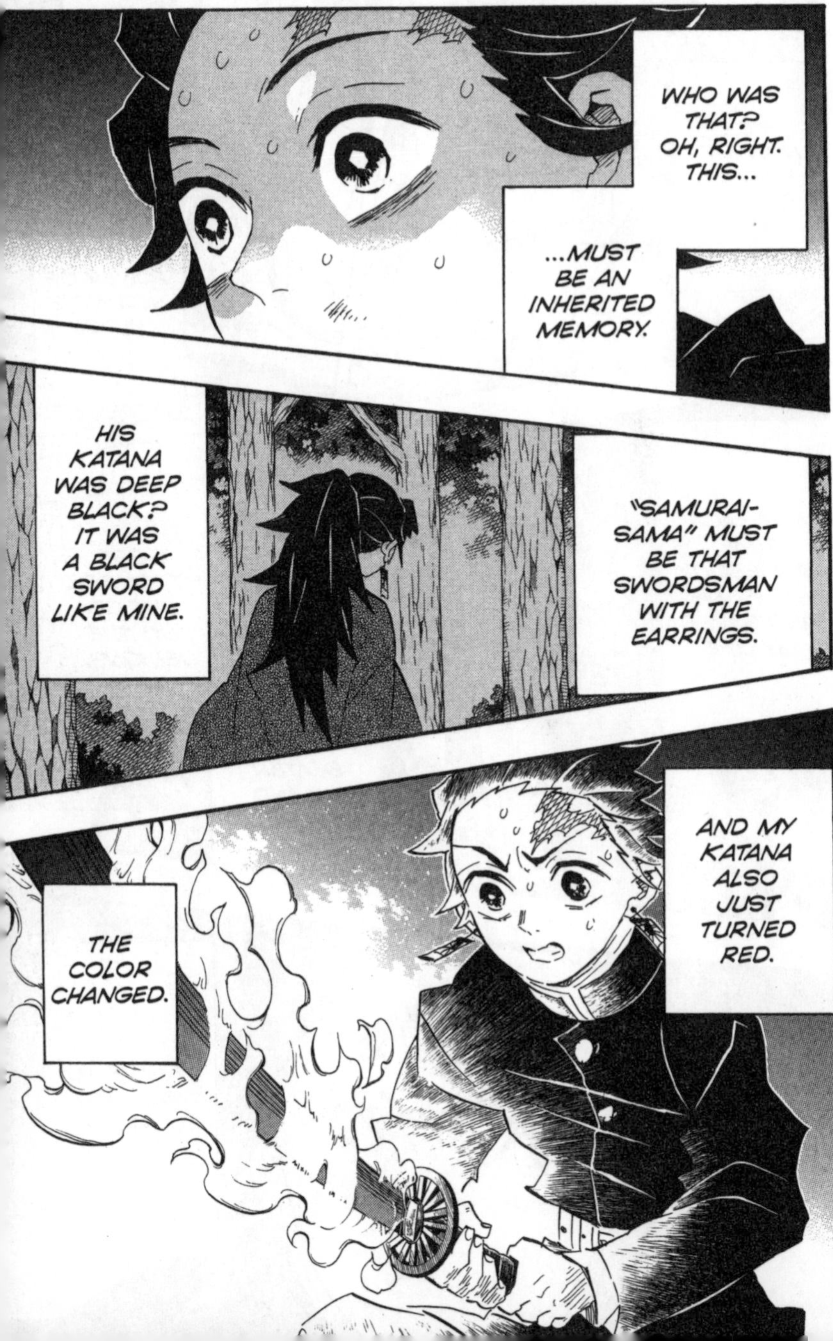
WHO WAS THAT? OH, RIGHT. THIS...
...MUST BE AN INHERITED MEMORY.
"SAMURAI-SAMA" MUST BE THAT SWORDSMAN WITH THE EARRINGS.
HIS KATANA WAS DEEP BLACK? IT WAS A BLACK SWORD LIKE MINE.
AND MY KATANA ALSO JUST TURNED RED.
THE COLOR CHANGED.

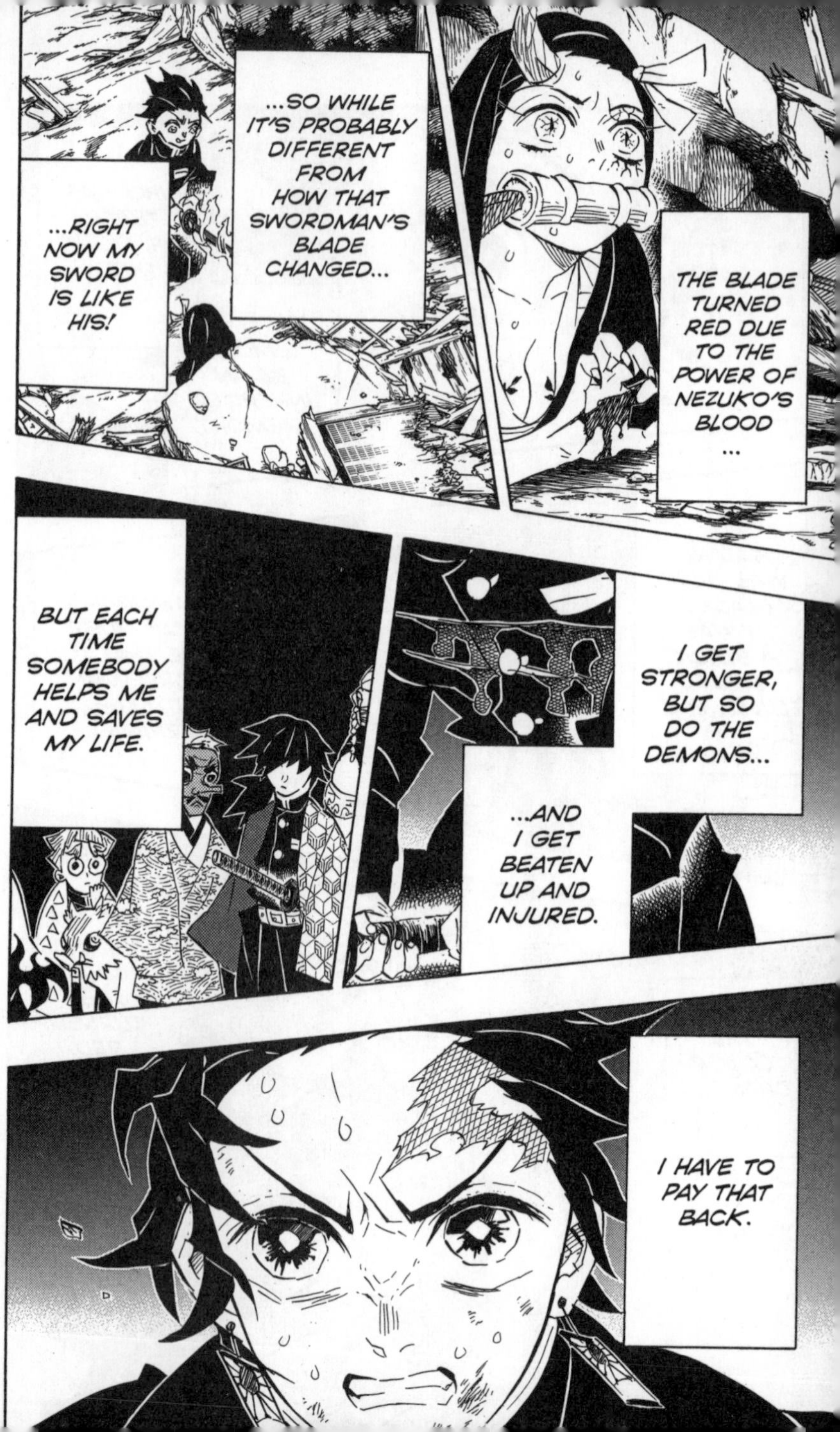
THE BLADE TURNED RED DUE TO THE POWER OF NEZUKO'S BLOOD ...
...SO WHILE IT'S PROBABLY DIFFERENT FROM HOW THAT SWORDMAN'S BLADE CHANGED...
...RIGHT NOW MY SWORD IS LIKE HIS!
I GET STRONGER, BUT SO DO THE DEMONS...
...AND I GET BEATEN UP AND INJURED.
BUT EACH TIME SOMEBODY HELPS ME AND SAVES MY LIFE.
I HAVE TO PAY THAT BACK.

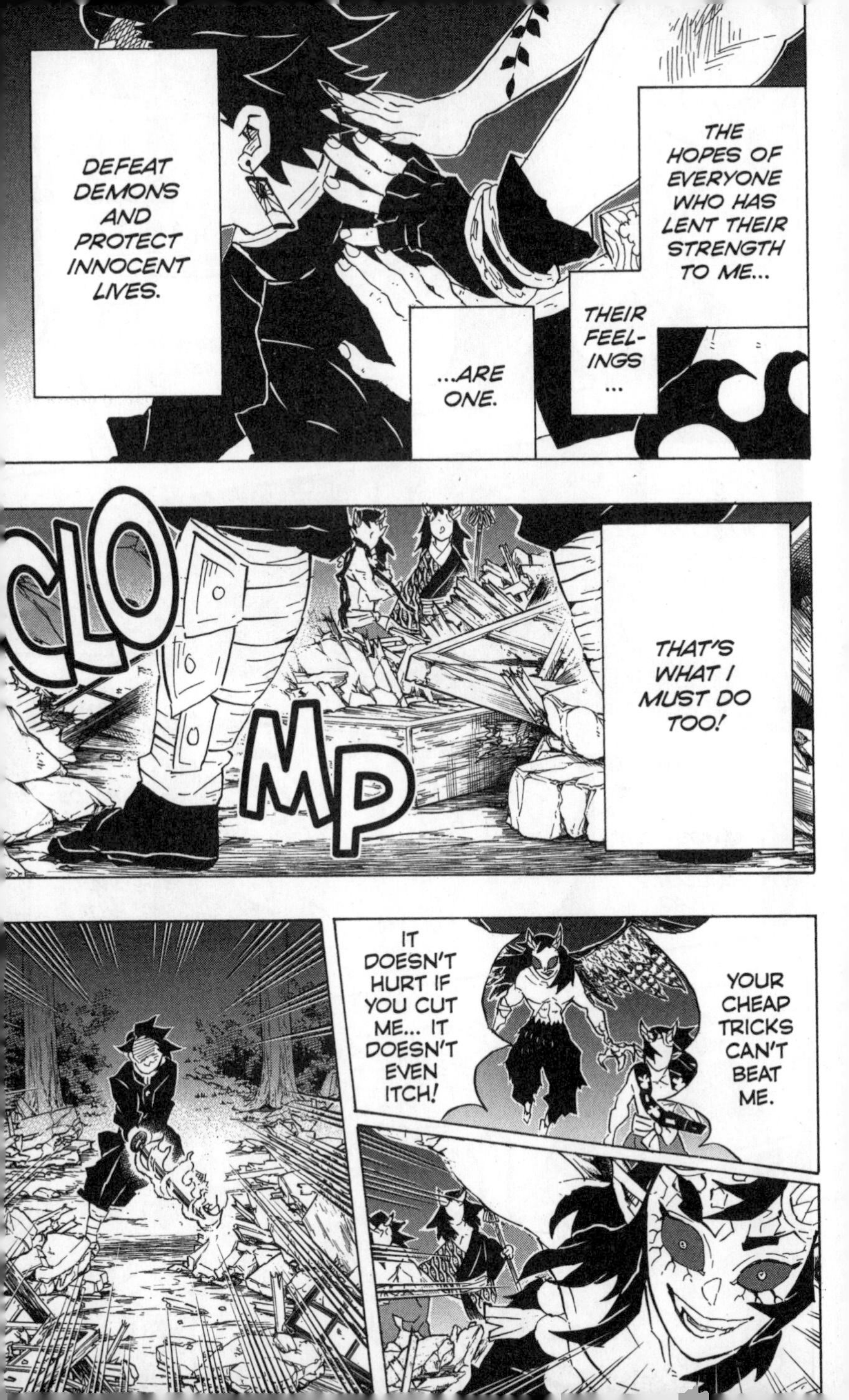
THE HOPES OF EVERYONE WHO HAS LENT THEIR STRENGTH TO ME...
THEIR FEEL-INGS ...
...ARE ONE.
DEFEAT DEMONS AND PROTECT INNOCENT LIVES.
THAT'S WHAT I MUST DO TOO!
CLOMP
YOUR CHEAP TRICKS CAN'T BEAT ME.
IT DOESN'T HURT IF YOU CUT ME... IT DOESN'T EVEN ITCH!

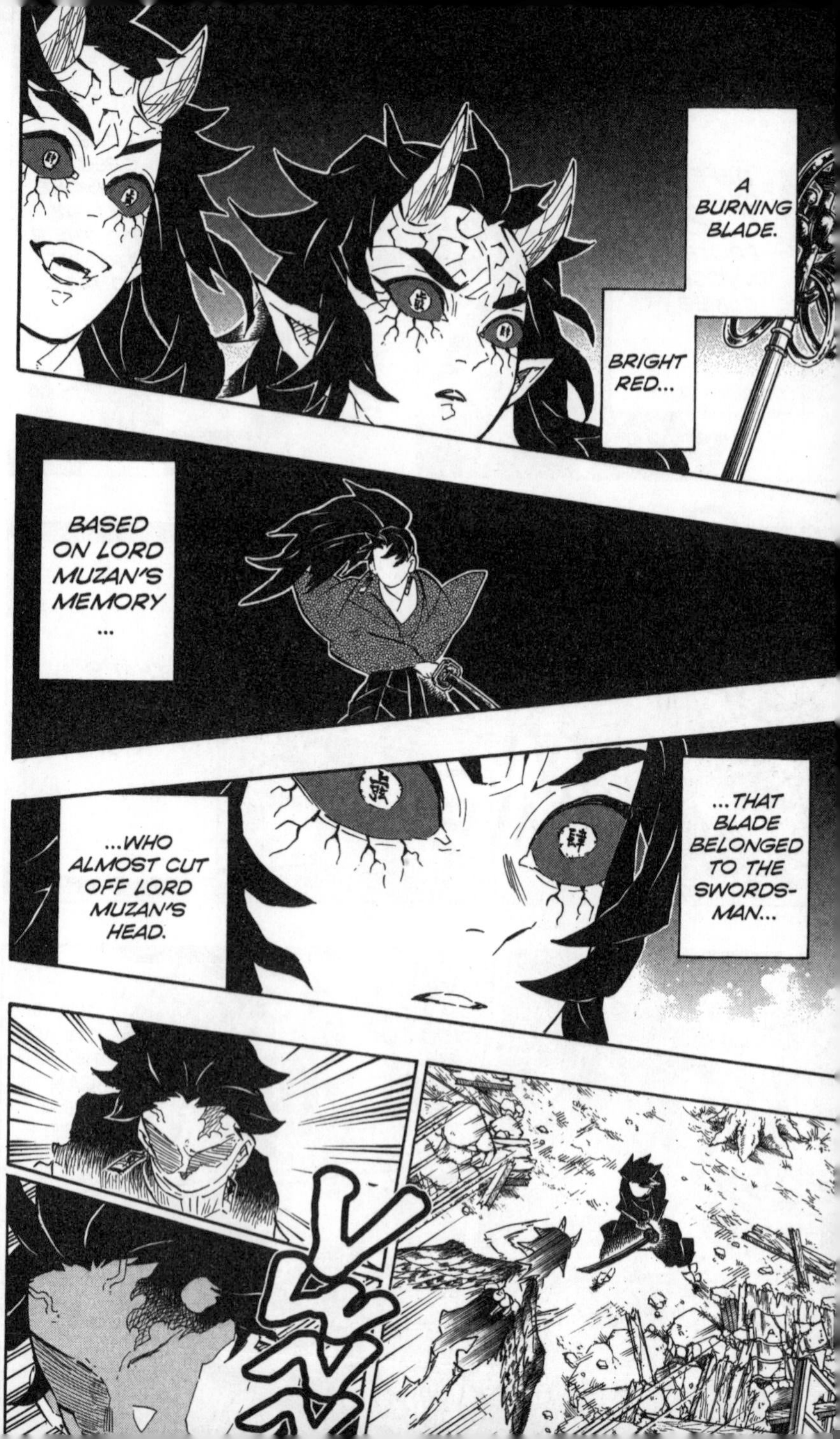
A BURNING BLADE.
BRIGHT RED...
BASED ON LORD MUZAN'S MEMORY ...
...THAT BLADE BELONGED TO THE SWORDS-MAN...
...WHO ALMOST CUT OFF LORD MUZAN'S HEAD.

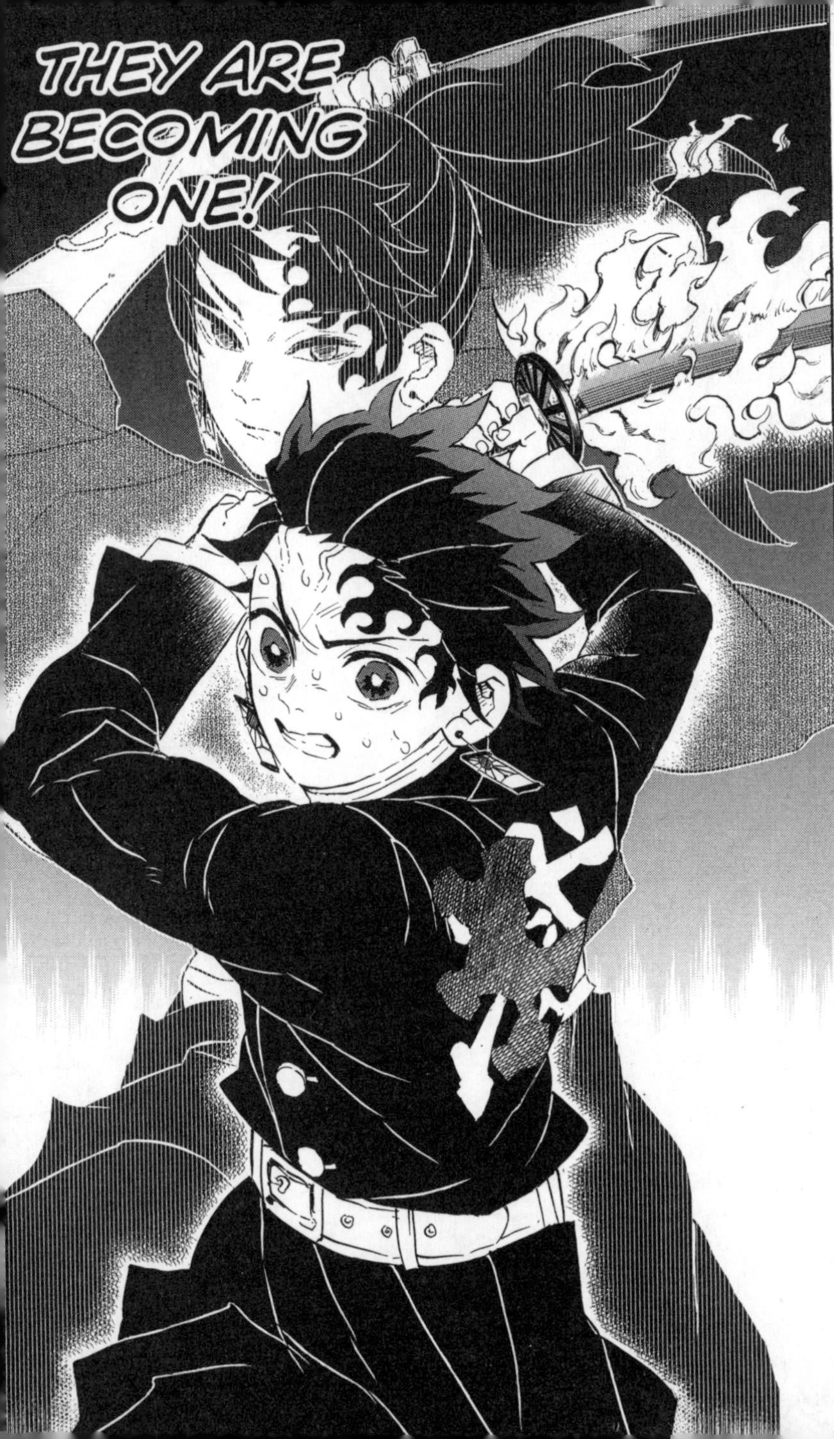
THEY ARE BECOMING ONE!

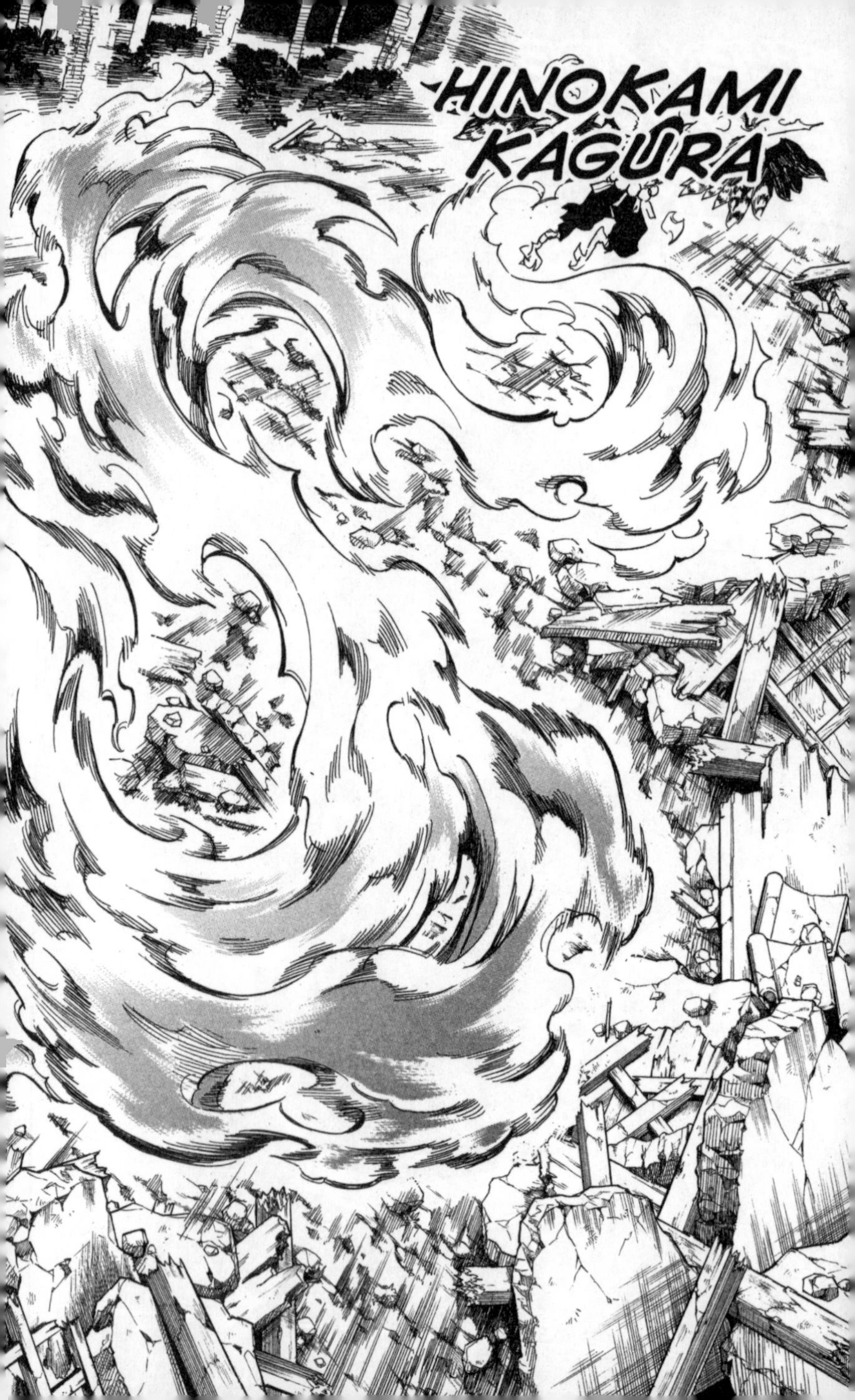
HINOKAMI KAGURA

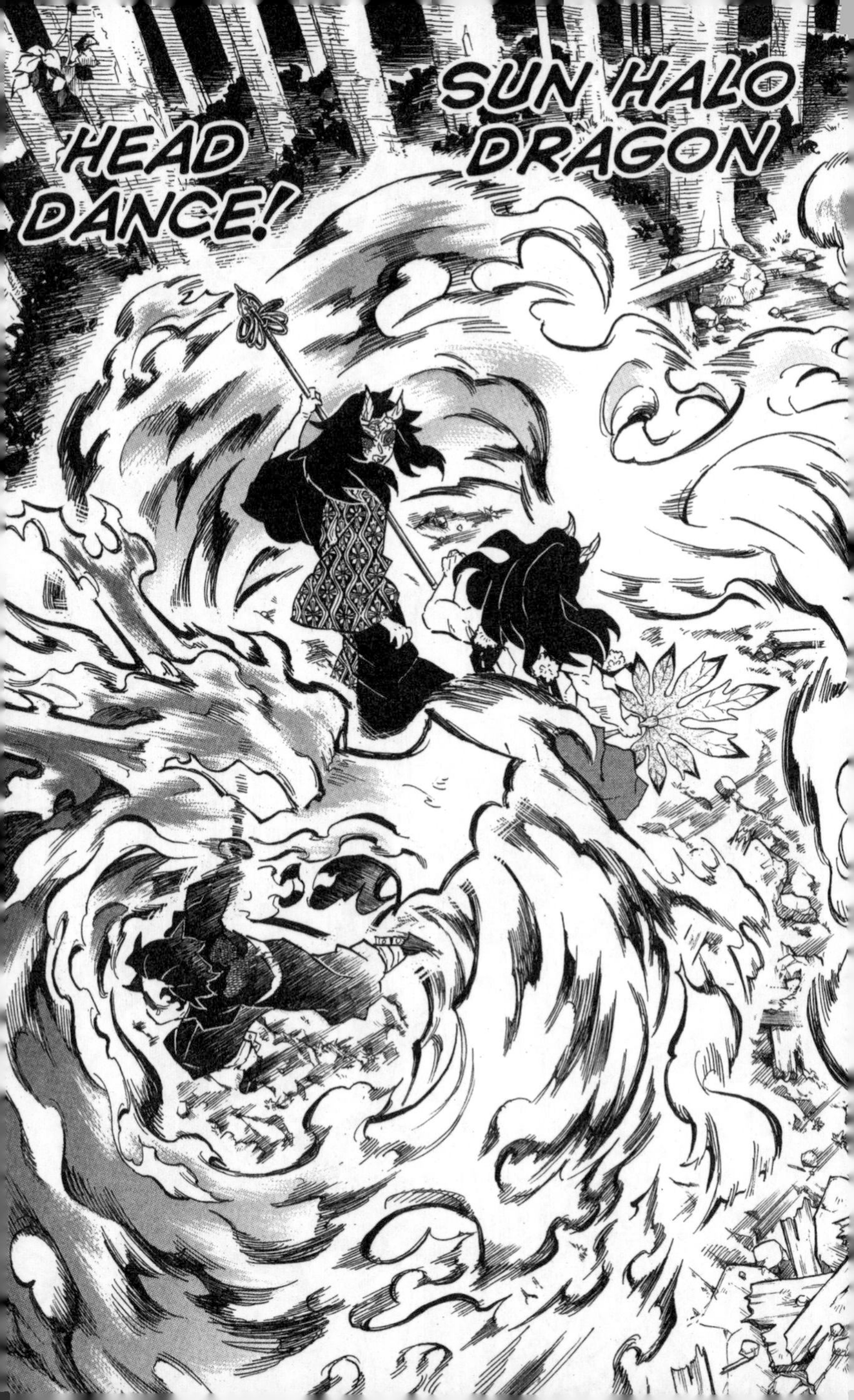
SUN HALO DRAGON
HEAD DANCE!

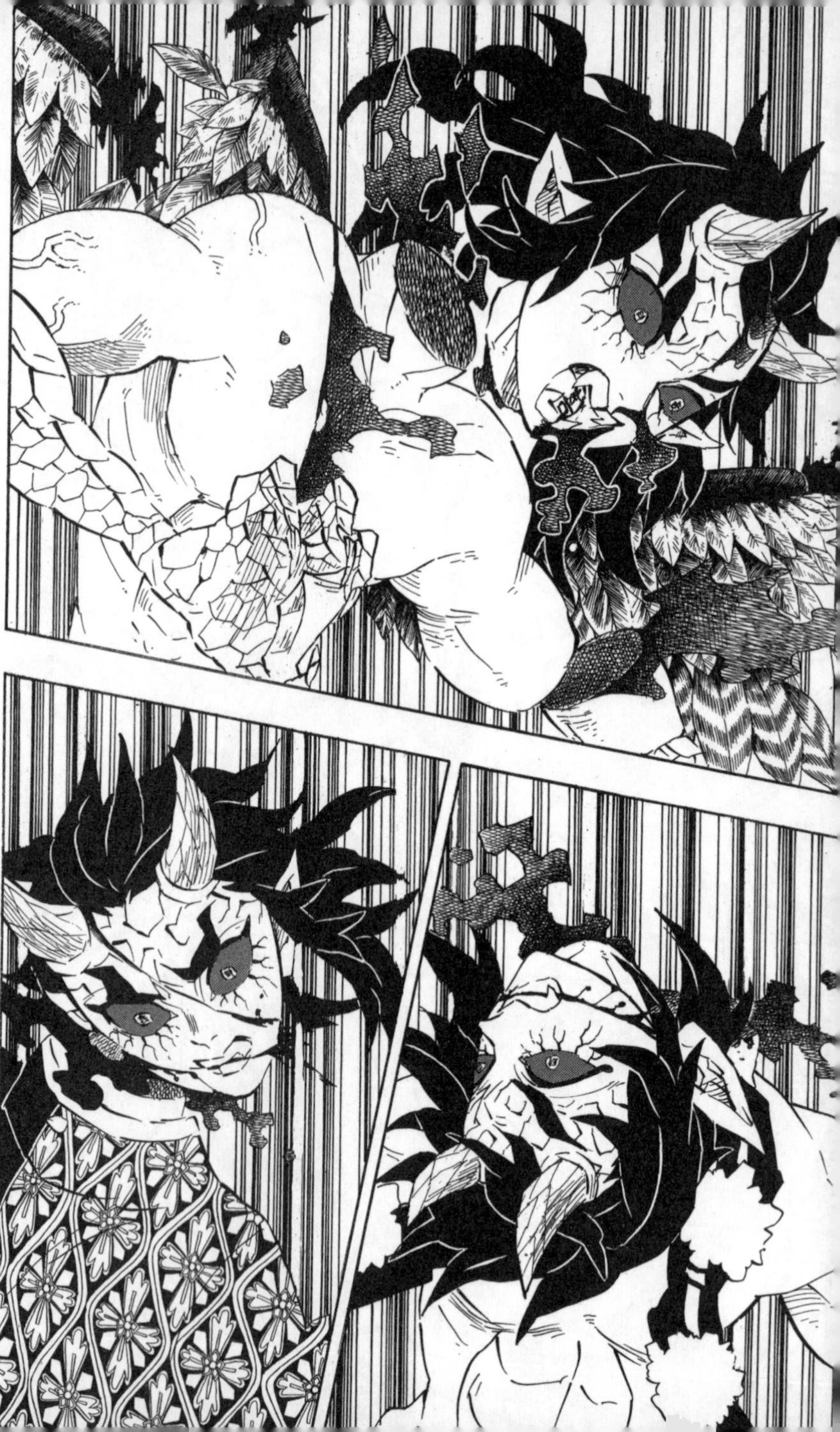

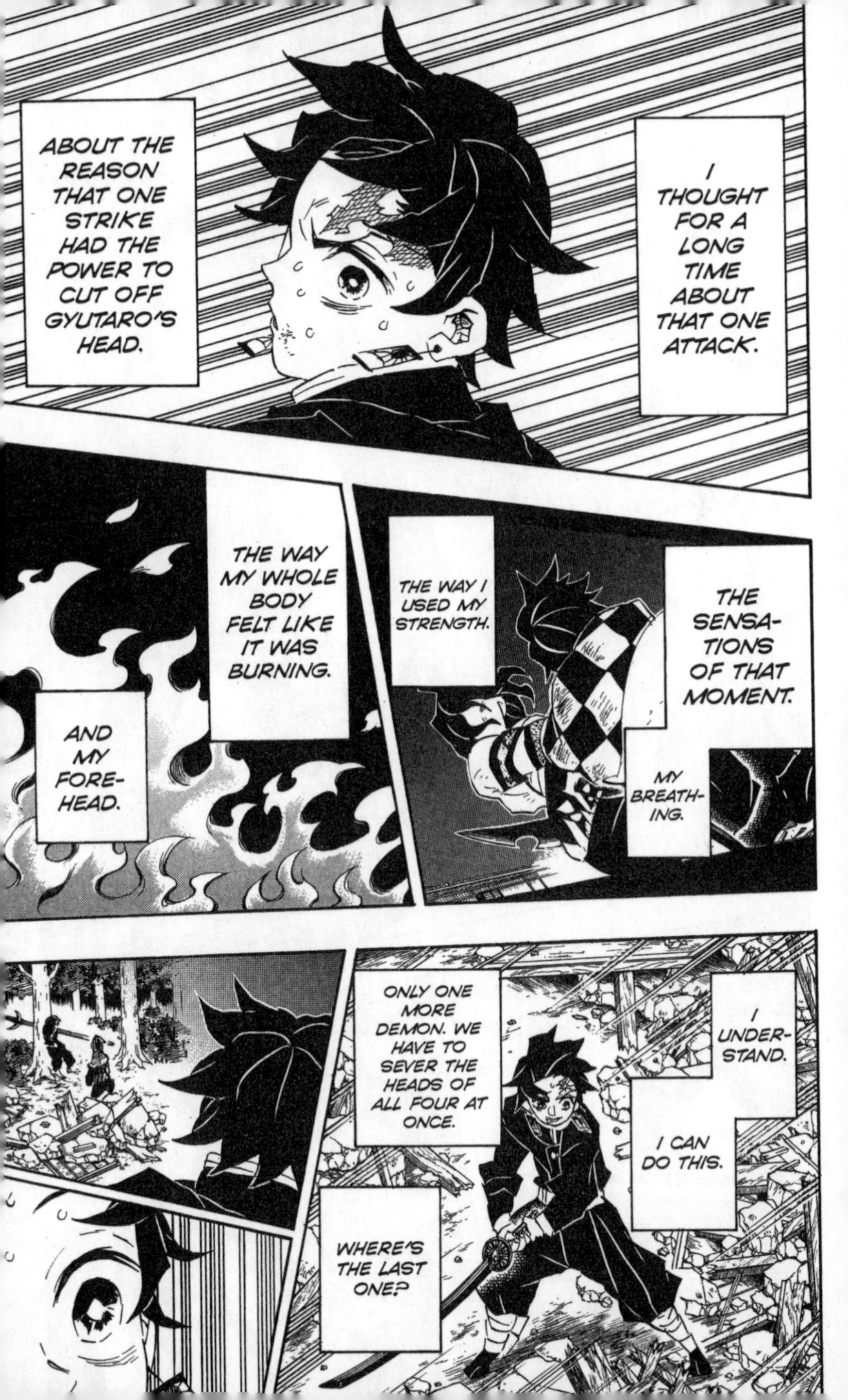
I THOUGHT FOR A LONG TIME ABOUT THAT ONE ATTACK.
ABOUT THE REASON THAT ONE STRIKE HAD THE POWER TO CUT OFF GYUTARO'S HEAD.
THE SENSATIONS OF THAT MOMENT.
THE WAY I USED MY STRENGTH.
MY BREATHING.
THE WAY MY WHOLE BODY FELT LIKE IT WAS BURNING.
AND MY FOREHEAD.
I UNDERSTAND.
ONLY ONE MORE DEMON. WE HAVE TO SEVER THE HEADS OF ALL FOUR AT ONCE.
I CAN DO THIS.
WHERE'S THE LAST ONE?

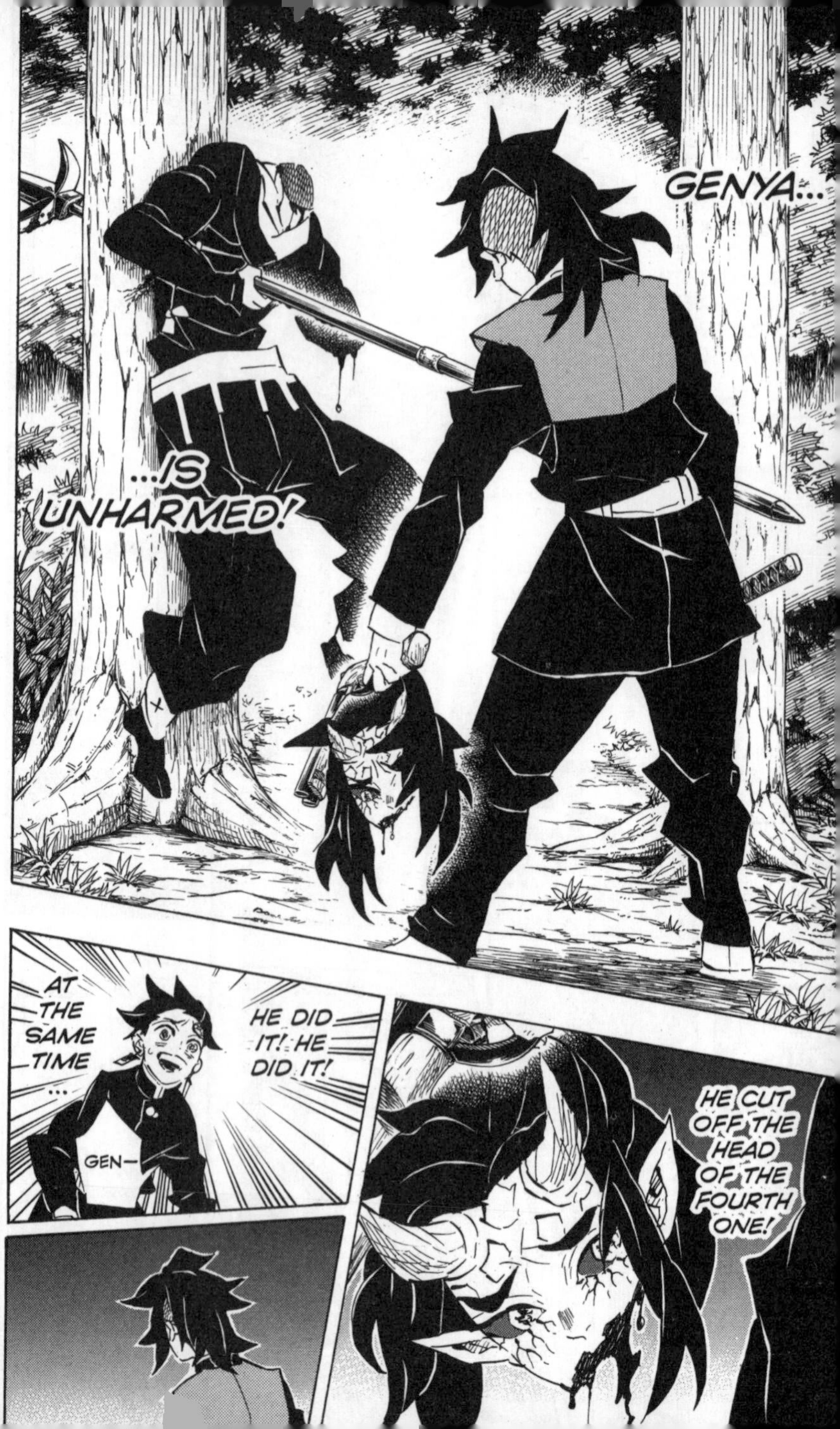
GENYA...
...IS UNHARMED!
HE CUT OFF THE HEAD OF THE FOURTH ONE!
HE DID IT! HE DID IT!
AT THE SAME TIME ...
GEN—

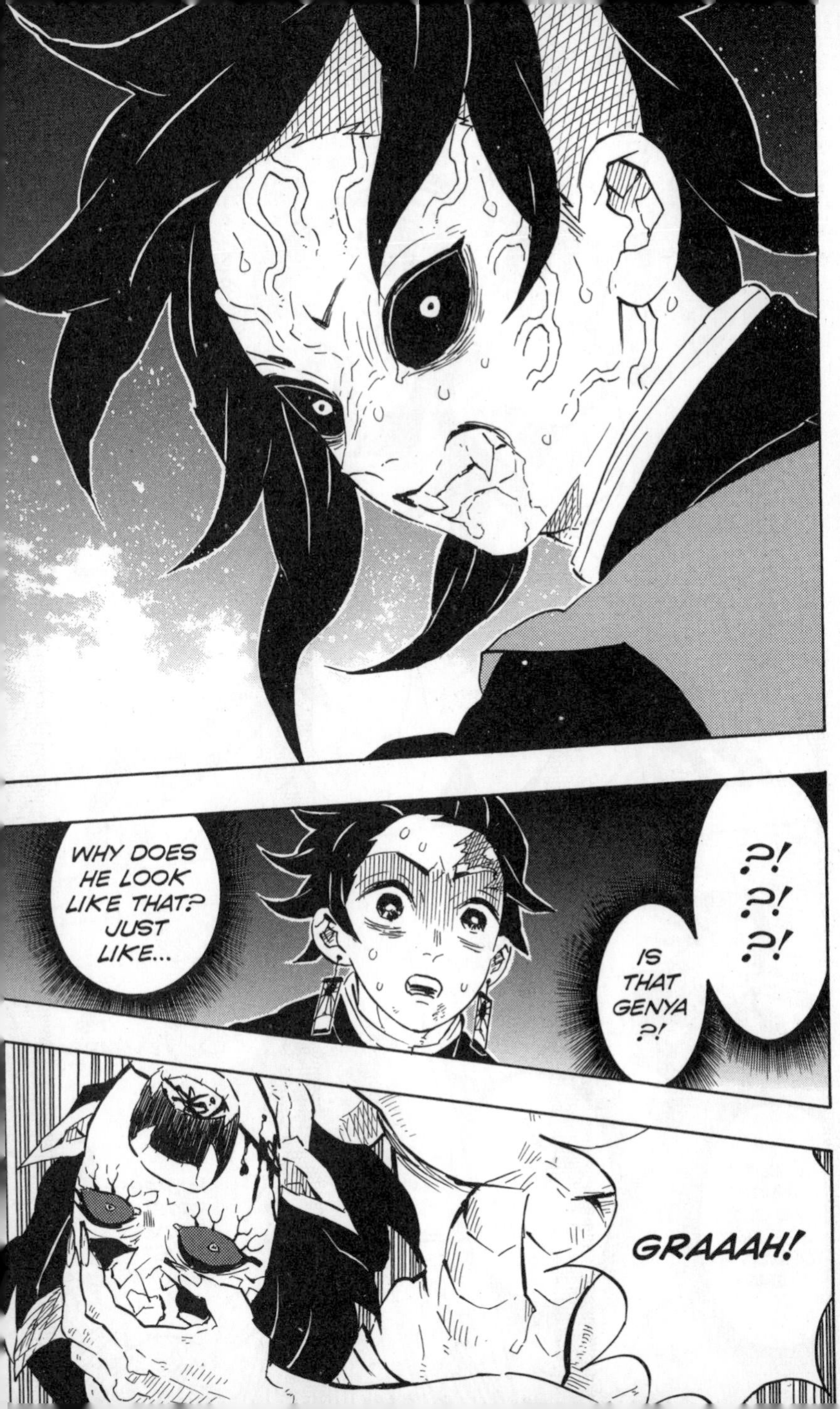
?! ?! ?!
IS THAT GENYA?!
WHY DOES HE LOOK LIKE THAT? JUST LIKE...
GRAAAH!

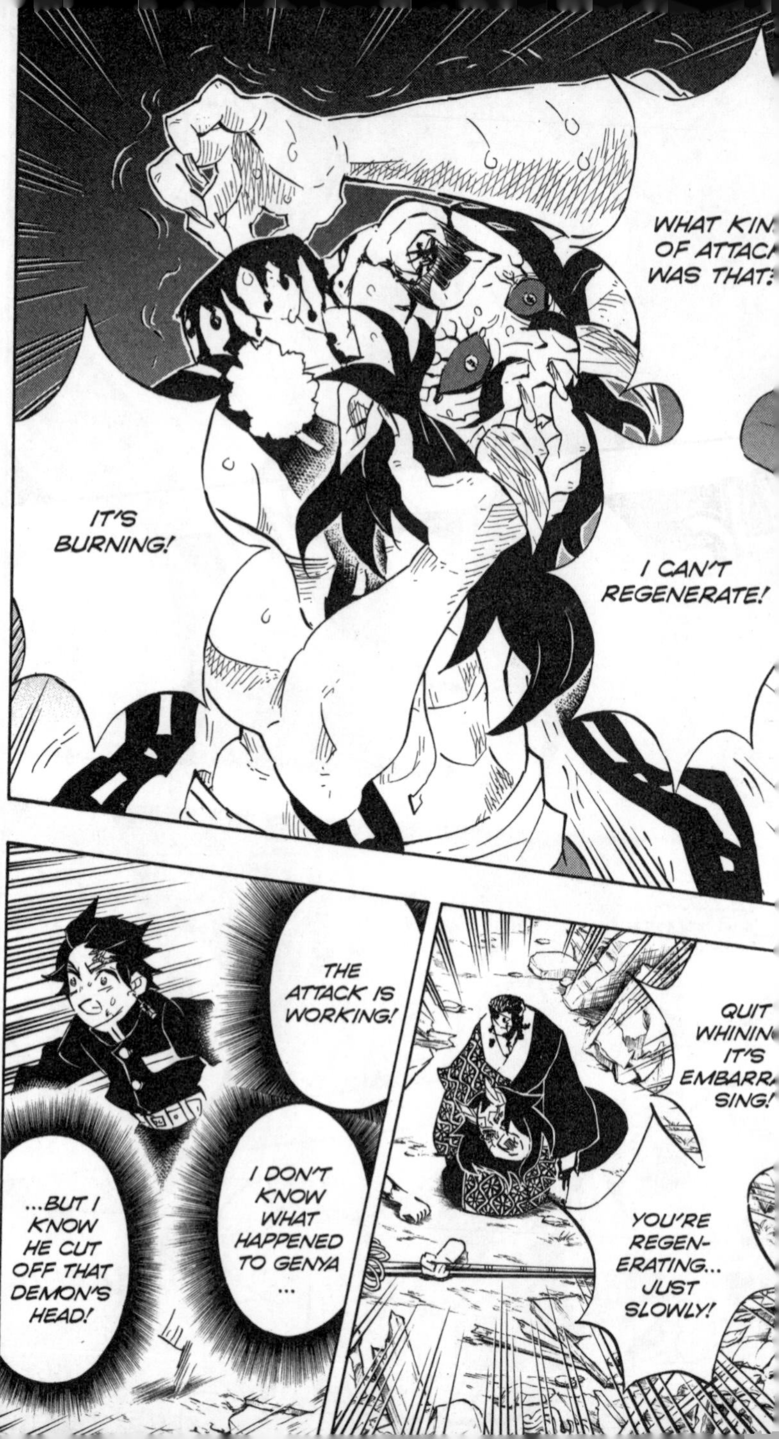
WHAT KIN OF ATTAC WAS THAT
I CAN'T REGENERATE!
IT'S BURNING!
QUIT WHININ IT'S EMBARRA SING!
YOU'RE REGEN-ERATING... JUST SLOWLY!
THE ATTACK IS WORKING!
I DON'T KNOW WHAT HAPPENED TO GENYA ...
...BUT I KNOW HE CUT OFF THAT DEMON'S HEAD!

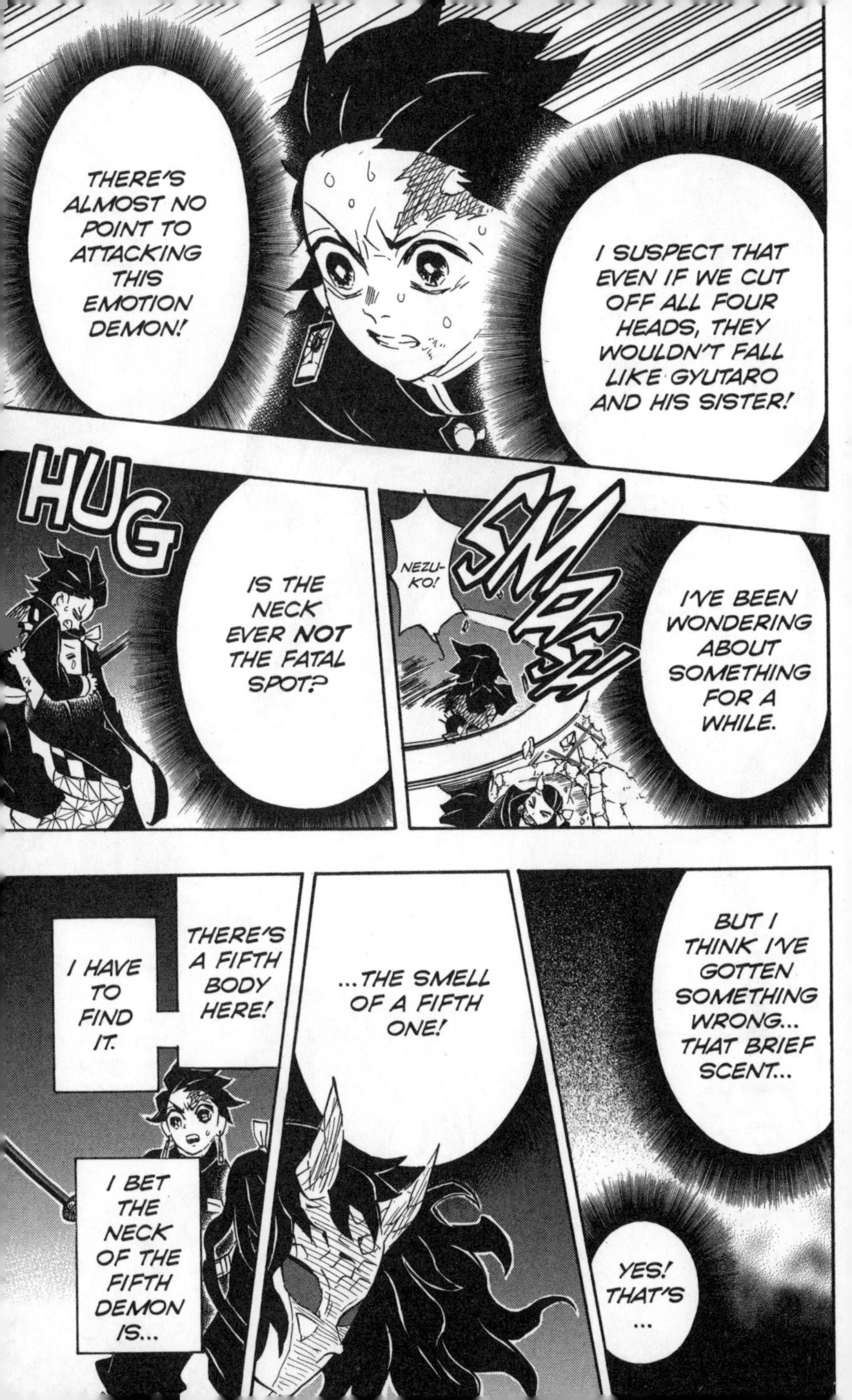
I SUSPECT THAT EVEN IF WE CUT OFF ALL FOUR HEADS, THEY WOULDN'T FALL LIKE GYUTARO AND HIS SISTER!
THERE'S ALMOST NO POINT TO ATTACKING THIS EMOTION DEMON!
I'VE BEEN WONDERING ABOUT SOMETHING FOR A WHILE.
SMASH
NEZU-KO!
IS THE NECK EVER NOT THE FATAL SPOT?
HUG
BUT I THINK I'VE GOTTEN SOMETHING WRONG... THAT BRIEF SCENT...
YES! THAT'S ...
...THE SMELL OF A FIFTH ONE!
THERE'S A FIFTH BODY HERE!
I HAVE TO FIND IT.
I BET THE NECK OF THE FIFTH DEMON IS...

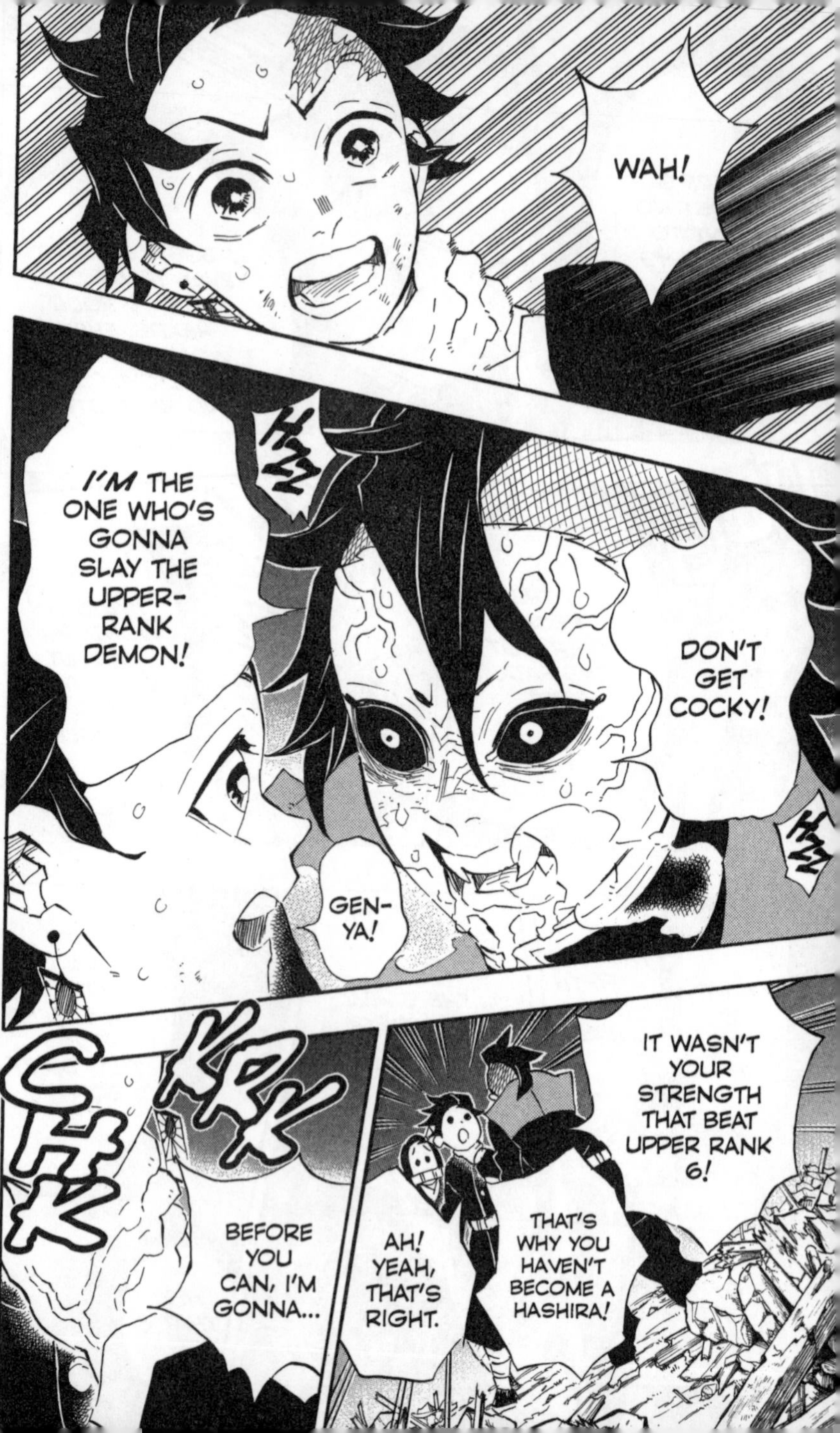
WAH!
DON'T GET COCKY!
HMM
GEN-YA!
I'M THE ONE WHO'S GONNA SLAY THE UPPER-RANK DEMON!
HMM
IT WASN'T YOUR STRENGTH THAT BEAT UPPER RANK 6!
THAT'S WHY YOU HAVEN'T BECOME A HASHIRA!
AH! YEAH, THAT'S RIGHT.
KRAK
CHK
BEFORE YOU CAN, I'M GONNA...

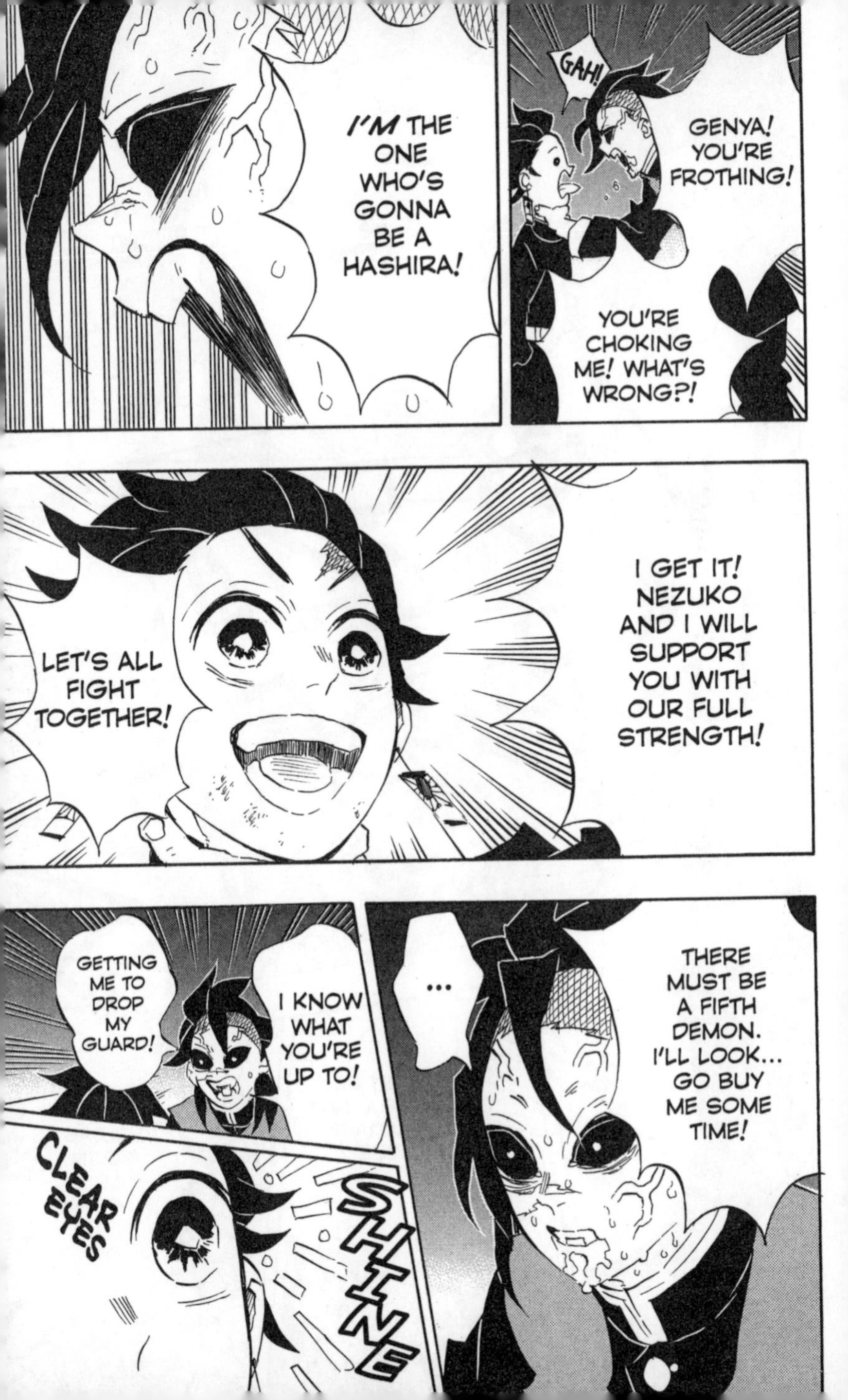
GAH!
GENYA! YOU'RE FROTHING!
YOU'RE CHOKING ME! WHAT'S WRONG?!
I'M THE ONE WHO'S GONNA BE A HASHIRA!
I GET IT! NEZUKO AND I WILL SUPPORT YOU WITH OUR FULL STRENGTH!
LET'S ALL FIGHT TOGETHER!
THERE MUST BE A FIFTH DEMON. I'LL LOOK... GO BUY ME SOME TIME!
...
I KNOW WHAT YOU'RE UP TO!
GETTING ME TO DROP MY GUARD!
SHINE
CLEAR EYES

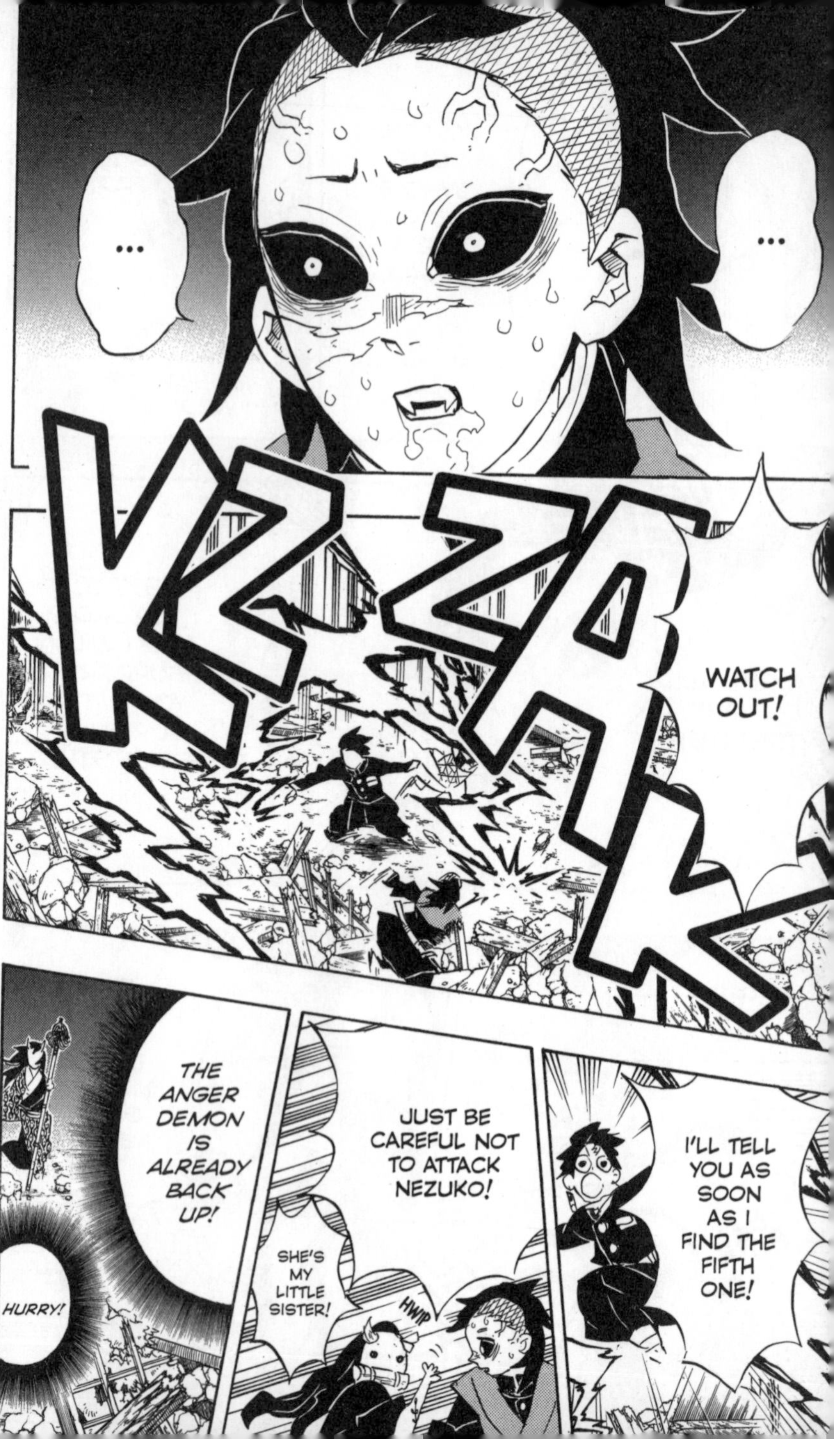
...
...
KZZAK
WATCH OUT!
I'LL TELL YOU AS SOON AS I FIND THE FIFTH ONE!
JUST BE CAREFUL NOT TO ATTACK NEZUKO!
HWIP
SHE'S MY LITTLE SISTER!
THE ANGER DEMON IS ALREADY BACK UP!
HURRY!

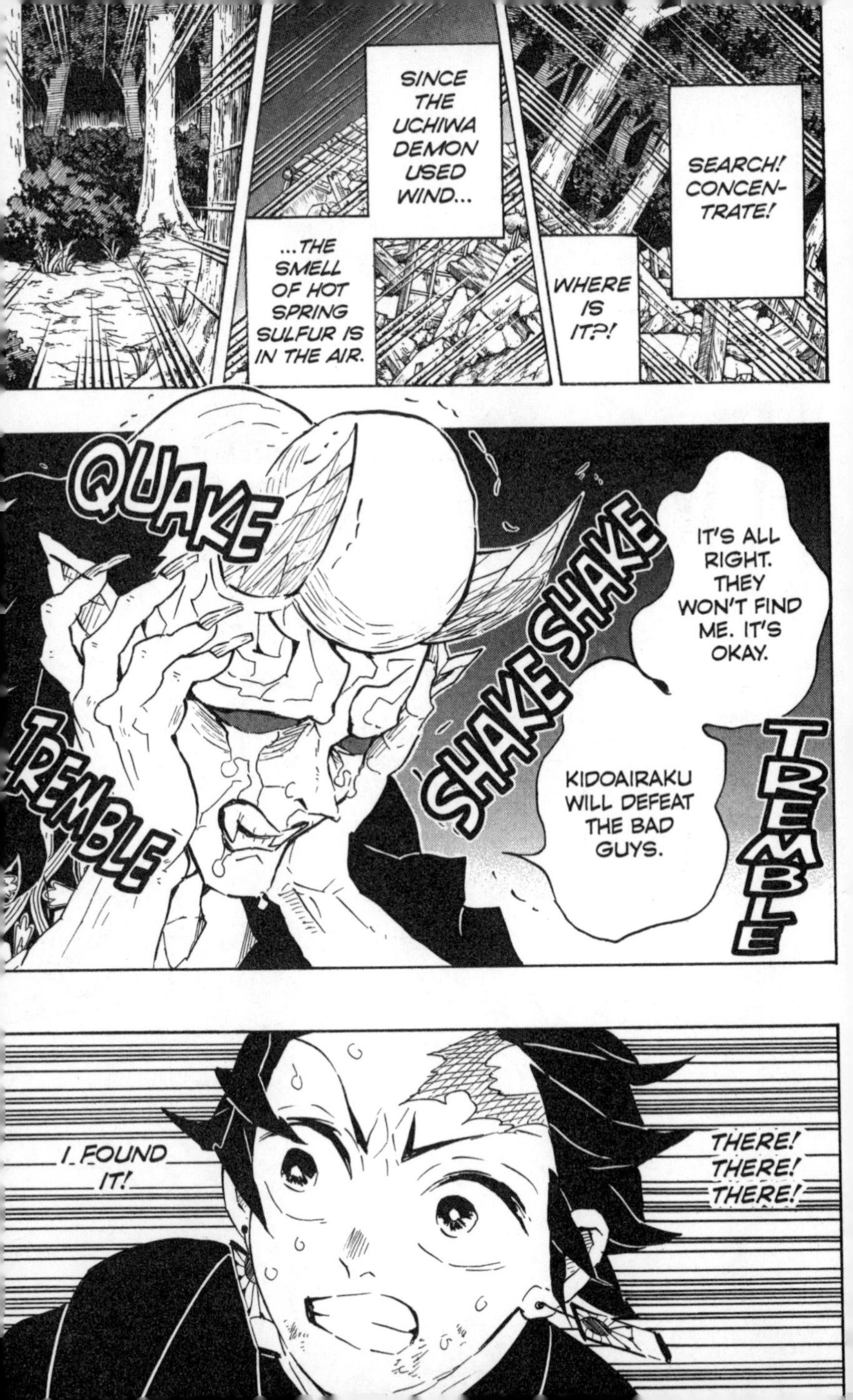
SEARCH! CONCENTRATE!
WHERE IS IT?!
SINCE THE UCHIWA DEMON USED WIND...
...THE SMELL OF HOT SPRING SULFUR IS IN THE AIR.
IT'S ALL RIGHT. THEY WON'T FIND ME. IT'S OKAY.
TREMBLE
SHAKE SHAKE
KIDOAIRAKU WILL DEFEAT THE BAD GUYS.
QUAKE
TREMBLE
THERE! THERE! THERE!
I FOUND IT!

TANJIRO'S ANCESTORS

SUMIYOSHI'S WIFE: SUYAKO

Apparently, she was someone who slept like crazy.

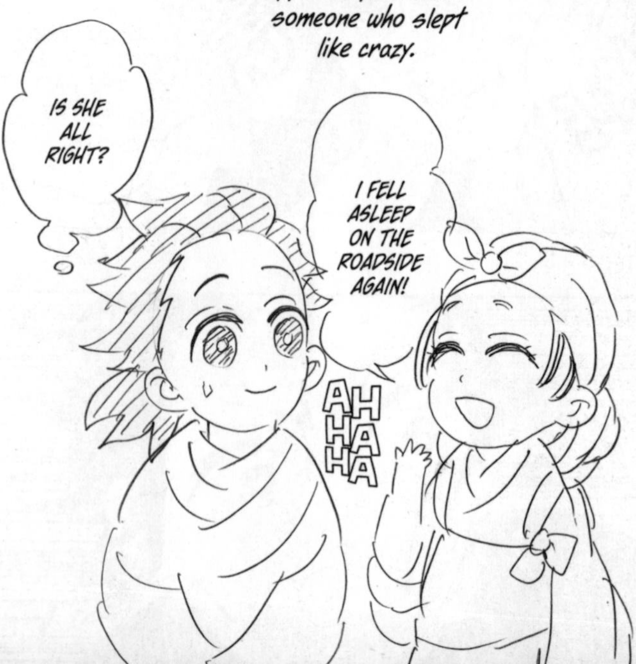

CHAPTER 114: WANTED: RESPECT

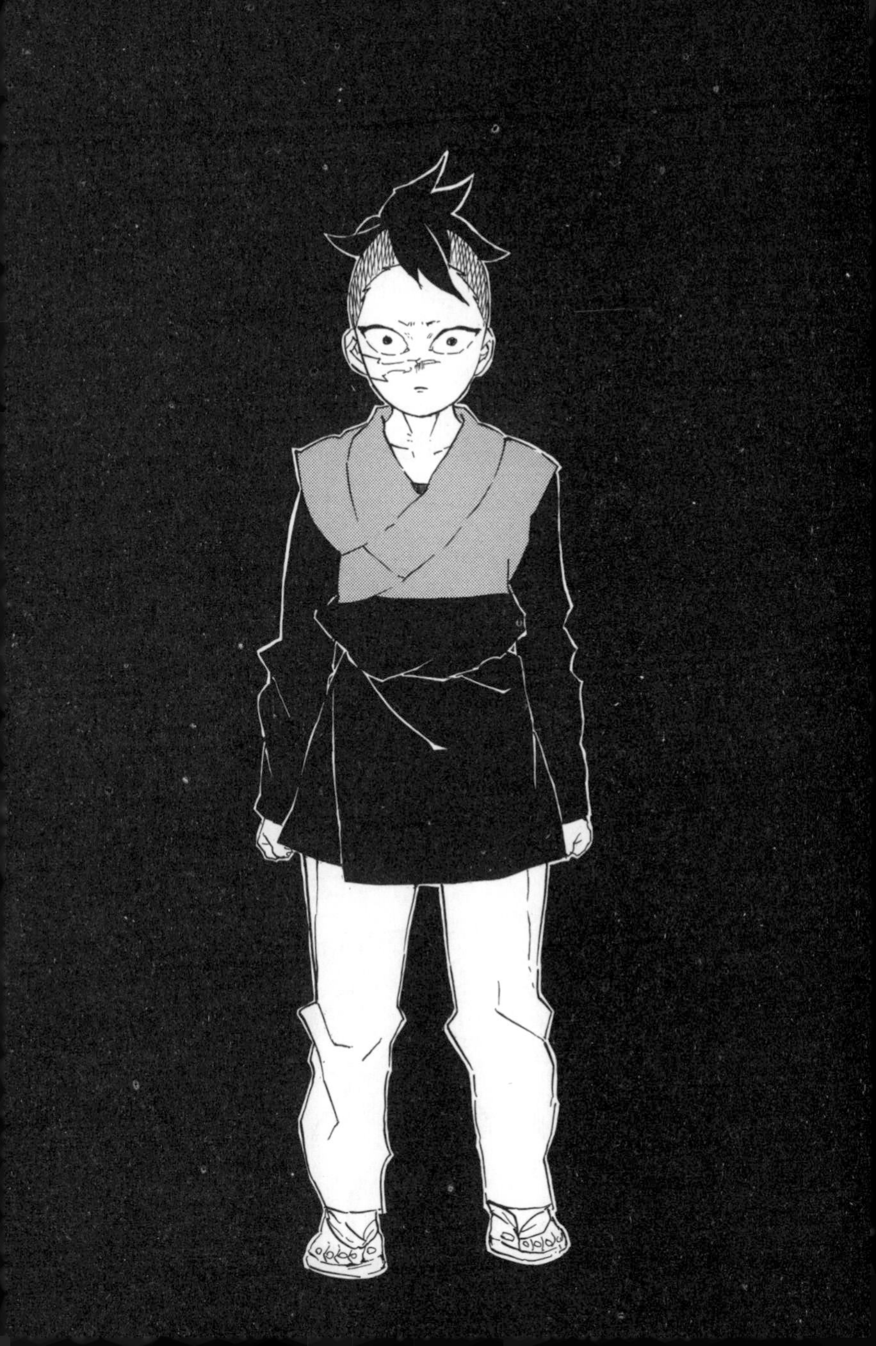

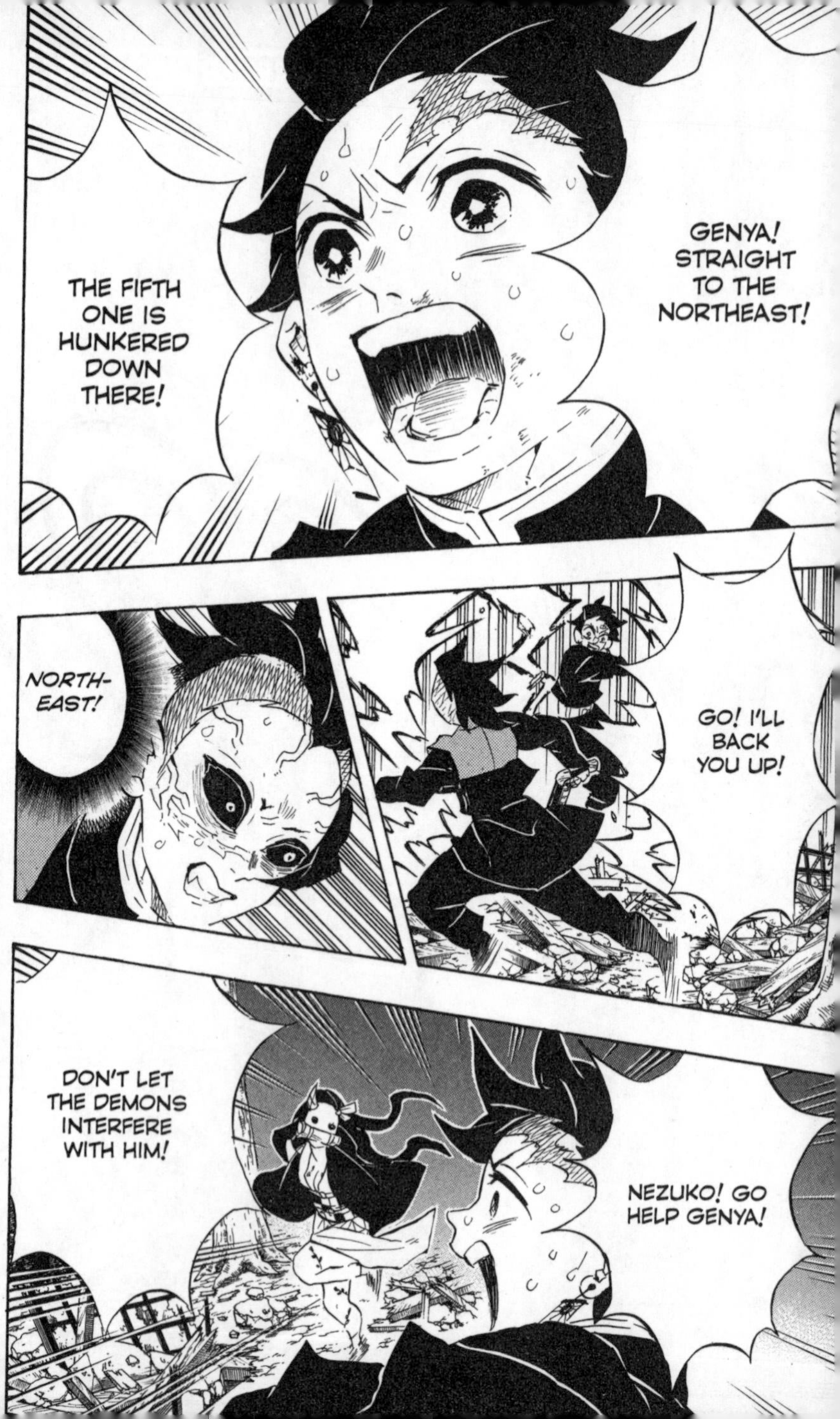
GENYA! STRAIGHT TO THE NORTHEAST!
THE FIFTH ONE IS HUNKERED DOWN THERE!
GO! I'LL BACK YOU UP!
NORTH-EAST!
NEZUKO! GO HELP GENYA!
DON'T LET THE DEMONS INTERFERE WITH HIM!

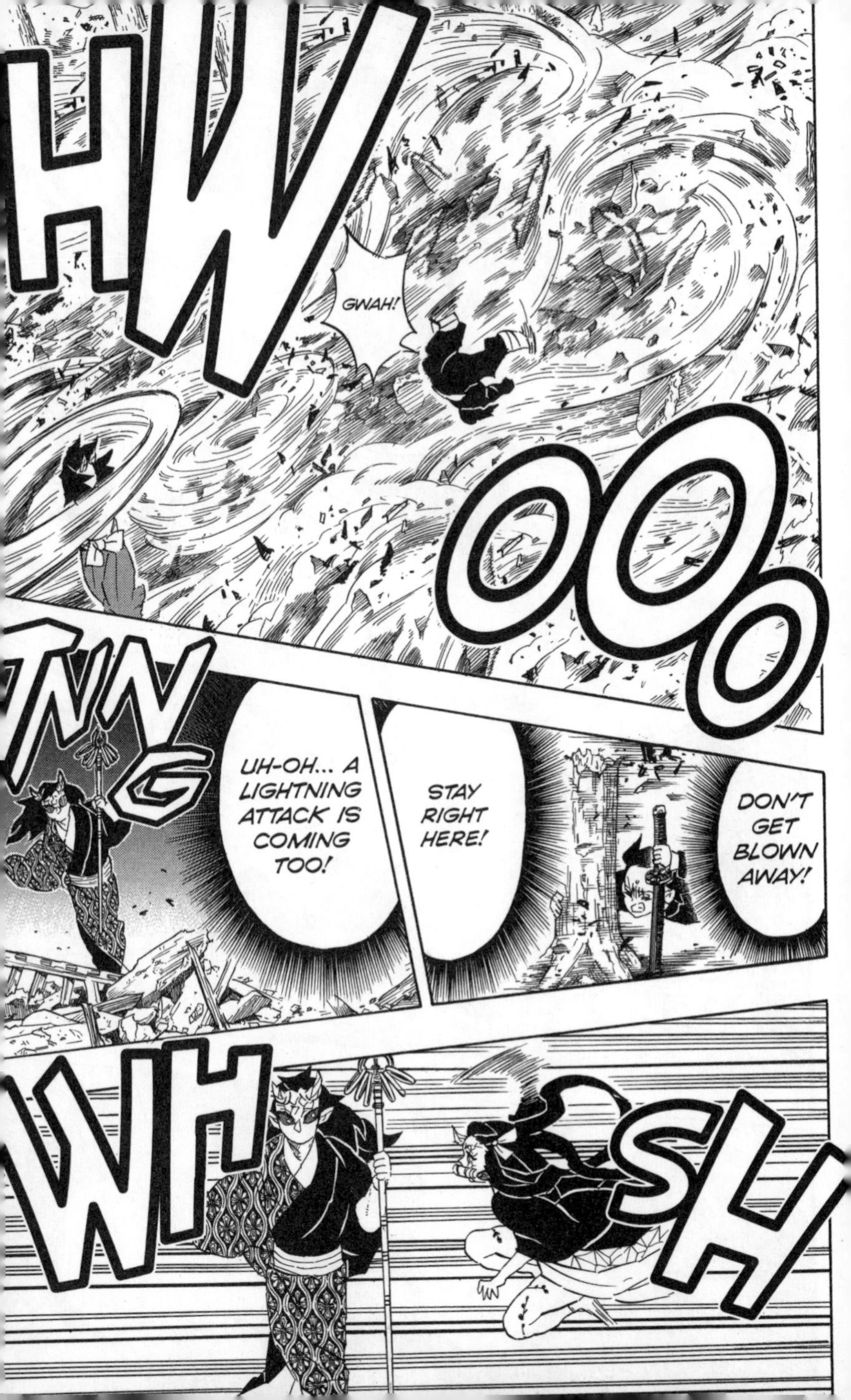
GWAH!
WHOOO
DON'T GET BLOWN AWAY!
STAY RIGHT HERE!
UH-OH... A LIGHTNING ATTACK IS COMING TOO!
TNNG
WHOOSH

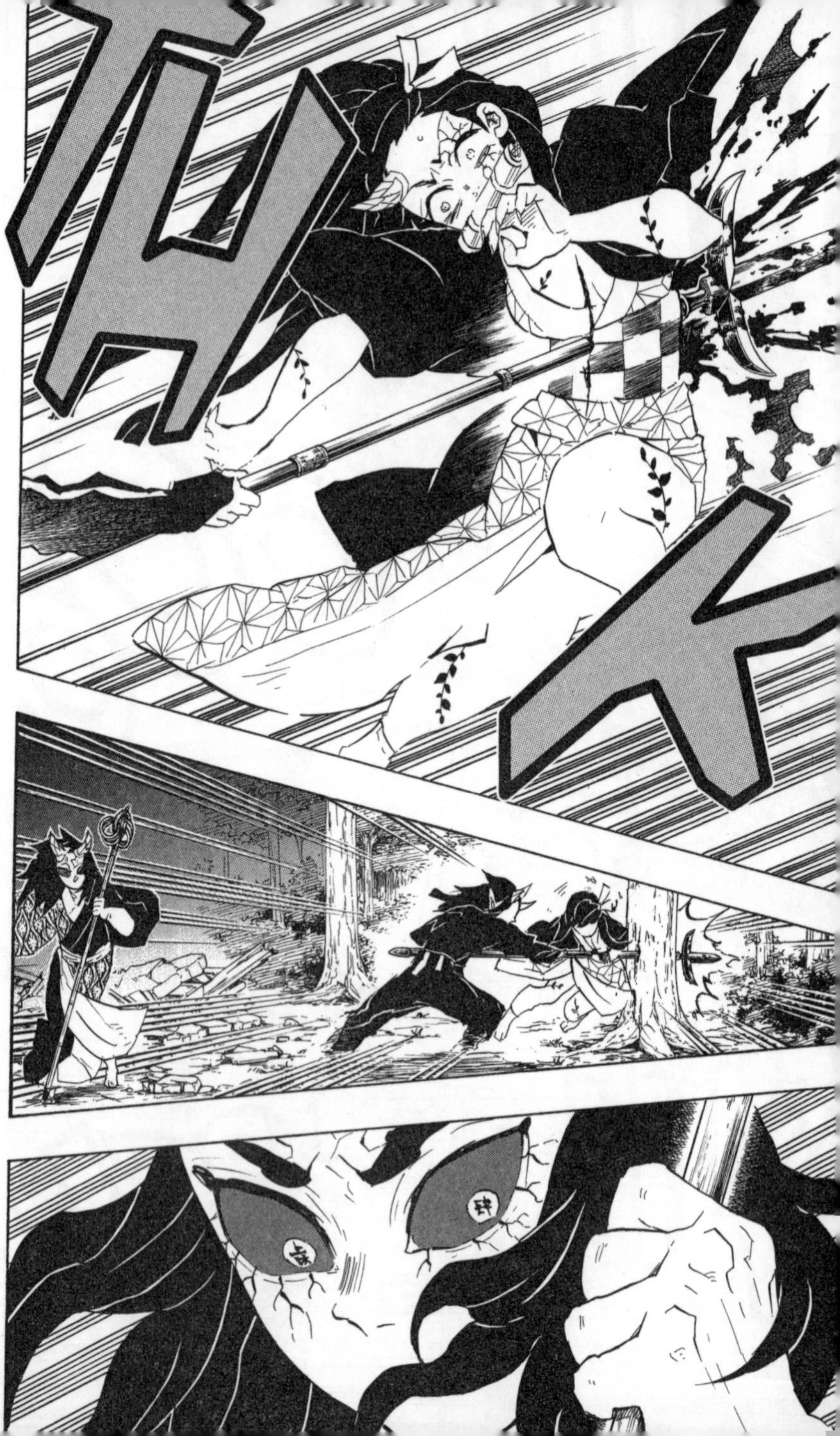

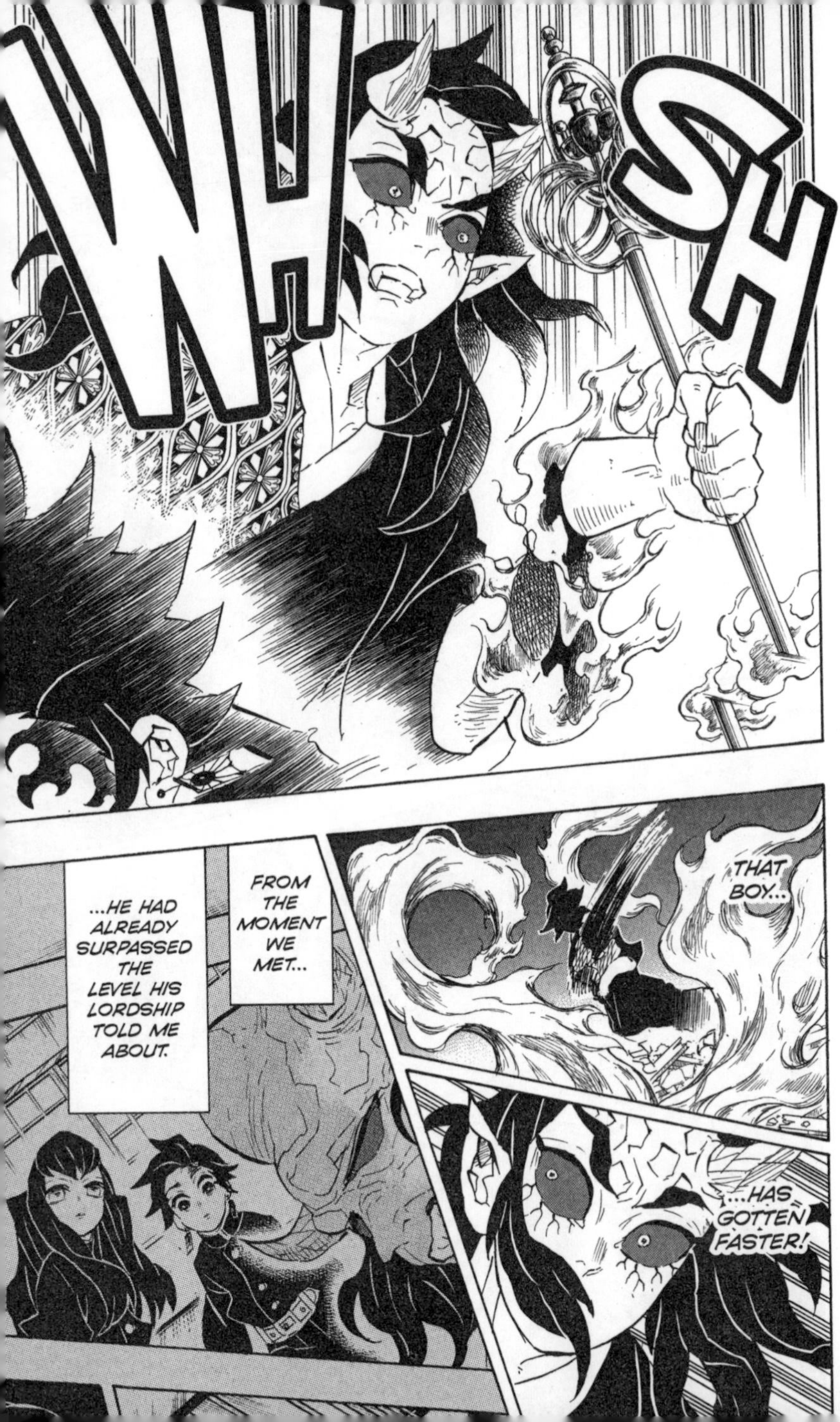
WHSH
THAT BOY...
...HAS GOTTEN FASTER!
FROM THE MOMENT WE MET...
...HE HAD ALREADY SURPASSED THE LEVEL HIS LORDSHIP TOLD ME ABOUT.

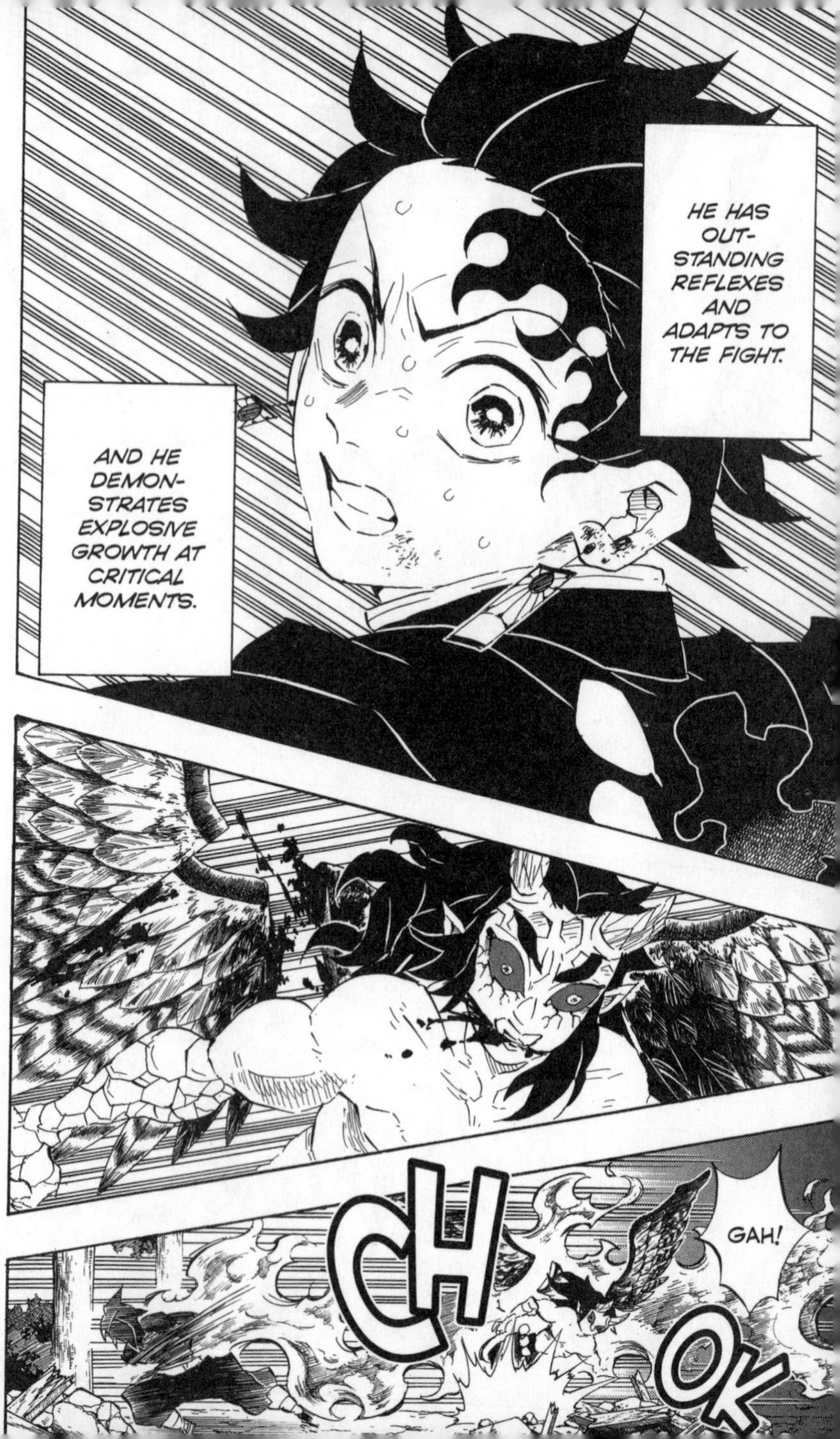
HE HAS OUT-STANDING REFLEXES AND ADAPTS TO THE FIGHT.
AND HE DEMON-STRATES EXPLOSIVE GROWTH AT CRITICAL MOMENTS.
GAH!
CHOK

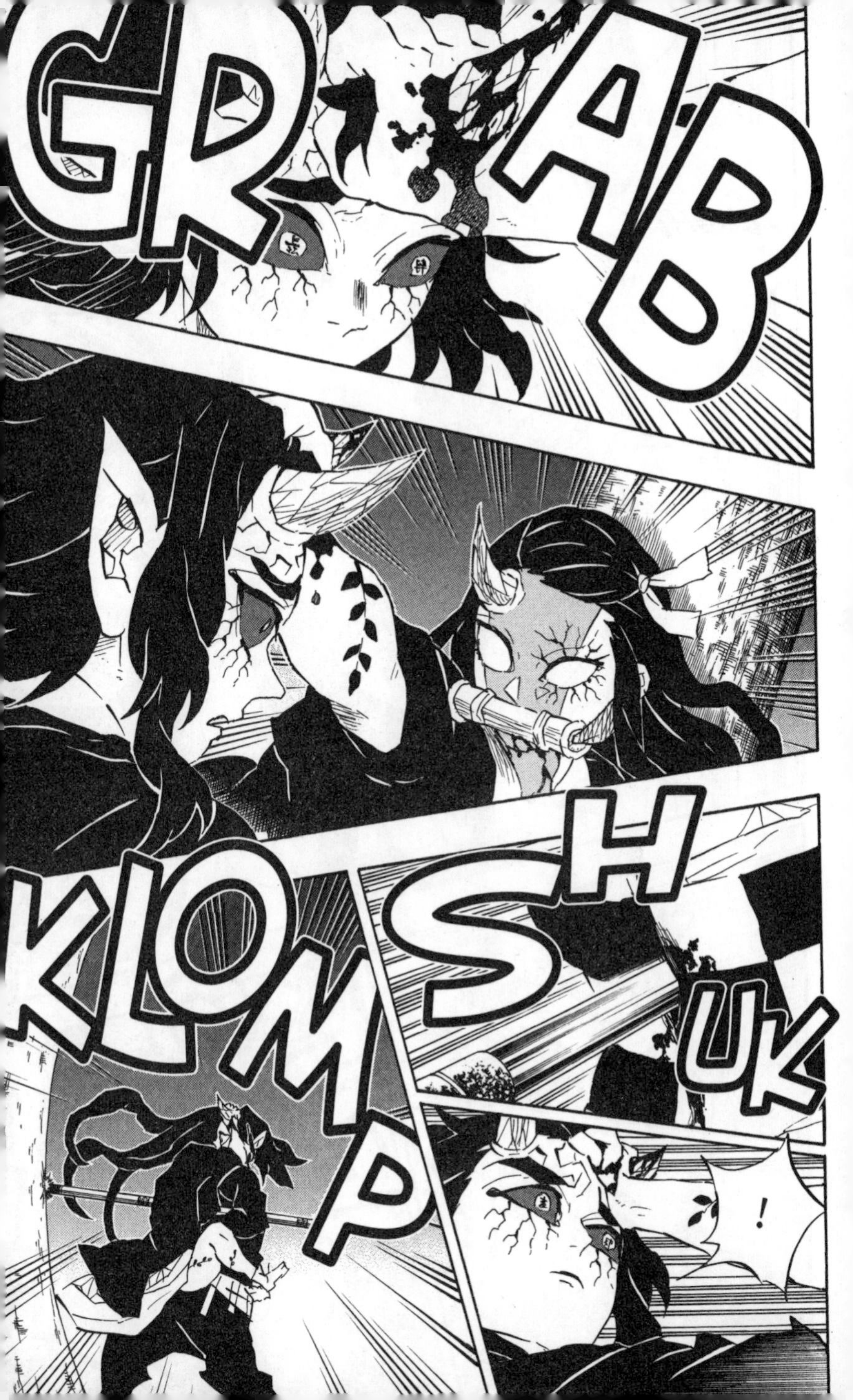
GRAB
SHUK
KLOMP
!

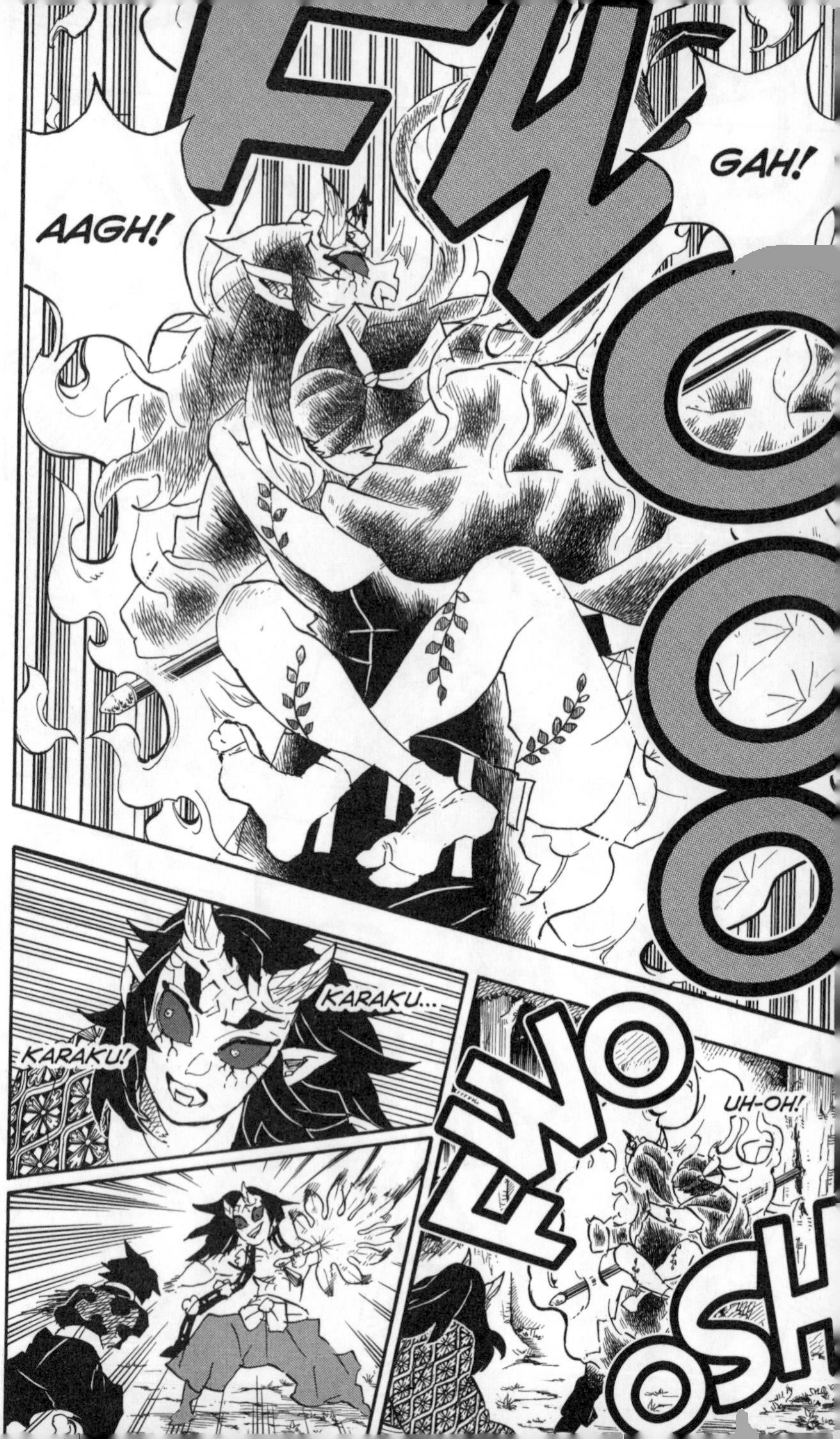
FWOOO
GAH!
AAGH!
UH-OH!
FWOOSH
KARAKU...
KARAKU!

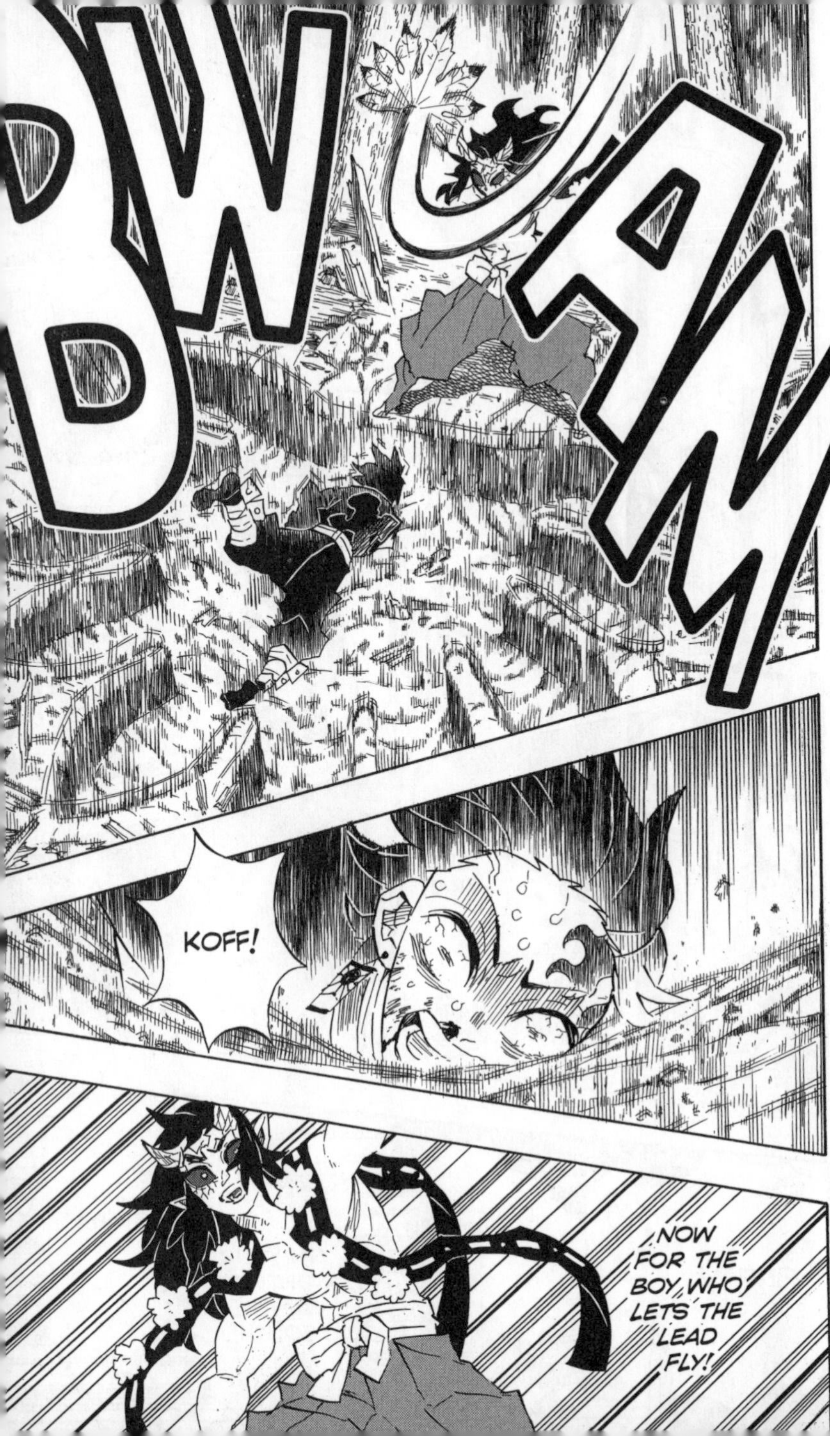
DWAM
KOFF!
NOW FOR THE BOY WHO LETS THE LEAD FLY!

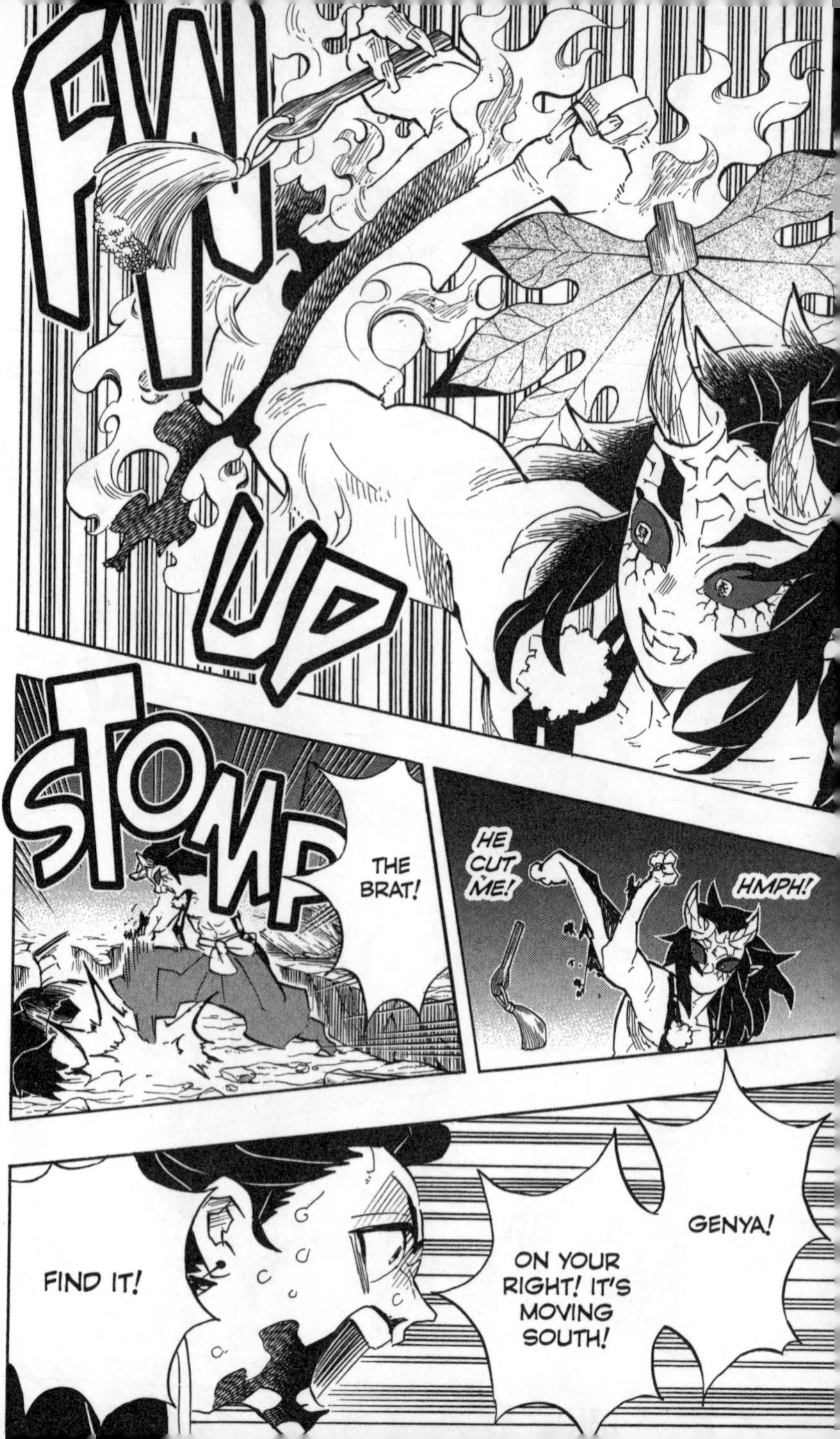
FWUP
HMPH!
HE CUT ME!
THE BRAT!
STOMP
GENYA!
ON YOUR RIGHT! IT'S MOVING SOUTH!
FIND IT!

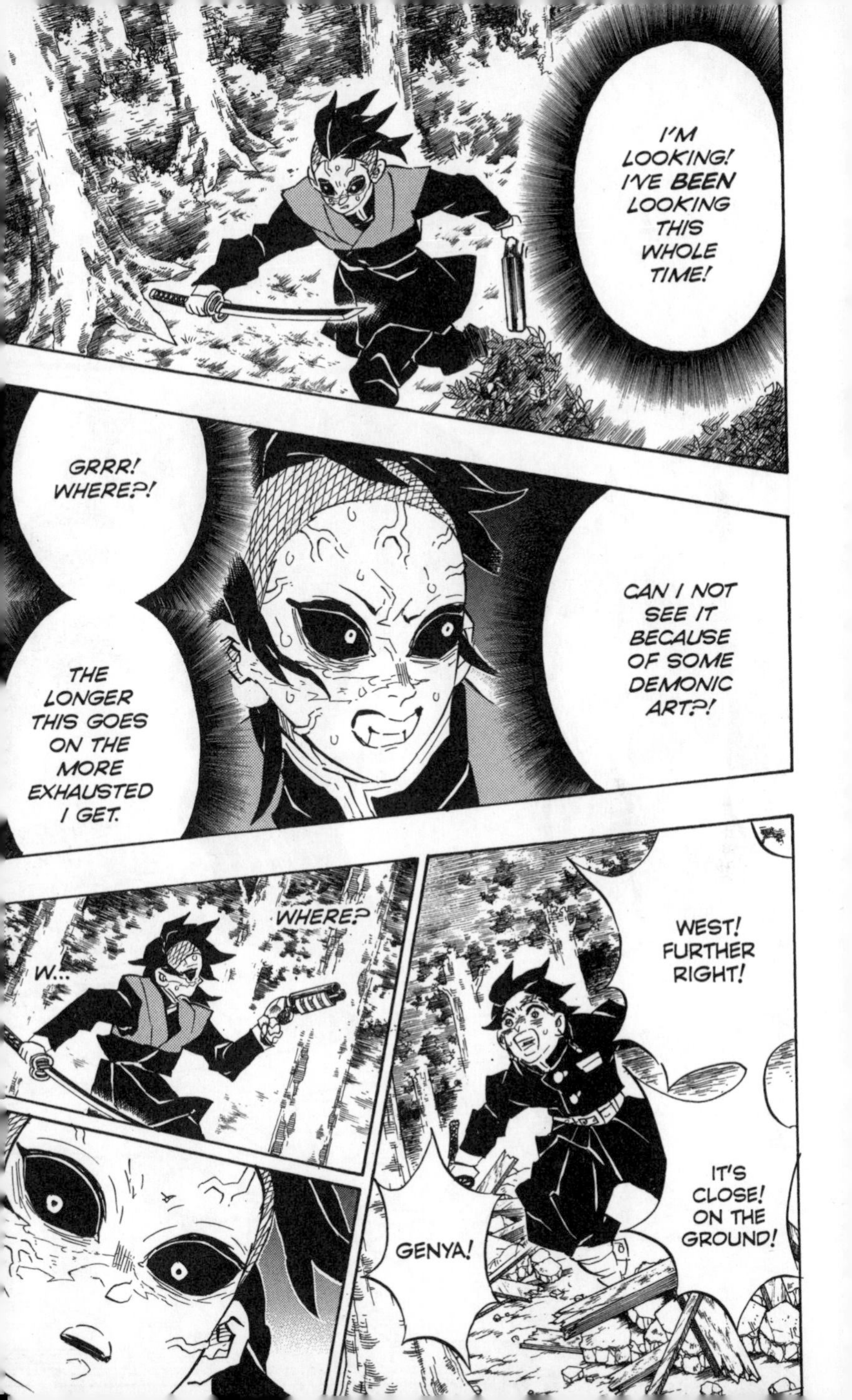
I'M LOOKING! I'VE BEEN LOOKING THIS WHOLE TIME!
CAN I NOT SEE IT BECAUSE OF SOME DEMONIC ART?!
GRRR! WHERE?!
THE LONGER THIS GOES ON THE MORE EXHAUSTED I GET.
WEST! FURTHER RIGHT!
IT'S CLOSE! ON THE GROUND!
GENYA!
WHERE?
W...

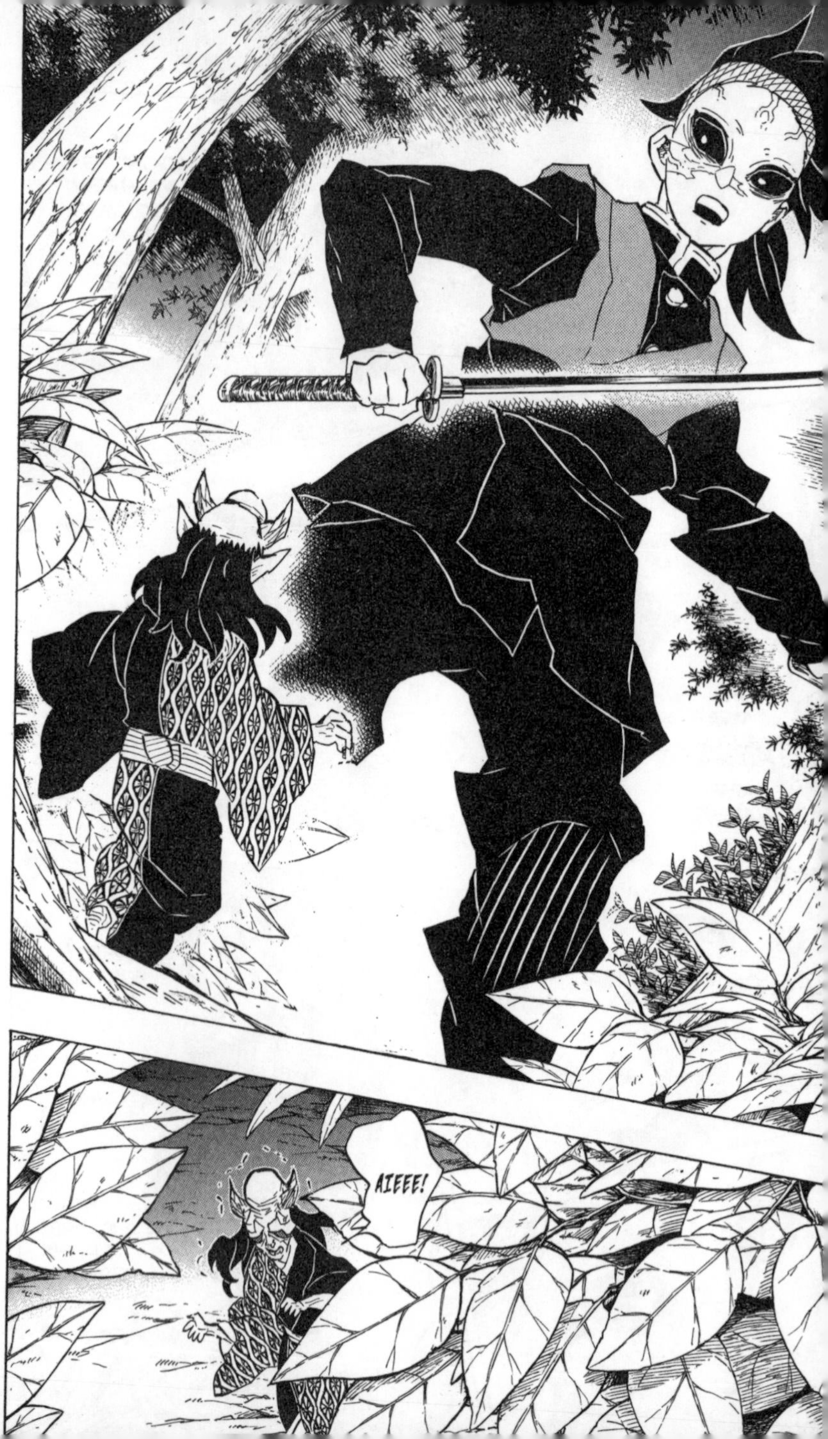
AIEEE!

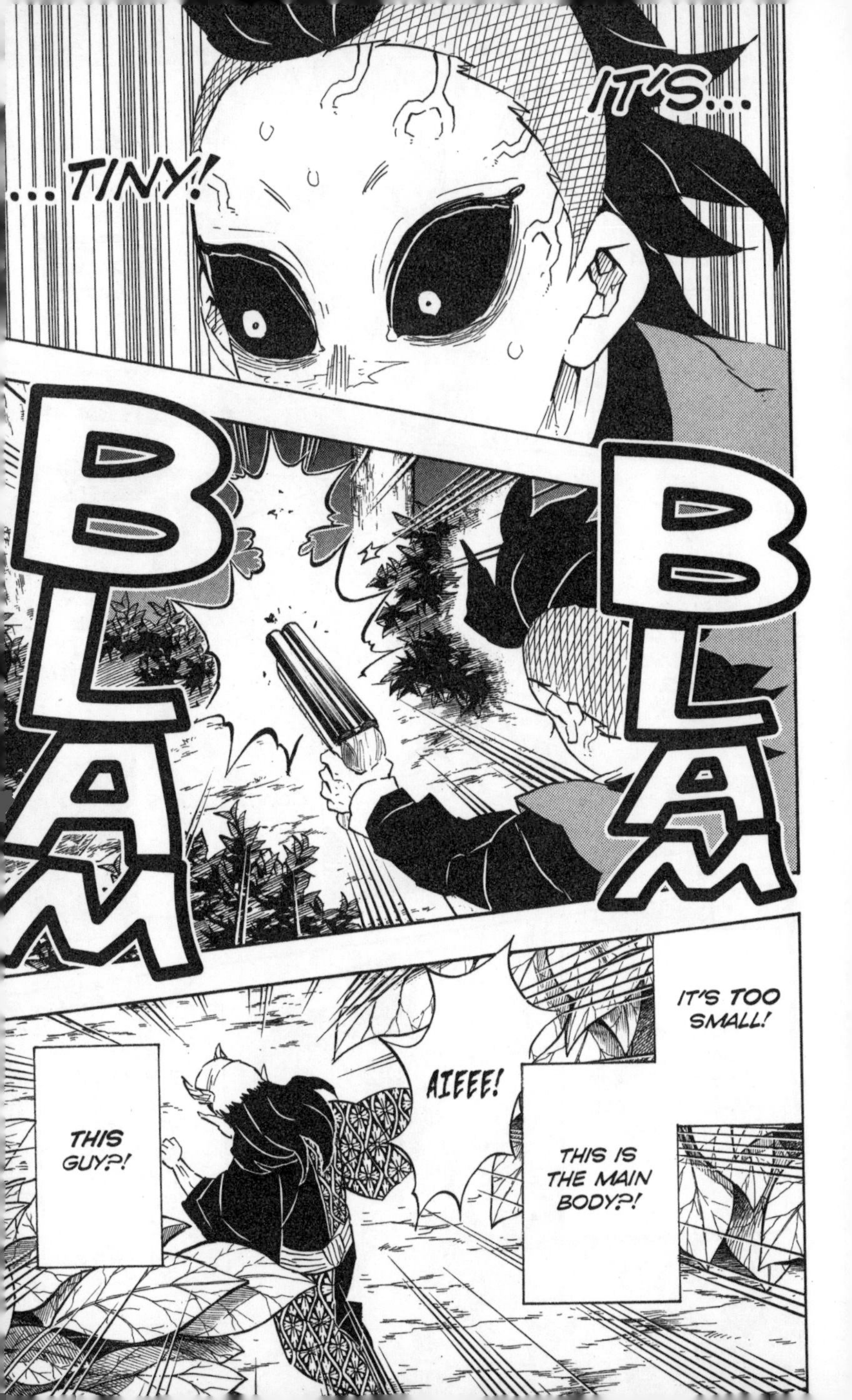
IT'S...
...TINY!
BLAM
BLAM
IT'S TOO SMALL!
THIS IS THE MAIN BODY?!
AIEEE!
THIS GUY?!

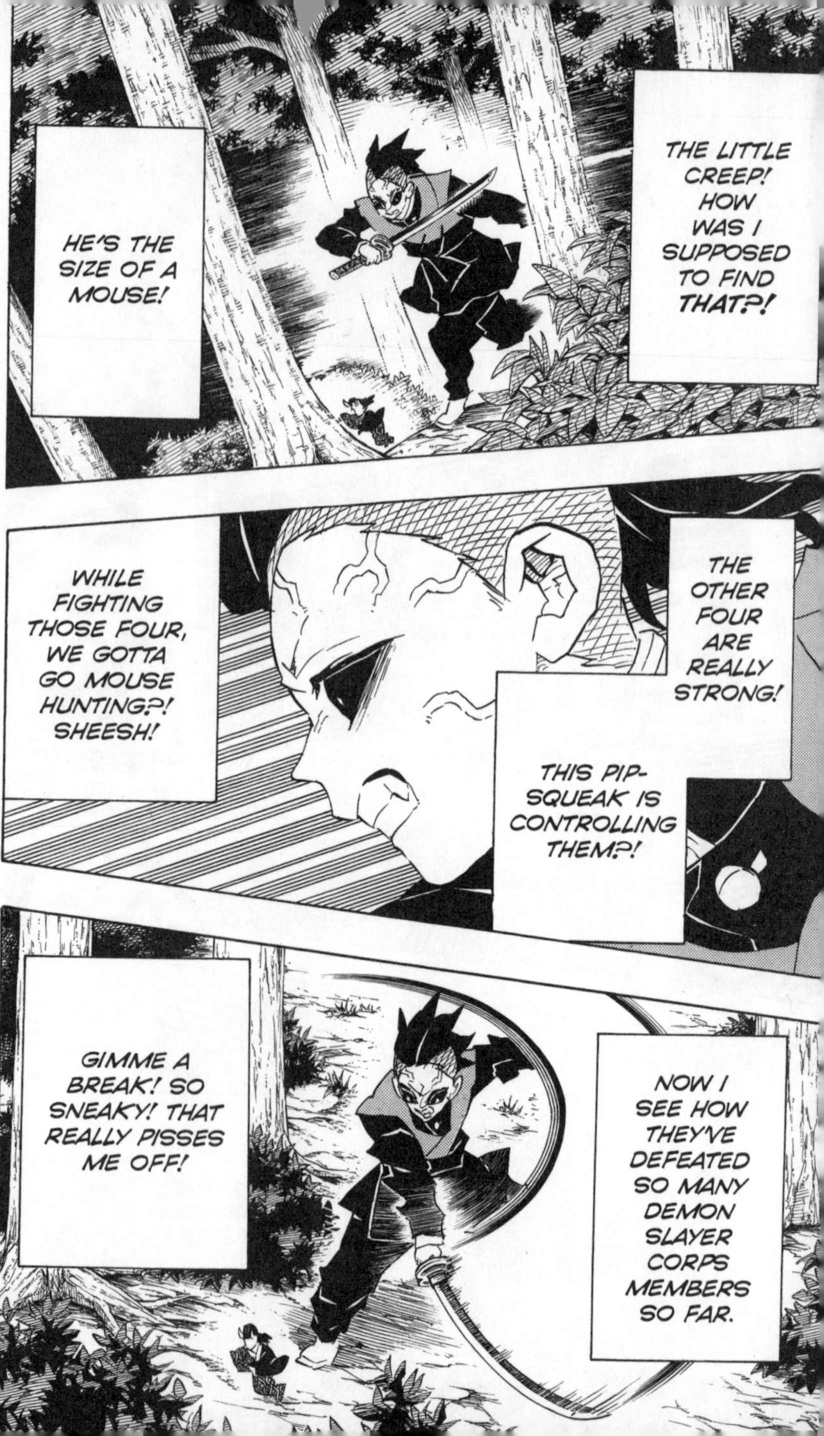
THE LITTLE CREEP! HOW WAS I SUPPOSED TO FIND THAT?!
HE'S THE SIZE OF A MOUSE!
THE OTHER FOUR ARE REALLY STRONG!
THIS PIP-SQUEAK IS CONTROLLING THEM?!
WHILE FIGHTING THOSE FOUR, WE GOTTA GO MOUSE HUNTING?! SHEESH!
NOW I SEE HOW THEY'VE DEFEATED SO MANY DEMON SLAYER CORPS MEMBERS SO FAR.
GIMME A BREAK! SO SNEAKY! THAT REALLY PISSES ME OFF!

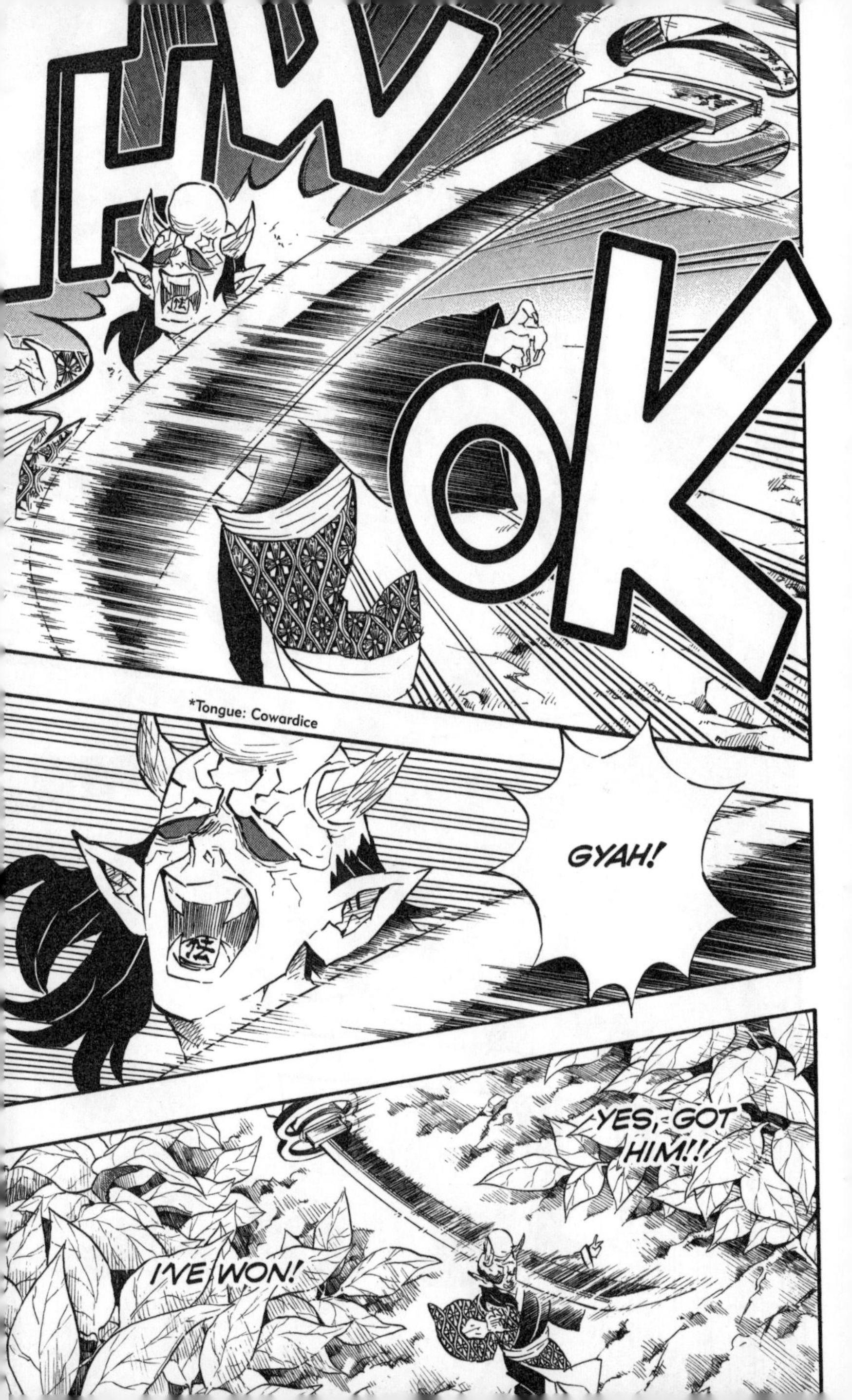
HW
OK
*Tongue: Cowardice
GYAH!
YES, GOT HIM!!
I'VE WON!

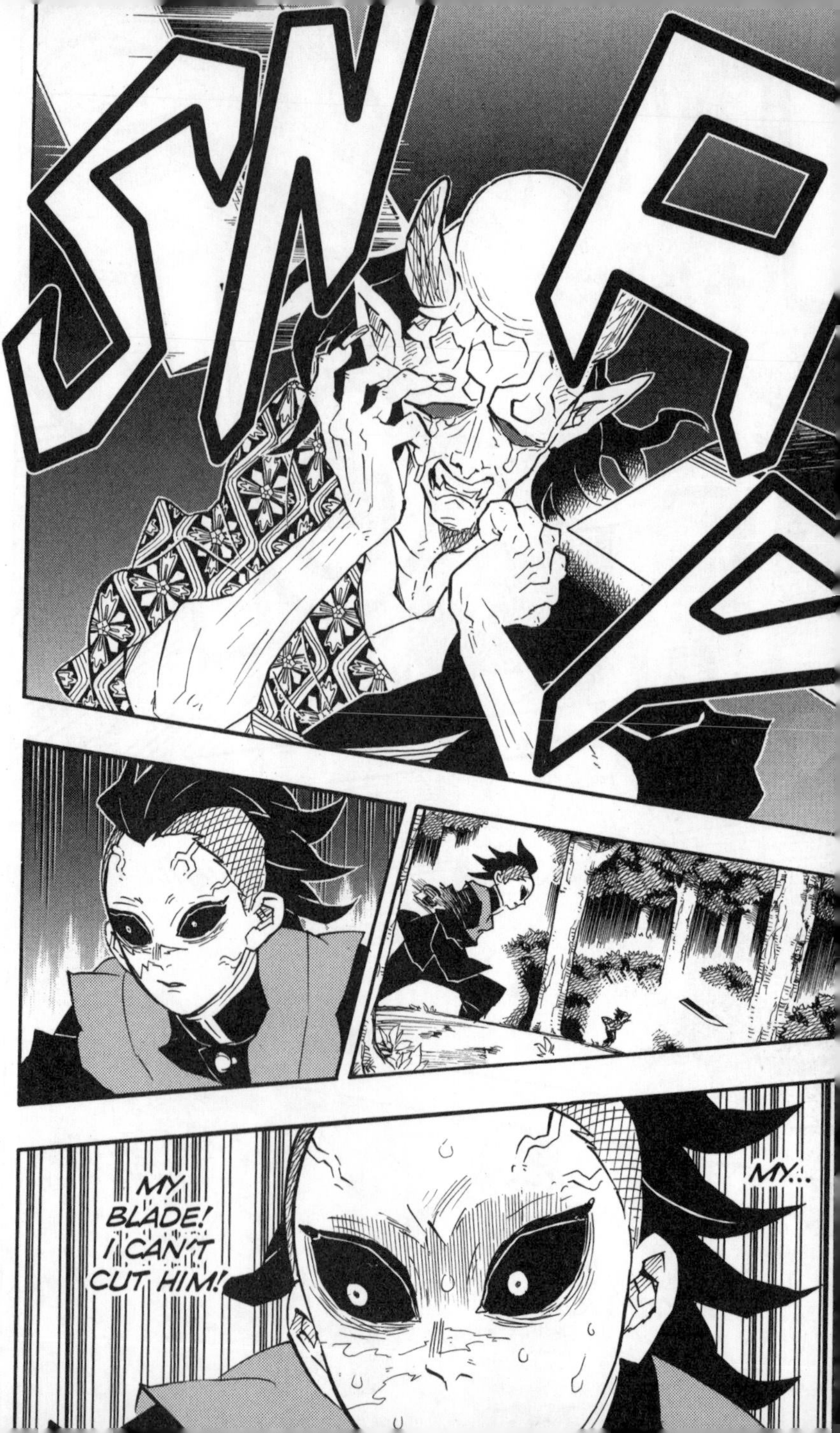
MY...
MY BLADE! I CAN'T CUT HIM!

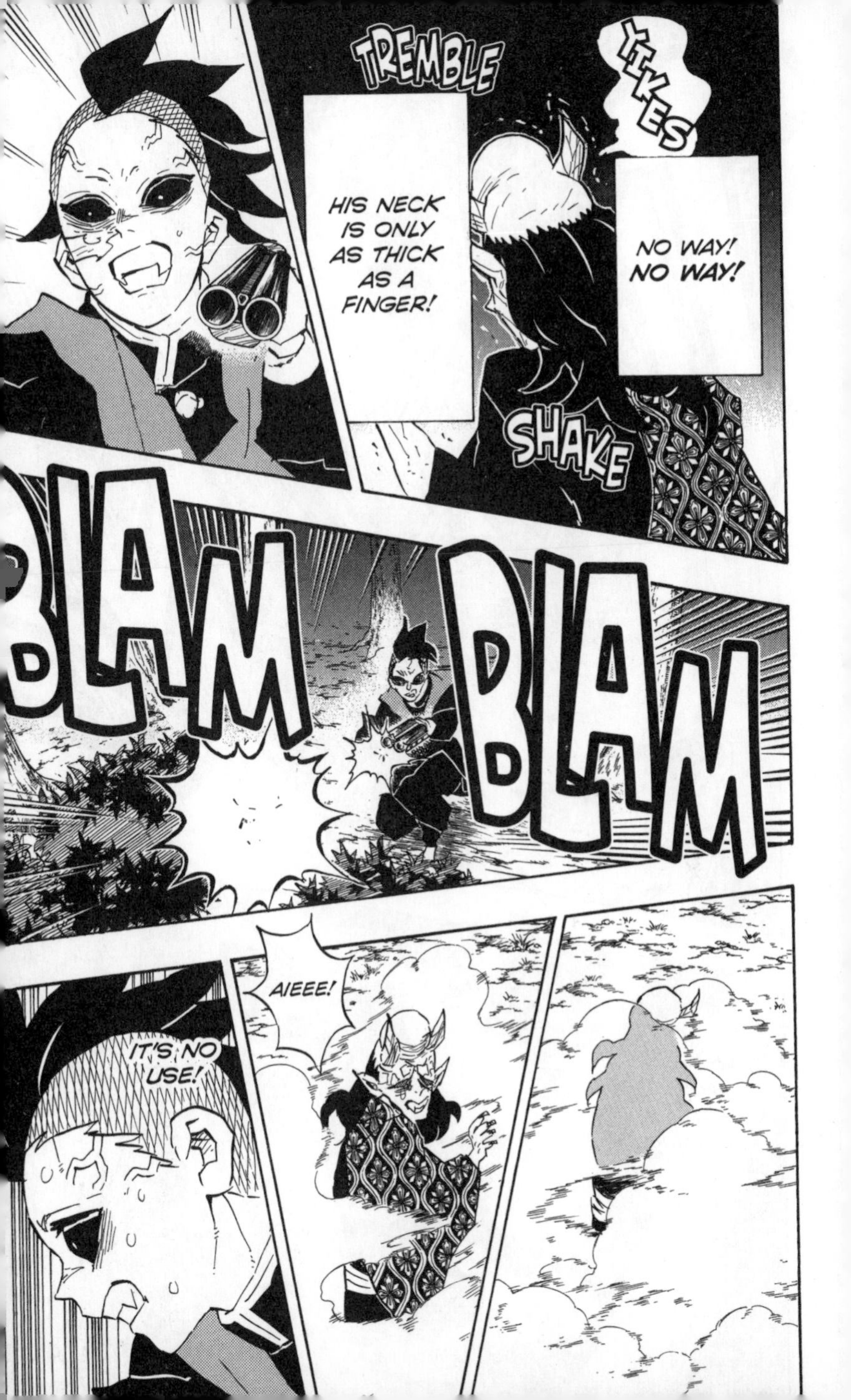
YIKES
NO WAY! NO WAY!
SHAKE
TREMBLE
HIS NECK IS ONLY AS THICK AS A FINGER!
BLAM
BLAM
AIEEE!
IT'S NO USE!

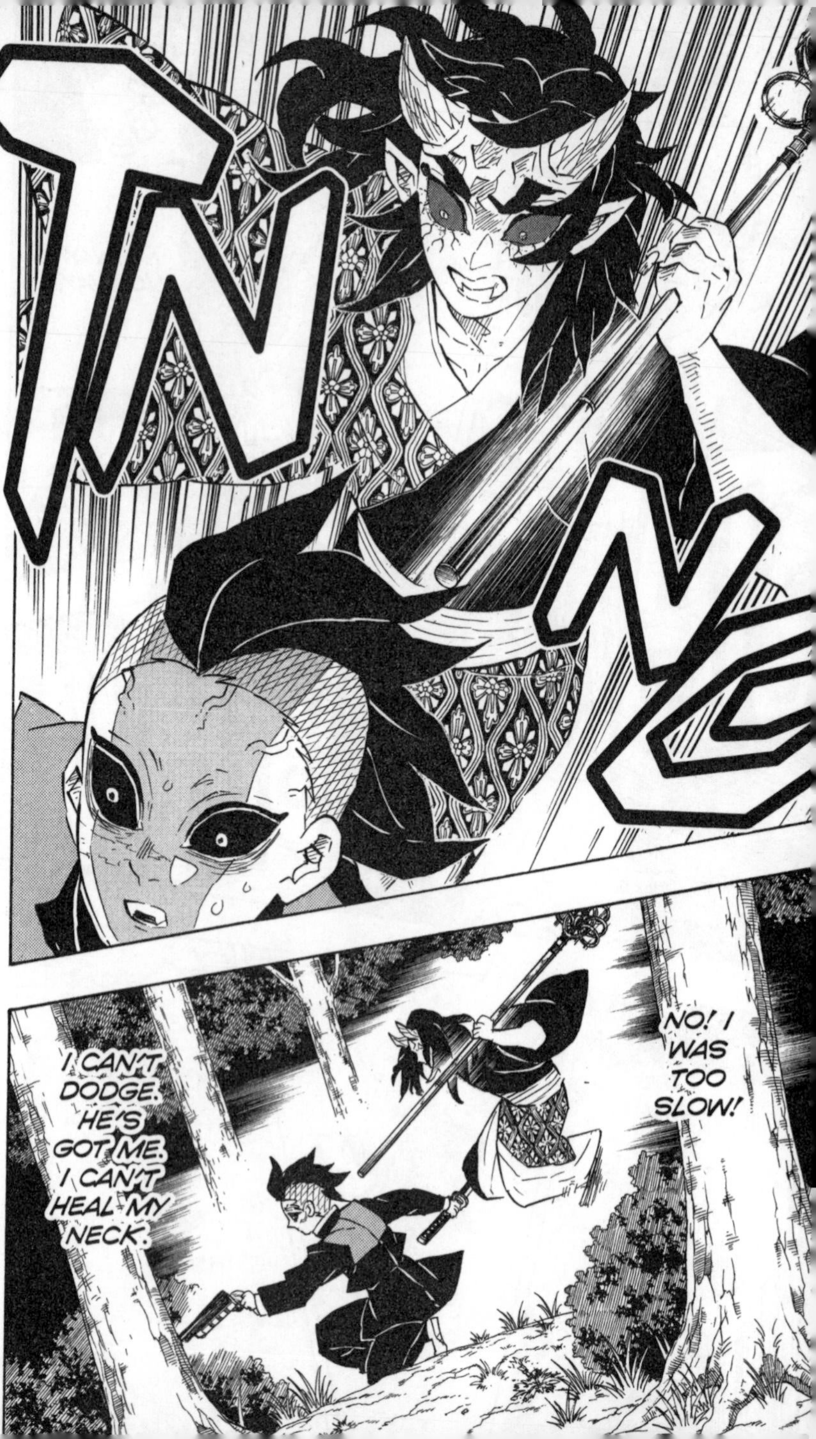
TNNG
NO! I WAS TOO SLOW!
I CAN'T DODGE. HE'S GOT ME. I CAN'T HEAL MY NECK.

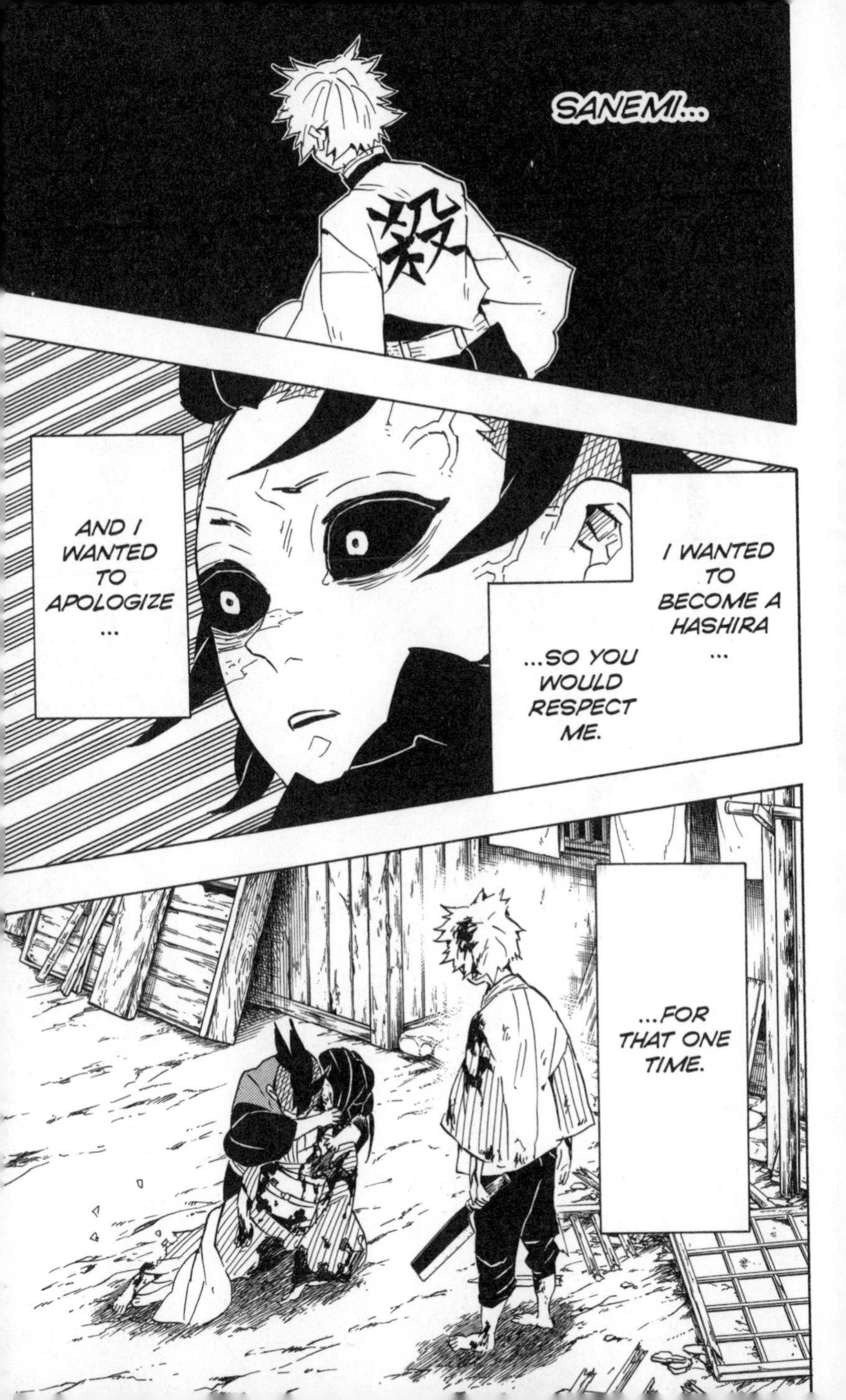
SANEMI...
殺
I WANTED TO BECOME A HASHIRA ...
...SO YOU WOULD RESPECT ME.
AND I WANTED TO APOLOGIZE ...
...FOR THAT ONE TIME.

Junior High and High School☆ Kimetsu Academy Story!

The Shabana siblings—the academy's foremost delinquents. They frequently get in fights and often clash with Tanjiro. The sister, Ume, is beautiful, so she has many fans giving her a never-ending stream of presents. She set a school record when 20 boys asked her out in a single day. She's one of the Three Great Beauties of the Academy.

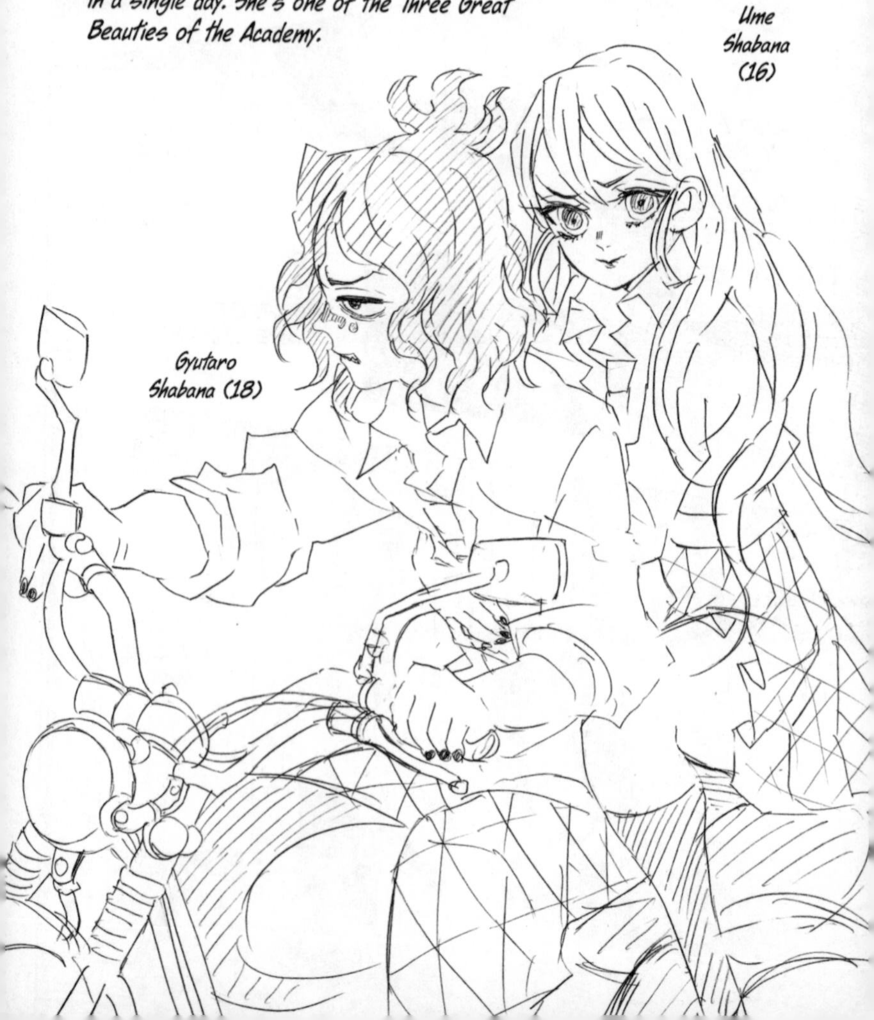
Ume Shabana (16)
Gyutaro Shabana (18)

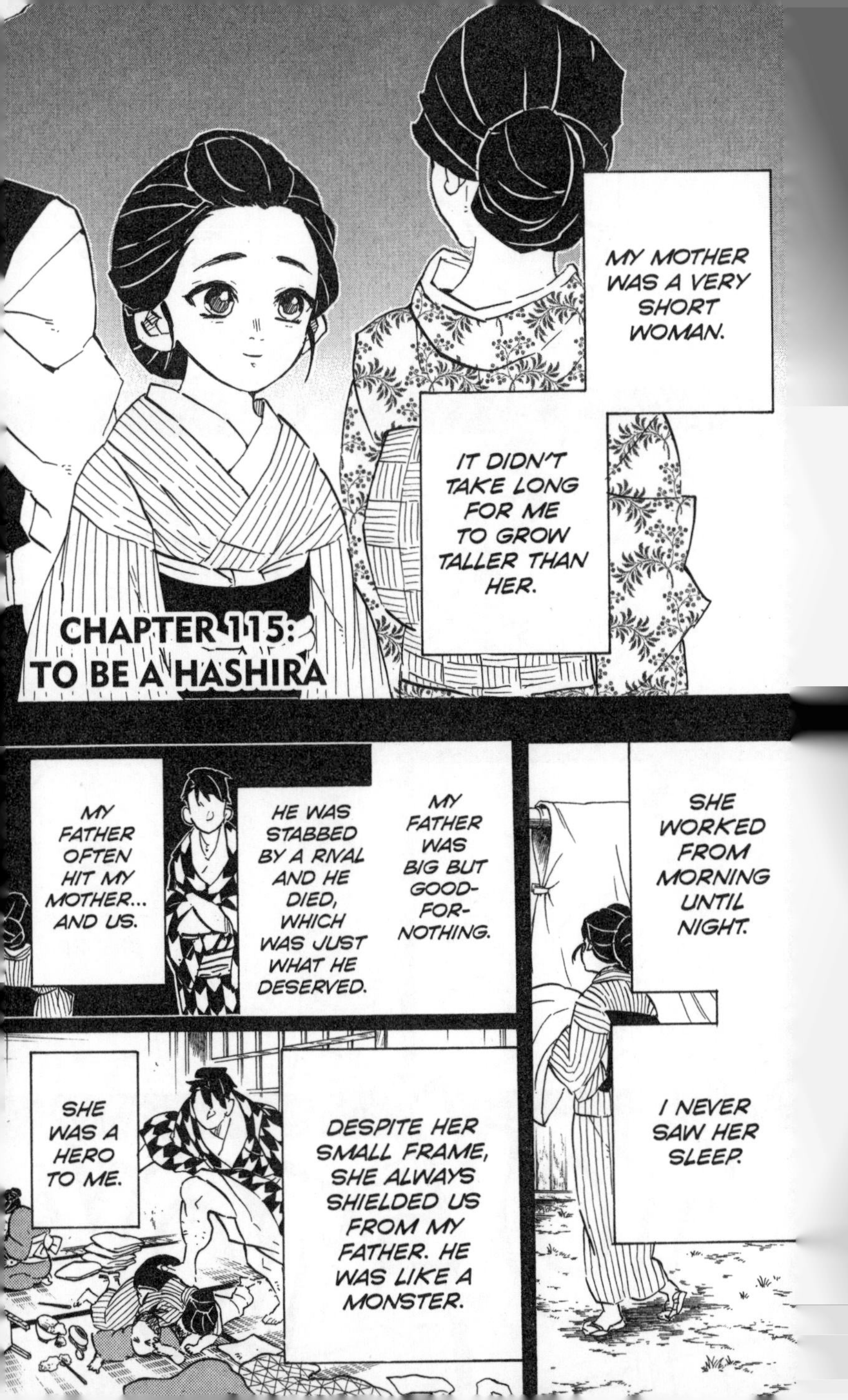
MY MOTHER WAS A VERY SHORT WOMAN.
IT DIDN'T TAKE LONG FOR ME TO GROW TALLER THAN HER.
CHAPTER 115: TO BE A HASHIRA
SHE WORKED FROM MORNING UNTIL NIGHT.
I NEVER SAW HER SLEEP.
MY FATHER WAS BIG BUT GOOD-FOR-NOTHING.
HE WAS STABBED BY A RIVAL AND HE DIED, WHICH WAS JUST WHAT HE DESERVED.
MY FATHER OFTEN HIT MY MOTHER... AND US.
DESPITE HER SMALL FRAME, SHE ALWAYS SHIELDED US FROM MY FATHER. HE WAS LIKE A MONSTER.
SHE WAS A HERO TO ME.

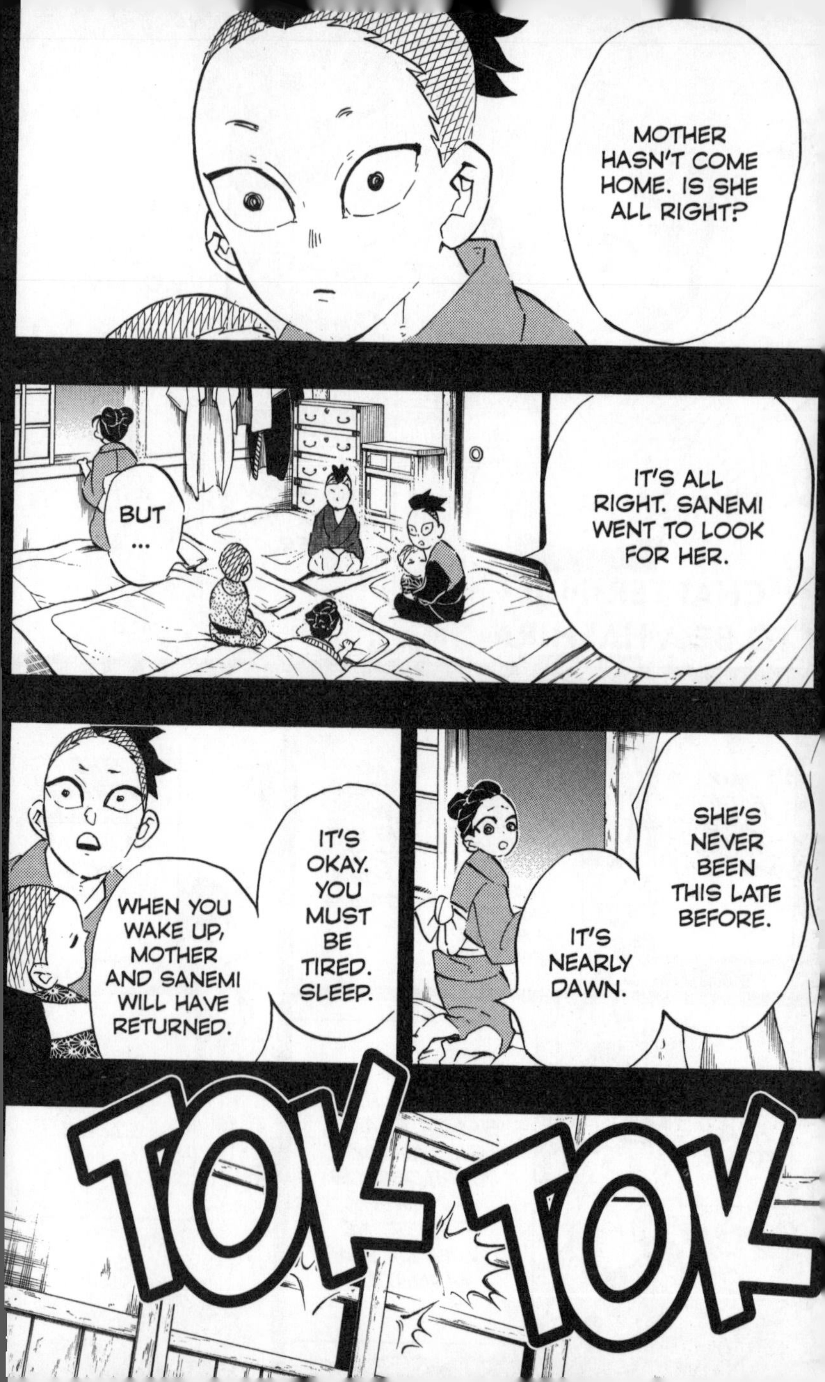

MOTHER HASN'T COME HOME. IS SHE ALL RIGHT?
IT'S ALL RIGHT. SANEMI WENT TO LOOK FOR HER.
BUT ...
SHE'S NEVER BEEN THIS LATE BEFORE.
IT'S NEARLY DAWN.
IT'S OKAY. YOU MUST BE TIRED. SLEEP.
WHEN YOU WAKE UP, MOTHER AND SANEMI WILL HAVE RETURNED.
TOK TOK

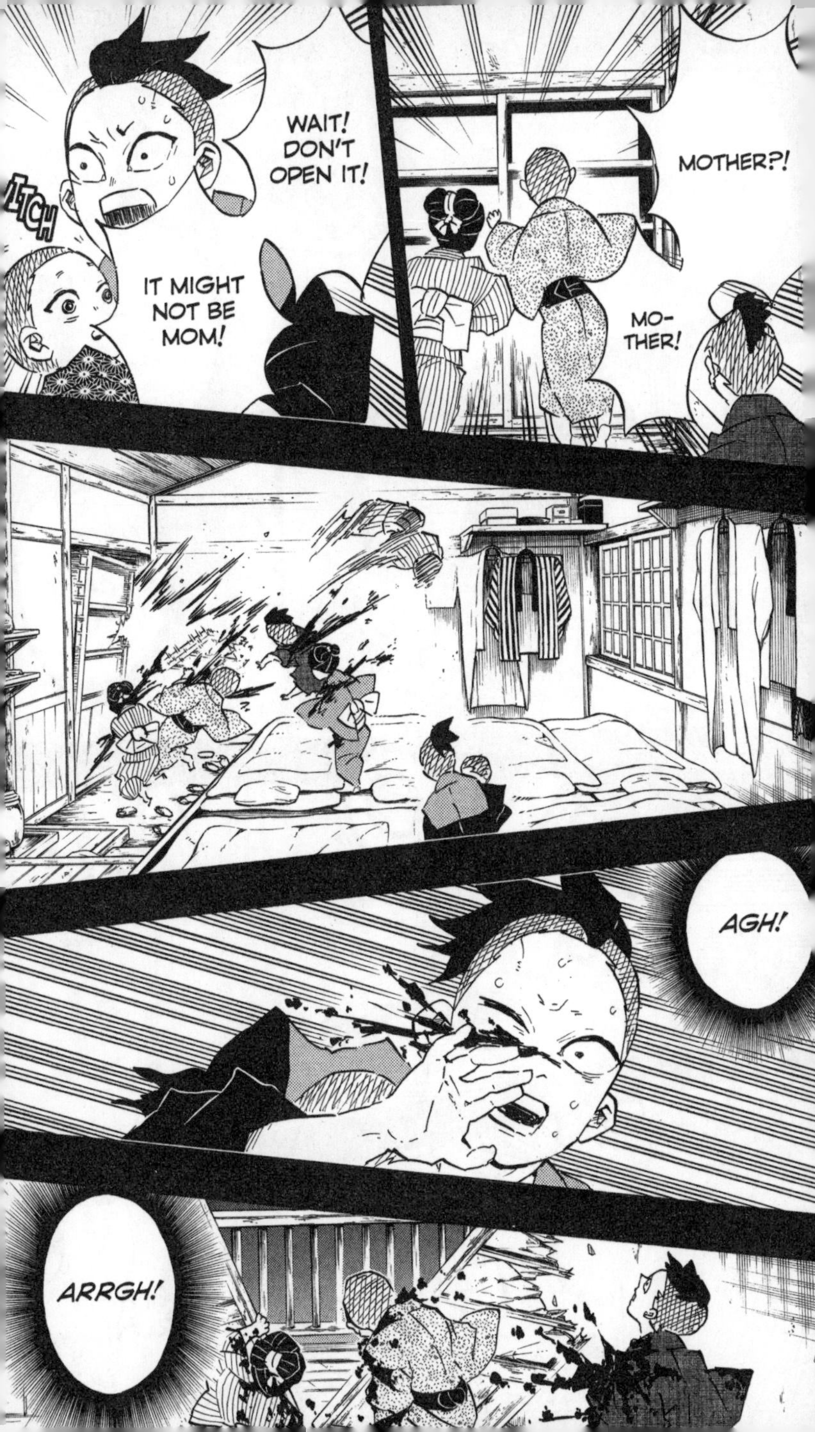
MOTHER?!
MO-THER!
WAIT! DON'T OPEN IT!
IT MIGHT NOT BE MOM!
AGH!
ARRGH!

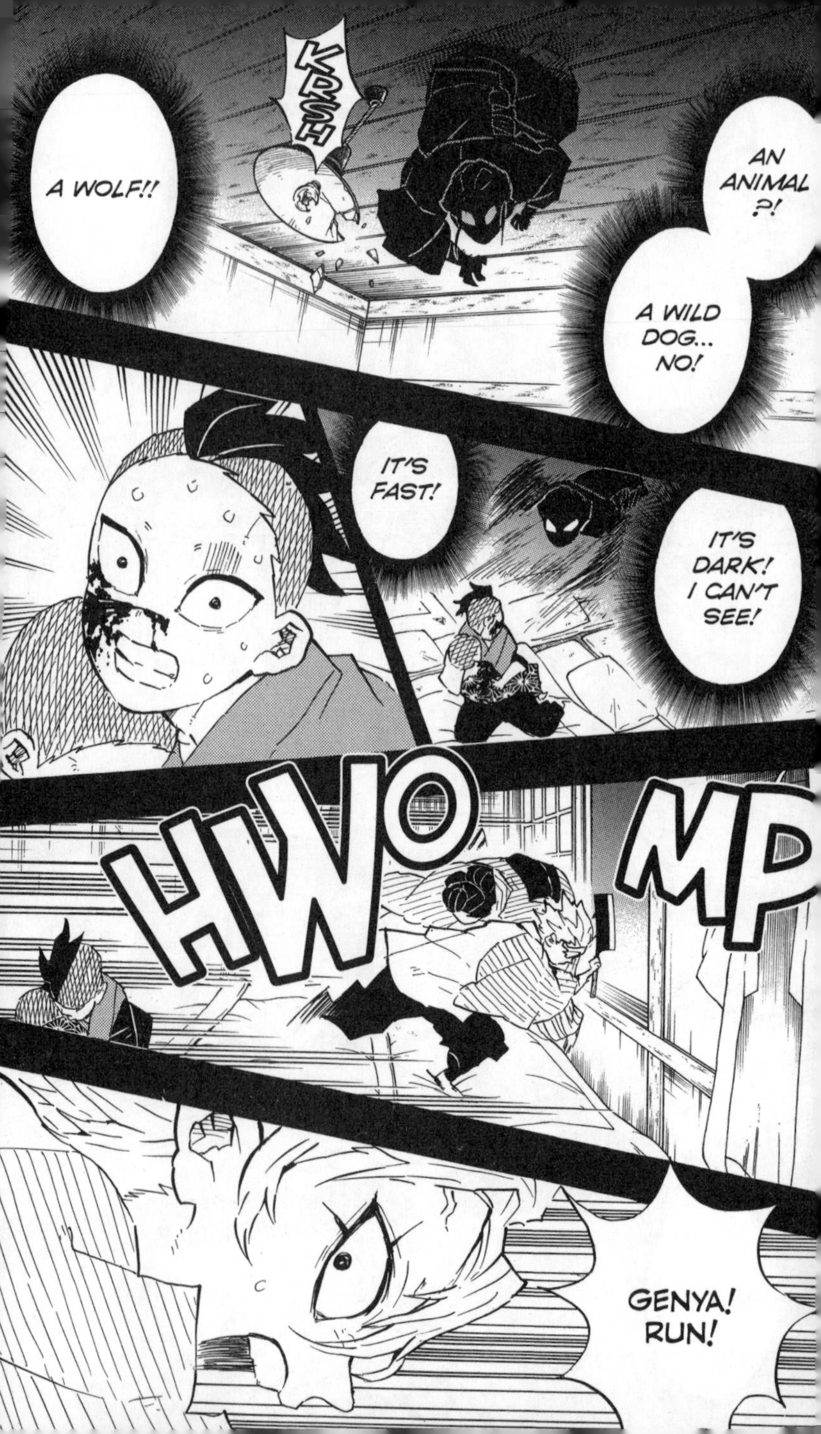
AN ANIMAL?!
A WILD DOG... NO!
KRSH
A WOLF!!
IT'S DARK! I CAN'T SEE!
IT'S FAST!
HWOMP
GENYA! RUN!

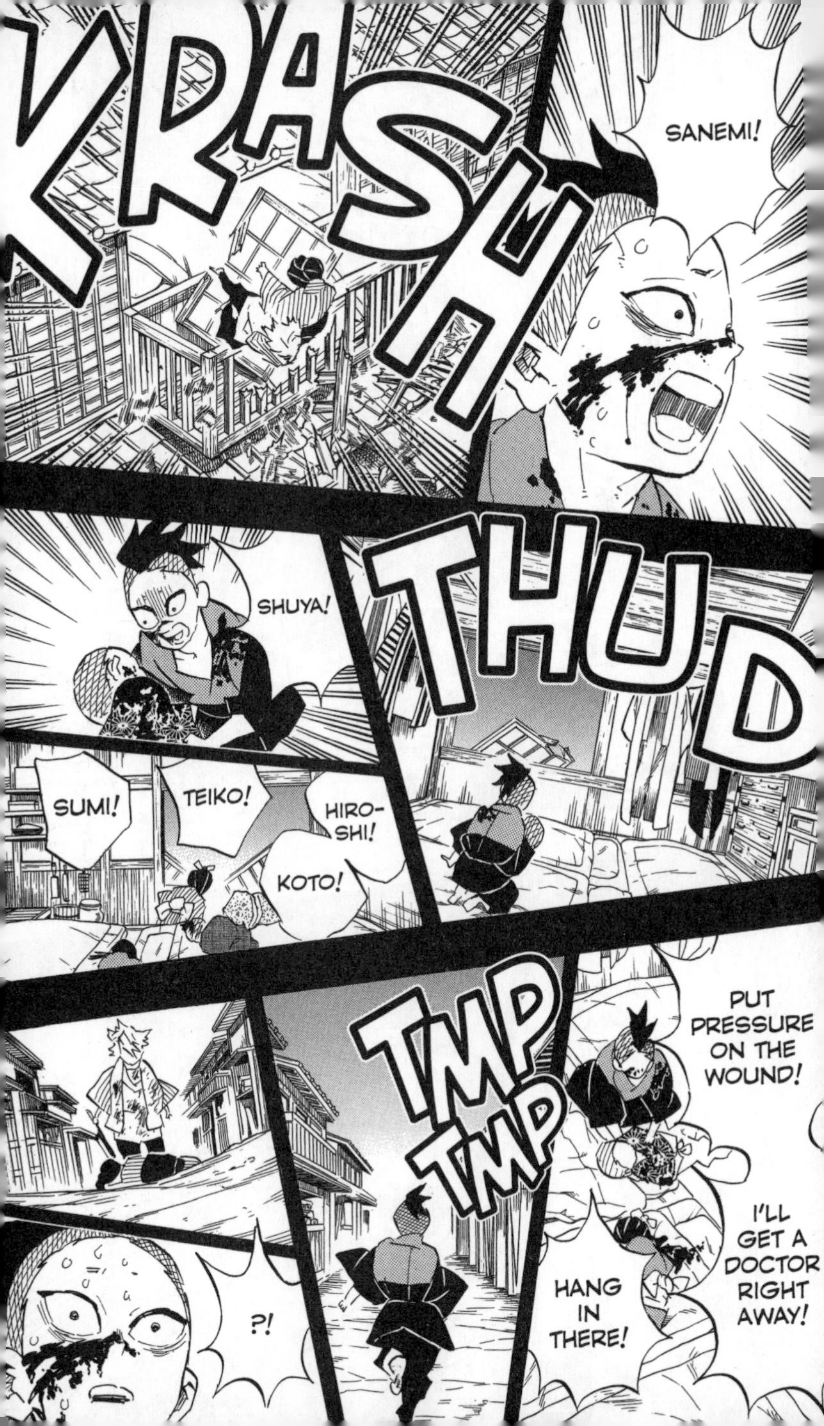
SANEMI!
KRASH
THUD
SHUYA!
HIRO-SHI!
TEIKO!
SUMI!
KOTO!
PUT PRESSURE ON THE WOUND!
I'LL GET A DOCTOR RIGHT AWAY!
HANG IN THERE!
TMP TMP
?!

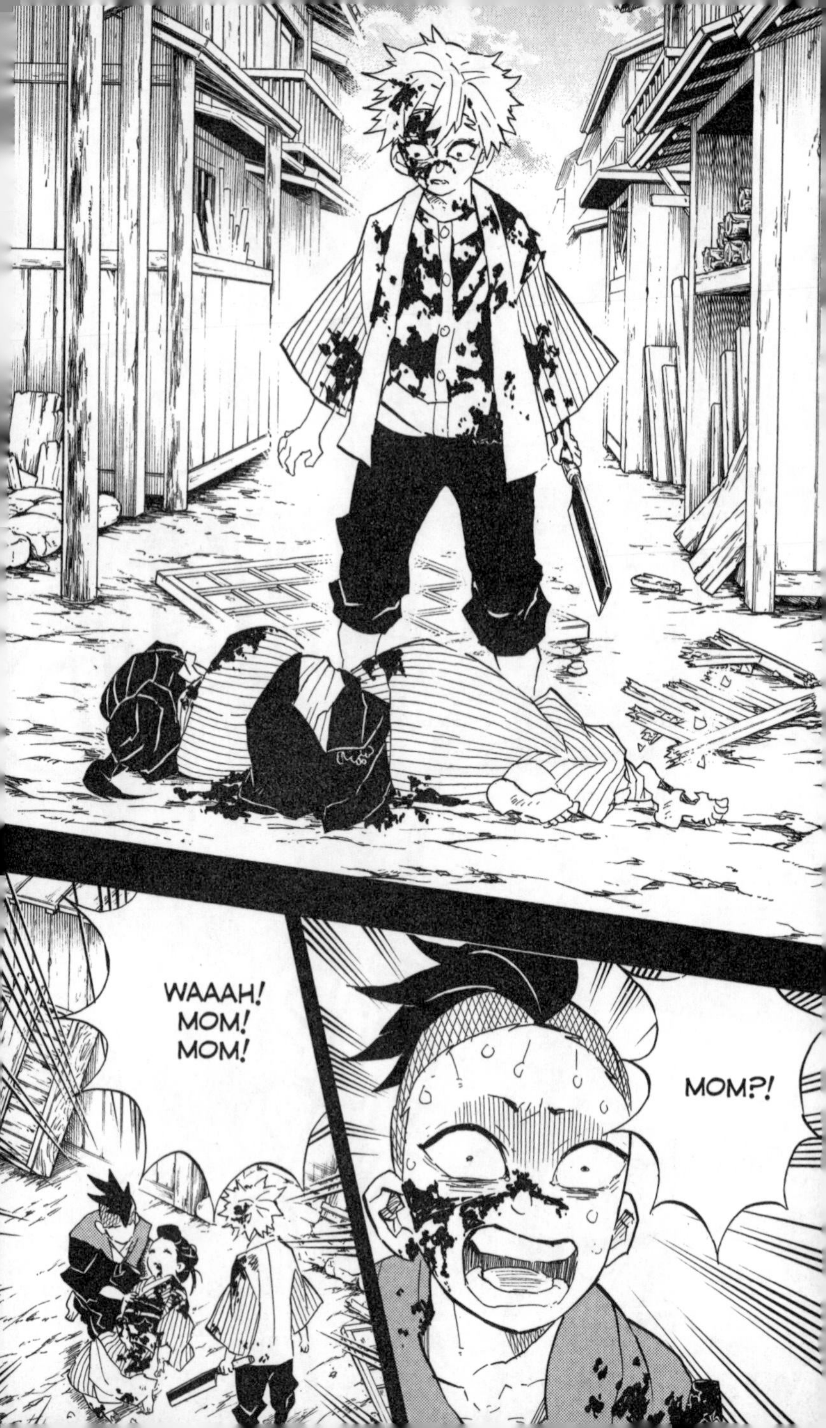
MOM?!
WAAAH! MOM! MOM!

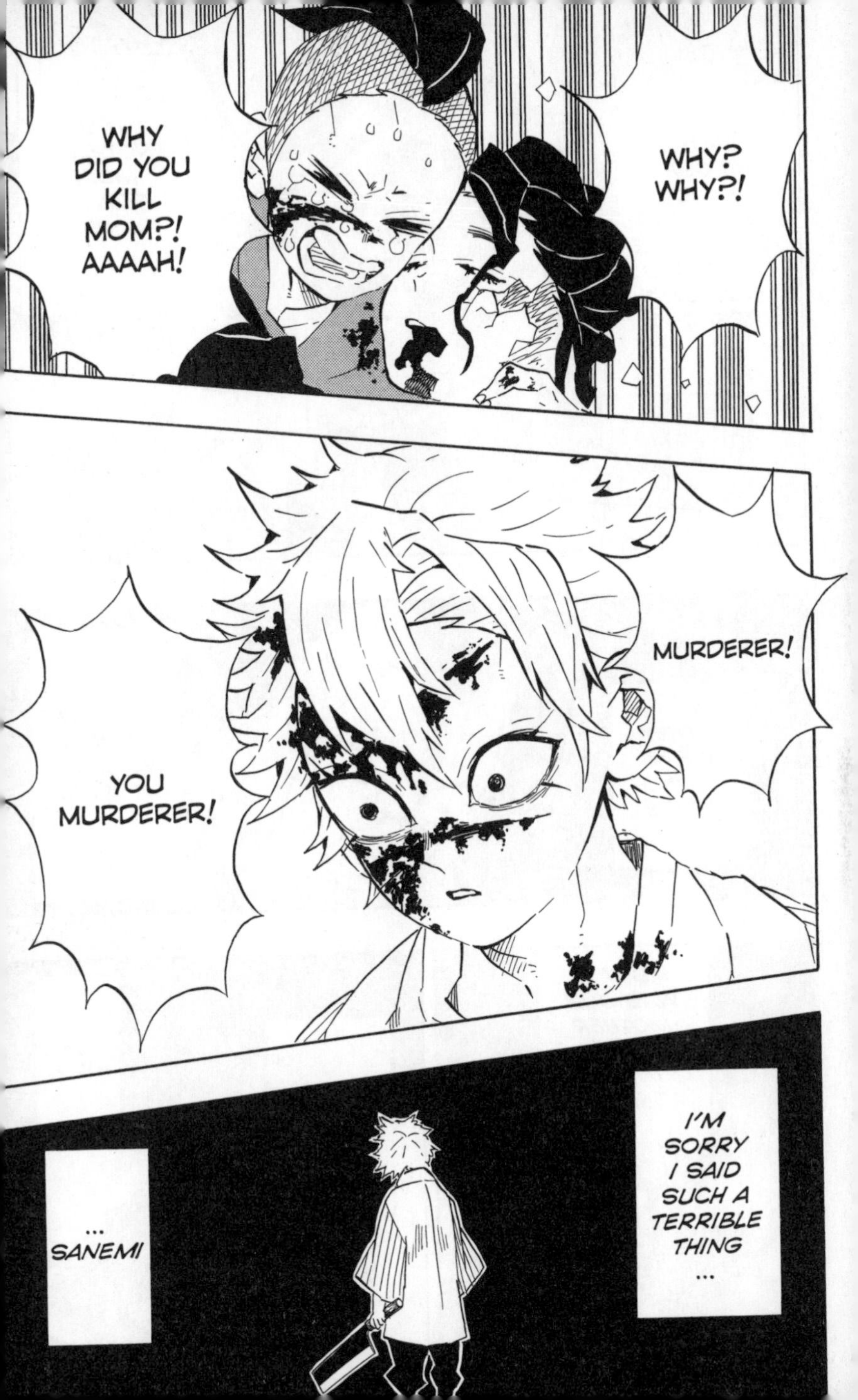
WHY? WHY?!
WHY DID YOU KILL MOM?! AAAAH!
MURDERER!
YOU MURDERER!
I'M SORRY I SAID SUCH A TERRIBLE THING ...
... SANEMI

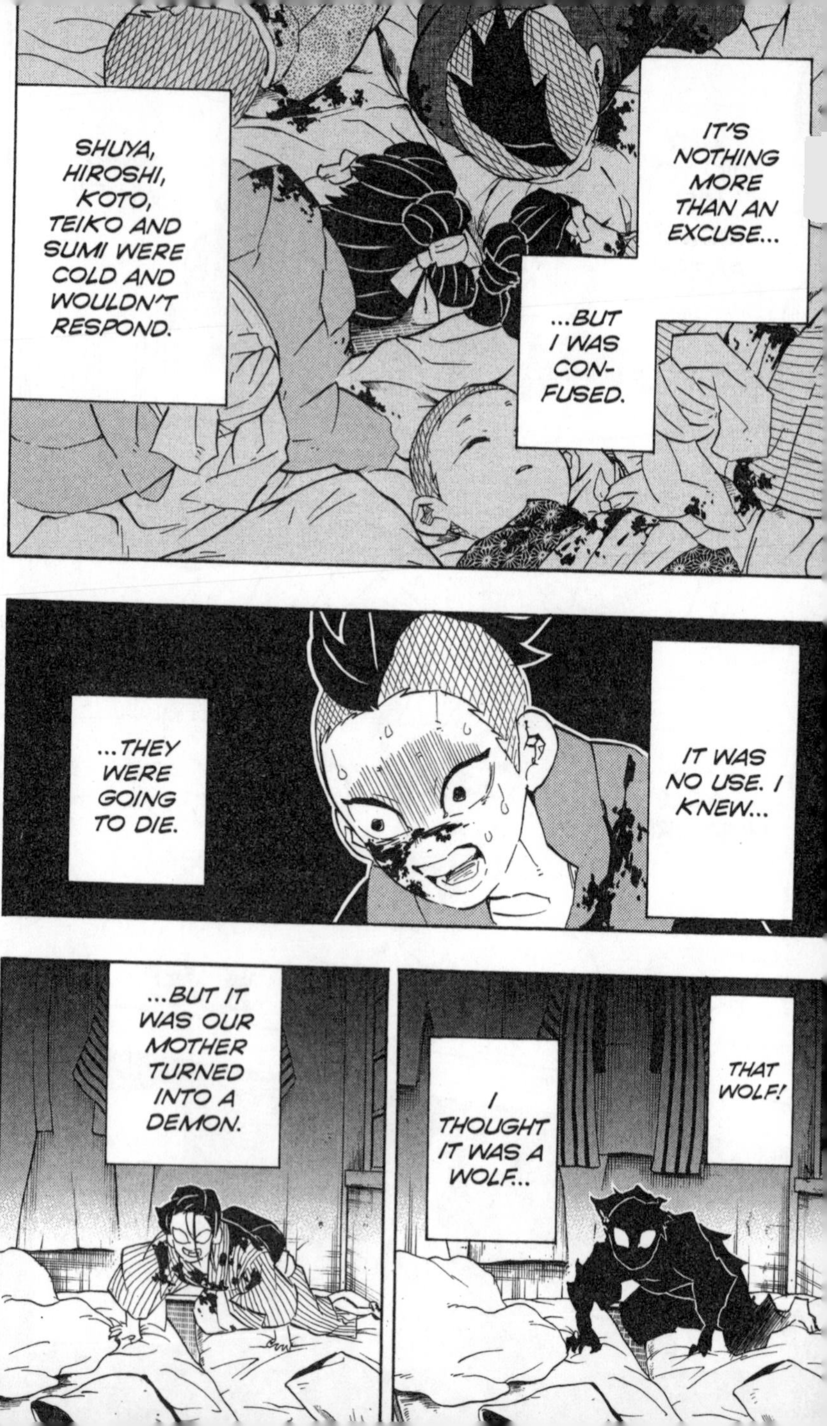
IT'S NOTHING MORE THAN AN EXCUSE...
...BUT I WAS CON-FUSED.
SHUYA, HIROSHI, KOTO, TEIKO AND SUMI WERE COLD AND WOULDN'T RESPOND.
IT WAS NO USE. I KNEW...
...THEY WERE GOING TO DIE.
THAT WOLF!
I THOUGHT IT WAS A WOLF...
...BUT IT WAS OUR MOTHER TURNED INTO A DEMON.

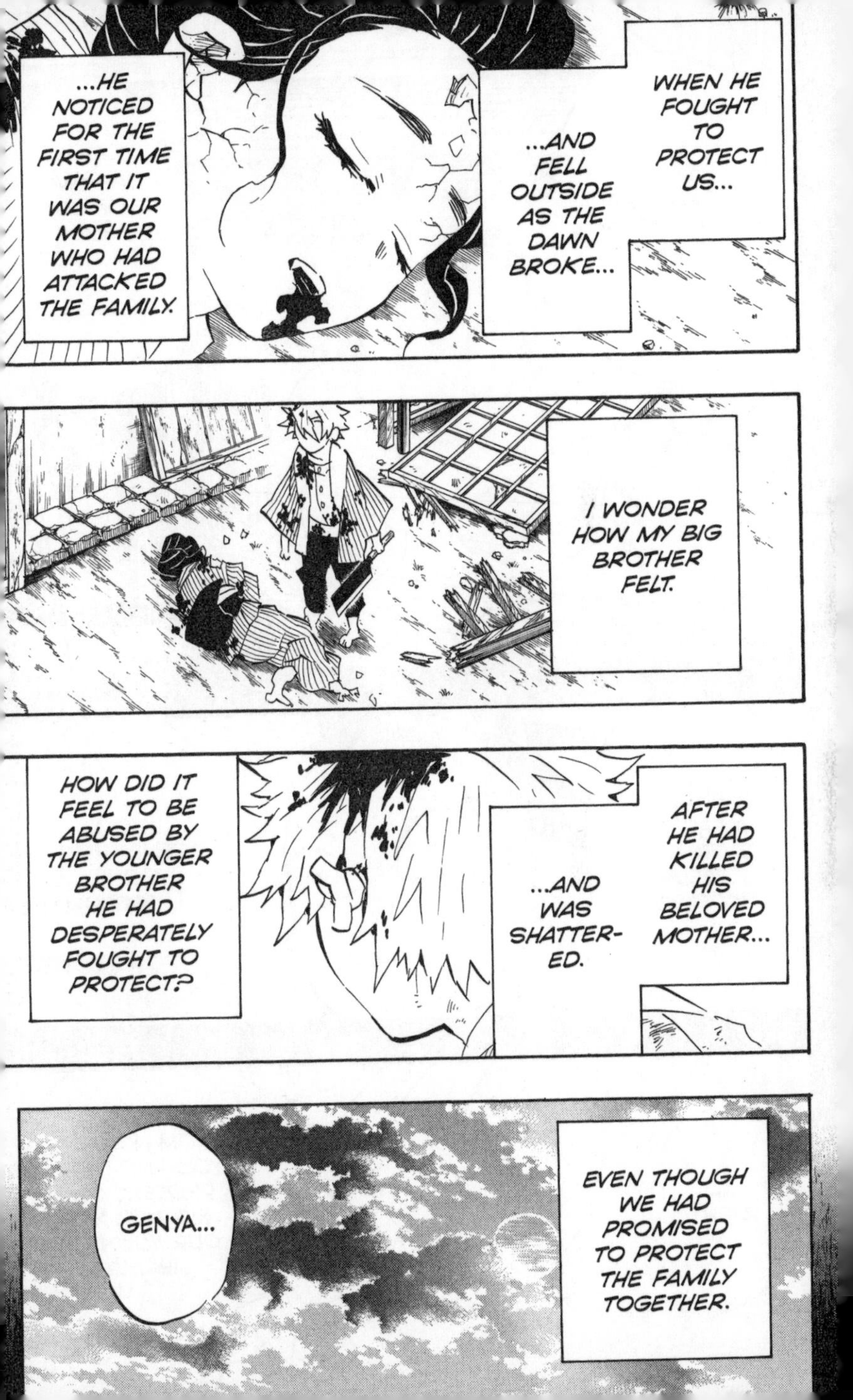
WHEN HE FOUGHT TO PROTECT US...
...AND FELL OUTSIDE AS THE DAWN BROKE...
...HE NOTICED FOR THE FIRST TIME THAT IT WAS OUR MOTHER WHO HAD ATTACKED THE FAMILY.
I WONDER HOW MY BIG BROTHER FELT.
AFTER HE HAD KILLED HIS BELOVED MOTHER...
...AND WAS SHATTER-ED.
HOW DID IT FEEL TO BE ABUSED BY THE YOUNGER BROTHER HE HAD DESPERATELY FOUGHT TO PROTECT?
EVEN THOUGH WE HAD PROMISED TO PROTECT THE FAMILY TOGETHER.
GENYA...

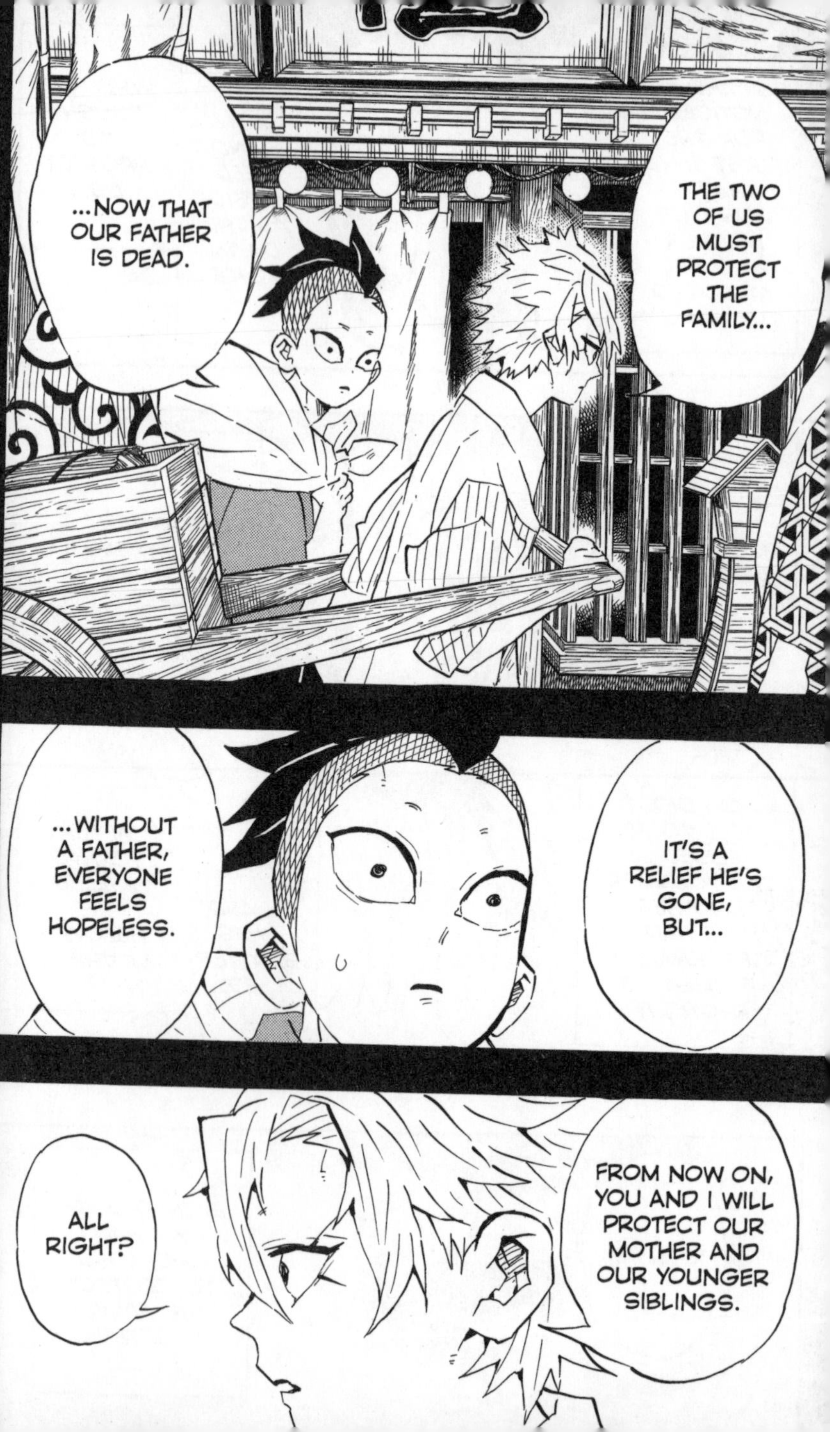
THE TWO OF US MUST PROTECT THE FAMILY...
...NOW THAT OUR FATHER IS DEAD.
IT'S A RELIEF HE'S GONE, BUT...
...WITHOUT A FATHER, EVERYONE FEELS HOPELESS.
FROM NOW ON, YOU AND I WILL PROTECT OUR MOTHER AND OUR YOUNGER SIBLINGS.
ALL RIGHT?

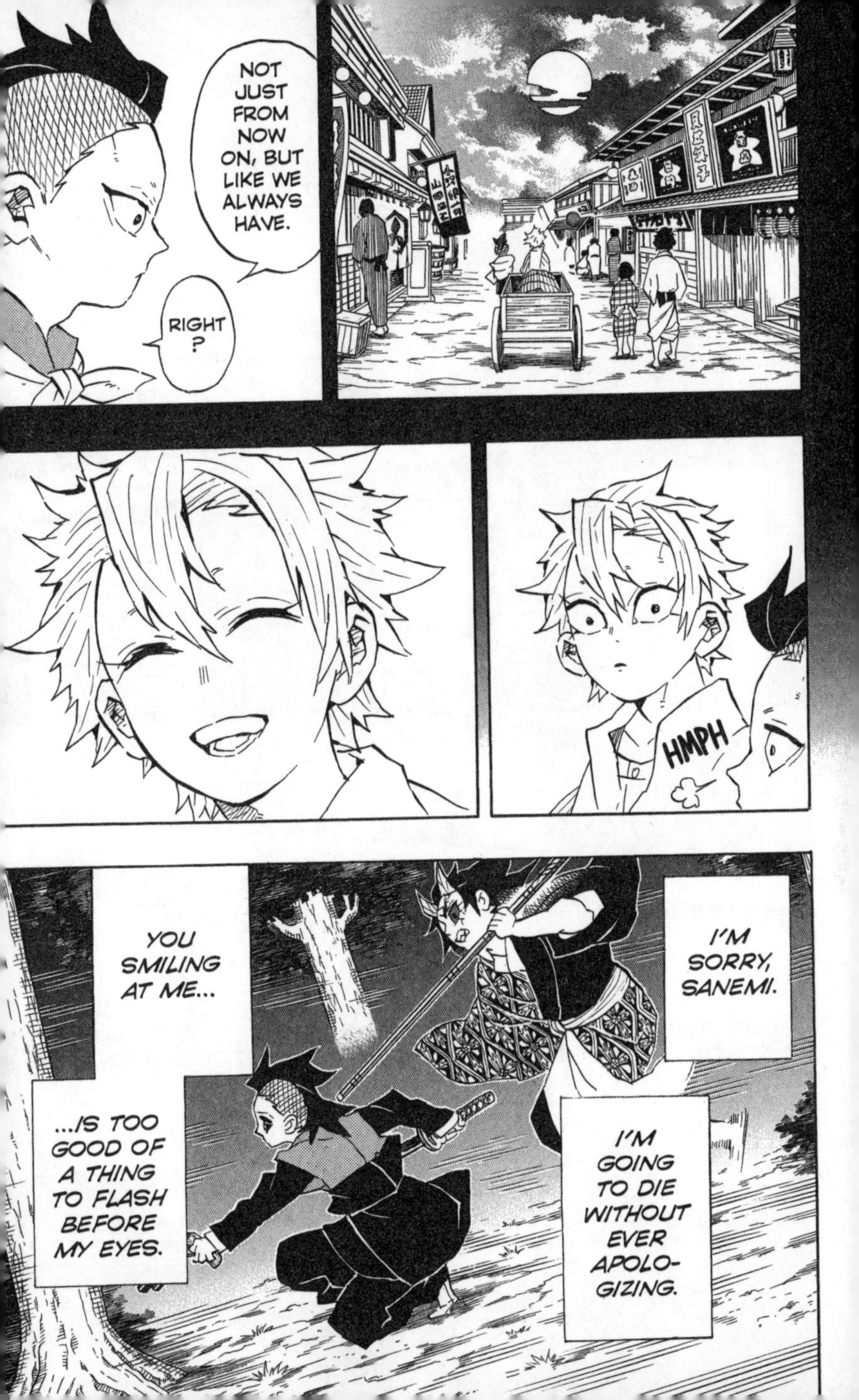
NOT JUST FROM NOW ON, BUT LIKE WE ALWAYS HAVE.
RIGHT?
HMPH
I'M SORRY, SANEMI.
YOU SMILING AT ME...
I'M GOING TO DIE WITHOUT EVER APOLOGIZING.
...IS TOO GOOD OF A THING TO FLASH BEFORE MY EYES.

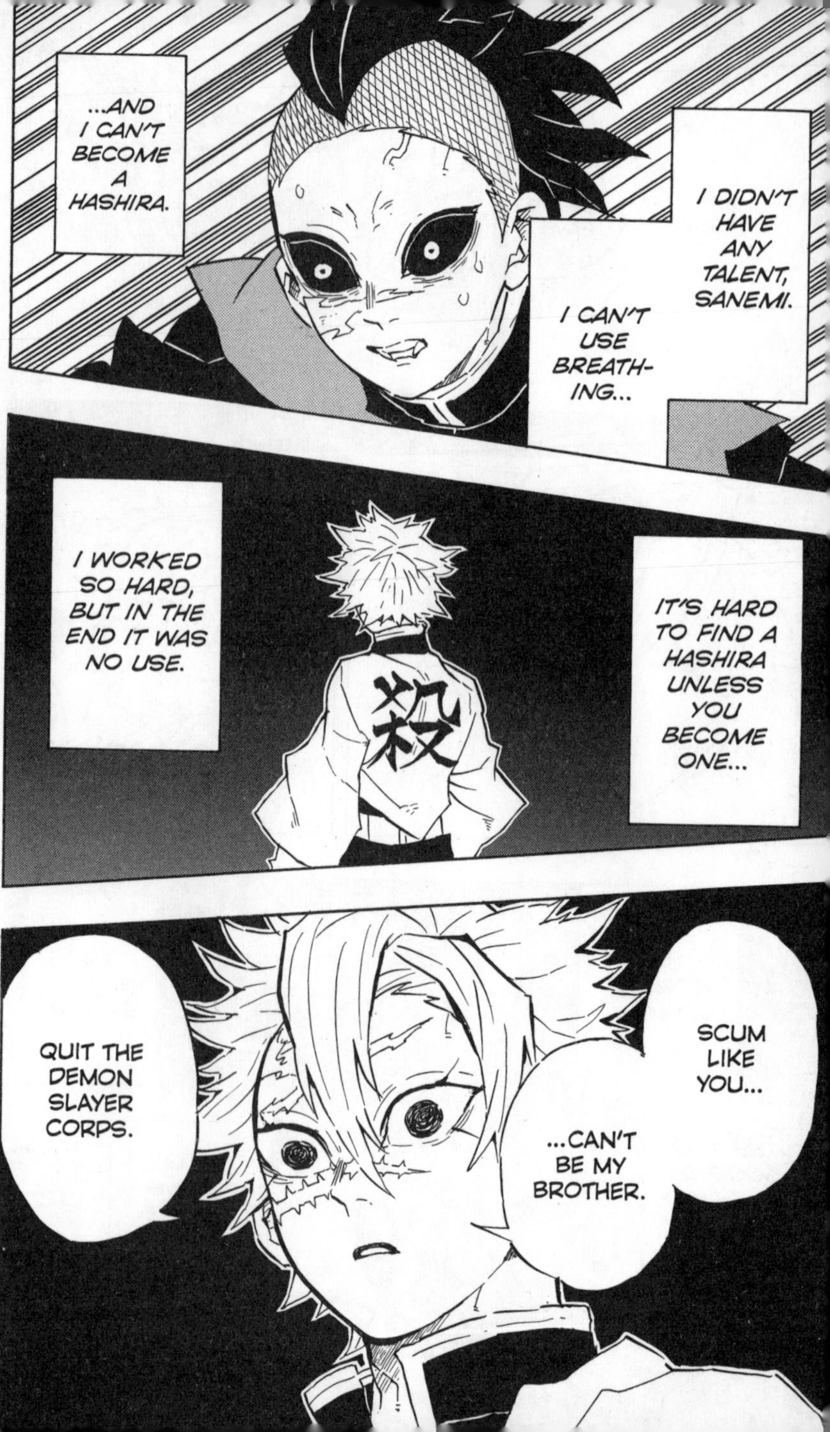
I DIDN'T HAVE ANY TALENT, SANEMI.
I CAN'T USE BREATHING...
...AND I CAN'T BECOME A HASHIRA.
IT'S HARD TO FIND A HASHIRA UNLESS YOU BECOME ONE...
殺
I WORKED SO HARD, BUT IN THE END IT WAS NO USE.
SCUM LIKE YOU...
...CAN'T BE MY BROTHER.
QUIT THE DEMON SLAYER CORPS.

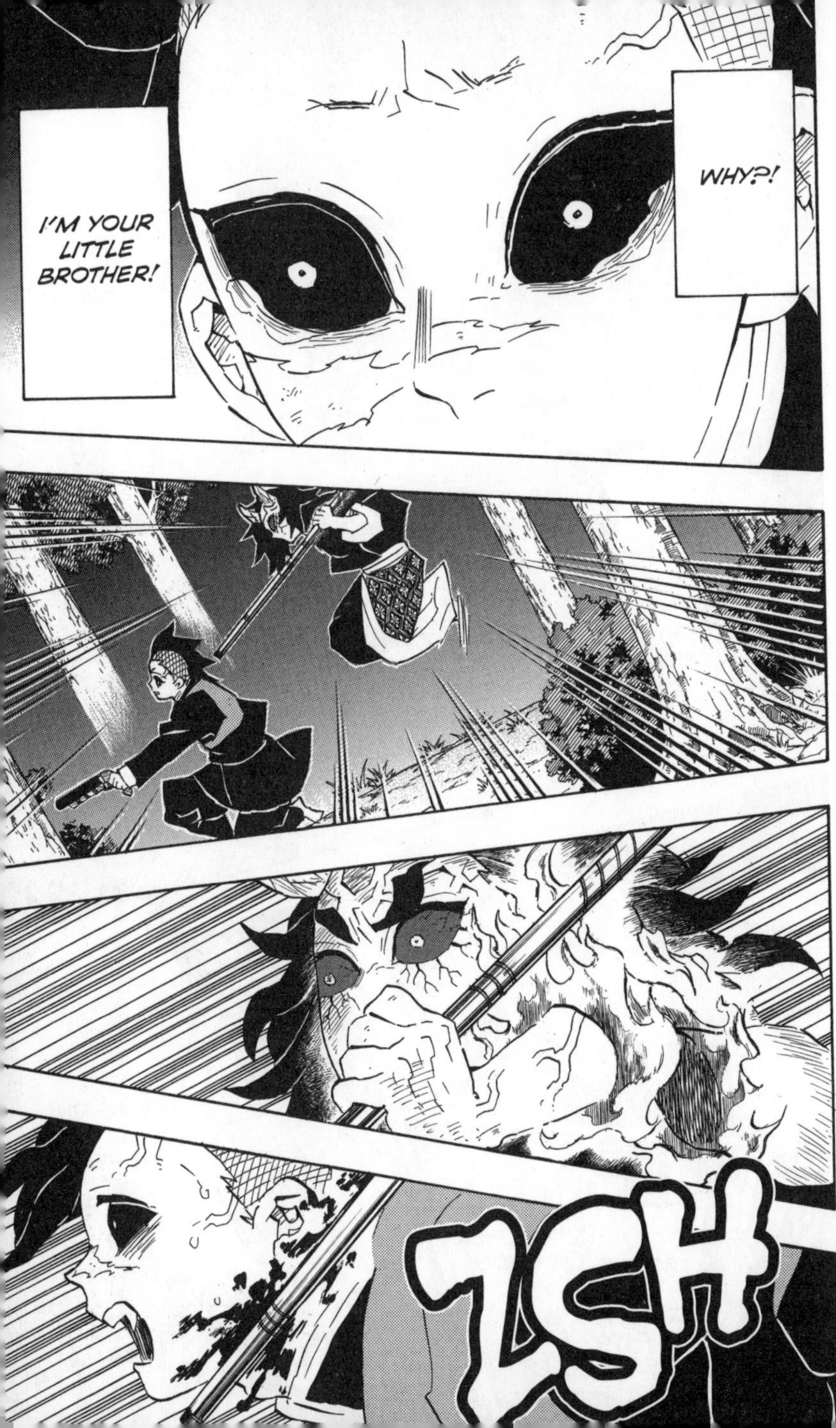
WHY?!
I'M YOUR LITTLE BROTHER!
ZSH

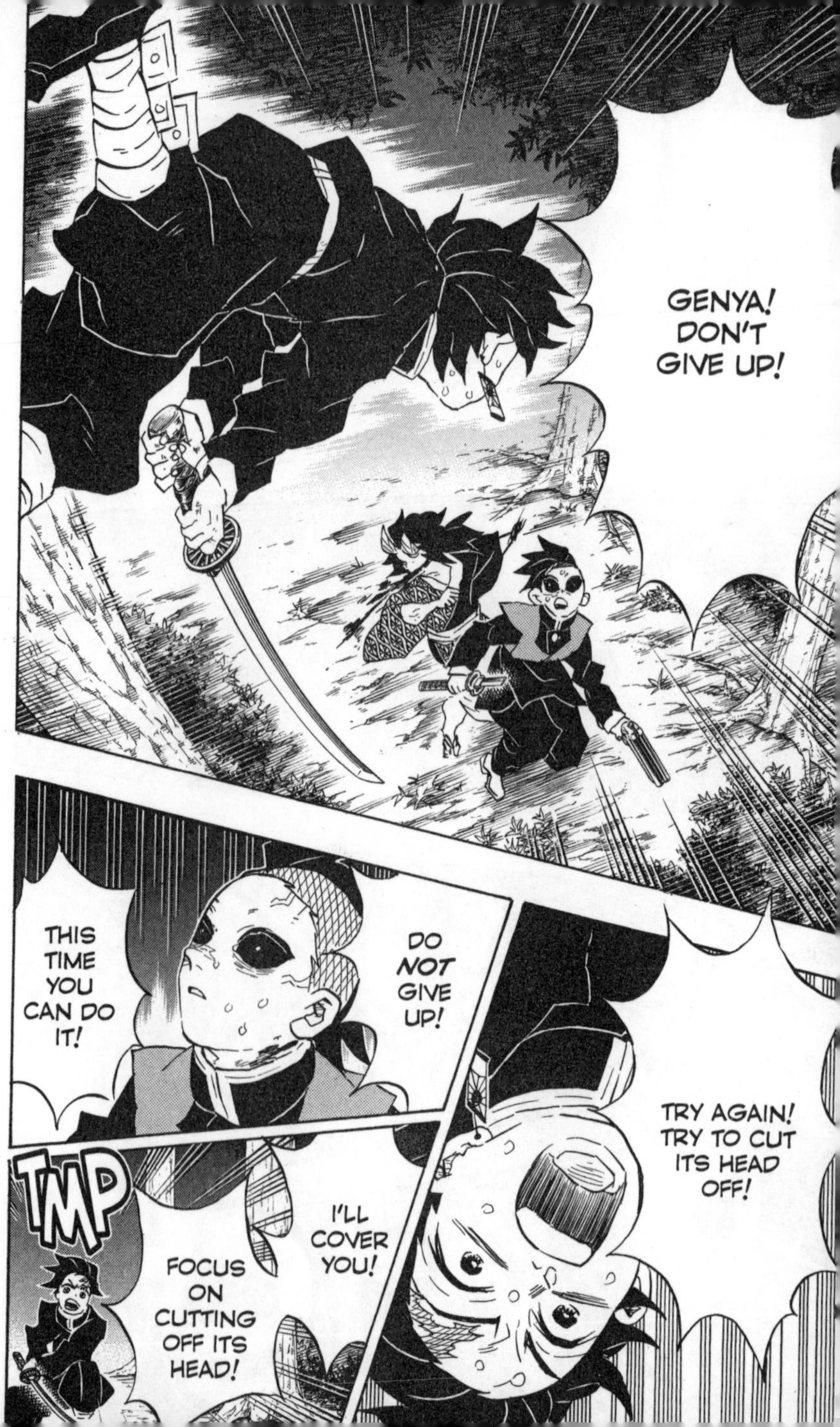
GENYA! DON'T GIVE UP!
TRY AGAIN! TRY TO CUT ITS HEAD OFF!
DO NOT GIVE UP!
THIS TIME YOU CAN DO IT!
TMP
I'LL COVER YOU!
FOCUS ON CUTTING OFF ITS HEAD!

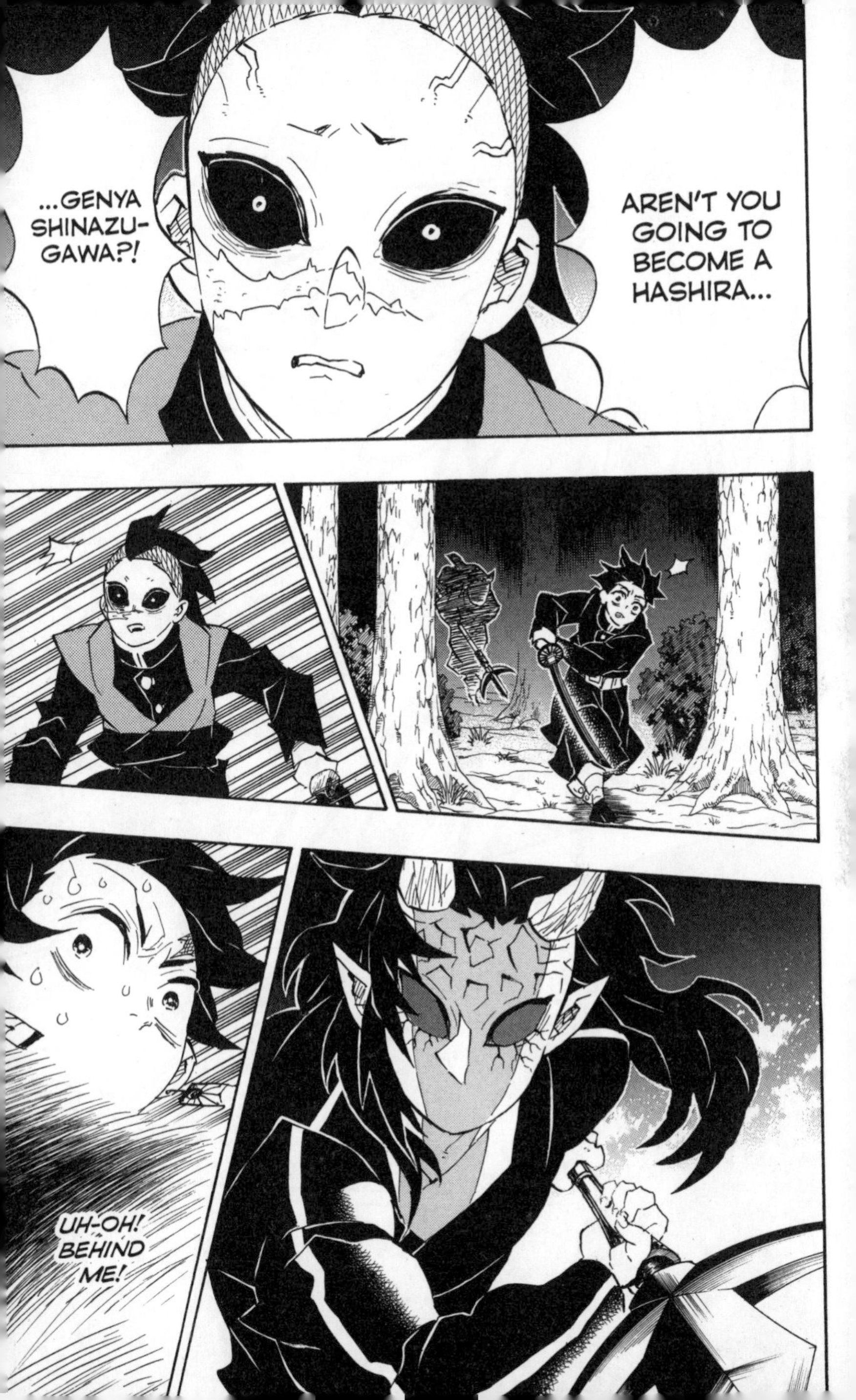
AREN'T YOU GOING TO BECOME A HASHIRA...
...GENYA SHINAZUGAWA?!
UH-OH! BEHIND ME!

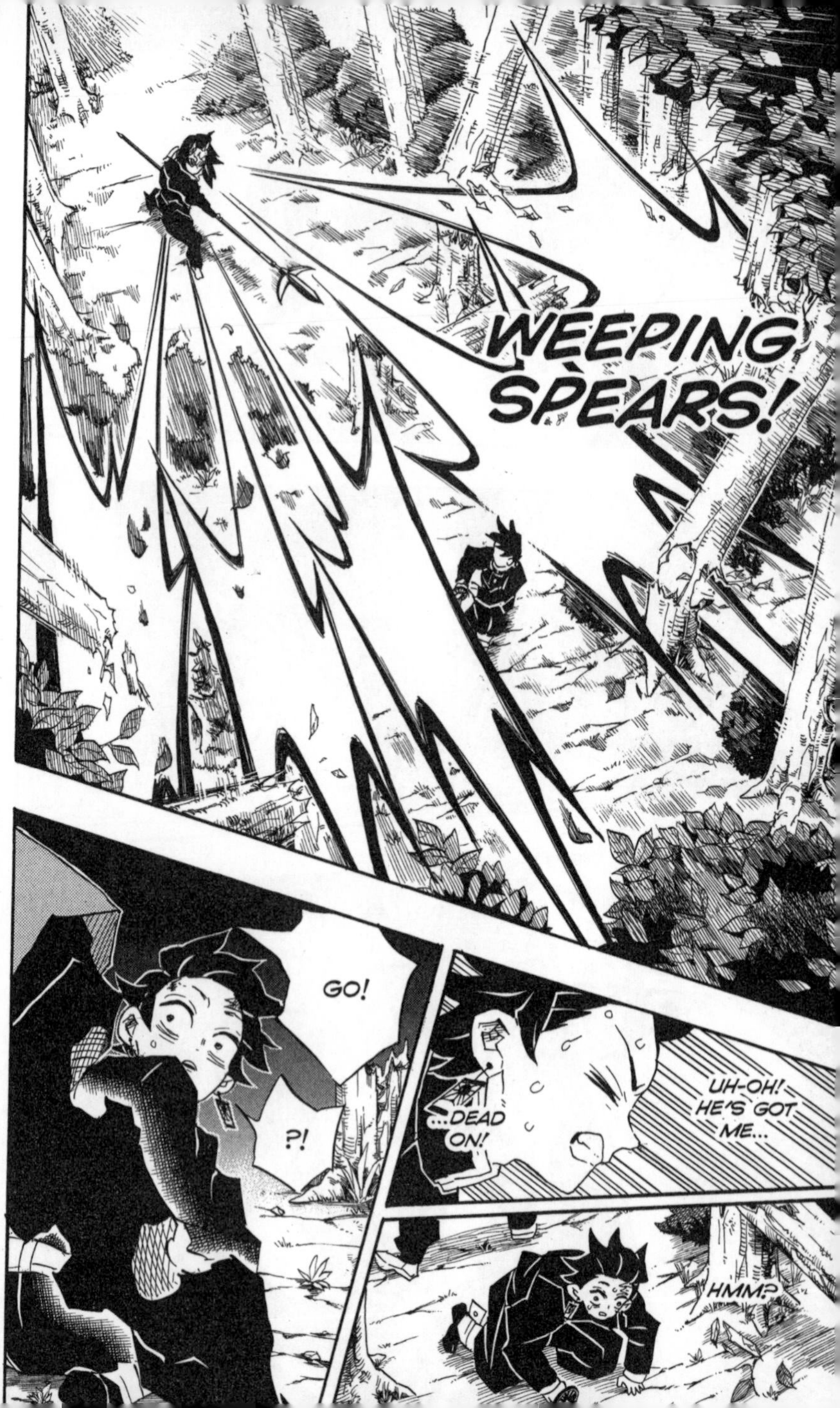
WEEPING SPEARS!
UH-OH! HE'S GOT ME...
...DEAD ON!
HMM?
GO!
?!

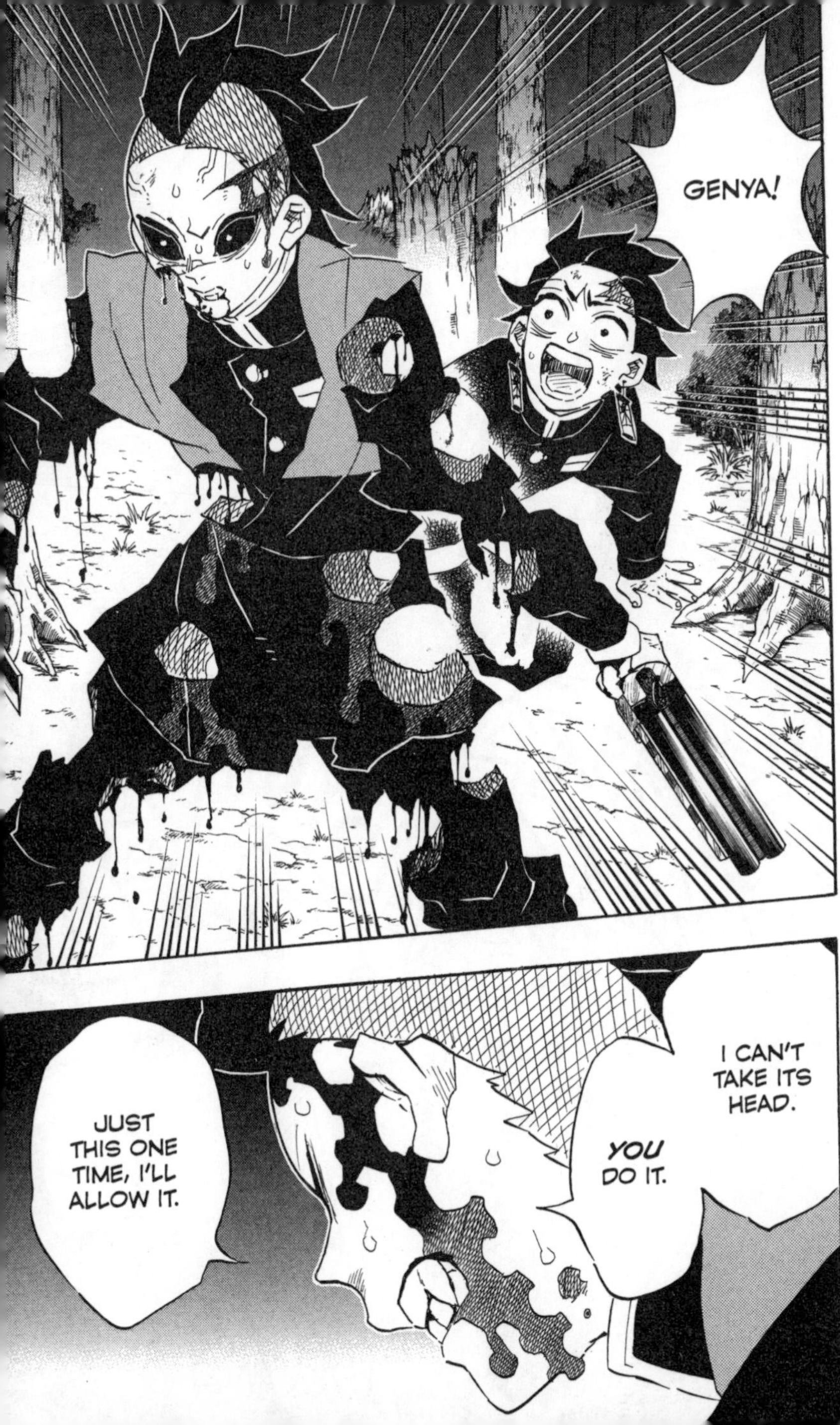
GENYA!
I CAN'T TAKE ITS HEAD.
YOU DO IT.
JUST THIS ONE TIME, I'LL ALLOW IT.

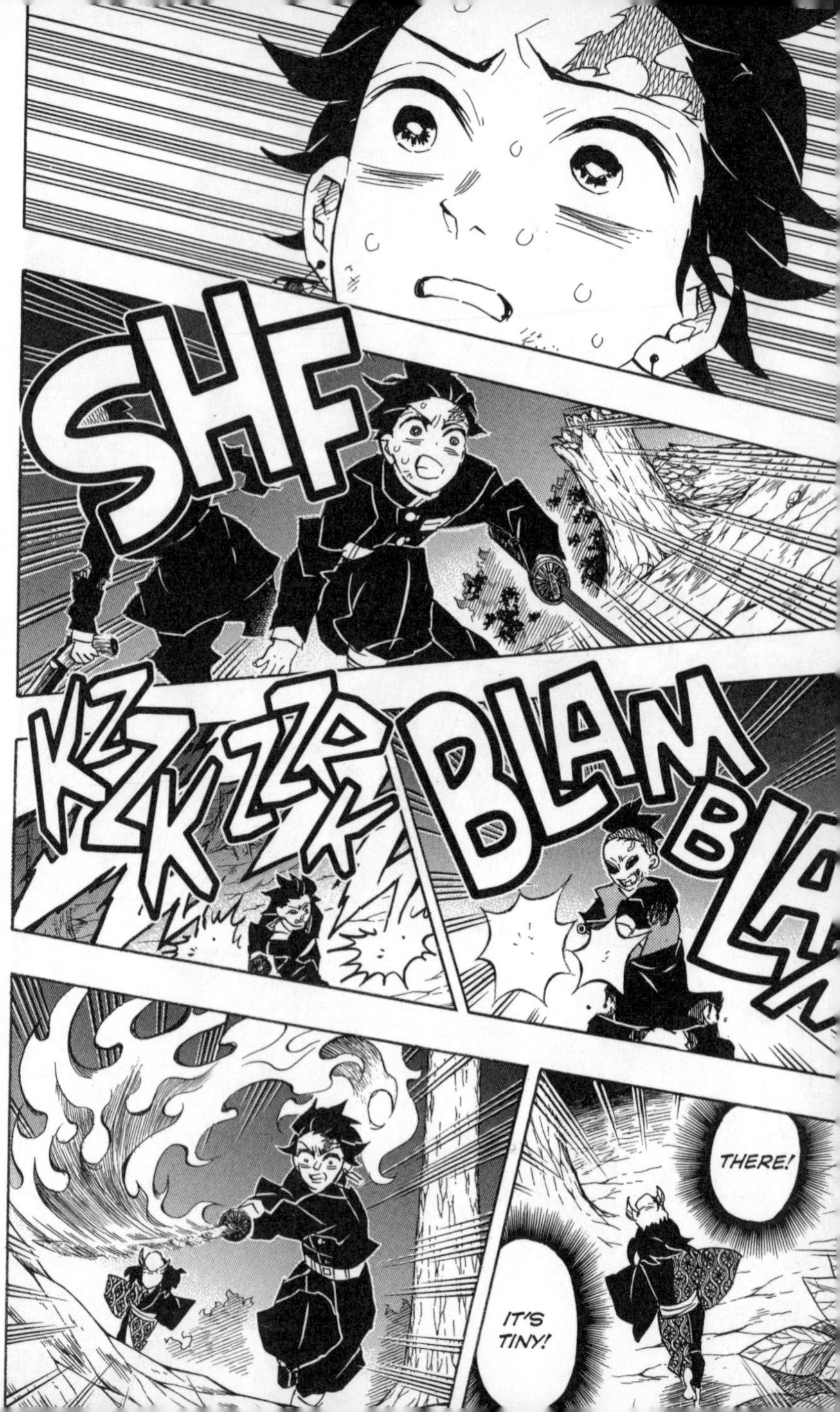
SHF
BLAM
THERE!
IT'S TINY!

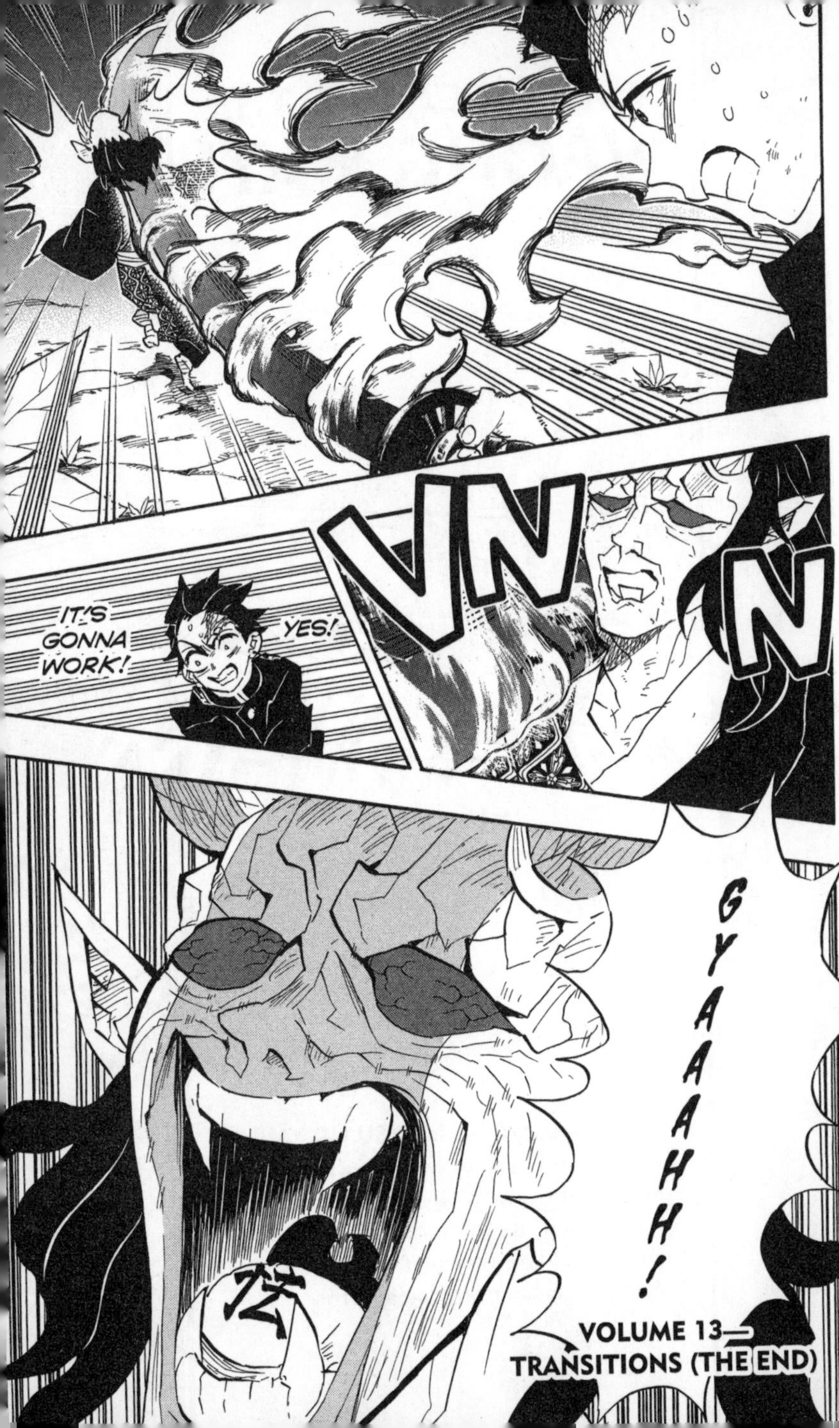
VNN
YES!
IT'S GONNA WORK!
GYAAAAHH!
VOLUME 13—TRANSITIONS (THE END)

YOU'RE READING THE
WRONG WAY!

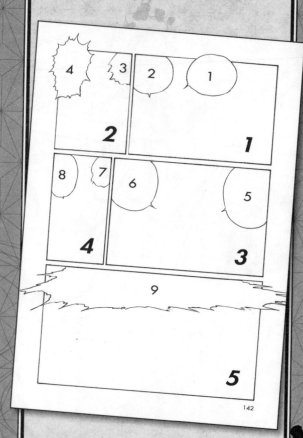

DEMON SLAYER: KIMETSU NO YAIBA reads from right to left, starting in the upper-right corner. Japanese is read from right to left, meaning that action, sound effects and word-balloon order are completely reversed from English order.